D1559602

VIOLENCE AS USUAL

VIOLENCE AS USUAL

POLICING AND THE COLONIAL STATE IN GERMAN SOUTHWEST AFRICA

MARIE MUSCHALEK

CORNELL UNIVERSITY PRESS
Ithaca and London

First published 2019 by Cornell University Press

Library of Congress Cataloging-in-Publication Data

Names: Muschalek, Marie A., 1978– author.
Title: Violence as usual : policing and the colonial state in
    German Southwest Africa / Marie A. Muschalek.
Description: Ithaca : Cornell University Press, 2019. |
    Includes bibliographical references and index.
Identifiers: LCCN 2019006493 (print) | LCCN 2019011860
    (ebook) | ISBN 9781501742866 (pdf) | ISBN 9781501742873
    (epub/mobi) | ISBN 9781501742859 | ISBN 9781501742859
    (cloth)
Subjects: LCSH: German Southwest Africa. Landespolizei—
    History. | Police—Namibia—History—20th century. |
    Violence—Namibia—History—20th century. |
    Germans—Namibia—History—20th century. |
    Namibia—History—1884–1915. | Namibia—Colonization.
Classification: LCC HV8273.5.A45 (ebook) |
    LCC HV8273.5.A45 L365 2019 (print) |
    DDC 363.2/3096881099041—dc23
LC record available at https://lccn.loc.gov/2019006493

Pour ma famille
To my family
Für meine Familie

Contents

ACKNOWLEDGMENTS

It is a very satisfying task to finally have the opportunity to thank at least some of the many people who have helped me to write this book.

First of all, I am deeply thankful to my *Doktormutter*, Isabel Hull, who has been the best mentor one could wish for. The great pleasure she takes in the calling of history is inspiring. I hope I can follow her example, and I am happy to call her my friend.

At Cornell University, I entered a stimulating environment of intellectual exchange. I thank my advisers Dominick LaCapra, Sandra Greene, and Robert Travers for welcoming me into this community. Each in their own way helped to make me a better historian. Moreover, I thank all faculty members and graduate students who gave their time and energy to discuss various papers and chapter drafts in the vibrant History Colloquium.

Since moving back to Europe to complete my project and to take on new ones, I have benefitted from many opportunities to present my work and from productive exchanges with other scholars. Birthe Kundrus, Michael Wildt, and Alf Lüdtke graciously welcomed me into their research colloquia. In Copenhagen, Søren Rud and Søren Ivarsson invited me to partake in the very interesting conversation of rethinking the colonial state. At the Marc Bloch Institute in Berlin, Fabien Jobard and Romain Tiquet invited me to join their discussions on the nature of policing in Africa. My gratitude also goes to the vibrant community of African Studies at Basel University, in particular to Dag Henrichsen, Lorena Rizzo, Giorgio Mischer, Brian Ngwenya, and Kai Herzog, with whom I enjoyed valuable and thought-provoking discussions. I am also grateful to my colleagues from the research network Gewalt—Geschichte—Gesellschaft, especially Alex Oberländer, Jonas Kreienbaum, Veronika Springmann, Alexa Stiller, and Franziska Zaugg, for their animated and theoretically rigorous debates on the history of violence.

In my new academic home in Freiburg, Sylvia Paletschek has given me her complete trust and continues to support me in every possible way. I wholeheartedly thank her.

I thank Franz Göttlicher, who, at the German Federal Archives in Berlin, brought my attention to my main corpus of sources. During my research in the Berlin archives I was furthermore well attended to by reading room staff and by archivist Ralf Engel. At the National Archives of Namibia in Windhoek, thanks to Director Werner Hillebrecht and archivists Martha Nakanyala, Laina Shaanika, Johanna Namulombo, Irene Isaacs, and Ndamian Hangula, my research stay was a very productive and pleasant one. I also thank George Iyambo at the University Centre for Studies in Namibia for arranging my housing in Windhoek and for his excellent company. In Basel, at the archives of the Namibia Resource Center, Dag Henrichsen assisted me in another way by helping me locate documents relevant to my project. Finally, Aïsha Othman, director of the Africa Collection at Frankfurt University Library, readily assisted me in my endeavor to find photographic material.

Scholarly work can be lonesome. Deeply felt gratitude therefore goes also to all my friends and colleagues who offered their moral support, their comfort, and their insights, making this endeavor a gratifying life experience. Christiane Hess, Marco Kühnert, Matthias Stelte, Julia Kramer, and Andreas Strippel were there when I took my very first steps in the discipline. In Paris, Marianne Beck pulled me out of the isolation of the archives and libraries. At Cornell University, Ada Kuskowski and Claudine Ang were my first friends in a strange land. To them, as well as to Oiyan Liu, Yael Manes-Goode, Emma Willoughby, Emma Kuby, Abigail Fisher, Kate Horning, and Mari Crabtree, go many, many thanks. Since the beginning of this project Michelle Moyd has been a constant companion in our shared interest in German colonial history. I consider her my big sister in spirit, and I thank her for all the things, big and small, she did for me over the years. Thanks go also to my colleagues and friends in Berlin, notably Susann Lewerenz, Dörte Lerp, Manuela Bauche, Kristin Weber, Julia Eichenberg, and Ulrike Schaper, for the innumerable talks we had about Germany's colonial past and the politics of doing history, as well as to Joël Glasman for introducing me into the African Studies community. Finally, I am grateful to my Freiburg colleagues, especially my wonderful office mates Christa Klein and Mirjam Höfner, but also to Miriam Bräuer, Yasemin Dasci, Isabelle Deflers, Antje Harms, and Angela Witt-Meral, for their support and inspiring conversations over Monday lunches.

I am very grateful that Roger Haydon's professional experience and his eye for the essential have substantially improved the book. Also at Cornell University Press, I wish to thank Ellen Murphy, Carmen Torrado Gonzalez, and Karen Laun for their patience and ready help on each step of the way. And I thank Bill Nelson for designing a great map at very short notice, and Sandy Aitken for an excellent index.

Finally, my family deserves my thanks for more reasons than I can enumerate here. My mother and father, my brother, and my sister have put up with me and my strange intellectual ways for as long as I can remember. Their generosity and love carried me all along the way, and I thank them from all my heart.

Ryan Plumley has been the most demanding critic of my writing, the greatest skeptic of my research, and a general pain in my ass. He has also made me a better writer, helped me refine my thinking, and been the love of my life throughout. To him, and to my two strong and smart girls, Zoë and Rosa, I dedicate this book.

VIOLENCE AS USUAL

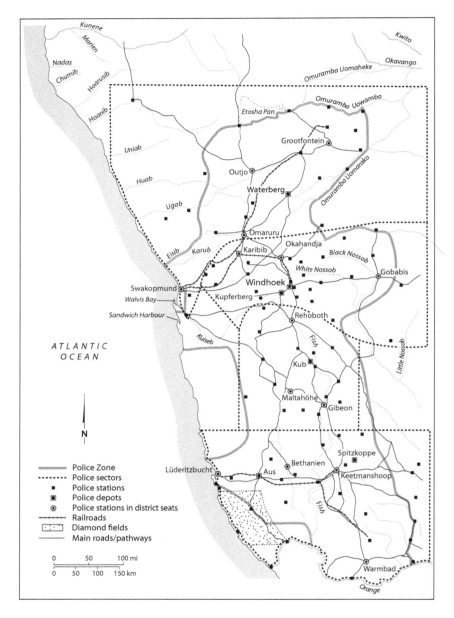

MAP 1. Police stations, police depots, and district seats in German Southwest Africa, 1909
This map was adapted from a sketch drawn by a police sergeant at police headquarters. In his map, the sergeant omitted the boundaries of the so-called Police Zone, the reduced territory that should in fact receive police "protection." It was added here. Map by Bill Nelson.
Adapted from: BArch Berlin. Lichterfelde, R 1002/2693, 115.

Introduction
Everyday Violence and the Colonial State

On March 14, 1909, at 10:30 in the morning, Police Assistant Hans, stationed at the southern edge of German Southwest Africa, shot himself with his service weapon. Earlier in the day, Hans had questioned a command he deemed unfair. For this, he had been beaten by his superior, Staff Sergeant Adolf Bauer. After his own punishment, Hans had then, in turn, himself hit a prisoner with the butt of his rifle. His supervisor, Police Assistant Daniel Pinnar, took the rifle away from him and went to report the incident. When Bauer heard that Hans had used the butt of his rifle, he told Hans that he should have beaten the prisoner with a *sjambok* (Afrikaans: whip) instead. Then Bauer handed Hans the whip—the very same whip with which Bauer had earlier beaten him. The latter then struck the prisoner three more times. Returning to his colleagues, Hans reportedly exclaimed that he did not want to serve in the police force any longer. Shortly thereafter, he killed himself.[1]

Bauer hit Hans, Hans hit an unnamed prisoner, Bauer ordered Hans to hit the prisoner again, and then Hans killed himself. Already confusing in itself, the story is further complicated by race: Police Assistant Hans and the prisoner were African, Sergeant Bauer was German, and supervising Police Assistant Pinnar was Baster (mixed-race).[2] The concatenation of events leading up to Hans's tragic end gives us a first indication of the complexity of "petty" violence in the colonial theater of German Southwest Africa. This short episode from the colonial archive shows that violence was pervasive but also highly differentiated: blows were dealt along social and racial hierarchies, with some tools considered more appropriate than others, and policing was often about showing rather than telling what acts of physical violence constituted proper social conduct. The official documentation evaluating Hans's death also shows that colonial violence was inscribed in an intricate system of official regulations and institutionalized meanings. What was at stake both in practice and in discourse was a theme raised time and again by colonial administrators and enforcers: the proper "treatment of natives."

For immediately after the incident, local administrators raised the question whether Hans's corporal punishment had been the reason for his suicide, and whether it had been authorized or not. Opinions on the issue varied. One official was convinced that the suicide was definitely the German policeman's fault and that, by beating Hans, Bauer had "rendered himself liable to prosecution."[3] Another official revised his initial belief that there was a connection between punishment and suicide, but felt that the beating had been irregular and thus deserved a disciplinary reprimand, while still allowing for "attenuating circumstances."[4] Yet another official admitted that the beating had been formally unlawful, but he saw no problem with the "energetic rebuke" of an African subordinate, referring to the German policeman's customary "right of paternal chastisement" and his overall good standing.[5]

The exchanges among officials discussing Hans's case demonstrate that the act of hitting an African man, although a run-of-the-mill affair, did not have one clear and simple meaning. Often, colonial bureaucrats struggled in their rationalizations, and their writings reveal that within the colonial state apparatus, the appropriate "treatment of natives" was laden with what Ann Stoler has called "epistemic anxieties."[6] The anxiety was about how much and, more importantly, *what kind* of violence was necessary to control indigenous labor and ensure colonial rule—and *who* were the proper wielders of this violence.[7]

This book is about the power of violence. Not warfare but the workings of *everyday* violence are its object of study.[8] Slaps in the face, kicks, beatings, painful cuffing, shoving, and forceful dragging: these are the quotidian practices of colonial life the book seeks to analyze. It asks about the meanings people attributed to acts of violence and about the social order built on such violent acts.[9] My analysis takes us into the settler colony of German Southwest Africa (present-day Namibia) at the beginning of the twentieth century. There, in the wake of a ruthless, genocidal war led by the German colonial army against the colonized population, a police force was given the task to reestablish a "peacetime" order. In this postwar regime, the quotidian, normalized violence that was orchestrated by the police force—what I call "violence as usual"—differed from the belligerent, destructive violence that had come before. If one pays close attention to these everyday practices of rank-and-file policemen, one can discover the workings of an improvised yet powerful colonial state.

German Southwest Africa: A Settler Colony

At the end of the nineteenth century the German Reich had become a colonial empire. Chiefly with military force, it had taken possession of territories in Africa, Asia, and the Pacific. German Southwest Africa became its settler colony. Military outposts were built, fences erected. Progressively, more and more valuable land and livestock went into the hands of European settlers. As a consequence, the population living there was increasingly unable to organize life in the forms it had done prior to German intrusion. Their pastoralist, seminomadic economy and usufruct claims to territory were displaced by a wage and forced labor agricultural and mining economy.[10]

Almost from the beginning, and unlike in other contemporary settler colonies, the German state took up a major role in the establishment of the rule of the few over the many.[11] It was a latecomer in the imperialist competition and sought to catch up by professionalizing and rationalizing its colonizing efforts.[12] With the help of its bureaucrats and soldiers, its surveyors and doctors, its laws, taxes, and road signs, the colonial state ventured to throw its net of influence over a territory one and a half times as large as the motherland. In many ways it did not succeed. Its territorial presence was thin and its resources limited, and its endeavors were met with resistance and evasion. Especially in the earlier phases of colonial dominion, German state control resembled more "islands of rule"[13] than a net, and, until the end, its power remained arterial rather than capillary.[14] What is more, the colony never made a profit.

The history of German Southwest Africa between 1884 and 1904 was characterized by a fragile system of alliances and "protective treaties" between German colonizers and local African political leaders.[15] In 1897 a cattle plague shook the African herder economy. The continuous expropriation measures and contemptuous treatment of the colonized by the growing settler community and the colonial administration led to an ever more unbearable situation. In 1904, the Herero and the Nama, two African groups living in the territory of Southwest Africa, took up arms against their oppressors. In a drastic attempt to fulfill the military "imperative of absolute victory"[16] over the rebellious forces, the German colonial regime committed the first genocide of the twentieth century. Between 1904 and 1907, the German colonial army, called the Schutztruppe, waged a ruthless war of annihilation against its opponents, killing about 80 percent of the Herero and about half of the Nama population.[17]

Still during the war, but particularly after it, the task of policing German Southwest Africa fell to the small force of about six hundred to seven hundred men called the Kaiserliche berittene Landespolizei für Deutsch Südwestafrika.[18] It operated in a land that was sparsely populated, harsh, and inhospitable. Constantly understaffed and lacking crucial resources, like most colonial police, the policemen of the Landespolizei struggled to assert their authority and their "claim to the monopoly of the legitimate use of physical force."[19] It had to limit its activity to a territory much smaller than the actual colony, called the Police Zone.[20] And yet, the men of the Landespolizei were crucial intermediaries for virtually every aspect of colonial life. Symbolic of the state as its most visible representatives, workers who built up and maintained infrastructure, brokers in the semi-free wage labor system, policemen were also themselves high-status members of the emergent social order. They were the sinews of the new social body.[21]

My study recounts the history of these policemen and of their daily deeds. It thus contributes to a scholarly field that, for a long time, has been dominated by literature on the rather distinct case of British colonial policing, but that has recently been revived by a series of excellent empirical research studies looking at Belgian, Dutch, French, and German examples. In these, we learn about the caste of indigenous men who—for one reason or another—had chosen to throw their lot in with the colonial power, and whose police work revolved around the distribution of "legitimate" violence.[22] But we also learn that the history of colonial police is as complex as the multiple sites on which they operated, whether they originated from a common European policing model or not.[23]

Notably in settler colonies, policing had a different dynamic than in non-settler colonies. There, the colonial social body comprised Europeans who, following a racist paradigm, could not be policed by colonized subjects. Police forces needed to integrate European men into their rank and file, and thus the Landespolizei was composed of about two-thirds German men. But it also employed about one-third African men, and these were, as we shall see, indispensable elements of the force. Settlers arrived in German Southwest Africa mainly after the war (aided and closely overseen by the German state). Yet, they were never as numerous as envisioned, and the ones who came did not necessarily meet the expectations put on them. In 1913, about seventy thousand Africans and fifteen thousand predominantly German settlers lived in the colony.[24] Southwest African German settlers did not have the same political impact (despite the formation of a self-government in 1909) as in other (notably older) settler colonies. Rather, their influence lay in their economic grip on the colony, especially after the massive land appropriations that took place during the war.[25] This study of policing a German settler colony can thus offer a narrative that might be slightly different from yet still comparable to the many predominantly British ones in settler colonial studies.[26]

Settlers complicated the colonial social order—even more so than missionaries or traders, for they were there to stay, claiming to build a new sovereign polity for themselves.[27] They competed with the colonial state for the command over the land and its people, for access to labor and profits. It is within this frontier context, in the daily interactions between state and nonstate actors, but also among African and German state actors themselves, that this book seeks to reveal the workings of colonial rule and state power.

The period that this book analyzes lasted less than a decade. This may seem fairly short, but despite the traumatic break of colonization and genocidal warfare, a "peacetime" society emerged with all the forms of conflict and cooperation typical of social order. It was, to be sure, prone to disruption, atrociously cruel to many, and unsatisfying even to its ostensible beneficiaries. But people made do. They sought an elusive stability through the regularized ways in which they built everyday lives, formed and reformed communities, and organized social life. The interwar period needs to be studied in its own right, not merely as postscript or prelude to even harder times.

Colonial State, Colonial (State) Violence

The colonial regime in German Southwest Africa after the genocidal war was characterized by a radicalized "native policy" and increasingly regularized labor extraction.[28] The state's aspirations were exceptionally high and all-encompassing: according to contemporary German state theorists and policymakers, every aspect of colonial life and all subjects, settlers and indigenous peoples alike, were to be brought under complete state control.[29] The "native ordinances" (*Eingeborenenverordnungen*), issued in 1907, are symptomatic of this concept of total rule and of the radicalization of the state. They stipulated that Africans were not allowed to own land, that they could not choose where to live, and that they had to carry identification tags as well as proof of employment with them at all times.[30]

The historian Jürgen Zimmerer has rightly described the German enterprise of all-encompassing colonial hold as a "utopia of absolute rule."[31] For these normative expectations were nowhere near fulfilled. To the contrary, the gap between aspiration and reality was considerable. The colonial administration still lacked the means and personnel to enforce its visions. Competition and conflict between colonial institutions thwarted the colonial government's plans. Moreover, settlers were unwilling to cooperate with the government, despite many shared interests. Last but not least, the project of absolute control was hampered by continued individual and collective resistance from the colonized even after their lives and social organization had been almost entirely destroyed.

Expanding on this argument, the historian Jakob Zollmann, who, like me, also focuses on the police force in German Southwest Africa, emphasizes the significance of space for the limits of police accountability, as well as the complexities of the rule of law, notably that it was often unfixed, fluid, and open to interpretation. His main argument about law enforcement remains, however, the same as Zimmerer's: just like the state as a whole, the Landespolizei was a weak organization and failed to make law and order reign. Especially in the peripheral spaces far removed from the centers of power, the police were, according to Zollmann, unable to effectively control settlers who acted like "little kings" on their farmlands.[32]

But what happened instead? What were the alternative workings of the colonial state, and how was it possible that it had nevertheless such devastating and transformative effects on the colonized society? This is where many historical narratives fall short, and where I wish to make a contribution. I believe that analyses of the nature of colonial states oftentimes remain locked in an understanding of the state that is too schematic and formalistic, and linked to this, in an understanding of violence in relation to state power that is too simple and instrumental.

To be sure, I am not the first one to point out the problems of a reductive, utilitarian model of statehood and to propose more complex explanations.[33] Moreover, a whole set of scholarly literature has tackled the internal contradictions of colonial states stressing connected and entangled aspects of colonial power relations, notably the importance of colonial intermediaries who acted as brokers for the colonial state.[34] Influenced by the school of subaltern studies, it shows how middlemen transformed the colonial enterprise, appropriating it to their own needs and cultural and social orders.[35] Nonetheless, despite the considerable scholarship that has been done on the various aspects of colonial statehood, and despite the wide acceptance of entangled histories and the multilateral complexity of colonial rule, the "modern Western state" (however idealized or even illusory) remains an absolute standard against which to measure political life all over the world. European colonialism, then, is construed as the endeavor to export that "world historical exception" and "European invention"—the modern state—into the non-Western world.[36] Inevitably, such narratives emphasize the limited success or failure of such an endeavor and list the various "deficits" of the colonial state.[37]

Violence, then, many scholars of colonial regimes currently assume, was the compensation for a perceived or actual lack of state power.[38] Or they see violence, notably excessive violence, as a particular trait of settler communities that states were unable to rein in. With respect to German Southwest Africa, Matthias Häußler claims, for instance, that settler "aggressiveness was boundless, undermining the weak colonial state entirely."[39] Our understanding of colonial state violence still lacks differentiation and specification, especially when it cannot easily be subsumed under the headings of warfare or excess.[40] Too often, students of colonialism have entrenched themselves in disputes over the question whether "the systematic employment of violence was essential for the colonial state's survival," or whether "violence was conspicuous by its absence."[41] And although the calls for a "deeper, more nuanced history of violence" are getting stronger, discussions about colonial violence usually stay on the level of assessing quantity, whether there was a lot or a little.[42]

I suspect that this understanding originates in a specific source situation: namely, almost exclusively excessive violence has made its way into the archive. The story of African policeman Hans's and an unnamed African prisoner's beatings, with which I opened this book, for instance, were documented only because of the deadly end this story took. Descriptions of such "normal," low-level violence that happened every day have rarely been recorded. Hence, the kind of violence that was accepted by colonial rulers, which in everyday practice was pervasive, does not become an object of study for historians.[43]

Another reason that might have led historians to distinguish simplistically between excess and containment of violence is projection of our present-day ethical and political condemnation of violence onto the historical situation. Unlike in the virtually hegemonic liberal political culture of the early twenty-first century, in the late nineteenth and early twentieth centuries, certain violent practices were valued.[44] And many state policies that had the goal of protecting and providing welfare, including the regulation of violence, were enforced in a violent manner. These violent acts had ambiguous meanings. They cannot simply be characterized as bad, illegitimate, or excessive, but they remained violent acts all the same. As Carotenuto and Shadle note, "Both African and European actors wielded violence . . . as a means . . . to justify both the strength *and the benevolence* of colonial rule."[45] Thus, I suggest initially avoiding moralizing in order to point out the more intricate workings of violence in their historical context. That colonial states were very violent—

especially to discipline and exploit labor—should not come as a surprise. What intrigued me when I was reading the sources in the police archives of German Southwest Africa, however, is that the discourses and practices of violence enacted by the state and its representatives were often produced in a logic of wanting to "do it right," to "treat well," and to care. Restricting or even abolishing violence was not the goal. The notion of the proper "treatment of natives" was about inscribing a specific meaning into a violent act. Policeman Hans's suicide, his beating, and the repeated beating of the unnamed prisoner before showcase this process.

Violence as Usual and the Improvised Colonial State

In *On Violence*, Hannah Arendt famously argued that the (excessive) use of violence reveals the limits of the power of its users. She insisted that one cannot treat violence and power as synonymous. Power, in her definition, is "the human ability to act in concert."[46] Violence, she claims, "can always destroy power," and power "can never grow" out of it.[47] However, taking a close look at the micro-mechanics of colonial life, I have discovered that there are forms of violence that can be characterized as productive and transformative rather than outright destructive.[48] If we shift our perspective away from the legal and institutional aspirations and structures of the state, and instead turn our attention to the everyday activities and encounters of low-ranking officials, a much different state comes into view: a semiofficial, informal, loosely organized state constituted by everyday social practices.[49]

Through their quotidian undertakings—their patrols, their workplace inspections, their office work, and so forth—the men of the Landespolizei interacted with almost everybody in the colonial theater. Despite their small number, they were probably the most socially present state actors. The police force's hybrid composition, though perpetually a sore point, allowed for its effectiveness. I have found that there was an overlap—a sometimes uncanny synchronicity—in the values and attitudes among the German and African policemen. Both were deeply invested in honor and the martial, masculine, professional identities attached to that concept. All of them valued their clientage relationship to the state. In the process of the everyday, their different notions of what honor and status implied mapped to a certain degree onto each other and became amalgamated into an organizational culture. The fact that honor is a code reliant on public reaffirmation helped this process. Policemen had to build their honor every day anew. Striving for status, they partook in a fluid "play" that situated them toward the public, generating an organizational culture based on improvisation and on-the-spot experience. The relationship between African and German policemen was not mutual understanding, nor was it cultural exchange. Rather, policemen worked together on a kind of "middle ground," a field of "creative, and often expedient, misunderstandings," which enabled them, on the one hand, to pull the colonial project in their direction, and, on the other hand, to relate to both the colonizer and the colonized populations.[50] However, the collegial relationships between German and African policemen were by no means equal. Instead, they can best be characterized as asymmetrical reciprocity.

Working from these smaller claims about violence and its agents, the larger claim of this book is a new conceptualization of the colonial state. It analyzes the recurring slaps in the face, the kicks, beatings, painful cuffing, shoves, and forceful dragging that were a quotidian part of colonial life. To many, these were (and sometimes even still are) not perceived as violence at all. Conventional research topics of state violence are war, state terror, or capital punishment, for instance. Instead, I focus on "unspectacular" violent acts orchestrated by the police force of German Southwest Africa. I claim that, instead of being built primarily on formal, legal, and bureaucratic processes, the colonial state was produced by improvised, informal practices of violence. Contrary to most social theories of the state, I argue that the organization of state power was not merely a matter of claiming the monopoly of force and thus proscribing any excessive, disruptive, and nonofficial violence. Rather, I discovered that colonial rule consisted in diffusing and regulating specific types of seemingly self-evident harm throughout society. These modes of violent interaction are crucial in understanding the production of colonial order. For they were instances in which exemplifying instruction about and negotiation over social organization took place.[51] Ultimately, these practices of normalized violence had constructive, ordering effects that were a fundamental and inherent part of the colonial state's power.

Everyday violence was constructive specifically when it was participative, shared, and routinized in nature. First, everyday violent practices were distributed to different actors in the colonial realm. They were shared out rather than restricted. They represented, to refer back to Arendt, a form of humans acting in concert. And the policemen of the Landespolizei were, if not the conductors, at least important players in that concert. The archival evidence thus bespeaks a colonial situation in which everyday violence was a form of cooperation.[52] Second, these practices drove legal and administrative rationalization, rather than the other way around. Through daily routines and the insistence on the primacy of experience, policemen established "commonsensical" ways of proceeding that often were retroactively justified and inscribed into written regulations or even law.

In short, I suggest going beyond an understanding of violence as solely destructive and instrumental and beyond the notion that modern states operate exclusively according to modes of rationalized functionality.[53] Thus, I propose thinking of state building—whether it is in the colony or in the metropole—as a process involving quotidian, "messy" violence on the ground rather than as a top-down, planned project.

Methodology and Sources

As pivotal actors in the everyday activity of colonialism, on the lower end of the administrative hierarchy, at the outposts of the colony, policemen provide a productive site for engaging in both a top-down and a bottom-up history of colonialism. My theoretical approach to this history draws from the disciplinary subfields of historical anthropology and Alltagsgeschichte.[54] Studying the everyday life of ordinary men can easily lead researchers to identify with historical actors, to believe they know the motives and states of mind of people from the past. The appeal of anthropological inquiry is that it casts the historian as a researcher of cultural differences who has the intellectual tools necessary to account for the complex relationship between researcher and object of study. My understanding of everyday history is moreover deeply indebted to Michel de Certeau's theoretical writings on the practice of everyday life. His work provides valuable impulses for thinking through questions of historical contingency and recurring commonalities when inquiring into what people do in the day-to-day.[55]

My study of the "common men" of colonial rule relies on a large body of source material that has not been thoroughly examined.[56] The holdings in question are the official files of police headquarters, the Inspektion der Landespolizei. These files, held at the German Federal Archives in Berlin, comprise about four hundred "subject files" and over eight hundred "personnel files." Specifically, the latter have proved a rich source of insight into the policemen's social and cultural backgrounds (for each German policeman there are considerable biographical data) as well as their everyday experiences. Likewise, among the subject files there are extensive patrol reports in which I have discovered details about daily practices and interactions. In addition to the records in Berlin, I have consulted the National Archives of Namibia in Windhoek. There, the official records of local administrations, the so-called Bezirks and Distriktsämter, offer further material with which to inquire into the micro-mechanisms of state control. Particularly the numerous depositions regarding grievances between different parties in the colonial realm have been of great use in reconstructing how policemen acted on a daily basis.

Contrary to their German counterparts, African policemen had no individual personnel files. Archival records unfortunately have little to say about African policemen. Usually, they are mentioned only in passing, and often their presence is not acknowledged at all. Nevertheless, it is possible to infer from the available source base who these men were and what their daily actions meant to them and to the colonial state. Working with very few and difficult sources is nothing new to Africanists. And I draw on their methodology to combine secondary literature with a careful amassing of available evidence in order to extrapolate plausible scenarios, reading sources at times "against the grain."[57]

Finally, a short comment on writing about violence is in order: it is difficult. Violence is "simultaneously a historical form of experiencing and a historical form of acting."[58] It is about bodies clashing, injury, pain, suffering, feelings of domination, elation, and internal experiences almost impossible to describe. In this study, I focus mostly on violent acts as forms of doing rather than forms of experiencing or being.[59] Moreover, especially with the sources at my disposal and the questions I am asking, the perspective of the perpetrators comes unavoidably to the fore, and the victims remain silent. What is more, detailed descriptions of violent practices demand a high tolerance for ambivalence and contradiction, a willingness to be unsettled in one's own comfortable distance from these events. When writing about the everyday of violence, identification with its victims or perpetrators, that is to say, getting too close to one's subject, is hard to avoid. I hope that my voice conveys respect for the victims of colonial violence while still accounting for the multiple perspectives involved in violent situations.

Chapter Overview

Chapter 1 offers a portrait of the patrolmen who made up the Landespolizei. Juxtaposing African and German life stories, it traces their socioeconomic and cultural upbringings and depicts the material conditions within which the policemen lived and worked while drawing connections to the values and identities these men aspired to. Three elements of identity formation are considered in depth: social class, soldiery, and masculinity. The chapter shows that the policemen's liminal social standing placed them at an uncomfortable albeit central position within the colonial power constellation. And although the men came from quite disparate cultural worlds, all were deeply invested in honor and a clientage relationship to the state—creating a peculiar overlap of moral codes and principles of social organization.

The police force was also semi-civilian and semi-military. Chapter 2 addresses this hybrid institutional setting within which police codes of behavior emerged. On the one hand, police leadership held on tightly to military notions of etiquette, proper appearance, comradeship, and loyalty. This attitude became particularly apparent in police training. Not legal knowledge or administrational skills, but an imposing military habitus and access to lethal force were to provide the foundation for quality policing. On the other hand, being charged with civilian tasks, the policemen of the Landespolizei created a professional culture that increasingly introduced administrational techniques as modes of validation and legitimization. To them, it mattered that the job was done in accordance with an ever growing complex of decrees as well as that it was documented in proper form. In short, policemen were men of guns and paper—they injured and killed people "by the book." This chapter returns to the significance of honor, demonstrating how the concern for proper appearance and performance was the most decisive factor in the emergence of a Landespolizei organizational culture.

The third chapter approaches practices of everyday violence through the lens of its material instruments. Three tools are examined in depth: the whip, the shackle, and the gun. Their specific use emerged as improvised responses to contextual constraints, refining ideological discourses and official policy along the way. The chapter reveals that violent technologies of policing were parceled out according to the system of status hierarchy that defined colonial order. Under what circumstances they were used, and how, were more important as a matter of social distinction than efficient practice. Symbolically, who used what tools in what situations clarified hierarchy, for instance in the general ban on Africans owning guns. Moreover, the expert or approved use of tools—professionalism—could also serve as a marker of social distinction that elevated the policemen, Africans included, above other colonial actors, such as settlers. This chapter offers a first substantiation of the thesis that police praxis drove legal rationalization. As the cases of corporal punishment and of weapons usage against fleeing subjects illustrate, policemen manufactured procedures that police headquarters reluctantly yet gradually accepted as the rule.

Chapter 4 investigates the nature of police work. It reconstructs the minutiae of policing in German Southwest Africa. Most of the policeman's day was filled with a series of established, unspectacular routines. Often, policemen appropriated the tasks at hand in a way that neither contradicted nor ignored given orders, but that executed them in a manner that would add distraction or excitement, or at least a sense of self-willed (*eigensinnig*) action to the task. In the field—in which immediate accountability was limited, resources were scarce, and nearly everything could seem to be part of policing—policemen proceeded according to what can best be described as a tactic of making do. Policemen frequently improvised; they mixed duty and sociability, and they deployed both formal and informal techniques. Trickery paired with bureaucratic rationalization featured prominently. As a result, an organizational culture emerged in which policemen insisted on the primacy of their own experience and established a "commonsensical" course of action. More often than not, making "short shrift," that is, resorting to the quick solution of violence, was the outcome. Integrated into daily routines, such violent behavior acquired ritualized features.

How this practice of (violent) improvisation played out in one important field of police activity, namely, the regulation of the labor market, is the subject matter of the final chapter. After the genocidal war, African labor was scarce. It fell to the police to capture those African men, women, and children who were still hoping to escape colonial control and to force them (back) into the semi-free wage labor economy. Further, police were charged to organize the distribution of workers among employers and to oversee their treatment on site. Concerning the treatment, or better, mistreatment of African labor, scholarship has fallen short in explaining the role the state played. The narrative of a stinted but genuine liberalizing effort through rudimentary protective labor laws by the German colonial government in the face of cruel and exploitative conduct by farmers, company owners, and foremen does not account for the complexities of violence. Colonial violence was not just excessively applied by some and limited by some others. The state, represented by its policemen, played a crucial role in fine-tuning labor coercion. It established a moral economy of normalized violence that was economically viable.

CHAPTER 1

Honor, Status, Masculinity

Violent Identity Formations

Who were the African and German men of the Landespolizei? Or rather, who did they and others think they were, or were supposed to be? To answer these questions of identity formation, this chapter examines the policemen's socioeconomic and cultural upbringings as well as the material conditions within which they lived and worked, while drawing connections to the values and identities these men aspired to.[1] Juxtaposing African and German life stories, three elements of identity formation are considered in depth: social class, soldiery, and masculinity. The chapter shows that the policemen's liminal social standing placed them at an uncomfortable albeit central position within the colonial power constellation. And although the men came from quite disparate cultural worlds, all were deeply invested in honor and a clientage relationship to the state. Striving for status—as soldiers and warriors, but also as family men and adventurers—they partook in a fluid "game of honor."[2] These men all understood themselves within a moral economy of status. This was so not simply because they all came from places with vestigial traditions of honor, but also because the new economy of status they produced for the colonial context enabled a dynamic negotiation of the hybridity that characterized the policing situation.

Honor

Some preliminary remarks regarding honor are necessary: it is a concept that has significance within both African and European history.[3] Thus, it is a useful focal point allowing me to include all policemen in the analysis of identity formations, and in doing so, to bridge to a certain extent the historiographical divide between the two fields of scholarship. But first, some general anthropological and sociological explanations of how honor works.

Authors who have written on the subject agree across the board on the relational character of honor. Honor is a social phenomenon. Without an onlooking public, honor does not exist. People establish, maintain, and defend their honor via the judgment of others. As Pierre Bourdieu notes in his ethnological study of the Kabyle honor system in the mid-twentieth century, the "point of honor is the basis of the moral code of an individual who sees himself always through the eyes of others, who has need of others for his existence, because the image he has of himself is indistinguishable from that presented to him by other people."[4] And because it is relational, honor has to be reciprocal. All members of an honor culture have to potentially be able to act honorably. They have "to be worthy of" participating in the culture.[5] In that sense at least, honor cultures are to a certain degree equalizing and inclusive— at least for those who are allowed to play the "game of honor."

Related to the features of relational character and reciprocity is that honor is also always situational. An honorable act within one group might be considered dishonorable within another group, or in another time or circumstance. Honor is therefore not a universal code of behavior. Bourdieu observes that "the ethos of honour is fundamentally opposed to a universal and formal morality which affirms the equality in dignity of all men and consequently the equality of their rights and duties. . . . The dictates of honour, directly applied to the individual case and varying according to the situation, are in no way capable of being made universal."[6] If honor applies to each individual and to each instance differently, it is rather misleading to define honor as a law or a right.[7] For ideally, these are supposed to apply uniformly and in an equalizing way to all members of a given society.

Accordingly, German sociologist Georg Simmel remarked in the time period that is of interest to me that honor, rather than being a law itself, was situated between the law and morality [*Sittlichkeit*]. He stressed the way in which honor connected the inner, spiritual life with the outer, social life. The function of honor, he claimed, was to perpetuate a given social order, to preserve and reproduce social strata, and to ensure cohesion within these. Honor was so effective in fulfilling its conservative purpose precisely because of its position between external, objective, generalized and internal, subjective, individualized means of establishing order:[8]

> If one were to bring these types of norm to their completely articulated expression, . . . law brings about outer purposes through outer means, morality effects inner purposes through inner means, and honor, outer purposes through inner means. . . . Honor takes a middle position: an injury to it is threatened by penalties that neither pure inwardness of moral reproach nor the corporal force of the legal sphere possesses. While society establishes the precepts of honor and secures them with partly inwardly subjective and partly social and externally perceptible consequences for violations, it creates for itself a unique form of guarantee for the proper conduct of its members in those practical areas that law cannot encompass and for which the guarantees through moral conscience alone are too unreliable. If one also examines the precepts of honor for their content, they always appear as a means for maintaining a social group's solidarity, its reputation, its regularity, and the potential to promote its life processes.[9]

The "triumph" of honor, Simmel argued, was that the individual was made to believe that the task of preserving his or her honor was "his most inner, deepest, most personal interest [*Eigeninteresse*]" when in fact it had a "sociological function [*Zweckmäßigkeit*]."[10] Simmel thus quite perceptively exposed the hidden logic behind the bourgeoisie's nineteenth-century liberalizing and democratizing effort to overcome corporate hierarchies. Namely, by connecting honor to internal qualities such as virtue and personal character (presumably achievable by everyone) instead of to external markers such as rank, birth, and estate, Enlightenment thinkers had produced a more surreptitious and more powerful tool to reinforce social structures than the early modern system of honor had ever been. Honor, in this interpretation, is a forceful disciplining device that inculcates conformist behavior, even or especially in times of social transformation. Historian John Iliffe, author of *Honour in African History*, claims that the strategic shift away from outward criteria toward an internalization of honor values can also, though to a lesser degree, be observed in colonial Africa, mainly due to the introduction of world religions on the continent.[11] I will come back to the historical specificities regarding honor at the turn of the twentieth century in the subsequent sections of this chapter.

Honor, we have learned so far, is relational and situational. Because of these features, practice is crucial in establishing what it is. "The system of the values of honour is lived rather than clearly conceived," Bourdieu writes.[12] Full comprehension and awareness are not required for the system to work. Without really being able to recite the exact rules, the members of an honor culture will still know how to act properly in any given case. However, often there is not only one right course of action, but several. As a consequence, honor operates in a highly flexible and adaptable fashion: "Everyone, with the complicity of public opinion, can play on the ambiguities and equivocalities of conduct."[13] It is these qualities—the flexible and adaptable character of honor—that make it a truly powerful mechanism with which communal life can be organized. This observation can be seen as complementary to Simmel's analysis according to which the effectiveness of an honor culture rests above all in its mediating ability between internal and external means of structuring society, between the law (and its executive power, the state) and morality.

Finally, in addition to relying on everyday practices for their perpetuation, systems of honor commonly depend on a series of punctuated rituals, religious or otherwise, structuring the lives of individual persons and groups into distinct sections such as childhood, adolescence, manhood, and elderly maturity. Rituals are, in Talal Asad's words, "symbolic activity as opposed to the instrumental behavior of everyday life."[14] However, Asad immediately calls into question this opposition between a figurative and a literal realm. For, at least in its original theological sense, the term "ritual" designated the script— that is, the instruction manual—that taught people how to practice religion. The tendency of modern scholars to surmise that "ritual is to be conceived essentially in terms of signifying behavior—a type of activity to be classified separately from practical, that is, technically effective, behavior"—obstructs our ability to understand rituals as both representing and at the same time practicing a moral economy.[15] Yet, it is precisely the way in which the various initiation rites and oath-taking ceremonies existing in the colonial theater were meant to symbolically represent while at the same time still upholding—at least to a certain extent—the function of effectively training or disciplining honorable selves that is of interest to me. For these were the moments in which honor had both a bodily, practiced, and immanent quality and a symbolic, transcendent dimension.

With these general observations on honor in mind, I now turn to the historical context and the actors within it to whom honor mattered.

African Men

In the relatively small corpus of secondary literature that exists on African colonial police forces as a whole, scholars have, until recently, characterized them in sweeping remarks as "vagabonds and adventurers," "ex-slaves," "freebooters and brigands," or "the foreign, uprooted, oppressed, and poor," often re-cruited from remote areas and not from within the colonized society they policed.[16] But the scholarly field is growing rapidly and adding complexity to the social makeup of colonial police.[17] A closer look at the nonwhite portion of the police force in German Southwest Africa suggests that they by no means came from the margins of society, nor from outside of it, but were rather at the core of a newly evolving social structure.[18]

Several peoples lived in Southwest Africa at the time of German intrusion. Broadly, they fall into three main categories: the Bantu-speaking (Ovambo and Herero),[19] the Khoisan-speaking (Nama, Damara, and San)[20] peoples, and the mixed-race Afrikaans-speaking Basters.[21] All of these peoples had migrated at some point into the area known today as Namibia. Very roughly speaking, first—that is, before European contact—the San, Damara, and Nama settled in, although when exactly is contentious among scholars;[22] then, between the sixteenth and eighteenth centuries, the Herero and Ovambo arrived; in the early nineteenth century, another wave of Nama (the Oorlam) and the Basters moved into the area.[23] Only Herero, Nama, Damara, and Baster men seem to have been employed in the Landespolizei.[24] Those are thus the relevant groups discussed in the following.

Beginning with the establishment of German colonial rule in 1884, or at the very latest after the German war against the Herero and Nama in 1904–1907, indigenous social structures, which had already been steadily evolving and changing since the mid-nineteenth century, were radically and irrevers-ibly altered. All colonized men and women who had survived the German genocide were forced to reposition themselves within the new postwar eco-nomic and political system. Many of the African men who were employed in the Landespolizei were born around the time German rule had begun. They grew up in a social constellation that was colonial. It is useful, however, to look briefly at precolonial socioeconomic structures and assess to what extent these had still an impact on African policemen's identity formations.[25]

Lineage, age, and access to means of production were the main factors according to which precolonial societies in southwestern Africa were com-monly organized. First, kinship—be it through patrilineage or matrilineage—significantly structured the distribution of political power and wealth and shaped communal life in general. As anthropologist Winifred Hoernlé observed regard-ing the social organization of the Nama, "A knowledge of [kinship] relation-ships is essential for an understanding of the whole moral regulation of the lives of the people."[26] Likewise, gender and age determined a person's posi-tion in the social hierarchy of a community. "Chief consideration," as stated by Hoernlé, was given to the "relative ages of the people concerned. Respect for age is inculcated in every possible way, and the whole social organization of the people is an illustration of the fact. In the family deference and respect must always be paid to elders."[27] Thus, reaching maturity and the householder position that came with it was an important stage in a precolonial Namibian man's life. Both kinship and generational relations were symbolically represented in the spatial plan of homesteads and sanctioned through various rituals in which ancestors played a crucial role.[28] Not least, the social order based on lineage was abetted by the repertoire of numerous praise songs. "In many African societies whose social order was structured through lineage," as historian Dag Henrichsen notes, "without genealogy a person had no identity."[29] And: "Especially persons 'with cattle' were (and are still today) remembered in [Herero] society."[30] In oral tradition, cattle ownership operated as code to indicate social and cultural belonging.

Hence, secondly, the economy shaped community and identities. All African societies in the region under scrutiny were, in anthropologist Edwin Wilmsen's words, "pastoral/pastroforaging social formation[s]."[31] Herding domestic animals and hunting were the dominant modes of production. In addition, some groups at times cultivated crops or extracted copper ore. Moreover, with the colonial expansion from South Africa all groups participated to a more or less intense degree in trade. Scholarship has shown that what most characterized these economies of southwestern Africa was their fluidity between different modes of production and their interdependence with one another due primarily to harsh nutritional and climatic factors.[32] Cattle, and specifically the accumulation of very large herds, were in these economies not just a means of subsistence, but also "relatively 'secure' economic, social, and symbolic 'capital,'" which was "particularly suited to be deployed in the organization of power and allegiance relationships."[33] This mode of regulating the social can best be described as a patron-client relationship, a particularistic "relation of mutual benefit"[34] that is "characterized by the simultaneous exchange of different types of resources, above all instrumental, economic, as well as political ones . . . on the one hand and promises of solidarity and loyalty on the other."[35]

The "status of a cattle owner . . . was a desirable one," and represented an important element of identity formation in precolonial Namibia, for it meant not only economic wealth, but also patronage that linked socioeconomic benefits and obligations with moral, political, emotional, and interpersonal ones.[36] Yet, this organizational logic was not without contradiction, as historian Tilman Dedering points out with respect to the Nama: "An internal contradiction existed between the semi-autonomous economic status of the basic productive units with free access to land on the one hand, and those social forces on the other that struggled for control over livestock and labour, using genealogical seniority in order to exert political power."[37]

Two major socioeconomic developments further marked the general setting in which we have to understand African precolonial identification processes in the region. In the early nineteenth century, groups of Nama called Oorlam-Afrikaners migrated north from South Africa into Namaland. Then, in the mid-nineteenth century "under the dual leadership of their missionary and their captain, some eighty or ninety Baster families trekked across the Orange River."[38] Linked to the expansion of trade capitalism and missions, both of these groups brought new forms of social and political organization, notably the militarized organization in small raider units called *komando* units.[39] The historian Nigel Penn explains the development of komando culture on the frontier of the Cape Colony in the late eighteenth century with the increased competition for natural resources: "Without the ability to appropriate more land, water and grazing for the increasing flocks and herds of its members, a pastoralist society is doomed to stagnation or decline. Without the means to protect livestock against predators, both human and animal, there could be no increase in the first place. At its most simple level, therefore, the commando was the military institution of a pastoralist society."[40]

Komandos were relatively small, armed, and mounted parties of men, a form of organization well suited to hunting, raiding, and trading. According to historian Brigitte Lau, among the Nama, komandos "began to replace kinship groups for both economic and political purposes."[41] Despite the komando's "quasi-democratic constitution," Nama society, she claims, remained "characterised by quasi-feudal forms of dependence which built upon the cattle-post system," in which other people—mainly the Herero and Damara—were incorporated serving as herdsmen and in other dependent roles.[42] However, less and less importance was given to pastoralist forms of production. By the middle of the nineteenth century, the Nama people had thus shifted their emphasis from herding to foraging and raiding.[43] According to Dedering, "The internal political structures of indigenous and immigrant [Nama] groups became more rigid with the growing importance of market-related raiding and trading activities."[44] Yet, this did not mean that older power relations resting on kinship were entirely displaced by new komando relations, but that the already very fragile political structures based on economic strength and "descent ideology" were reinscribed into a more centralized political system "at the expense of an economic dependence on the Cape market."[45]

In the second half of the nineteenth century, partly as a reaction to Oorlam-Nama incursions, the Herero invested heavily in horses and firearms while also adapting their cattle-raising methods to the new situation (more directed breeding). They too organized in komandos. The result was a re-pastoralization of Herero society and the emergence of big cattle ownership and accumulation of wealth and political power in the hands of few.[46] "At this stage, the identification of men with guns and horses became part and parcel of a modern Hereroness, not only of modern Herero masculinity, but also in similar ways to the identification of Herero with pastoral society in general and with cattle in particular," Henrichsen observes.[47] As a consequence of the Hereros' successful competition within an economy of relatively scarce resources, other groups, particularly the Damara and the Nama, were impoverished.[48]

Fighting for and defending the few resources available was essential in these southwestern African economies. The two key tools were horses and firearms. Henrichsen describes nineteenth-century Herero and Damara communities as "gun-owner societies."[49] To sustain their lives, they—as well as the Nama and the Baster—relied on military prowess. As we have seen, Nama, Herero, and Basters varied in their adaptation of the komando system.[50] But they all generated forms of warrior identifications with it.

This warrior hero was a man who could expertly handle his rifle while on horseback, who could track, reconnoiter, and prey, and whose courage was measured by his cunning and assertiveness in skirmishes and other encounters with man or animal.[51] Thus, the increased presence of firearms and horses redefined ideals of African soldiery.[52] Besides other weapons, firearms were now included in male rituals such as the Herero *ozombimbi* rituals, those victory dances or parades of armed hunter or combatant groups that celebrated and mobilized men as heroes.[53] Display and symbolic practices were crucial, as Iliffe observes with respect to the example of Zulu warrior ideals: "The heroic ethos . . . stressed physical strength and beauty, whether displayed in the near-nakedness of daily life or the elaboration of military costume and personal adornment carefully graded by age and rank. Dance was a further means of display, replacing military drill and demonstrating athleticism, discipline, and solidarity."[54] The introduction of rifles had a deep social and spiritual impact on male subjectivity. There is evidence that Herero men, for instance, had ecstatic experiences during battles against Nama-Oorlam groups when using their newly acquired weapons.[55]

Moreover, komando units fostered forms of authority and power that were not reliant on kinship. For "the power of the commando system . . . far exceeded the potentials of a system based solely on kinship."[56] Some of the male relationships and identities that evolved within these warrior groups were characterized by homosocial, nonkin interactions. Again, the Herero example is well researched.[57] Among Herero, the nonkin male bonds were called *epanga* (otjiHerero: friendship). Within the *omapanga* relationship (otjiHerero: allies, friends) cattle were exchanged, and sometimes wives were shared to strengthen the male fellowship.[58] They were thus another form of organizing cattle re-distribution, sex, and power. And they cultivated male warrior identities that emphasized companionship.

Finally, an essential precondition for the forms of existence described above was free mobility. Particularly for the male members of Herero and Damara clans, constant movement along a wide and complex network of wells, graz-ing grounds, and trading posts gave the rhythm to their everyday lives.[59] This was also true for other groups living on the territory, for "both flexibility and mobility were vital to survival in this fragile ecology, where water was usu-ally short, drought frequent, and pasture and other resources could quickly become exhausted."[60] Furthermore, the Basters in particular specialized in transportation, a trade they had in common with the Boer and that was based on their trek tradition.[61]

Hence, to recapitulate, the formative aspects of precolonial socioeconomic structures, the main principles according to which Herero, Nama, and Damara societies had been arranged, were kinship, gender, and age on the one hand, and access to livestock and/or firearms and horses on the other. Following his-torian John Iliffe, these socioeconomic principles of organizing society were embedded in an honor culture. He argues that "African notions of honour survived vigorously until the colonial period and then fragmented, partly surviving, partly disappearing, but chiefly transmuted and absorbed into other ethics, which themselves were most effective when drawing on traditions of honour."[62]

The historian Philipp Prein has shown how, up until the aftermath of the war of 1904–1907, social relations were consistently described in pastoralist idioms—even when pastoral life was no longer possible—partially due to the way in which flexibility was inherent to the patron-client logic.[63] And I would add that this also held true for the continuation of komando idioms. Prein claims that pastoralists "continued to understand their social relations in their own idioms of paternalistic domination. Clients were still seeking better pa-trons and young male and female dependents still challenged senior author-ity. Yet, at the same time they were increasingly weaving European items and idioms into their conflicts. In this process they did not feel they had to make a choice between defending a 'traditional' mode of thinking and conforming to a 'modern' one. They drew creatively from all available sources when rene-gotiating social relations."[64] Some of these available sources were new, that is, they had become available through German colonialism. And anthropologist Alan Barnard notes, "It is all too easy to see Nama society in terms of a pre

1904 and post 1904 dichotomy. . . . The political organization was destroyed, but elements of the ideology which generated it did remain."[65] Hence, if honor cultures and pastoralist and komando ways of talking and thinking about social relations continued to have validity, finding a way to obtain a horse or a weapon, to create a household, to acquire and accumulate stock, and in that manner to gain social status and warrior honor remained a significant life goal for many young African men. This objective was, however, drastically curtailed by the cattle plague of 1896/97 and, especially, by the German colonial regime, its expropriations, land seizures, fences, taxes, restrictive legislations, forced and wage labor, and so on. Entry into the police force renewed access to the above described pastoralist, forager, raider, nomadic forms of social identity. In the police, African men regained the possibility of obtaining a gun, a horse, and even livestock. And their mobility was increased, too.

The question of lineage and age had a more ambivalent impact on African policemen's identities. Age might have played a role in whether or not men would join the police, either to conform with precolonial standards or to go against them. Africanists have long since pointed out that gerontocracy and patriarchy were "systems of order and/or dynamic tension," and that "formal rituals such as initiation and marriage . . . endow[ed] Africans with status, control over resources, wisdom, and civic virtue," but that these were "in no way fixed or immune to internal or external pressures." Thus, "patriarchal discourse and ritual served as references and anchoring principles that were inherited, contested, and reinvented over time."[66] Young Herero Andreas Kukuri, for example, recalls entering the service of the Schutztruppe because this was what men "his age" were expected to do.[67] But signing a contract with the police might have also replaced other initiation rites, providing an alternative honor source. Thus, joining the police might have amounted to a form of challenge to the preeminence and prescriptions of older generations. John Iliffe observes that "European conquest . . . destroyed much of the rationale for African notions of heroic honour."[68] The result, he claims, was that African "sensitivity to issues of rank and vertical honour"[69] increased. As power relations were reconfigured, conservative movements to defend old elite structures, patriarchy, and the precedence of age emerged. Yet, at the same time, "European control offered the enterprising new avenues to distinction and the young new opportunities for respect. The only certainty was that defeat brought great confusion in which the pursuit of honour remained a guiding principle."[70] Thus, by becoming soldiers or policemen in the German colonial administration and entering the wage economy, "many young men defied their elders by seeking 'accelerated seniority.'"[71]

The *Bambuse* System

Onto these older influences of identity formation we have to add more immediate social facts: African police recruitment was organized on the local level. Each police station disposed of a budget dedicated to remunerating, equipping, and feeding African policemen.[72] Men were approached by German police sergeants on the beat, or the men presented themselves at the nearest police station. Often, they had been in contact with colonial institutions for quite a while. Many came from the Schutztruppe and from missionary schools at first.[73] Yet, by and by, African police assistants, Polizeidiener, as they were depreciatingly called, were increasingly recruited from within the police force.[74] The sons and nephews of policemen and all the young boys and adolescents who lived in the vicinity of the police stations made themselves indispensable. Almost every German and quite often the African policemen as well had at least one if not many young batmen—so-called Bambusen—who would carry out chores such as collecting wood, making fires, cleaning, and attending to the horses.[75] Once grown up, these young men frequently signed up for police service.[76] Often German policemen took their subordinates with them when they were transferred to another post.[77] From the perspective of the recruiters, it was only commonsensical and practical to employ men they already knew or those who had been recommended by a colleague, who already knew the German language, and who were familiar with military discipline. From the perspective of the recruits, entering the police force meant above all a stable and relatively high income provided by an employer they often already were acquainted with and whose reliability they thus had had time to assess.[78]

A brief account of a recruitment scene illustrates how African policemen relied on their clientage relationship to German policemen. Senior Staff Sergeant Max Ehrlich in Okahandja reported about the way in which Baster Petrus approached him to get hired:

> On the occasion of a police servants' clothing muster in front of the office building I saw Baster Petrus standing nearby. At first, I did not take notice of him. But when he greeted me with the words "good day, Staff Sergeant," I remembered that I knew Petrus from Windhuk from the police mess room. During my stay in Windhuk Petrus had ridden a longer patrol with me. I asked him what he was doing in Okahandja. He answered that he had been put on leave, and that he was working for farmer Dewitz. I then asked him why he had left the police, and he replied that it hadn't been nice [*schön*] with the police any more, and

that he preferred to work for Mister Dewitz. But he kept pointing at the police servants' things and stated that one did not have these with a farmer, and that also his old employer [*Herr*] (Pol[ice] Sgt. Dohndorf) was in Germany.[79]

To what extent Petrus was attracted by the uniforms or by other police equipment, notably weapons, does not become clear in this passage. What does become apparent, however, is the way in which he reassessed his situation several times, and that his relationship to an individual police superior (patron), as well as access to uniforms, weapons, and probably horses, was crucial in the choices he made. The fact that usually German policemen gave their old uniforms and instruments to their African subordinates fostered even further the connection between patron-client relationship and accoutrement.[80]

Another incentive to join the police force was the prospect of material advantages such as bribes or booty, or, conversely, simply the lack of material alternatives. Thus, the police force harbored on the one hand long-term African members with career paths such as those sketched out above, and on the other hand those drifting men who took what they could get to get by, including on-and-off service in the police force. An African man called Seemann, for instance, was police assistant at Bühlsport station when he was sent to the hospital to be treated for a sexually transmitted disease. This ended his service for that station. After his recovery, he traveled to Rehoboth, where he was employed by a Baster to make bricks. During a visit to his parents' hometown a Sergeant Lahmeyer recruited him as a construction worker for the police station in Hornkranz. After a while, he again became a policeman at Gosorobis station.[81] Employment in the police force could also provide easier access to cash. African policemen borrowing money from their German superiors was a common practice. This pecuniary dependency must have fostered the existing patron-client relationship between African and German policemen even further.[82] What is important for my overall argument regarding identity formation among policemen is that reaching a certain level of revenue meant also achieving a position of social influence in one's own community and thereby securing honor. As Michelle Moyd observed of the Askari, African soldiers in the German East African military, they "aspired to and pursued a kind of respectability . . . that was characterized by the accumulation of large households, herds of livestock, and the ability to act as wealthy patrons and power brokers to others."[83] Equally important is that this socially grounded form of honor was tightly linked to the African policeman's access to violence: to his possessing weapons and to his overt or covert exploitation of the policed population.

To sum up, African policemen can best be described in terms of their relative proximity to localized power nodes. The main criterion for recruiting the men was their degree of immersion in the colonial system, as substantiated by their qualifications, experiences, and prior employment. This factor made up a great part of their identity formation. Moreover, complying with precolonial social standards of cattle, horse, and gun ownership, they nevertheless overcame to a certain extent older social ideals (which had lost almost all material base) as soon as they entered the colonial socioeconomic web. Dag Henrichsen has called them appropriately the "lost generation": young men whose entire social organization and their place in it had collapsed with the German war against the Herero and Nama.[84] But in the process, these men became the African "new men," those men who seized the opportunity to insert themselves within the new social structures rather than trying to evade them.

German Men

As much as the colonial regime depended on an enterprising generation of African men, it relied equally on German men to construct its racialized order. The social background of German policemen shows surprisingly similar patterns: coming from economic niches that were becoming obsolete, they perceived the state as a patron in their quest for regaining lost respectability.

The sample data I have collected from the personnel files of the Landespolizei show that a significant majority of its German men were artisans or artisans' sons, followed by agricultural and domestic workers.[85] There were few industrial workers. Almost all of them were born in the late 1870s and early 1880s.[86] With little variation, this occupational and demographic makeup of the German police body corresponds very much with that of noncommissioned officers (NCOs) in the Kaiserreich, the group from which virtually all German policemen in Southwest Africa were recruited—a fact to which I will return shortly when discussing the military as a crucial site of socialization.[87]

Statistical records indicate that men who became NCOs were not born in concentrated pockets but all over the Empire: in the countryside, small towns, midsize towns, as well as large cities. The number of men from densely populated agglomerations (over one hundred thousand inhabitants) was slightly lower, however.[88] NCOs originated largely from small peasantry as well as from lower-middle-class professions such as elementary school teachers, artisans, shopkeepers, and clerks—that is, from the "old" middle class (Altmittelstand).[89] Moreover, it is quite likely that an important percentage of the men who later chose to become NCOs moved away from their birthplace in order to find employment someplace else. Migration within the German Reich was intense at the turn of the nineteenth century. This did not mean that men necessarily ended up in highly industrialized settings. Up to World War I, despite rapid industrialization and urbanization, German society remained greatly marked by its rural constitution. In the 1870s two-thirds of all German town-dwellers lived in middle-sized communities (two thousand to twenty thousand inhabitants). In 1910, 40 percent still lived in rural areas, that is, in communities with less than two thousand inhabitants.[90] Historian Wolfgang Mommsen has argued that the development of the German economy needs to be seen as an irregular, nonuniform process. Some branches of the economy grew faster than others, and with them the social structures surrounding these economies. He also claims that around 1880 "the full impact of industrialization on the social structure was yet to make itself felt."[91] Simultaneously, however, huge demographic changes had taken place, which did make themselves felt at least around the turn of the century. These changes had a powerful impact on many Germans, at least in terms of their repertoire of cultural self-representation. One can assume that. speaking in very general, proportional terms, most NCOs had been born and remained living and working in rural or moderately urbanized areas. Their line of work and that of their fathers was mostly within the agricultural, artisanal, small trade, or lower public sector. Their perception of the social order was, however, saturated with images of heavy industry, factories, bustling metropoles, and tenement houses, and marked by the uncertainties of modern economies.

Sergeant Otto Müller, for instance, can be taken as typical. He was born in 1881 in Osterwieck, a Prussian town of about four thousand inhabitants in the Harz Mountains. At that time, Osterwieck was growing rapidly due to its glove manufacturing. But it could by no means be compared to industrialized centers such as the Ruhr or Rhein-Main areas, and Osterwieck's economic growth would soon slow down again. Otto Müller, the son of a miller, was himself trained as a miller before he joined the military in 1901. In 1904, as with so many of his police colleagues, he arrived in Southwest Africa having volunteered to join the war against the Herero. Then, in 1907, he transferred from the Schutztruppe to the Landespolizei.[92] Many of his German colleagues had similar life stories. They were carpenters, cobblers, or carvers, following their father's occupation. Occasionally, some policeman or other had been a waiter, a farmhand, or a miner. And, very rarely, you can find a salesman, a day laborer, or a factory worker. Compared to NCOs in general, policemen came more often from artisan rather than peasant, clerk, or shopkeeper families because the Landespolizei explicitly gave preference to artisanship: craftsmen were by far more useful to the police in the colonial environment than any other trade.[93]

So why would specifically the men from the "old" petty bourgeois strata seek employment as NCOs? The appeal can be explained with one set of reasons in particular: they were the generation that had grown up in the "long depression" that had followed the initial "take off into sustained growth" of the 1850s and 1860s;[94] consequently, they increasingly felt the (real or imagined) pressures deriving from the demands and constraints of a newly emerging technological and economic order.[95] To pick one example among many, fewer and fewer coachmen or saddlers were needed in a transportation system that relied less on horses. There are what seems to me a disproportionally high number of coachmen and saddlers in the personnel files of the Landespolizei.[96] With little political organization of their own, men from the Altmittelstand might have entered the military as NCOs in the hope of laboring for the preservation of the old corporate order in which they had enjoyed a certain social standing.[97] Similar to the bourgeois groups who, once integrated in the officer corps, appropriated the corps' *ständisch* (corporate) thinking, they took comfort in supporting the "authoritarian state," as Mommsen has characterized the Kaiserreich's ruling system.[98] In a rapidly changing social order, challenged by an increasingly politicized working class as well as by an equally politicizing bourgeoisie, NCOs were the "underdog" pillars of the old regime.[99] They traded the class honor (*Standesehre*) they believed they had lost for another, military caste honor. Like the African men who entered police service, they associated certain material and economic resources (importantly horses and arms) with a tradition of social standing. And, as with the African policemen, this form of procuring social rank and respectability involved violence: armed, disciplined potential to use physical force.

Moving into the colony might have been another attempt to escape the strain of modernity. But little can be found about such a supposition in the police sources.[100] The imagination and phantasies of the German bourgeoisie about the settler colony of Southwest Africa as a nostalgic, premodern place had little to do with individuals' decisions to settle there.[101] What is clearly substantiated by evidence, however, is that men sought to relocate to the colony in order to better their financial situation. The prospect of earning an "expatriate income" (*Auslandsgehalt*) on top of the regular civil servant salary was attractive to many. Policeman Otto Olkiewicz, from a small town in Holstein, for instance, stated that his salary was low and thus "since I want to better myself it is my sole wish to get employment in the police force in Southwest Africa."[102] Police officer Max Geyer noted that he was forced to change his current permanent position because he had "only 900 M[arks per year] with which I have to provide for my wife and children."[103]

Those recruits who were already in the colony, namely, soldiers from the preceding war, were also motivated by material incentive. Participating in a war, like the one against the Nama and Herero, usually meant expedited promotion and a higher income.[104] After the war, when large portions of the military were demobilized and sent back to the homeland, joining the Landespolizei was a way of securing a decent salary and one's stay in the colony.[105] Indeed, it was likely the best method to do so, since the offer of advantageous credits for soldiers of the Schutztruppe who wished to buy a farm and settle in the colony had ended in 1906.[106] To employ former colonial soldiers was also in the interest of police headquarters and the Colonial Office in Berlin, for these men already had knowledge of the colony.[107] That the terms of employment would be as good as for those who remained within the military— these were, among other benefits, a one thousand mark bonus after twelve years of service (*Dienstprämie*), guaranteed state employment after service (*Zivilversorgungsschein*), and an ample pension—was not clear in the initial phase after the war. Several examples document that men hesitated therefore before they agreed to transfer over to the police.[108] But the police leadership realized quickly that it was crucial to offer favorable conditions and at least moderate career possibilities in order to attract men.[109] How important a sizable, steady income and other financial benefits were to these lower-middle-class men is expressed in letters Sergeant Hermann Strunck wrote to his brother. With relief he looked on the upcoming bonus and entitlement to a full pension when he rejoiced that "only one more year to bear, my brother, then I can say, it is done! . . . A goal of my dreams will then be achieved." And in another letter looking forward to his home leave he reckoned that with his colonial income "one can do all sorts of things over there!"[110] That quite a few men joined the police not out of conviction but rather out of economic necessity is documented by the repeated orders issued to remind recruiters that "human wrecks who apply to the Landespolizei only out of momentary money trouble" had no place in the police.[111]

The NCO Type

In the metropole, recruitment practices for police forces were similar to the ones implemented in the colony. There too, most policemen were formerly military.[112] We can therefore learn much about Landespolizei identities if we look at their peers in the motherland. There, an arrangement, codified in 1874, guaranteed that noncommissioned officers (NCOs) would find employment in the civil administration after they had served their term of service.[113] For many men with few skills other than the ones learned in the armed forces, a career in the police or gendarmerie (or sometimes also as prison guards, night watchmen, and similar professions in the security sector) seemed the only possible option. A caricature published in the *Vorwärts* in 1892 captures quite strikingly how the lives of many of these men must have unfolded: "Born in Farther Pomerania, went to village school, pulled beets, became a soldier, signed up for the twelve-year service, was promoted to NCO, learned a little writing and sums, drilled recruits, was promoted to sergeant, drilled recruits, staff sergeant, still drilled recruits, got his guaranteed spot in the civil service, and, finally, became a policeman."[114] Note the different components of police identity formation evoked in the quote: the rural background I already addressed in the preceding part of this chapter; the low but nonetheless existent educational level also already touched upon; and, finally, the lengthy and repetitive character of that military life.

The quoted passage illustrates quite clearly that the average German policeman was not just a discharged soldier, but a very specific type: the long-serving NCO. What characterized the NCO most was his role as a drill sergeant. Enlisted usually for a minimum period of twelve years of service, he instructed men day in, day out.[115] This too is well depicted in the *Vorwärts* quote. But the NCO type was also a man who served.

"Whoever would become an upright, virtuous NCO, who would act according to the heart of our highest Commander-in-Chief and to the pleasure of his superiors, he must immerse himself, the longer the better, in his professional and class duties [*Berufs- und Standespflichten*] so that he is completely filled by them. Only in this way can he become a worthy member of the corps of non-commissioned officers and live up to his difficult task: to form the soldiers entrusted to him into virtuous, duty- and honor-loving men."[116] Thus read the introductory sentences from a 1909 manual for NCOs. According to the rationale expressed here, the NCO's primary duty was to serve his superiors (even to please them), and to know and accept his assigned place in the social order. This duty stood in first place. It was the necessary condition for his actual task, namely, to train the troops. Before being able to deal with and be an example for those beneath him, he needed to be absolutely aware of and compliant with those who were above him. Accordingly, his duty included acting according to the "heart" of the emperor. He was to be the epitome of a loyal subject. Given their long terms of service in the military and the likelihood of continuing that service in the civil sector, (ex-)NCOs had ample time to "prove" their loyalty. Or rather, their career paths condemned them to a life of servitude and loyalty. Their social and political identity was strongly shaped by the idea of a lifetime of service to the state and its monarch. In the romanticizing words of a monographer, "For them the notion of service [*Dienen*] meant the absolute fulfillment of a self-imposed task."[117] The quote captures well the way in which the NCO persona was thus also built on notions of self-sacrifice and devotion.

Ideological incentives like these were crucial to NCOs, for their relatively low pay and the poor conditions of their service were not conducive to creating the social prestige to which NCOs were supposed to feel entitled and that was supposed to set them apart from the lower classes.[118] Nor was education much valued: the shorter a candidate's school education, the higher his chances of being accepted.[119] What is more, there were no career paths that rose above the NCO rank. Except within technological units, not one single NCO was made officer in the decades before World War I in the Prussian-German military.[120] Historian Wilhelm Deist has therefore rightly observed that their "social prestige was attractive only to certain petty bourgeois strata."[121] They were the necessary complement for the creation of a well-defined and elevated officer class. Historian Detlef Bald comments on the deep divisions internal and external to the military:

> The rejection of the NCOs from the officer corps paralleled the social distance from other classes that the high bourgeoisie had established. This tension within the military was carried over into society through the civil employment of NCOs who became civil servants, who in the public administration embodied discipline, orderliness, and reliability. The "attitude of absolute obedience" of the former NCOs increasingly came into conflict with the bourgeois circles that were turning against the authoritarian state. The Prussian-German NCO . . . became the negative symbolic figure of the German military.[122]

The NCOs' uneasy, conflicted position between officer caste and draftees also becomes evident if we look at their use of physical force. The many instances of abuse against troops in their care, discussed at length in the press, made NCOs appear as cruel oppressors or brutish boors, depending on the angle from which they were observed. Common soldiers feared and loathed them for their ruthless discipline, and officers despised them for their participation in necessary but "dirty" tasks. Violent behavior—unauthorized but perceived by some as a necessary evil for the greater good of forming hardened defenders of the nation—was thus an integral part of who NCOs were expected and understood to be.[123]

In a society in which the military as a whole was held in the highest regard, NCOs did nevertheless enjoy a certain renown, as did all men in uniform. Many historians have by now shown how the military increasingly gained preeminence in the Kaiserreich era, and how society in Imperial Germany was permeated by a "double militarism," that is, by an official and a populist drive for militarily organizing society and politics.[124] And Ute Frevert has compellingly demonstrated that "the army steadily evolved into an extremely influential and valued instance of socialisation."[125] The mentality of militarism thus pervaded all social levels and almost all aspects of life. Most German men's identities were saturated with the military spirit, whether it came from their education, their nationalist sentiment, or their notion of masculinity.[126]

And so, inevitably, the "school of the nation," as the military was called, had put its mark on the men who would become policemen—in the motherland as well as abroad in the colony. The tradition of recruiting policemen from the military existed since the creation of police institutions in German states.[127] This was not an exclusively German model. Most continental European countries—contrary to Anglo-American traditions—governed and regulated their populations with militarized or (para)military police forces in the nineteenth and early twentieth centuries.[128]

To sum up, we have to picture the German policemen of the Landespolizei as specimens of the NCO type I have tried to describe here: long-serving military men whose assigned role within the institution and within society was overdetermined by notions of dutiful subservience, whose everyday practice, however, had mainly consisted in commanding and (violently) disciplining others. Their place in the military was a liminal (and uncomfortable) one: neither simple soldier nor officer, neither lower class nor bourgeois. However, as bearers of uniforms they held a prominent and privileged position and were used to ordering people around in an Imperial German society.

Husbands and Adventurers

Being a soldier necessarily also meant being a man. Ideally, all German policemen were supposed to be married to German women so that they would embody the colonial state's valorization of white bourgeois respectability. In 1907, Chief of Police Joachim Friedrich von Heydebreck wrote in his position paper regarding the general organization of the Landespolizei of the "desire and aspiration to recruit married policemen."[129] Contrary to the military, whose members were organized for the state of war, the policemen were to exemplify civic life and durability. Stations manned with only one man were, "if at all possible," to be staffed with married policemen.[130] In 1910, Senior Executive Officer Hugo Blumhagen wrote: "No doubt, the advantages of policemen's marriage outweigh by far the disadvantages. . . . It certainly should not be underestimated how important it is for the development of the colony if married policemen are stationed permanently on the same outposts and thus provide a strong framework for the settlement efforts."[131]

Yet, in practice, the living conditions were such that they were not deemed fit for European women. Blumhagen deplored the situation in which stations did not meet the standards that would at least "tolerably comply with the requirements for white women."[132] In August 1910, he thus suggested strictly controlling marriage and, if necessary, forcing policemen to postpone indefinitely their marital plans.[133] The Colonial Office in Berlin sanctioned a directive to that effect a month later.[134] At first, it had insisted on continuing to support the marriage of policemen, pointing toward the threatening "increment in the bastard [Mischling] population," and reiterating that matrimony among civil servants was crucial to promote European settlement.[135] But fear of losing honor and prestige trumped even fear of miscegenation and long-term settlement plans. Chief of Police Heinrich Bethe stressed the connection between "worthy" housing for policemen's wives and the image the police wished to convey when he reminded local administrators of the need to monitor marriage requests: "I ask you to instruct the policemen thoroughly on this issue and to explain to them in particular that this directive is in their own interest, and has been decided out of consideration for the reputation of the body [Beamtenschaft] of policemen, which can only suffer if policemen's wives have to cope with apartments that are unworthy of a German woman. For our reputation would be severely harmed, not only in front of the white population but also in the eyes of the natives."[136] By that time, about a third of the German police force, or maybe slightly less, was married.[137] In the remaining years of German colonial rule, the numbers first increased but then decreased again, for "married policemen hinder[ed] too much their deployment," and were thus less and less recruited.[138]

The "unworthy" conditions were not all that made marriage difficult. Prospective wives were also subjected to close scrutiny. In 1911, the chief of police crafted a telling decree to this effect that I wish to quote at length:

> Much to my regret I have ascertained more and more cases in which policemen plan to enter marriages that are not compatible with their status. From the human perspective, one should not think too harshly about these failings [Verirrungen], which often originate in the absence, for months, of intercourse with the white woman, or in plenty of alcohol consumption [sentence struck out of the final draft—M.M.]. I am unable to keep a man, who is a keeper of the law, in the police force whose wife does not enjoy an impeccable reputation. . . . If the reputation of the [German—M.M.] woman in question does not accord with the dignity of

the police corps, and the policeman does not relinquish the engagement, he is to be dismissed without further ado [*rücksichtslos*], for he is no longer suitable for colonial service. The influence of a woman not befitting one's rank will make itself felt on the moral qualities of the husband and can only harm the individual and the collective. Also, it cannot be expected from married policemen and their wives to accept an inferior person into their closer acquaintance. . . . The gain for the police force will be much greater if it dismisses proficient men who marry below their rank, rather than keeping only one policeman with an inferior wife in its circles.[139]

Possibly the chief of police was referring to the small number of European prostitutes who operated in Windhuk and the coastal towns.[140] In any case, the suspicion that female promiscuity would tarnish the institution's reputation was taken seriously by police headquarters. Typical of sexual moralism of this kind, blame was unevenly distributed. On the one hand, the police leadership did not trust in its men's resilience. On the other hand, their moral failing was caused by women. Sergeant Reichelt's wife, for instance, was considered the main culprit for his conniving tendencies.[141] The consequences would be catastrophic, the chief of police feared, "on a lonely police station . . . where, among several unmarried [men], sits one married official whose wife soon falls back into the habits of her former, not so blameless lifestyle."[142] He thus kept women as far removed as possible from his men, even when that meant that he could not achieve the goal of a police force constituted of bourgeois husbands, and that he would lose good men.[143] Everyday realities and identification references for policemen were conditioned by a tension among bourgeois aspirations, considerations of honor, and economic and other constraints, in this case, the lack of "respectable" German women. Conceivably, a police force that formed an all-male community was in many ways more appealing, for it was perceived as less disruptive, less challenging.

Regarding African policemen, there is, as usual, less direct evidence for their family situations. They lived in close proximity to their German superiors, but not in the same building. Their families, if they had one, lived with them in the *Eingeborenenwerft*, the "natives' quarter." The general notion seems to have been that the German administration let families stay together if possible. Pictures from the period show African police assistants posing as proud patriarchs in front of their homes with their household members and belongings.[144] African wives received food, but no pay, although it was expected that they worked (usually assisting their husbands with domestic labor).[145] Later on, this understanding was turned into a rule, and family members who were not contributing in some way or other to the German administrational economy were removed from the police stations' perimeter.[146] My impression is that, as a rule, African policemen sought to build families after having acquired enough wealth to sustain them. As I have alluded to before, founding a household might have been a motivation for joining the police, for it assured social standing and respectability. Given the much higher number of African women compared to European women living in the colonial realm, and the extent that police headquarters, and the colonial administration in general, were less concerned about regulating the sexual and moral behavior of African men, one can assume that African policemen were more likely to live with a wife or mistress than their German counterparts, that is, at least more likely to do so openly than their German counterparts. In relation to this, since African women must have been quite present, maybe even on remote outposts, it should not be underestimated how they themselves shaped everyday life at stations, whether they were in matrimonial, concubinary (both with African and German policemen), or no relationships at all.[147]

Thus, all policemen—the African and the German alike—were supposed to and to some extent did embody ideals of family life and patriarchal masculinity. However, they were far from living a bourgeois life in the material sense. And all of them, the married and the single men alike, regularly went on long patrol rides in small units of usually two to four men. So, whether married or not, the policemen spent a large part of their time in homosocial groups roaming the wide spaces of the colonial territory. Indeed, their everyday resembled much more an earlier, precolonial form of social life, that of the all-men raiding party.[148] And as we shall see now, the bourgeois and family man identities were not the only masculinity concepts available to policemen.

Birthe Kundrus distinguishes between two kinds of German colonial masculinity. A first, more traditional model was based on notions of homosocial comradeship and adventure; a second model relied on a more modern, liberal-nationalist, bourgeois concept of the heterosexual couple and the family. Kundrus calls the former kind of masculinity "pioneer," the latter "head of family."[149] The policemen of the Landespolizei exhibited features of both of these kinds of masculinity. To speak in the terms used by Raewyn Connell, who stressed the dynamism of gender as a social practice, the policemen were living two divergent "gender projects."[150] Depending on the situation, on their public, on the task at hand, they sought to achieve masculine honor by enacting either the one or the other, or something in between. Violence was performed in relation to the one or the other standard of manliness. Or, conversely, violent acts made them more the one or the other kind of man.

Likewise, as Iliffe stresses in his work on the history of African honor, notions of heroic and householder honor coexisted in African societies. They were linked to different stages in a man's life. Only a man who could provide for a family could be regarded as a fully grown man. But first, he had to have proven himself worthy through brave deeds. "Male honour," Iliffe notes, "related strongly to age and notions of masculinity, distinguishing the heroic behaviour expected of the young warrior from the civic honour appropriate to the adult householder."[151] When African men joined the police, passing over or accelerating important stages of growing into manhood, heroic and householder identifications merged together, similar to the oscillation between European adventurer and head of the family masculinities. Thus, both German and African policemen needed to reconcile young and courageous with mature and patriarchal male behavior in their everyday actions.

In this regard, space mattered. Men had to adjust between the all-male environment of the patrol and the context of larger settlements that included women and, all in all, more people. Furthermore, there was a similar vacillation regarding age. In the case of African policemen, although primarily determined by the colonial discourse on the "childlike" nature of Africans, there are signs that some individual district administrators and police superiors esteemed Africans' seniority and experience in their local community. Magistrate Zastrow from District Office Grootfontein, for instance, observed that older, "seasoned" policemen's influence among their community "cannot be overestimated."[152] In the case of German policemen, police headquarters' take on age was equally ambivalent. These men were supposed to be young, but have the qualities of age and maturity. At first, the Landespolizei recruited men not older than thirty, and then not older than twenty-seven.[153] Older men would not be able to "cope with the physical strains" of the colonial theater, police headquarters claimed.[154] Nevertheless, young men would not be up to the "difficult demands of a certain independence and inner strength of character," the Colonial Office in Berlin declared.[155] Policemen were required to be young and physically fit, yet they were expected to bring a certain experience and sophistication one could only have acquired after a certain age.

In general, a paternal, caring kind of violent masculinity pervaded the characterization of what a good policeman was. For even though he was primarily supposed to be a soldier, he strove for something more: qualities that would dignify him as a member of a modern, rational state, not a traditional, atavistic, military institution. His honor was founded on bourgeois, Christian values of masculinity such as sober-mindedness, restraint, and temperance. Honor, in this context, was fulfilled through duty and service. Police Sergeant Johannes Boll, for instance, "showed great calm and sensitivity [*Gefühl*] in his dealings with the public."[156] And Sergeant Josef Alefelder was described as having "composed and humble" manners.[157] Commendations of individual policemen stressed above all their calm and self-possessed conduct in difficult situations. Especially in the field, violence was to be wielded in a controlled and dispassionate manner.[158] Strong emotions and urges were to be repressed. Senior Staff Sergeant Otto Donicht's leadership of a patrol, for example, was praised as an altogether "thoughtful" [*umsichtig*] enterprise.[159] On the patrol in question, he had raided several settlements, forcefully captured men, women, and children, and most likely burned their dwellings and belongings. His interrogation techniques had included depriving people of water and had resulted in the death of one man.[160] These actions, though brutal, were understood as legitimate because they were undertaken in a spirit of rational and conscientious duty. The language used in patrol reports did not draw the picture of heroic, courageous, or belligerent men. "Prudent," "attentive," or "conscientious": those were the terms with which superiors described subalterns, with which lower-rank policemen described their colleagues, even their African associates.[161] And those were the descriptions of their actions as well, including violent acts like the ones committed during Constable Donicht's patrol.

But precisely due to the many caring, protective, and welfare expectations of police work, the men of the police were at times depicted as effeminate or weak. Sergeant Lippke, for instance, was accused of passivity and was yelled at by a farm steward: "You're too limp for the job, you're too limp!"[162] The local newspapers were filled with articles deploring the loss of the military troops that were being disbanded after the war, complaining about the impotence of the Landespolizei that had been deployed to replace them.[163] It is in this context, then, that violent practices had an important function in thwarting emasculating, enfeebling images and in constructing tough, fearless, relentless, pioneer-type masculinities instead.

Policemen recurrently regarded women and children (mostly African) as prey and property. As a number of documented cases attest—one must assume that many more undocumented ones took place—they raped, abused, and quarreled over who got to "keep" or to "have" them.[164] This too was a form of affirming a more forceful, vigorous masculinity.[165] Cases of physical fights between policemen themselves were also not rare.[166] These could operate as violent rituals with which the men of the Landespolizei proved and reaffirmed a certain kind of boisterous, adventurous, comradely manliness. All these behaviors were accepted as long as they did not undermine the appearance of cohesion, loyalty, and comradeship, and thus did not harm the honor of the institution.[167]

Finally, German policemen also built their masculinity on the back of their African subordinates, not rarely through paternally chastising them. They declared that African men were childlike, that they could never reach paternal maturity. German policemen practiced the same kind of "petty" violence toward their African subalterns. Within the collective identity of wielding violence together, racial hierarchy was preserved. German policemen had larger horses, more powerful weapons, and different tasks of violence. Consequently, these acts fostered not only a certain kind of masculinity, but also a racial order. Thus, the construction of African masculinities was overshadowed by racist ideology. As historian Stefanie Michels notes, Africans' own "patronage systems and masculinity concepts . . . contradicted the idea of clear 'racial hierarchies.'"[168] German colonial representations "de-masculinized" and anonymized African men. They aimed at excluding the possibility of African men "representing themselves as the head of households, often including several women, many children, and servants."[169] However, practices of everyday violence might have operated slightly differently than the hegemonic representations Michels describes. As a cultural practice they might have produced moments in which a "mutual recognition of what it meant to be a man" was possible across the color bar while still upholding the racial hierarchy.[170] The daily challenges and dangers of policing led policemen to put great value on physical strength and the ability to wield violence. And their violent trade might have brought both African and German policemen to valorize each other's masculinities—without undermining the racial order.

Material Conditions and Status Anxiety

The pay of an African policeman was about twenty to forty German marks per month, or in rare cases up to sixty marks.[171] This corresponded to about a tenth of what a German policeman usually earned (three thousand to forty-two hundred marks per year contingent on rank and seniority),[172] and did not include all the social benefits the latter received.[173] An African police assistant or his family could be granted financial support from the colonial state in cases of disability or death, but this was not guaranteed by law.[174] In addition to their pay, police assistants were given free shelter, board, and equipment. The daily food ration for an African policeman included a pound of meat, a pound of some form of starch, coffee, sugar, salt, and some form of fat. On weekends he received a portion of tobacco.[175] The German policeman bought or made his own food. However, what he could get depended largely on what was available at the local store, restaurant, or officers' mess and was usually fairly expensive.[176] Thus, the fact that policemen in German Southwest Africa made about three times as much as their peers in the metropole has to be put into relation with the inflated living costs and deficiency of goods in that colony. Like their African colleagues, German policemen were provided with equipment and housing. Except in the few "urban" centers like Windhuk, Swakopmund, and Lüderitzbucht, housing conditions were bleak. Most of the time, policemen lived in former military buildings that had been constructed hastily during the periods of conquest and war, and that were quickly deteriorating due to the climatic conditions. But even those buildings that had been more recently erected by policemen were usually wanting and lacked basic equipment such as household tools or furniture.[177]

The African policeman's right to raise small livestock was strictly regulated, but in many cases accorded. The German policeman's right to do so was much more limited, as was his right to hunt game.[178] He remained fixed in his income class with no other possibility of substantially bettering his situation. In terms of material conditions, despite the undeniably substantial difference in pay, one could argue that the African and German men of the Landespolizei were quite close to one another, meeting somewhere in the middle of the social spectrum of colonial society.

If we look at photographs the policemen had made of themselves, their families, and their homes, one can observe two features that reappear in all of them. On the one hand, the pictures betray the plain and austere circumstances in which the everyday life of most of the men unfolded. On the other hand, they display a desire on behalf of the men posing in them to convey a certain lifestyle, certain material values, a certain pride in their way of living and their status. In the case of the German men (figure 1) this ambition can best be described as bourgeois. In the case of the African men (figure 2), it can be related to the status of "big men," that is *omunene* (in otjiHerero) or *gáo-sab* (in khoekhoe).[179] The photographs illustrate how economic necessities and constraints collided but also merged with status aspirations and other cultural paradigms.[180]

German policemen in German Southwest Africa were responsible for virtually every aspect of colonial administration: the maintenance of the legal order, the organization of the economy, the development of knowledge about the territory and population, and so on. I will elaborate on their range of responsibilities in chapter 4. For now, it suffices to note that their situation was overwhelming while at the same time instilling self-aggrandizing delusions. The inflation of one's own importance and the pressure to meet the public's as well as the command's impossible expectations generated insecurities and anxieties of failure in policemen. Sergeant Sterzenbach, for instance, stated, "'I have not been instructed on this' . . . on every occasion he was asked to do something."[181] Sergeant Uhde was "one of those, for whom duty easily becomes too much to handle."[182] And Sergeant Czarnetzki confessed that "since the duties of an

Figure 1. Two unnamed German policemen in dress uniform wearing their military decorations pose with family members and dogs in front of a simple stone house. Place and date unknown. Bildarchiv der Deutschen Kolonialgesellschaft, Universitätsbibliothek Frankfurt am Main. Photo No. 014-2171-03.

enforcement officer are so manifold, I feel I am not able to fulfill these by myself."[183]

African policemen, on the other hand, were supposedly responsible for nothing. They were meant to be merely a "support" for the German policemen.[184] In fact, however, they had multiple, unacknowledged, and often crucial responsibilities. This situation could be equally anxiety-producing. Moreover, one has to assume that, from the perspective of the colonized, the hopes and expectations projected onto African policemen as important brokers of the colonial regime must have been quite high. There is evidence that the colonized made use of the police in a bifurcated way, addressing the official, bureaucratic German apparatus for some concerns, and seeking support or justice from the African police for other concerns.[185] Since most of these cases were not recorded, we cannot say how common they were. But we can assume that African policemen experienced worries about not being able to fulfill all that was expected from them.

The historian Roger Chickering argues in his social psychology of right-wing, reactionary middle-class men in Imperial Germany that "their self-concepts tended to be tenuous and insecure." This was due to the fact, he claims, that

FIGURE 2.   Several unnamed African policemen in uniform pose with family members in front of a simple hut near Sendlingsdrift, 1909. Bildarchiv der Deutschen Kolonialgesellschaft, Universitätsbibliothek Frankfurt am Main. Photo No. 020-2209-14.

these were either men "with prolonged exposure to a foreign environment" whose identity was "insecure for having incubated in a state of tension with the cultural environment," or were men who were "recent arrivals in roles that carried high status" and whose "status and respect . . . were clouded by incommensurate social background or by credentials that had yet to find unqualified acceptance."[186] Without wanting to stretch the comparison too much, one could apply these observations regarding status insecurity to the German and African policemen of the Landespolizei: to the former for their insertion into a foreign environment (in addition to the insecurity related to their belonging to a social class on the wane); to the latter for their arrival in a newly created, high-status social group. Moreover, the historian Mohamed Adhikari frames anxieties of mixed-race men in South African history also in terms of social status, claiming that "the basic dynamic behind the assertion of coloured identity . . . was to defend [their] position of relative privilege," which "engendered fears that they might end up losing that position and be relegated to the status of Africans."[187] Again, without wanting to strain its explanatory value too much, I think that this form of status anxiety might also have been existent among Baster policemen of the Landespolizei. Across the board, then, the men of the Landespolizei were likely anxious about their social position as well as their excessive responsibilities.

To conclude this chapter, who were the African and German policemen, socially speaking? There were the African men who had seized the opportunity of securing social standing and consequently honor in the colonial system. They had done so by holding on to some of the economic principles of an older social order while abandoning some of the ancestral, generational principles. And then there were the German men who had found refuge in the armed forces as a stable employer and as a representative of the old regime. In the military and by extension also in the colony, these men had found compensation for their perceived loss in social prestige and class honor. Thus, although the men came from two quite different social and cultural backgrounds, the similarity between the two in terms of self-understanding is striking. Both groups strove for and were anxious to attain traditional forms of social standing (honor) through association with certain economic resources (horses, guns) and a particular patron (the state). And the experience of living and working together in the existing conditions in the colony made both groups of policemen come closer to one another in material and social terms.

Social and cultural backgrounds, class, gender, race, the policemen's identities as adventurers and paterfamilias, all informed their professional identities. But their identities also grew out of their specific experiences in the colony: out of their interactions with one another and with the policed population, out of the mixed-race composition of the force, and, in particular, out of their emerging organizational and professional culture.[188] This culture was defined by two facets—that of the soldier and that of the bureaucrat. German policemen had typically lived a martial identity for quite a while before their entry into the police force, and this experience continued to have a significant effect on how policemen perceived themselves and their work. The clerical side of identity formation was often new to them, but it was nevertheless crucial, for it set policemen apart from their military counterparts. Likewise, two main paths generally led African policemen to enter the police: either via the Schutztruppe or via a missionary school, or both. What is more, missionary schooling resembled in many respects military training: the young African men were subjected (as had been German policemen in their home country schools) to a rigorous disciplinary regime that oftentimes inculcated language and scribal skills by means of military drill.[189] How military and bureaucratic characteristics came together in a complex, at times ambivalent, way to form German and African policemen's professional culture will be addressed in the next chapter.

CHAPTER 2

Soldier-Bureaucrats

The Primacy of Proper Bearing

In 1910, Chief of Police Bethe stated that "the Landespolizei stands or falls with its military organization."[1] Bethe, like his predecessor Heydebreck and others of the head staff, repeatedly stressed how important the "military spirit" of their policemen was.[2] Within their understanding, just as in the German metropole at the time, the police were first and foremost a military institution.[3] This was also true for other continental European police forces at the turn of the century, notably the French and those that had come under Napoleonic influence.[4] Thus, unlike the British case, where a decentralized, community-grown, mostly unarmed civilian style of policing had evolved in the metropole, the heavily militarized character of colonial policing was not in contradiction to, but in congruence with, the centralized, ruler-appointed, mostly armed, militarily organized police in most other European metropoles.[5] As a consequence, policemen of the Landespolizei were almost exclusively recruited from the military. With the exception of some few auxiliary policemen, it was mandatory for the German men who wished to enter the force to have served at least six years and reached the rank of an NCO.[6] Regarding the African members, police recruiters (as well as the recruits themselves, as we shall see) regularly insisted on a military or warrior imprint as well.

This notwithstanding, the police force was also a civilian institution. Being charged with civilian tasks and being subordinated to civilian authority, the policemen of the Landespolizei increasingly relied on clerical techniques as modes of validation and legitimization. Their administrative tasks gained importance in an expanding colonial bureaucracy. Their job needed to be done in accordance with an ever growing complex of decrees, and it needed to be documented in proper form. Thus, policemen were at once soldiers *and* bureaucrats, or "bureaucrat-soldiers," or "bureaucrats in uniform," as other historians and sociologists have called them.[7]

The hybrid institutional setting of a semi-military, semi-civilian institution within which police codes of behavior emerged is the focus of this chapter. It addresses the institution's professional and organizational culture at the nexus between "administrative work and the administering of violence."[8] Expanding on the first chapter's emphasis on status and respectability, I argue here that honor and proper bearing were, in many respects, the glue that held the two different strands of policing together. Or phrased differently, in order for policemen's violence to be honorable, it had to be bureaucratically correct. Thus, bureaucratic procedure was primarily a pro forma act because its purpose was to display legal correctness rather than to rationally organize social life. And since the honor of the colonial state and that of the individual policeman were always intertwined and reciprocal, the Landespolizei, as an institution, relied heavily on its individual members' performances. Policemen were expected to represent a state that trusted in notions of station, standing, and rank (estate) and of splendor, display, and presence (stateliness), rather than in statehood as governance (statecraft).

The War

The German war of 1904–1907 "left deep marks on the society and collective memory of Namibia's population."[9] As a pivotal transformative event, it needs to be factored in if we want to understand the creation of the police and their culture. In its aftermath, German Southwest Africa was suffused with anxiety and paranoia, and the war had a crucial impact on how the colonized related to men in uniforms. To many onlookers, military and police personnel were simply not distinguishable. Or, if they were, they often meant the same thing: repression, control, and recurring violence. Tellingly, scholars who collected oral testimonies on the war have never come across recollections of the police force.[10] Many colonized simply experienced the postwar persecutions, forced labor, and ongoing military and police manhunts as a continuation of the state of war in which everyone had to fear for their personal safety well into the 1910s.[11] The historian Dag Henrichsen summarizes in a few striking sentences what the war meant for the region and its African populations:

> When war broke out . . . , the whole of southwestern Africa plunged into unprecedented violence and suffering. Never before in the known history of this region had so many people died. Never before had so many people been imprisoned and/or forced into flight on such a wide regional scale and across colonial borders. . . . The Southwest African war . . . developed into genocide of various pastoral societies, notably otjiHerero-speaking Herero and Mbanderu communities of central Namibia and various Khoekhoegowab-speaking Nama communities in southern Namibia. This war changed the political, social and economic landscape of the region decisively. Tens of thousands of Africans were killed during the war, perished due to their enforced flight into the harsh Kalahari Desert of eastern Namibia, or died in the concentration camps for prisoners-of-war.[12]

On the German side, the war remained ingrained in the settler community's and administration's memory as a drastic, traumatic event culminating in political radicalization and, as Helmut Bley states, a "circle of violence, hate, and hysteria about security."[13] One does not have to go as far as Bley, who claims that the war made everything that came before irrelevant for the historical analysis of what came after.[14] But it is not wrong to ascribe a significant role, or "independent significance," as he terms it, to the war and especially to the deep-seated fear of another uprising in shaping German postwar colonial rule.[15] As Gesine Krüger notes, the German settlers' "distrust, arrogance, and lordly presumption had turned into hate and hysteria."[16]

For some in the colonial administration, this anxiety influenced deeply their way of conceiving of a postwar society and of the Landespolizei's role. Vice Governor Brückner declared that the police force's principal purpose was to replace the Schutztruppe as a standing army to be deployed in case of emergency.[17] Almost all men of the Landespolizei had participated in the war—on one side or the other. Warlike mentality, friend-foe thinking, and a profound fear continued to influence people's behavior well after the armed conflict had ceased. Rumors about a resurgence of the war, about people being "stolen" and brought to other colonies, and other panic-based and panic-inducing stories spread throughout the colony. Most of these were told by settlers and the colonized.[18] But the police and local administrators were not immune either. At the beginning of 1909, for instance, District Office Keetmanshoop reported about a series of "uncontrollable" rumors among farmers living near the South African border suggesting that "the *Orlog* [Afrikaans for war—M.M.] might break out again."[19] And although the report observed that these settler stories were "nothing tangible, nothing positive," and that "nothing [could] be done at the moment," the apprehension about a renewed rebellion was so strong that the office instructed its police stations to arrest "all natives without work and without a pass," and to remove them from the area. The office's magistrate considered the Nama, especially "the border crossing Bondels [a group of Nama—M.M.] and other rabble [*Gesindel*]" to be particularly dangerous in this respect, "despite the Bondels Commissioners' reassurances to the contrary," and thus ordered them to be deported all the way to the north of the colony, to Grootfontein.[20] "What made a rumor or a legend powerful was that people believed it," as Luise White points out.[21] The example shows that in spite of their awareness that they were dealing with unverified gossip, local police agencies could not help acting upon it.

For rank-and-file policemen, their war experiences had divergent impacts on what kind of militarized men they perceived themselves to be. The sources, at least, make no common thread appear. In chapters 4 and 5, which go into everyday policing practices, I draw out those dynamics that can be attributed to behavior internalized in wartime and those that broke with such patterns.

For African policemen, the war had destroyed most of their identifying structures and values. Their social and cultural foundations had come apart, and they had to find or invent new forms of identification. Krüger observes that with the war in 1904 initiation rites for young Herero of the same age group ceased to exist. Only in 1923 were they reintroduced into Herero culture. "Thus, not only did an important male socializing experience disappear, but also a foundation of group unity beyond kinship in Herero society."[22] The procedures that entry into the German police force entailed (signing a contract, receiving clothing and equipment, standing at attention, and so on) might have provided a replacement "initiation" ritual for young African men. In fact, historian Jan-Bart Gewald points out that German colonization—especially after the war—offered conflicting initiation "alternatives" with competing power sources attached to them: "Given that Christian conversion came to replace initiation, conflict arose between the Herero Christian converts and those whom [sic], in their eyes, were the uninitiated youth. However, these uninitiated youths were very powerful, for they served in the army and the police. This is not to say that the bambusen who became soldiers [or policemen—M.M.] were not initiated; all recruits are initiated into an army."[23]

In short, the war affected Germans and Africans in quite different ways, but nevertheless served as a foundational event for both groups. For the former, it was in many cases the first—that is, in a sense "initiating"—experience in the colony. The war impressed them not only as soldiers but as colonial soldiers.

For the latter, it destroyed most of their identity founding structures. But at the same time, the war brought into the colonial theater one of the two major institutions that shaped their new identities and became sites of initiation. As a "foundational myth" the war has been central to the identity of both Africans (notably Herero and Nama) and Germans in Southwest Africa and Namibia even long after the colonial era.[24]

Regulations

In an effort to exclude the German parliament from the decision-making process, colonial legislation was directly linked to the administrative body of government (the Kaiser, the chancellor, colonial office, governor), thus creating a regime of executive orders (*Verordnungsstaat*) rather than a *Rechtsstaat*.[25] Colonial society was to be organized by the state, not by its citizens nor by the settlers in the colony, and even less by the colonized subjects. Unlike in British settler colonies where claims to political participation had already gained some ground, aided, among other things, by a governmental style of relatively small administration and indirect rule, settlers in German Southwest Africa, whose numerical strength never reached critical mass, faced increasing executive interference "in a state-centred colonization organized by an authoritarian state."[26] From the perspective of a British observer in 1915, this German style of colonial rule was overbearing and insensitive to local circumstances:

> There is no British territory in South Africa which is so little developed as this colony, but it is burdened with more official ordinances and regulations than would be required to run an Empire. . . . A former British colonist of the South-West, while testifying to the progressive qualities displayed by the German farmers, has described the administration of the colony as mischievously autocratic. In his words: "There is far too much government. There is one official out of every three in the population and it is a great burden on the country. Take a place like Keetmanshoop. . . . [There] they have a Deputy-Governor with a secretary and about half-a-dozen clerks, in addition to ten or a dozen policemen who are also largely engaged in clerical work. . . . I have no great opinion of the German as a coloniser, for one thing, because he wishes to do everything on the same lines as he does it in Germany. The system of Government is an elaborate machine not at all suited to a thinly-populated country like German South-West Africa.[27]

Present-day historians have characterized the German state's aspirations in the colony as a utopian view of absolute control and order.[28] In this vision, even the tiniest facet of colonial society needed to be brought under state direction for, within nineteenth-century German state theory, only a state that could establish perfect order was a strong state.[29] As the British observer quoted above derogatorily remarked, German home administrations served indeed often as templates for the colonial state's (illusory) aspirations. District Office Swakopmund used both a Prussian gendarmerie code from 1820 and a Berlin police regulation book from 1899 for the police of its precinct, for example.[30] But at the same time, German colonial administrators referred frequently to and were well informed about the structures and practices of the neighboring British colonial administration in South Africa while building their own.[31]

For the policemen of the Landespolizei, the regime of executive orders meant that directives absolutely needed to be enforced, even when settlers insisted on customary rights or other "laws" such as tradition, racial supremacy, "survival of the fittest," or maximization of profits. It also meant for the policemen that orders were issued at all different levels of the colonial administration. Decrees could come directly from the Colonial Office in Berlin and from the central colonial government or police headquarters in Windhuk, as well as from any local administrator, that is, from the magistrates (*Bezirksamtmänner*) and district chiefs (*Distriktschefs*) who were the immediate civil superiors of all policemen in the field.[32] These orders sometimes contradicted each other. Not seldom, policemen were simply unaware of orders that theoretically applied to them.[33] More generally, the entire framework of rules regulating the police was vague and obscure.

A first charter of the police had been worked on since 1900 and circulated as early as March 1905 when the Landespolizei was officially created.[34] But the text had little consequence while the war was raging. The individual policemen's legal status was regulated partly by civil service laws (*Reichsbeamten, Kolonialbeamtengesetz*) and partly by military codes (*Schutztruppen-Ordnung, Mannschaftsverordnungsgesetz*).[35] In October 1907—the year in which the comprehensive and momentous "native ordinances" were issued—the police force finally got its own codification in the form of an executive order from the emperor.[36] But that order merely determined the policemen's legal position, mostly by referring to the general laws mentioned above. The decree's so-called implementation rules (*Ausführungsbestimmungen*), which were intended to provide crucial explanations about how the police should function, took much longer to be drafted and were never officially sanctioned by Berlin. These rules were meant to revisit the 1905 charter and to redefine the institution's organizational structure, internal allocation of competencies, and position within the postwar colonial administration. The head of police was well aware of the "misunderstandings and differences of opinion" that might arise between the different, notably military and civil, branches of the institution. In the hope that a clear formulation of such implementation rules would forestall "any disadvantageous dualism," he had a first draft circulated to all magistrates and district chiefs, as well as other divisions of the colonial government in September 1907.[37] The revised text, which was sent to the Colonial Office only one and a half years after its initial drafting, represented a compromise between different forces within the colonial theater.[38] After an unconvinced response from the Berlin office and yet another draft, local military leaders joined in on the conversation.[39] When State Secretary Dernburg came to visit German Southwest Africa in September 1909, the police's organizational structure was yet again put on the agenda.[40] At this point, colonial leaders were still debating whether a more militarized form of organization, that is, a gendarmerie, possibly under Schutztruppen command, would be preferable to the existing one.[41] A number of ancillary concerns remained contentious issues as well: for instance, whether six years of prior service in the military were really necessary; who should be allowed to discipline policemen and whether they should be put under civil or military jurisdiction; and whether police sergeants should be offered more substantial career prospects, introducing the rank of *Oberwachtmeister* ("in the Cape police, a deserving policeman can advance to [the rank of] officer," the vice governor argued).[42] In October 1909, Governor Bruno von Schuckmann told the Colonial Office in Berlin that "now [I] can say with certainty that we are on the right path regarding the organization [of the police], and that a fundamental alteration is not necessary."[43] There is no evidence that the implementation rules were ever ratified by Berlin or published in an official gazette. The long-running discussion and the many uncertainties that prevailed about the police's basic organizational makeup did, in any case, not help to give clarity to the lower ranks.

While police headquarters sketched out the "implementation rules" of the 1907 decree, it simultaneously initiated the effort to standardize police work in a general instruction manual, the so-called *Dienstvorschrift*. Here again, several drafts as well as extensive comments from officials within the colonial government and military, and from magistrates, district chiefs, and inspection officers, are preserved in the archives.[44] This little book was designed to give each policeman "in brief form, an instruction about his status [*Stellung*] and his behavior."[45] It was "to contain everything the [police]man should know."[46] Together with their service book (*Dienstbuch*), policemen were expected to have one on hand at all times. Or at least each police station was supposed to have one available for the policemen to consult. A decree from September 1909

ordered, since the manuals "still have not been distributed by some district offices to their subordinate police stations," to report in December every year
whether "all police stations [had been] supplied with at least 1 copy," and stipulated that if the offices did not have enough, to have them replicated.[47]

The manual focused on form and formalities. In the first section (there were
five total), two pages were dedicated to the various kinds of salute or address
policemen had to conform to depending on the rank and station of an encountered person.[48] Paragraph seven, entitled "Oral Reports and Notifications,"
detailed how policemen had to hold themselves when reporting to their superiors: "When giving oral reports and notifications the policeman's address
has to be short, decided and clear, and must not be accompanied by any il-
lustrative [erläuternd] gestures, hand or body movements."[49] Correct uniform-
ing was meticulously spelled out over another four pages in the annex.[50]
Usually, the middle management first had to supervise form before attending
to other aspects of policing. Senior staff sergeants, for instance, had to visit all
their sector's police stations once a month and check on "military demeanor
[and] appearance."[51] Only thereafter did the Dienstvorschrift instruct the senior
staff sergeants to inquire into "overall training and overall police duties," closing
the paragraph with yet another list of issues about proper form, namely, "the
keeping of the daybooks, horses, weapons, ammunition, and equipment."[52]
Photographic evidence documenting the inspection visit of an officer (figure 3)
shows a police station's crew standing to attention in front of their office building while holding out their equipment. The form I am referring to here was
thus primarily related to appearance, to the outward aspects of the policeman's
body, his uniform, movements, material, to the image of the police he conveyed, and less to the formalization of action-reaction routines. As argued in
chapter 1, the Landespolizei was particularly anxious to uphold its own and
each individual member's reputation and honor, and the manual precisely reflected this concern, for the instructions about proper appearance were mostly
about attaining and retaining authority through dress and comportment.

Accordingly, the entire second section of the handbook was exclusively dedicated to the policemen's professional and social standing and to the duties
and codes of behavior that were prescribed by his status (Berufs- und Standespflichten). "Obedience towards all superiors, discipline [Manneszucht], sense of
honor, and a comradely mind"—those were the principles policemen had to
abide by.[53] The manual prescribed "sober, virtuous, and honorable conduct,"[54]
and stipulated "reputable behavior"[55] both during and outside of duty. To as-
sure the policeman's reputation, wives and children were to be "kept under
order and discipline."[56] Policemen had to be free from debt, and their uniforms
had to be clean. Accepting gifts was prohibited, as was drinking alcohol while

FIGURE 3.   An inspection officer reviews a police station. German policemen stand at attention in front of their station building presenting their gear. Place and date unknown. Bildarchiv der Deutschen Kolonialgesellschaft, Universitätsbibliothek Frankfurt am Main. Photo No. 019-2132-09.

on duty or engaging in any form of trade. Moreover, policemen were not allowed to join political organizations.[57] In several passages, the *Dienstvorschrift* urged policemen to pay close attention to their manners and behavior. They had to be "polite and obliging," and to "keep a calm composure at all times" as well as maintain "self-possession."[58] These prescriptions were thus more of the order of self-discipline rather than detailed recommendations on how to navigate particular encounters when representing the colonial state. In this sense, and borrowing from Clifford Geertz's useful reminder of the tripartite etymology of the state, the manual reflected notions of estate and stateliness, rather than statecraft.[59]

Among the fifty-seven paragraphs, several annexes, and an additional series of bulletins, the "treatment of the natives" received merely four paragraphs.[60] Initial drafts had stated that "one of the most difficult and most important tasks of the policeman is the treatment and education of the natives, [and] justice must prevail in particular in those cases in which the policemen have the difficult task to rule on disputes between whites and natives."[61] Both the idea that policing Africans was the hardest and most important part of policing and the admission of difficulty when it came to mediating between colonizers and colonized were edited out of the later drafts.[62] What remained in the final version was ambiguous counsel based on racist assumptions. It cautioned policemen not to interfere in "petty" conflicts among Africans, or between them and their European employers. Especially regarding the latter relationship, the handbook recommended "keeping reticent," just to remind its readers immediately thereafter that this was true only if compatible with their duty to police labor relations.[63]

The overall "guiding principle" (*Richtschnur*) that the manual suggested was to show "severity which must not degenerate into harshness or cruelty."[64] Policemen were to "abstain from any kind of swearwords towards natives or even assaults accompanied by gross swearwords," yet had to make sure that Africans would not "be spared" their "deserved punishment," for "indulgence is not interpreted by the natives as benignity and clemency but as weakness."[65] The manual stated that "a kind word toward natives is often advisable to instill trust or to laud their work. But one is to desist from joking and banter."[66] In order to "assess the natives fairly," the manual recommended that policemen learn about their "minds and characteristics." Two lines further down, however, it already provided such an assessment when it noted that "on the one hand, the native is not yet a mature member of humanity, on the other hand, his natural dispositions [*Naturanlagen*] make him in various abilities superior to men of culture [*Kulturmenschen*]."[67] In short, the *Dienstvorschrift* reflected common racist views advocating a paternalist while vigilant attitude toward the colonized, resulting in rather equivocal directions as to when to use what measures, notably violence.

At the end of the manual, in the last section, hidden between some general explanations about the police's overall structure and training and a couple of paragraphs on disciplinary actions in case of transgression, were some concrete and fairly detailed guidelines as to how to proceed in specific situations. These remaining paragraphs were clearly modeled on gendarmerie and police manuals from the homeland, and thus made sense only to a limited extent in the colonial context.[68] The directives covered filing charges, making arrests and confiscations, house searches, proper weapon usage, overseeing mass gatherings, transporting prisoners, and handing out deliveries.[69] In theory, these applied to policing both the colonizer and colonized populations. But since the latter had received attention in a separate section, this last part of the handbook could easily be perceived as irrelevant to the African population and was most likely not pertinent to the bulk of everyday police work.[70]

Both the 1907 decree mentioned above and the entire *Dienstvorschrift* gave not a single word to the African staff, detailing neither their legal status and rights nor their tasks and conduct toward the public.[71] In the original 1905 charter, African police assistants had still had a whole paragraph dedicated to them. But since their mention could be interpreted as including African policemen in the body of civil servants of the German state, an interpretation colonial administrators wanted to rule out at all costs, their role was left out of the new regulations entirely.[72] In an internal note in 1907 on the organization of the Landespolizei, Chief of Police Heydebreck noted that "the solution to the native question [meaning Africans who were employed in the police force, policemen included—M.M.] encounters difficulties which will have to be reported on separately."[73] I have found no evidence following this statement of a general definition of the African police staff's role and status. Revealingly, the rare minor directives that did pertain specifically to African policemen concerned primarily questions of appearance and standing. This becomes evident in the repeated orders emphasizing that African policemen were not allowed to wear military insignia.[74] Also, police headquarters found it necessary to decree expressly how police assistants had to salute superiors and what their correct posture toward Europeans in general should be.[75] In July 1914, although it was done too late to go into effect, Chief of Police Bethe prohibited disciplining African policemen with corporal punishment.[76] Inspection Officer Medding had already laid out the issue, having discussed it among magistrates and other officials. His wording, on which Bethe's ordinance was based, testifies to the way in which even this crucial matter was unfailingly discussed in terms of honor and prestige. What mattered was, on the one hand, to fare well in comparison to the British Empire, and, on the other, to instill a sense of honor in the African members of the Landespolizei in order to distinguish them from the rest of the colonized.[77] Medding's letter is moreover a telling confirmation of the German police force's dependence on its African counterparts:

> At the border where there will always be the comparison with English natives and their different treatment, we will only have good natives who fulfill the very important and indispensable position of police servant, who can read tracks well, and who are particularly well suited as interpreters, if we treat these natives differently than the average of our natives, especially if we don't punish them with "corporal chastisement." A Rietfontein Baster who was a police servant in the Aruab District reported a little while ago that someone called out to him at the border: "Why do you even stay with those sjambok Germans!"—and he actually did not stay with us.—The police servant has to feel himself in a "superior position" [gehobene Stellung] toward the other natives.[78]

More explicitly than Medding was Bethe when he stated in his decree draft that "one will never instill [erziehen] a sense of honor in natives with corporal punishment, and a sense of honor is what we must and can inculcate police servants with."[79]

In the discussions around the manual in general, one magistrate went so far as to ask if written guidelines were necessary at all. He suggested that one should leave the instruction of both the German and the African policemen to the local authorities, that is, to men like himself. He specifically objected to formulating rules of conduct regarding contact with Africans. "Such rules of action," he wrote, "should rather belong in verbal instruction, they should remain unwritten, for they might raise wrong ideas."[80] Other magistrates, on the other hand, were impatient to receive written directives. One of them declared that he would soon write his own.[81] Windhuk colonial officials and local administrators debated for almost two years over the instruction manual, and when it was finally sent out in June 1909, authorization by the colonial ministry in Berlin was still pending.[82] Moreover, local administrations did not or could not necessarily forward the manuals to their outlying police stations.[83] Or if they did, it was not guaranteed that the handbooks would be read. Vice Governor Hintrager noted in January 1910 that "although the offices have reported that the *Dienstvorschrift* has been distributed and is known to all policemen, investigation has shown that the policemen were unable to provide information on the simplest topics, such as superiors, professional and social duties, weapons usage. During briefing they utterly failed."[84] Eventually, in that same year, a printed version of the manual was published in Breslau. Two years later, in 1912, when police headquarters suggested an alteration regarding recruitment requirements, the Colonial Office in Berlin claimed that it had still not given its final approval for the initial manual.[85] By then, having made do without a manual, or with minimal knowledge of the content of the existing one, policemen had constructed their own code of conduct.

Other, more specific policing rules, notably those pertaining to the use of force—regarding the usage of weapons, for instance—remained indeterminate and qualified by exceptions until the end of the German colonial period. Notably, the question of whether African policemen should be allowed to carry firearms was debated throughout the colonial period. I address the development of weapons usage in more detail in the chapter on technologies of violence. Likewise, uncertainties about disciplinary powers—who was authorized, and in what way, to reprimand policemen—took a long time to be resolved. Here, the conflict was first and foremost about whether the civil or the military arm of the police force was responsible, and which was more capable.[86]

It appears, then, that a majority of administrators at police headquarters and in the local offices felt that, to a certain extent, the less they put in writing about handling concrete situations, the better it would be. Or at least they hesitated to consolidate such guidelines on paper, because they did not want to be hemmed in by the law. I am not sure how conscious a decision this was, but it supplemented the structural inconsistencies—the hybrid institutional makeup as well as the uncertainty of what pertained to the realm of policing. Hence, despite an insistence on absolute order, and despite the will to regulate each and every part of life through executive orders, to a large extent the official state left open the question of *how* to bring about that order. This observation pertained particularly to the realm of violence and its relation to race. There, the colonial state officials who debated and decided on police regulations seemed to rely on an under-articulated ideology, on unquestioned and ostensibly shared assumptions, on notions of honor and duty, which would somehow guide the policeman in the field and indicate to him how to act.[87]

Furthermore, pragmatic considerations fed into this understanding. Some administrators were well aware that the limitations and constraints of the colonial system granted individual policemen room for maneuver that they would not have enjoyed in the homeland. Magistrate Todt, for instance, noted that "remote police stations must be granted a certain independence when making decisions. Otherwise the organization of orderly conditions will be made illusory as a result of delays caused by great distances."[88] State Secretary Friedrich von Lindequist affirmed that the "difficult exigencies" of the colonial theater demanded "a certain independence and inner strength of character" from policemen.[89] And if one read the *Dienstanweisung* very carefully, one could find that even there independent initiative was allowed when the situation asked for it: "In urgent cases, it is the duty of every . . . officer of the Landespolizei, even if he has not been assigned to or commissioned by an office, to independently initiate police action."[90] Depending on their disposition, policemen perceived this leeway as an opportunity or as a burden. Either way, it forced the men to come up with procedures and ways of handling things by themselves.

The Institution

The compound organizational structure of the police force caused frequent internal conflict. In theory, chains of command were parceled out according to different functions: the military division, that is, notably the inspection officers under the chief of police's command, was responsible for the policemen's initial (military) training, their physical form and bearing, and their deployment; the civil division, that is, the magistrates and district chiefs under the governor's command, were responsible for additional training and gave orders with respect to day-to-day business.[91] In reality, roles were not that well separated. Since recruits who were still in training already carried out actual police duties, their instructors, that is, the inspection officers, were in fact also in charge of everyday police affairs. And magistrates and district chiefs often decided on deployment questions by way of commissioning mandates that called for additional staff at some station or other.[92] Moreover, these magistrates and district chiefs found it particularly difficult to accept directives from the chief of police, who was the highest commander of all policemen, but ranked equally with local administrators; he was not their superior. District Chief von Frankenberg perceived police headquarters' "tone of patronizing censure" as "misplaced and offending," for instance.[93] Equally tense was the relationship between the police and the military in general. Major Estorff, the commander of the Schutztruppe, complained in 1907, for instance, that he had to send out military missions on false information because, in his eyes, the police had not done their job.[94] In return, an inspection officer from Bethanien bemoaned the fact that, in 1911, the military had not even taken notice of the police's existence.[95] Thus, scholars are in principle right when they state that discord internal to the colonial administration hindered the development of a well-oiled state apparatus.[96] Not all conflict between the two branches resulted in malfunction, however. In some cases it caused both magistrates and inspection officers to urge their policemen to more activity. The long-lasting dispute between District Chief Frankenberg and Inspection Officer Hildebrandt, which prompted both men to spur their subordinates on, is a good example of this.[97]

The most grievously felt limitation of the police force, from the perspective of its members, was the lack of manpower. This grievance was nothing unique. Most police forces, both colonial and metropolitan, complained about being understaffed. In a time when governments were still uncertain about the exact purpose of police, notably its advantages over a domestically operating military force, and thus wanted to keep costs of these agencies rather low, police representatives unremittingly repeated that more men would entail better policing.[98] In German Southwest Africa, local administrators claimed time and again that if only they had sufficient staff, things would run more smoothly.[99] The most vocal among them was District Chief Wasserfall from Bethanien whose tone ranged from imploring plea to open threat when he requested more men for his locality.[100] As a matter of fact, although manpower rarely reached the level authorized in annual budgets, the discrepancy was not as severe as some accounts would have us believe.[101] The initial budget sanctioned by the Reichstag in 1907 had foreseen a size of 720 German and 370 African men. Just one year later, the budget was cut to an authorized size of

470 and 260.[102] In early 1908, only about 160 German but already 220 African policemen were in the Landespolizei. Yet, by the end of that year, boosted by sustained recruitment from the metropole, the number of German recruits had surpassed 400.[103] By 1912, they were at a high of circa 570 and 320, respectively. In 1914, the numbers decreased again to around 470 and 370 men.[104]

Granted, this was not an exorbitant number of men to police a population of about 70,000 Africans and 14,800 settlers (1913), on a territory of approximately 501,000 square kilometers.[105] Other European colonial administrations met similar challenges.[106] In Algeria in 1881, twelve gendarmes were responsible for the surveillance of 22,500 North Africans and 500 Europeans living across a surface of 2,332 square kilometers.[107] In Kenya in 1902, a British police officer found himself "administering and policing a district inhabited by half a million well-armed savages . . . the size of Yorkshire" with only two other British men, twenty African soldiers, and fifty African policemen.[108] Moreover, circumstances differed not substantially from rural areas in the German motherland as well, except that there territories were generally less sparsely populated.[109] Berlin, the most heavily policed city in the Kaiserreich, had a ratio of 1:288, compared to Windhuk with 1:175.[110]

Police stations of the Landespolizei were usually manned by two to six men while keeping a slight white majority. Ideally, all stations were supposed to have five, but at least three German men. "Less than three white men are inexpedient because they cannot fulfill the purpose of constant readiness," the head of police noted.[111] Thus, stations with only one German man were not meant to exist, but they frequently did. In December 1908, the distant northern district Grootfontein had three stations with only one German man.[112] An overview from 1911 lists 101 outposts, of which more than half were manned with less than three German men. Six were unstaffed entirely. One police station was occupied by a simple constable helped by four African men (Kauchas), and one was even operated by an African policeman alone (Spencer Bay).[113] Larger town stations attached to district offices garrisoned ten to thirty, and the police depots up to fifty men.[114] The 1911 list documents a slight predominance of German over African personnel, yet, notably on small stations, the proportion between African and German staff evened out. And on patrols, the racial breakdown was often 1:1.[115]

Interestingly, the Landespolizei was initially meant to be an exclusively German force, merely helped by a few African men serving as messengers, guides, and prisoner guards.[116] But police headquarters quickly realized that particularly as trackers and interpreters, and "to mediate in negotiations with the native population, a sufficient number of loyal and dependable native police servants are an absolute necessity."[117] Indeed, in many respects, the

African police assistants were the linchpin of policing. Without them, little would have worked. An experiment in 1912 to create a police unit composed of Basters only—the so-called Bastard-Feldkornett—who would be allowed to operate independently and police their own people in the Rehoboth area, thus making the force "whiter" while keeping personnel costs low, was considered a failure and abandoned after a year.[118] And thus, although it was seen as an annoyance, the police force kept its racially mixed composition of about two-thirds German and one-third African policemen until the end of German rule, as the numbers above confirm.

In colonial Africa, such a racial makeup was unusual. Police forces in which European men also manned the rank and file and did not act exclusively as superior officers to a largely African (at times also Asian) force existed only in colonies with European settler populations. Algeria, South Africa, and Southern Rhodesia had primarily white police forces or gendarmeries.[119] Yet, in other African settler colonies, notably Kenya and Northern Rhodesia, police forces did not reach such high levels of European rank and file.[120] Moreover, scholarship suggests that, broadly speaking, colonial administrations did not merge indigenous and European men, but had them police their respective racial communities.[121] In German Southwest Africa, however, African and German policemen worked together. In fact, as will become clear in subsequent chapters, in many cases, police work could only unfold and be effective because it was practiced as an interracial project on the ground.

Regarding colonial officials in general, Assistant Secretary of State Heinrich Schnee admitted in 1911 that "one has not always the very best civil servant material at one's disposal," but that if only trained properly, "even mediocre civil servants can achieve something useful."[122] The available "human material," as Governor Schuckmann called the men of the Landespolizei, was certainly not always the best.[123] Promotion prospects were minimal, which deterred more accomplished men from transferring from the military to the police. A policeman with a sizable criminal or disciplinary record was no rarity. In its 1910 annual report, police headquarters observed that the military was not sending them the "worst of the worst" anymore, but that "former Schutztruppen members poll[ed] badly with regard to penalty figures."[124] A survey of the military rolls in the personnel files of the Landespolizei supports this assessment.[125] The Colonial Office in Berlin stated in 1911 that repeated examples had shown that it was "not dependable" to ask the candidate himself whether he had committed any crimes prior to his enlistment in the military and police.[126] Accusations raised by the settler parliament (Landesrat) that African policemen in particular had been former criminals led to an internal investigation that revealed that this was not the case.[127] The magistrates' and district chiefs' reports show, however, that African police assistants were as likely to have previous convictions as were their German sergeants or staff sergeants.[128] Moreover, both African and German policemen were disciplined for smaller and greater breaches on numerous occasions during their time in the police force.[129] As Chief of Police Bethe noted, "Unfortunately, there are only a few ideal types among the policemen."[130]

Oftentimes, policemen were bereft of one set of skills entirely, but proficient in another. For example, many men who were recruited for their artisanal expertise could barely read or write. In the end, a lot depended on how sensitive inspection officers or magistrates were to the problem. If they knew where to deploy what sort of men, affairs usually ran more fluidly.[131] But that was not always the case. Sergeant Strunck, for instance, noted in a letter to his brother that "me, with my lousy handwriting, they have now ordered to the office, and now I have to run the whole shebang."[132]

Working Conditions

The police force had little equipment. Furniture, horses, paper, uniforms, and even entire buildings were lacking. The old firearms and the insufficient housing gave particular cause for complaint.[133] A more peculiar deficiency was the use of camels instead of horses in some places. Camels seemed to be not at all useful, even to make an impressive entrance: Sergeant Gentz complained bitterly about this fact. He was frustrated that there was no way one could ride the animal and keep one's dignity (or honor, as he framed it).[134] Often, policemen had to rely on outside help such as buildings provided by farmers or equipment made available by the military.[135] The many privations, and hence dependence on material support from other actors in the colonial theater, made policemen long for a strong professional culture and identity that would distinguish them and would accord with their official standards of social standing. One can detect this desire in the way individual policemen spruced up their uniforms and their sparsely furnished apartments.[136]

The climate was another taxing factor. Namibia's environment is hostile, comprising mostly desert or arid highland. Very high and very low temperatures are common, scarcity of water is punctuated by heavy rainfalls, and numerous pathogens accompanied the policemen's daily efforts. A significant number of men—especially the Europeans—were regularly unavailable because they were sick or exhausted. A 1912 report estimated the proportion of men on sick or home leave at 25 percent.[137] Police Sergeant Kowalke at Police Station Chairos, for instance, "suffer[ed] constantly from fever."[138] Concurrently, his

station colleague Sergeant La Croix was hospitalized at the district's headquarters location Outjo with malaria. "He had broken down on his way
hither ca. 40 km outside of Outjo, and had to be retrieved by a medical sergeant."[139] The station's senior, Sergeant Dawedeit, fractured his collarbone
and was also off duty, which must have left the station manned with the sick
Kowalke and two police assistants. Contrary to racist preconceptions of their
adaptation to harsh environments, African men fell sick too. Sergeant Dufring,
for instance, had to abort a patrol because one of his police assistants had
fallen ill.[140] Almost the entire staff of Police Depot Kub, whatever their race,
contracted malaria during the heavy rains of 1909. Five Africans died in the
incident.[141] Coping with harsh climatic conditions often became the main
achievement in police narratives. Coupled with the material deprivations, these
exploits seem to have fostered romanticized notions of an adventurous, dangerous life. Doctor Zachlehner promoted the idea when he told police headquarters that policemen in the colony had to be and were indeed tougher than
their peers in the metropole.[142] And Vice Governor Brückner stressed that the
extraordinarily hard lot of policemen and their secluded work demanded that
they be tougher than Schutztruppen soldiers.[143] Police reports became more
detailed, sometimes even florid, when danger had been involved. Sergeant
Hagner's overwritten report of a patrol on which he was attacked by San
people with bows and arrows is an example for this.[144]

Space significantly determined the manner in which police work developed.[145] Communication and transportation of supplies took a great deal of
time. Policemen spent long stretches of time on horseback crossing the wide
expanses of German Southwest Africa. Sergeant Link reported, for example,
that on a patrol he and his African colleague had covered an average distance of
six kilometers per hour. During the patrol in question they had traveled 488
kilometers in a span of twelve days.[146] The very orderly patrol book from Police
Depot Spitzkoppe listed in 1911: "January, 16 patrols, 2248 kilometers covered;
February, 14 [patrols], 2014 km; March, 18 [patrols], 2534 km."[147] An outlying
post could operate on its own for weeks, even months, before it would get a
visit from its inspection officer or a senior staff sergeant.[148] As a consequence,
accountability was only sporadically guaranteed. Policemen could get away
with things as long as they were not caught by their superiors or exposed by the
public. That policemen would let themselves go without regular superinten-
dence and "go native" under the malign influence of the African climate was a
constant fear of superiors.[149] Inspection officer Freytag of Depot Spitzkoppe
worried in 1909, for instance, that his men on remote posts had been "smoth-
ered by the rather bleak conditions." "On many stations a colossal sloppiness
[Schlendrian] reigns," he observed, and "the good life, drinking and other enjoy-

ments are the main thing."[150] Thus, a year later, he sent several men back to the depot to be reminded of military discipline, "for it became noticeable that some of them could not bear the long freedom without strict supervision."[151]

Training and Appearance

That the policemen could not be experts in all the domains they were asked to administer is obvious. All men went through a quick training (usually six to eight weeks) at the police depots, focused primarily on military skills and those abilities useful in the colonial terrain, before being deployed to their station.[152] Not seldom, instruction at the depot was inconsistent and patchy for various reasons. One inspection officer noted that instruction had to be canceled several times because of too much fluctuation in personnel, and because repairing the depot's buildings was more pressing than training.[153] Sometimes, because of shortages in personnel, policemen were sent out almost immediately.[154] It could happen that sergeants were deployed even though their exam results were "barely sufficient" and their "teaching was not yet completed."[155] Acting Magistrate Krafft was particularly unsatisfied with the "insufficient training" at police depots. According to him, said limited training was the key problem in light of the ongoing settlement of the colony that had increased the "insecurity and incorrect behavior of individual policemen towards the public."[156]

Once deployed, ideally, policemen were supposed to be taught administration and legal skills by their local civil superiors. This training in civil matters was a continuous enterprise for which policemen were required to return regularly to their district's head offices. It took them away from their duty and took time, though. Thus, oftentimes, local administrators preferred to keep their men in place to the detriment of their further learning. District Chief Frankenberg, for instance, claimed that his men were not able to attend regular instruction sessions or other meetings because the police stations of the Omaruru district were too far away and did not have enough men.[157] Some magistrates and district chiefs passed instruction responsibilities down to their senior staff sergeants; some took them upon themselves. Whereas superior administrators were learned men, usually in the law, staff sergeants were simple military men who had barely received any specialized training themselves. Only about half of the senior staff and staff sergeants of the Landespolizei had attended classes at the police school in Windhuk.[158] Others were advanced in rank based on their seniority.[159] Or they simply fulfilled the function without having been officially promoted. Sergeant Melzer, for instance, notorious for his disruptive and insubordinate as well as violent behavior, was nevertheless recommended for advancement, simply because he had "already served as staff sergeant."[160] And since he already "had all the proficiencies and qualities necessary" for that position, the recommending inspection officer asserted, he did not need to attend the police school in Windhuk.[161] The schooled knowledge of the men of the Landespolizei, even the more senior ones, could therefore have been only fragmentary. And on-the-job training was, as just suggested, equally difficult to sustain for structural reasons.

When it did actually take place, police training focused to a large extent on riding and shooting—not on legal knowledge, administrative skills, or other civil competences.[162] Military loyalty and comradeship were highly esteemed values, and military protocol was a constant concern among police officials. The police archives are filled with cases of quarrels over whether a salute had been executed correctly, whether hierarchies had been respected, or whether a uniform had been properly worn.[163] Sergeant Hugo Baudeck, for instance, was reprimanded for not having recognized a Schutztruppen officer's rank, but more because he "left one hand in his pocket while he gesticulated with the other, [and] moved his upper torso back and forth."[164] In this fashioning of the ideal type of martial policeman, external physical features were regularly intertwined with internal character traits. A man who was corpulent, for instance, was thought to lack the suitable mental faculties for police work.[165] Men who applied for posts in the police sometimes sent photos and physical descriptions of themselves to support their candidacy, often emphasizing that they were tall and strong.[166] Being of vigorous, soldierly physique and able to exert violence, so they implied, they would make good enforcement officers.

Regarding the African policemen, a number of them had gone to missionary schools to learn the German language as well as reading and writing.[167] Once in service, they were hardly trained at all. Mostly, they learned how to salute and how to stand at attention.[168] Their other skills, it was assumed, were "natural" and did not need to be taught. On occasion, beginning in November 1910, they received training in shooting, but only in the presence of an inspection officer or a senior staff sergeant. Twenty-five shots per year was the allowed practice rate for African policemen.[169] In 1914, the number of allowed shots for training purposes for African policemen was increased to seventy-five per year, and the supervision could be performed by the station eldest.[170]

The quality of the Landespolizei rested hence on the capacity of each individual policeman to embody state authority through an impeccable exterior and an interior martial self. Especially the higher ranks had to be of "immaculate military form."[171] If that standard was not met, the honor of the police force was harmed, with detrimental effects on the colonial state as a whole. Police Sergeant Arnold, for example, was a former NCO who had served eleven years in the military, and was described as "a highly literate, absolutely independent worker."[172] But Inspection Officer Hollaender regarded him nevertheless as "totally unfit for the Landespolizei," for he "had had the effrontery [*sich nicht entblödete*] to repeatedly cry out for help during riding exercises and to make an exhibition of his infinite fear in every possible way. . . . No threat, acrimony, or appeal to [his] sense of honor," Hollaender reported, had helped. Sergeant Arnold was bound to "harm in an irreparable way the reputation of the Landespolizei."[173] Arnold's case prompted the chief of police to issue a circular noting that such "riding caricature" was unacceptable in the police force, and that "all policemen must be kept at the depots until their military training is accomplished."[174] Constable Türk, on the other hand, was considered by the same inspection officer a useful addition to the force, precisely because his "good military demeanor" had made up for his "limited physical and mental abilities."[175] And Sergeant Thelen, who did not know how to write properly when he entered the police force, and who, after two years of service, had still only "sufficient" knowledge of police work, was nevertheless recommended for promotion, because besides being diligent and ambitious, he had a "dashing and energetic demeanor and good form," and he was very much liked by his comrades.[176]

What counted in the end were features that mattered externally, that polished and honed the public face of the institution. Policemen needed the ability to perform symbolic power through an honorable military persona. And violence was always present in that identity as a potentially lethal threat inherent in the disciplined, martially trained, armed, and mounted bodies of the policemen.[177] Military obedience and discipline structured every aspect of policemen's activities. Military training provided internalized behavioral patterns that helped in those many situations where action was left to individual discretion, especially since there were neither clearly delimited areas of competence nor positively defined rules. Military habitus by itself was supposed to inspire awe among the population. Besides, the military offered a large pool of disciplined recruits who were loyal and obedient servants of the state, who could function as visible and exemplary representatives of state power. The precedence given to military background and conduct applied also to Africans, although they had not received the same military training as German NCOs. Inspection Officer Hollaender, for instance, deemed four African policemen particularly competent because they had "all [been] former native soldiers."[178] Thus, the primacy of military values pertained to German and African members of the police force alike.

Yet, in many ways, African policemen were "almost but not quite" like German policemen, to paraphrase Homi Bhabha's famous formulation of the ambivalent concept of mimicry.[179] This becomes particularly clear when we look at physical appearance again—in this case at uniforms. The uniform was the most visible marker of the African policeman's belonging to the German colonial state. But it signified more than that. It became a marker of belonging to another social organization, a new "caste" of African men.[180] The uniform can thus be analyzed as an indicator of the complex system of alliances and allegiances in which African policemen operated. The uniform of a police assistant resembled in all aspects the one his German fellows wore with the exception of military insignia. Instead, he wore two large metal letters—L.P.—on the side of his hat and a red armband with the same letters (figure 4). Many African policemen did, however, carry badges of rank. As the commander of a Schutztruppe unit in Keetmanshoop complained to the local police in July 1909, "Many natives disobeye[d] the law prohibiting the 'wearing of military insignia,' especially the native police servants who almost all [had] cockades attached" to their hats, and who acted quite surprised when reminded of the ban.[181] Baster policeman Friedrich Boekis, for instance, appeared on duty dressed in a uniform with aiguillette and cords on his shoulders.[182]

Africanist scholars have extensively studied this mimicking appropriation of military signs of power especially by the Herero people.[183] Wearing a German uniform, the African policemen of the Landespolizei were not only servants of the German state, *Polizeidiener*, they were also *ovasolondate* [otjiHerero: soldiers] of the *oturupa*, representatives of "new systems of authority in keeping with their own ideals of (male) identity."[184] In the oturupa, African men reenacted, or "played," German military culture. Anthropologist Larissa Förster observes that these troop performances were "not simply an imitation, but also a symbolic usurpation, a parodic commentary and counter-narrative."[185] Scholars argue that this form of social organization "embodied opposition" and a form of "mastery through mime."[186] It provided status to its members and was a means of asserting or reaffirming one's warrior masculinity and the honor denied by local and colonial elites. By participating in those groups, younger men—especially those with access to weapons, but with no wealth in livestock or kinship—appropriated and partially usurped older precolonial elites with their "traditional" *komando* structures, and against those colonial authorities who had taken over the roles of "chiefs" or "kapteins," that is, German missionaries and military commanders.[187] Referring to the 1890s, missionary Jakob Irle recalled the soldiering performances of three different groups of young African men, who identified themselves with different colors: "A spirit of disobedience and insolence against the elders and the missionaries arose among the male youth of all stations. Playing soldiers began. . . . We had now not only White and Black Boys [Oorlam and Nama groups—M.M.], but also the Red Boys [Herero group—M.M.], who developed to a dangerous element. It was as if a

FIGURE 4. Group of six African policemen in Lüderitzbucht who, against regulations, wear military belts, shoulder straps, and pistols. Their posture exudes confidence. Date unknown. Bildarchiv der Deutschen Kolonialgesellschaft, Universitätsbibliothek Frankfurt am Main. Photo No. 019-2133-13.

spirit of rebellion moved with these red bands among the youth. There was drilling, swearing, boozing and aping the German soldiers."[188]

At the same time, the self-organization of young African men into military-style groups resulted from as well as furthered their close insertion into the German colonial web. Their lives were marked by the experience of living in proximity to the Schutztruppe. As Henrichsen points out, "Whatever the immediate reasons may have been for the attraction the colonial military had for these African boys and youths, the fact remains that until 1904 large numbers of youths and men in central Namibia received military training in the German forces, or were at least able to experience an everyday military reality."[189] Thus, the immersion of young African men in oturupa and military culture was key in producing African police personnel. Whether it sprang from usurping imitation or actual employment, the Landespolizei, to which proper bearing mattered so substantially, could capitalize on these enactments of drill and military posture. Often, individual relationships between German and African men had already been formed in the Schutztruppe. Evidence shows that many

African men knew some German policeman or other from their previous careers in the military. Nama policeman Jan, for instance, served in the colonial military for ten years before his former commander found employment for him in the police force.[190] And Police Assistant Zacharias had served twelve years in the Schutztruppe prior to his employment at Police Depot Kupferberg.[191]

Group Dynamics

Because of these long acquaintances, often, German policemen projected concepts of European military loyalty onto their African subalterns. A sense of mutual obligation sometimes emerged out of the shared experience of careers in military service. In July 1908, for example, at the request of an unnamed African policeman, Senior Executive Officer Müller from police headquarters arranged for the release of the man's wife, who was still in war captivity, and had her brought to live with her husband at the police's "native" quarters.[192] In another example, when a settler had his dog attack an African policeman's wife, Inspection Officer Freytag gave credence to his subaltern's account rather than believing the settler's version and went out of his way to have the settler penalized.[193] And Captain Streitwolf noted in his journal about one of his African policemen who died from a disease that he "felt deeply for him . . . this Herero who in most loyal fulfillment of his duty for Emperor and Empire has given his life."[194] To the African policeman, employment in the Landespolizei meant entering a patron-client relationship with an individual German superior, who, in an ever-threatening and ever more restrictive colonial setting was most likely to be able to provide goods, pay, and a desirable warrior status. One cannot exclude that the above-mentioned Herero friendship or male bond concepts were, from the perspective of the African policemen, mapped onto German notions of military loyalty and comradeship. However, some apologetic narratives of the German colonial era have taken these relationships as proof of Africans' unwavering loyalty to the German nation, even after it had ended.[195] The example of Police Assistant Josef Frederik, who in 1927 wrote a letter to his former superior, Sergeant Bruno Vogel, giving his latest news, but above all asking for some clothes, has been interpreted in such a way.[196]

As I already pointed out regarding the policemen's masculinities, violence within the group itself was common. German policemen were violent against German colleagues, either to settle a conflict between equals in rank or to remind the lower ranks of military hierarchy. Sergeants Petruschkat and Garstecki and Staff Sergeant Wirtz got into a fight with the owner of a bar and other guests.[197] And Sergeant Melzer provoked a brawl in another bar.[198] Fistfights and petty violence among policemen generated and strengthened male bonds. An integral part of an NCO's life, these everyday violent practices against members of the own group had become a habit and continued to exist within the police force. When the fight was considered to have harmed the police force's reputation, it could, however, result in a policeman's dismissal.[199] More frequent than petty violence between men of one racial group were the slaps in the face, kicks in the buttocks, and so forth that African policemen were subjected to by their German superiors.[200] All of these forms of everyday, irregular violence were part of the interpersonal dynamics among policemen. They were expressions of the often tense, emotionally charged conditions under which policemen operated, and as such they were intrinsic to police organizational culture.

Officially administered corporal punishment as disciplinary action against African policemen was, however, rare and controversial. In 1913, Chief of Police Bethe requested all local administrations to provide him with information about the numbers and kinds of punishments African policemen had received. The replies show that corporal punishment was rare and decreased over the years, to be replaced by imprisonment.[201]

"The police servants must feel themselves within a higher position towards other natives, or else we will never be able to find and keep useful and good elements for the Landespolizei. . . . We will never educate the natives to a sense of honor with corporal punishment. And we must and will educate the police servants to a sense of honor.[202] Thus read the explanation Chief of Police Heinrich Bethe gave in July 1914 when he finally decided to prohibit this disciplinary method entirely. The African policemen's belonging to the colonial state made them different in the eyes of the German administrators, a difference they meant to cultivate. As Inspection Officer Medding noted, for the sake of availing oneself of able African policemen, it was necessary "to treat those natives differently than the average of our natives."[203] In fact, he referred to a decree regarding the proper salute for African policemen to suggest that, since they were military men, they were entitled to honor.[204]

When it comes to honor and race, the profound contradictions within colonial ideology in German Southwest Africa become most evident. The desire to "educate" this group of men to a sense of honor sat uncomfortably between two common received ideas about "native" honor. The first one stipulated that the colonized did not have a concept of honor and were thus impervious to being humiliated through corporal punishment. The second idea stated the exact opposite, that is, that Africans, especially Herero, had such a high sense of honor that they would be most severely humiliated by corporal punishment. In any case, both ideas left no room for an inculcation of honor. And none of the ideas took into account the understanding of honor of African policemen themselves.

This notwithstanding, honor did extend to African policemen. As such, it was transracial. A sense of professional honor, or "pride in the office" (*Amtsstolz*), as Zollmann calls it, was not just promoted from above.[205] African policemen claimed it for themselves, as much as German policemen did. "Sergeant, I am not a bambuse, I am a police servant," Baster Police Assistant van Wyk was reported to have said when he was insulted by his superior.[206] This professional honor relied heavily on military traditions, both African and German ones.[207] But beyond that, the policemen conceived of their professional honor as a group ethic that they had created within a specific historical situation: being military men charged with civilian tasks.

Bureaucracy

Given that their training, their socialization, and their demeanor were considerably military in nature, the policemen of the Landespolizei were most of the time poorly trained bureaucrats who learned their administrational trade on the beat, supervised by the local magistrates and district chiefs, formed in relation with the policed population. Their bureaucratic reality was in gross contradiction to Max Weber's ideal-type official who was a highly specialized, objective, rational man. In Weberian theory, state officials, including policemen—whom Weber ironically characterized as "representatives of God on earth"—were supposed to execute bureaucratic tasks with the precision of a machine, entirely neutral toward the public.[208] Their professional ethos lay in their treatment of all cases "irrespective of a person's status," he claimed. That is, the ideal bureaucrat did not pay attention to *ständisch* notions of honor. Herein lay the bureaucrat's honor. Thus, paradoxically, the honor of the bureaucrat rested on his impartiality, his ability to be blind to status honor.[209]

The historian Ann Goldberg has recently demonstrated how libel suits played a crucial role in modernizing and democratizing German honor culture during the Kaiserreich. She rightly points out that honor and modernity should not be viewed in a simplistic dichotomy, but instead one should look at the way in which German honor culture was "juridified," was transformed and introduced into modern life "at all levels of society."[210] According to Goldberg, honor lawsuits were both tools of state repression and of democratic emancipation. They "made sense in a society where status and identity remained closely bound up with honor."[211]

A similar process of adaptation can be observed in the colony. The laws pertaining to honor and reputation were also valid in the colonies; policemen could appeal to the courts in defamation cases, and they regularly did. Sergeant Rach filed for libel against a farm manager who had called him "insolent [*frech*] like a Kaffir," Sergeant Sternberg against a farmer who had called him "dim-witted [*dämlicher*] dog."[212] Even Africans were allowed to make a case if they felt that their honor had been harmed. Interestingly, the implicit acknowledgment that Africans had honor and a right to defend it was given in a half-sentence when "defamation" was named as one example to specify which "minor offenses" Africans were allowed to bring before the law personally. Major offenses had to be prosecuted by a higher colonial official, usually the "native commissioner" or magistrate.[213]

However, it was more often the bureaucratic state rather than the judiciary that was appealed to by policemen. Just as Goldberg observes for the metropole, colonial policemen held on to the codes of military and masculine respectability that defined them. But they introduced them into their everyday working routines and thus, by doing so, altered them. Their endeavors to establish an institution, to define a profession, to build a state had an impact on how honor was achieved. Their professionalizing ambitions can best be seen in their attempts to validate police duties through acts of writing—in reports, notes, or book entries—or through reference to written texts—to laws, decrees, or regulations. For the policemen, this was a crucial, self-defining moment. State violence and bureaucracy were thought of and practiced together as one concerted effort to claim the legitimate use of force and to fashion one's professional self.

Obviously, it is in the nature of reading bureaucratic sources that bureaucratic procedures will appear to have played a prominent role in the policemen's work. But I wish to push this matter a bit further and suggest that bureaucracy, that is, authority and authorization through documentation, was a form of building professional culture for these men. The bureaucratic archive is itself a product of the intense emphasis on bureaucratizing police practice: every patrol had to be documented, every shot bullet had to be accounted for. Part of what made everyday violence into policing was the fact of its being recorded, organized, and justified in relation to inscribed codes of behavior and normativity that were distinguishable from wartime rules. Here are some examples of how these processes unfolded.

Policemen could get retroactively authorized for their violent deeds merely by indicating that the individual policeman's honor and the honor of the state were interchangeable, that they were one and the same. The state took very seriously the idea that its respectability and the individual policeman's honor were reciprocal, a concept that found expression in the "special definition of the [German] criminal code against 'insults of officials' [*Beamtenbeleidigung*]."[214] This is a phenomenon that can be observed for other German state institutions, and for other colonies, as well. The German postal services, for instance, "were, above all, concerned with the image they conveyed, with their reputation," a study of the colonial Reichspost affirms.[215] But take Senior Staff Sergeant Karl Schlink, for instance, who had arrogated to himself the authority to pronounce corporal punishment sentences in the absence of his depot commander. Asked to explain himself, he noted that "several natives have expressly refused obedience, have behaved themselves against police officials in such an insolent manner, that in order to prevent any further setbacks and to avoid undermining the reputation of a police official, I have made use of this right to punish."[216] To support his argument he referred to "written communication from the Imperial District Office Keetmanshoop in 1912 (I cannot exactly recall date and I[dentification] n[umber])," and added that all German policemen who had been present at the time could testify.[217] Schlink's official and procedural gesturing was successful. He had been able to mobilize his bureaucratic expertise, as limited as it was, to make his superiors accept his justifications. No disciplinary action was taken against him. When the reputation of one individual policeman was at stake, as Schlink made sure to mention in his statement (it was not even his own), the whole police institution had to rally to his cause.

Another example in which police actions were retroactively authorized, or at least attempted to be settled and renarrated in a way that would preserve a policeman's reputation, was Sergeant Julius Streibel's case. Stationed in Windhuk, he filed a complaint against an African police assistant. In the grievance, Streibel observed that "since a couple of days ago, the natives . . . mock me when I have to pass them or come near them."[218] The reason for this, he claimed, was that one of his African subordinates, namely, policeman Gottlib, had told lies about him. Reportedly, Gottlib had related the tale that Streibel had chased Africans from their dwellings, beaten them, and then been reprimanded for unauthorized police action. Interestingly, Streibel did not want to refute that he had been violent. Not at all. Rather, he wished to be cleared of the suspicion that his violent behavior might have been unauthorized. He closed his statement noting that "my reputation with the natives has suffered."[219] On the one hand, Streibel framed the issue as a defamation case, that is, as a matter of defending his name. On the other hand, he was concerned about the fact that the public could view his use of force as having been wielded outside the given set of rules. The two reference points for him were honor and the bureaucratic state. There is no record of whether Gottlib was censured or not. But the short episode offers insight into German policemen's professional culture by means of retroactive bureaucratic confirmation.

In other cases state authorization was at the onset of police action. In these instances, policemen were authorized to authorize. They were the ones who monitored violence within the colonial theater by whomever it was deployed. And one essential monitoring means in this undertaking was again bureaucratic procedure.[220] Whether authorized retroactively or in advance, practices of bureaucratized state violence functioned as techniques of distinction and professionalization. The policeman's use of his firearm is a good example. The rifle was the attribute that most visibly marked the policeman's identity as a wielder of violence. But many actors in the colonial theater possessed weapons. Thus, the specific manner in which policemen made use of guns became important to distinguish their actions from those of others in the colonial realm. They had procedure. The bureaucratic practice of inserting violent acts into narrative formulas formed police identities. These acts were undertaken by men who prided themselves in being respectable state servants who honored the law.[221]

Other textual and administrational techniques—distributing passes or pass tags, taking identification pictures and fingerprints, drafting biometric profiles according to the Bertillon system, and so forth—contributed, furthermore, to the police's professional identity. In these instances policemen not only advanced their professionalization with bureaucratic practice but also sought to achieve it through technological progress.[222]

The extent to which bureaucratic practices included the African policemen or excluded them from this aspect of professional culture is debatable. There was a tendency among German policemen to literally write their African subalterns out of the record. African policemen are for example rarely mentioned in patrol reports even though they were practically always present. They also have no individual personnel files. Yet, the numerous depositions in which African police assistants brought forward their own grievances or conveyed the voice of the colonized show evidence that they were well aware of the importance of certain wordings and procedures, and of paperwork in general. Moreover, African policemen could have recourse to their familiarity with written culture from before the German colonial era.[223] The historian Gesine Krüger demonstrates compellingly that it was actually colonial officials who forcefully insisted that Southern African societies were more illiterate than was the case, thus laying the foundations for the myth of African cultures as exclusively oral cultures.[224] Also, especially during and after the war, Africans were wary of producing written documents, knowing that German authorities were suspicious of their literacy.[225] Warning each other in letters not to share or record experiences in writing, they perversely contributed to the disappearance of their written archive.[226]

Evidence that African policemen served as scribes in the colonial administration is scant. Zollmann found evidence that at least some of them—how many is unclear—were taught not only the German language but also how to read and write at missionary schools.[227] There is plenty that testifies to African policemen's crucial role as interpreters.[228] A good translator was of great value, as Sergeant Eckel knew when he requested to be allowed to take Police Assistant Franz Boy with him when he was transferred to a new assignment.[229] And even if the majority of police assistants were not employed in clerical positions, as messengers and translators they were situated at a pivotal point of communication and inscription. Thus, they did in point of fact quite considerably participate in the bureaucratization of police practices and professional culture. This position guaranteed them an exclusive standing in their own community, for it situated them closest to colonial power in terms of production of administrational knowledge.

In brief, bureaucratic modes of fashioning professional police culture did not replace martial and masculine patterns, but instead were layered onto them. Thus, codes of honor were not abandoned for the sake of an exclusively rationalized state. In Weberian terms, the traditional and the bureaucratic kind of authority overlapped. Both contributed to the constitution of the colonial civil servant's honor.

This and the preceding chapter have laid out the complex historical constellation of a group of men who to many onlookers were the state. The German and African policemen of the Landespolizei were men invested deeply in honor and proper appearance: in their social status, in their masculinity, but especially in their professional identity as soldiers and bureaucrats. The numerous systems of honor and identification (German—African; adventurer—head of family; drill sergeant—hero warrior; military—bureaucracy) sometimes worked together, sometimes did not. The rules of the "game of honor" were not necessarily sound, but rather a "casuistry."[230]

German policemen executed power as members of the colonizing society. But as lower-rank civil servants coming from the lower middle classes of their home society they were liminal figures dependent on support from their superiors and African subordinates. The exercise of power by African policemen—as limited as it may have been—stemmed from their hybrid position, their performance of "bricolage" identities that at the same time appropriated and accepted colonial power.[231] Underlining the commonalities between African and German soldiers, Stefanie Michels stresses "how similar the *habitus* of 'black' and 'white' soldiers, troops and 'war lords' was in German Southwest Africa, and how established the shared military culture in the contact zone" was.[232] Despite fundamental cultural differences, as intermediaries of the colonial regime, German and African policemen drew nearer to each other and built a joint organizational culture. And this proximity reinforced the overlay of their respective honor codes.

Nevertheless, the interracial nature of Landespolizei was a fragile concoction, for, as has already become clear in these first two chapters, the men of the state were not ideal-type bureaucrats, but feeling men with a strong sense of honor. Policemen's emotions were part of who they were and accordingly affected how they policed. Ann Stoler proposes to include "affective states" as a significant element of the art of statecraft in the analysis of colonialism. She argues that scholars of colonial regimes have focused too much on the Western celebration of reason and rationality and have thus failed to account for the ways in which "strategically reasoned forms of administrative common sense informing policy and practice were grounded in the management of . . . affective states, in assessing both appropriate sentiments and those that threatened to fly 'out of control.'"[233]

If we give up the analytical distinction between emotion or embodied experience on the one hand and cognition or thought on the other, we can see that these motions were, in a way, one and the same thing to the historical actors in question (a notion that may be difficult for us as post-Weberian, not to mention post-Cartesian, scholars).[234] Doing so, one can see how colonial statecraft was not simply rationally performed, but rationally and sensorially felt. As policemen went about their daily work, they were expected to be "men of reasoned feeling," that is, to regulate their own emotions even as they contributed to regulating public life, and hence the emotional expression of others.[235] Yet, the archives show that policemen were not always able to keep in check their feelings, notably their fears and frustrations. Thus, policemen weaved apprehensive nervousness into statecraft.[236] In that sense, German Southwest Africa was an affective state. Keeping in mind that affects were a significant part of the practices with which policemen produced a colonial order and state, the following chapters delve into the heart of this book's subject matter: the everyday of policing.

In the everyday, both African and German policemen were to a large extent left to learn their job on the beat—by doing it. Savoir faire was acquired through practice, rather than through instruction from above or from handbooks. In response to the harsh conditions, the shortage of manpower, and the lack of a definite body of regulations, an attitude emerged that celebrated precisely this reality. In a written exam, a sergeant wrote that "practice and one's own experience are and remain the best teachers."[237] An ideology of the primacy of practice and experience had taken root.

CHAPTER 3

Of Whips, Shackles, and Guns
Tools and Technologies of Policing

European empires in the nineteenth and twentieth centuries believed firmly in their technological superiority. The idea of progress was deeply fixed in Western peoples' minds and had found entry into the colonizing project under the heading of "civilizing mission."[1] Convinced that their ingenuity and productivity had assured their economic wealth, and supported by the faith that history was proving them right, Western empires set out to force their innovations and technical inventions onto colonized societies.[2] Colonizers relied heavily, almost blindly, on their railroads, telegraphs, vaccines, and machine guns to seize and dominate foreign territories and populations. Unsurprisingly, they were at a loss when their machines did not produce the desired effect, when victory and welcoming awe failed to appear.

Some scholars seem to mirror this imperial discourse by attributing a determining, causal role to technology in imperial conquest. For instance, in *Tools of Empire*, Daniel Headrick boldly claims that "Western industrial technology has transformed the world more than any leader, religion, revolution, or war."[3] However, other scholars have tried to reverse this causal link, emphasizing the way in which imperialism itself was an important motivator for technological development and stressing the importance of racist and other ideologies in shaping and justifying the deployment of Western technologies.[4] Moreover, current studies on the history of technology stress the various forms in which historical actors used or consumed technological devices and the way in which these were embedded in discourses about race, gender, and class, thus refuting the notion that tools drive history.[5]

Based on these latter insights, and having focused on the actors and the institution in the previous two chapters, I turn now to the police force's tools in order to get a more minute understanding of how police activity was grounded in the material. As with so much else, policing technologies emerged as improvised responses to contextual constraints.[6] One constraint stood out above all others: the need to provide definitive and hierarchical social distinctions in an unstable situation of rule. While access to whips, chains, and firearms certainly did give the German colonizers an edge in some contexts of conflict, like many colonizers they were quick to overestimate their own ability to coerce compliance to colonial rule. More importantly, technologies of violence helped establish and refine the system of (pseudo-consensual) status distinctions that defined colonial life: colonizer/colonized, white/black, police/settler, high/low rank, and so on. The expert or approved use of policing implements—professionalism—also served as a marker of social distinction that elevated the policeman (and by extension the colonial state) above other colonial actors (like settlers). Finally, the devices themselves ensured a physical distance, an immediate distinction between the bodies that did violence and the bodies that were violated.

In early 1909, the author of a short newspaper article entitled "Jujitsu in the Colonies" expressed his doubts regarding the introduction of this specialized fighting technique into the police force of German Southwest Africa.[7] The article closed: "In addition to Jujitsu one will still need the rifle and the whip. For no bodily agility, no sleight of hand will help against a bullet. And once a thieving or robbing native has been apprehended, the whip will do."[8] For the author of the article, elaborate fighting techniques and potential bodily proximity to the colonized were a distraction from the core technologies of colonial rule: the gun and the whip. To his list, I will add a third: shackles. These three implements (the whip, the shackle, the gun) were embedded in three technological practices, each central to the system of social distinction, including police professionalism: flogging, binding, and shooting. The three sections that follow address in turn each of these three tools and practices. They demonstrate how an interplay of ideology, bureaucracy, and daily practice honed and fostered social hierarchies, modified and adjusted official policy, and in the process produced an effective regime of police violence.

The Unnamed Tool

The *sjambok* was a heavy, stiff leather whip, usually made of hippopotamus, giraffe, or rhinoceros hide. In 1905, the Governor of German Southwest Africa had chosen the sjambok as the "approved" tool for corporal punishment, describing it as follows:[9] "It has to be about 80–100 cm long, has to be round and smooth at the end with a diameter of one cm. Under no circumstances can it have knots or other bulges, and no wire or such similar may be sewn into the crease of the hide."[10] Yet, beyond this description it is striking that this apparently fundamental technology of rule—and a globally recognized "expression of white sovereignty"—simply disappears from the official sources of the lower echelons of the German administration.[11] Just as African policemen were often written out of the archive, the whip was erased from official documentation. This is even more true for other beating instruments such as birches or sticks. Police stations' inventories enumerate at length even the most insignificant items, such as horse combs or shoelaces, but none record whether a police station or an individual policeman was in possession of a sjambok or other beating devices.[12]

Whips did not make it into the public record most likely because they were privately rather than publicly owned tools, and because they were deemed a matter of course. In a rare mentioning of the whip in an official record, Staff Sergeant Bauer is quoted to have hit African Police Assistant Hans "with *my* sjambok."[13] State Secretary Dernburg observed in a secret report in 1907 that "nearly every white walks around with a whip," and that public offices had them lying "on the table, . . . directly next to the inkwell."[14] The sjambok was omnipresent—carried at the belt or placed in convenient places, available at any time. It was quite visible in everyday colonial life. In the metropole as well, it was a frequently seen object.[15] There were even postcards of posed floggings circulating.[16] Their ubiquity and self-evidence might explain their absence from formal colonial documentation.[17]

Another possible reason for the silence surrounding whips in official records is the deep ambivalence the colonial regime exhibited about their usage. A symbol of colonial rule, the sjambok was also deemed a lowly tool. For that reason, it was to be wielded only by African subalterns. "Officials entrusted with judiciary functions may never carry out the birching or flogging themselves," the general directive "regarding the application of corporal punishment" of 1907 ordered.[18] Although at least one German official, and if possible a doctor, had "always . . . to be present" during punishment, it sullied a white man's honor to carry out punishment personally.[19] "It is beneath his dignity," Schutztruppen officer Heinrich Fonck wrote.[20]

In theory, the legal rationale within which a beating was administered determined who wielded the whip. Floggings were carried out within the framework of either criminal or disciplinary justice (performed by Africans against Africans after a formal sentencing), or within the logic of paternal chastisement (performed by Europeans against Africans on the spot).[21] In the latter case, colonizers were in fact handling the instrument themselves. It is conceivable that they more or less consciously differentiated between the two legal principles. But this reasoning fits only awkwardly into a code that disdained "dishonorable" punitive technology altogether. Moreover, paternal chastisement was sometimes delegated to Africans, while official sentences were sometimes carried out by Europeans. Missionary Brockmann, for instance, asked the African teacher at his mission to chastise two domestics in his stead—in all probability with a cane or rod. "I had the teacher give the girls a proper beating [*ordentlich durchprügeln*]," he wrote to his superior in 1911.[22] And, notably in remote areas, German policemen sometimes enforced their own sentences in person. Sergeant Franitzek, for example, reported that on patrol he sentenced a man to "15 blows with a stick," adding that "the sentence has been executed [*vollstreckt*] by the signatory."[23] Thus, the sjambok was often used by a variety of actors without much attention to the subtle distinctions of regulation.

In the case in which Staff Sergeant Bauer beat his subordinate Hans (with which I open this book), the German policeman seemed to be confused about regulation while at the same time insisting on the proper usage of the whip. Bauer had whipped Hans, which was against regulation. But after Hans had then beaten an African prisoner with the butt of his rifle, Bauer told him that "that was not what the rifle was there for, that if a prisoner did not want to obey he should beat him with a sjambok. I hereupon gave Hans my sjambok with which he struck the prisoner . . . three times. Hans should see out of this that the rifle is not there for the abuse of prisoners."[24]

The actual technique of whipping or beating that was being performed on the ground is also hard to extract from the sources, but one rare testimony gives some insight into everyday practice. Herero Police Assistant Richard Kainazo, stationed in Omaruru, described the procedure as follows:

Petty cases were dealt with summarily by the sergeant merely on verbal information by the white master. For instance, if a German brought his native servant to the sergeant and said the native had been idle or negligent or cheeky, the sergeant would immediately order me to take the native and prepare him for flogging. I and my assistant had then to take the native to the kraal near the police-station, strip him and make

him lie over a tub or a box. We generally used a tub. The sergeant
would then come along and in his presence and that of the German
master I was ordered to give the native 15, 20, or 25 lashes with a heavy
sjambok. The sergeant counted and generally told me when to stop
beating. We nearly always kept on beating until the blood began to flow.
I often had to beat men whom I knew well.[25]

What meaning Kainazo ascribed to the floggings, whether he and his African
colleagues endorsed them or not, remains unclear, especially since his testimony was collected for the purpose of discrediting the German colonial
regime.

What kind of "expertise" the agents of floggings had is difficult to identify
as well. Was there common knowledge about how to flog "properly," a shared
practice of flogging? At least for the Togolese context we know that "individual 'specialists' were consigned to" the task of flogging.[26] But were these
"specialists" chosen because they hit particularly hard, or because they hit particularly accurately (striking the backside and no other parts of the body)?
For many German policemen, meting out blows was a well-rehearsed practice from their days as NCOs.[27] The punishing device, however, was not the
same. For some of the African policemen, physical punishment was reserved
for parents toward children, or took the form of domestic violence against
women. But as a judicial penalty it was probably as well quite foreign.[28] Furthermore, they oftentimes were on the receiving end. My sense is that both
German and African policemen felt inexpert with respect to the sjambok and
insecure about how to wield it. But there are few evidential grounds on which
to base speculation about the whipping technique of state servants in German
Southwest Africa.

The infamous *Strafregister*, the books that recorded each punishment meted
out by the colonial regime, are of little help in clarifying everyday practice,
since they indicate only the number of blows, not how the whip was employed.[29] However, we can get a little closer to practice by looking at the implications of regulations. The Berlin Colonial Office's 1896 decree on corporal
punishment of natives focused on who could be punished by how many blows
of what kind: only men (under the age of sixteen only with birching), limited
to twenty-five at once (twenty for birching).[30] It moreover forbade corporal
punishment against "natives of a better status."[31] And the overseeing official
or physician was permitted to interrupt the flogging if he felt that the recipi-
ent's state of health demanded it. A further directive in 1905 urged those colonial officials who oversaw punishments to "pay heed that the body above
the buttocks is protected by clothes, sacks, pillows or the like from blows that

go astray."[32] Additionally, it reduced the number of permitted blows during "marches and other physical efforts" to ten and fifteen for birching and flogging respectively.[33]

Although colonial regulations provided no clear relationship between the degree of penalty and the nature of an offense, nor any clear indication of what offenses merited a flogging, German colonizers did worry over the effects of using the sjambok.[34] First, it was apparently as shameful to receive a whipping as to give one, hence the prohibition against corporal punishment of the higher orders of Africans. Second, the differentiation of punishment according to body type (male/female, adult/youth) and environment (on the march or not), combined with some attention to where blows were struck (below the back) and the recommendation that a doctor be present to assess the health of the person being flogged, all indicate that flogging was a dangerous, potentially mortal activity.

One does learn more about the sjambok in those rare sources that describe its effect on victims' bodies. In 1907, governmental proponents of the sjambok (from Southwest Africa and East Africa) and proponents of the rope (from Cameroon and Togo) had a dispute about the "usefulness" of the two different tools that revolved primarily around the different wounds they caused.[35] These exchanges are an exception to the silence about the sjambok that otherwise reigned in official papers. They reveal that, above all, the sjambok quickly tore the skin.[36] The open wounds produced were susceptible to infectious diseases of all kinds. And, despite the officials' declarations to the contrary, these lacerations could cause long-term damage through trauma to subcutaneous fat tissue.[37] The reality of corporal punishment was permanently mutilated bodies and grievously injured victims. Farmer Engelhard, for instance, complained to the local colonial authorities of Omaruru in 1913 that Karl, one of his African herders, had been punished excessively. The eleven gashes, he wrote, had been as deep and large as a finger. His "boy" had been unable to work for five days, and even one and a half years after the incident, one could still see the scars.[38]

The gruesomely cynical discussion between colonial officials about "appropriate" disciplining tools produced a racist medico-ethnographic discourse that justified the use of the sjambok in the context of local conditions, indigenous cultures, and African bodies. Sergeant Maletz, who had ordered Karl's punishment, described the penalty as "vigorous" and "appropriate."[39] He claimed that beatings were indispensable for Africans he deemed "uncultivated [and] bereft of all sense of honor." Indeed, he continued, had the high politicians in the metropole—who, he intimated, were entirely unfamiliar with the conditions in the colony—abolished corporal punishment, "the natives themselves would have been highly astonished."[40] Moreover, colonial officials, German policemen included, complemented the notion that corporal punishment was part of indigenous tradition, rather than that of the Kaiserreich, with a discourse on the supposedly special texture of African skin.

The skin of "black-colored natives," Governor Schuckmann declared, was "particularly hardened" and "not sensitive at all." Only maybe the "yellow skin" of the Nama, the governor added, was "more delicate."[41] Overall, he concluded, the sjambok had "no detrimental consequences."[42] In a contrary logic, Sergeant Maletz stated that he had instructed his Police Assistant Gustav "explicitly not to beat too hard, . . . not to hit the side, but, according to regulations, hit the backside. I do not wish to exclude the possibility that some blows hit the loins. The strokes were such that some of them made the backside's skin crack up in fibers. . . . The native 'Karl' seems to have delicate skin."[43] The doctor asked to examine the scars came to the conclusion that "the superficial lacerations were kept in a permanent state of irritation by means of . . . pepper or similar," insinuating that some indigenous custom of scarification had prevented the proper healing of Karl's wounds.[44] Thus, whether African skin was too thick, too thin, or subject to superstitious native practice, the sjambok remained an appropriate tool of punishment. As inconsistent and contradictory as the ideas about African skins were, they nevertheless justified punishment on the body of the colonized.

Given the colonial regime's concern for economic productivity and the permanent shortage of African labor, it may seem difficult to understand the extremity of floggings as practiced in German Southwest Africa. They were obviously counterproductive insofar as they regularly incapacitated laborers.[45] Hence it is important to recall that corporal punishments were also performances, a mise-en-scène of the colonial order. According to Michel Foucault's now classic narrative, early modern European punishments were bloody spectacles focused on the committed crime that symbolically restored the social order, while modern penal systems were refined disciplinary systems focused on the individual body of the criminal.[46] Colonial floggings were clearly both. The description by African policeman Kainazo above indicates that punishments were carried out at the kraal, that is, in an enclosed or secluded area. Though visible, they were not spectacles in the sense of being announced ahead of time or ritually enacted on specific days for spectators. However, other German colonial capitals (in Cameroon and German East Africa) did have "beating days."[47] And postcards of dramatized flogging scenes fed the European imagination, illustrating the racial order in a crude and graphic manner.[48] As the historian Florence Bernault observes, "In Africa, the prison did not replace but supplement public violence."[49] At the same time, as evidenced above, the use of the sjambok was also ostensibly calibrated to the individual body and the individual crime of the punished person.[50]

To sum up, the presence of the sjambok was so self-evident that no one saw the necessity of itemizing or describing it in detail, much less discussing its usage in practical or legal terms. There was also a certain discomfort in addressing its existence and usage because corporal punishment was widely considered a degraded and degrading activity.[51] The sjambok was the dirty but open secret of the violent regime of German Southwest Africa. It was the tool of public violence that cemented racial order in settler colonial settings.[52]

More importantly, while corporal punishment was a quintessentially European institution that existed in schools, prisons, and the military until well into the twentieth century, policemen put great effort into defining whippings as indigenous.[53] As Schröder observes, "the common practice of corporal punishment and 'paternal right of chastisement'" in the metropole had to be "adapted to the colonial situation."[54] The importance attributed to a very specific version of the whip—the sjambok—was designed to locate the instrument in a precolonial tradition and within the exigencies of the colony. Thus, whereas in the metropole the sjambok stood for the exceptional, excessive violence of the colony,[55] in the colony it evoked the idea of normality and common law.[56] With little professional culture to inform and form their own usage of the whip, German (and maybe even African) policemen espoused the rationale that made punishments with this particular tool a local affair that the remote bourgeois sensibilities of the metropole could not understand.[57] Affirming such presumed local knowledge and experience, they ultimately sought to frame their usage of the tool, or their oversight of its usage, as regular and professional.

As will become clear in the following, similar processes were at play when policemen manipulated binding instruments. Here too, improvisation and aspirations to professionalize characterized their actions. Yet, regarding shackles, it was the men's resourcefulness in designing and adjusting the technology rather than their invention of a tradition that came to the fore.

An Improvised Restraining Regime

In January 1910, the chief of police sent out a circular to all districts to gather information about existing fetters (*Schließzeug*)—their properties, conditions, and quantities—and about practical experience with them.[58] The circular encouraged local authorities to make "recommendations with regard to altering the existing, or to acquiring new, practically tested chaining implements."[59]

This invitation to participate in the refinement of the technologies and techniques of the colonial restraining regime was met with excitement. Detailed replies came from all levels of the administrative apparatus, and even low-ranking sergeants had something to say about restraining tools. The sheer mass of documentation hints at the significance policemen and local administrators assigned to this aspect of their job.[60] From the even larger documentation of reported escapes—not only from prisons and prisoner transports, but also from workplaces—it is fair to conclude that various forms of detaining and restraining were an everyday concern for the police. As discussed in more detail in chapter 5, the archives are filled with accounts of captures, escapes, and recaptures. From the perspective of the police, the colonial theater must have, at times, appeared like a big carousel in which the colonized were constantly moving into and out of their grasp. Hence, instead of being able to fix their colonial subjects into a firm order, the policemen were obliged to be mobile too.

Almost all the reports about fetter technologies stated that the shackles, cuffs, and chains were too large, too old, and too heavy, and that they were quite easy to open or to slip out of.[61] District Offices Gibeon and Okahandja and Police Depots Spitzkoppe and Kupferberg reported that their police stations had no handcuffs or fetters at all.[62] Swakopmund, however, had about a hundred old leg irons, over fifty dysfunctional handcuffs, and about four hundred neck rings, a remainder of the concentration camp nearby (for an example of prisoners chained in iron neck rings, see figure 5).[63] Two reports observed that the construction of the cuffs was such that putting them on regularly resulted in struggles between policemen and arrested subjects.[64] The state and design of the bonds allow at least two remarks regarding the fate of those who had to wear them. While the devices probably provided more opportunities to free oneself than there would have been with less deficient material, they certainly must have caused more pain and injuries. The existing tools of detention thus engendered an unstable system of everyday violent practices.

Above all, such circumstances prompted the men at the police stations to improvise. Sources testify to the cruelly resourceful ways with which policemen tied up their victims. Some devised restraints out of rope, wood, wire, tendons, or intestines.[65] Often, they used simple chains to tie people to all kinds of objects: a cart, a tree, a post.[66] These methods were anything but regulated or standardized. There was no decree that prescribed what kind of implements were to be used and what procedures were to be followed regarding the detention of people.

However, as we will see was the case with firearms as well, policemen's written discourse indicated otherwise. In their reports, policemen emphasized

FIGURE 5. A group of African prisoners, men and women, chained together with neck irons, guarded by one German and two African policemen. The African policeman on the right carries, against regulations, a firearm. Place and date unknown. Bildarchiv der Deutschen Kolonialgesell-schaft, Universitätsbibliothek Frankfurt am Main. Photo No. 014-2175-14.

that the restraining had been done according to regulation and in a professional way. One such instance was the case of the presumed cattle thief Taweib, captured by some farmer's employees and delivered to the police. Sergeant Maywald had chained the man to a cart wheel, and, overnight, Taweib had died. The sergeant's superior, Magistrate Vietsch, asked for details about the incident. In his additional report the sergeant affirmed that he had "personally examined the ties of the prisoner in the evening. At this occasion, I did not notice any signs which would have indicated that one should fear for the prisoner's demise. Otherwise I would have left the farmer's natives with the prisoner to watch over him. The chain with which the prisoner was attached to the cart wheel had so much leeway that it is impossible that the restriction could have caused the death. The cause of death must have been lack of solid food, for there were no external wounds on the body of the deceased who must have been about 16–18 years old."[67] The magistrate noted casually in the margins of the document that no incriminating act had been committed and that no further steps were necessary.[68] His inquiries had not been about the death of a man, but about whether an imprisoned person had been restrained

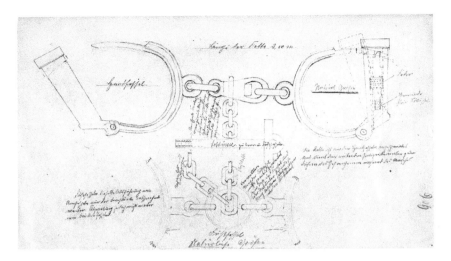

FIGURE 6. Sketch of handcuffs and foot irons with extensive commentary pertaining to their suggested manufacture and usage. Police Depot Waterberg, February 1910. BArch Berlin Lichterfelde, R 1002/2670, 13.

properly, in compliance with the rules. Thus, the police's improvised and apparently deadly violent technique was normalized through bureaucratic procedure.

All police stations asked for more modern, more reliable, and lighter fetters, drawing on an apparently broad knowledge of existing techniques. Policemen knew about the technologies used by prison guards and police forces in Imperial Germany and about those deployed by the British police in South Africa.[69] Based on that knowledge, they proposed their own inventions, claiming that these would be more adapted to local requirements. Some even attached drawings to their reports.[70] Some police stations tried out new devices on test persons.[71] And others even designed their own prototypes, advertising their many advantages and asking for the material in order to produce a greater number of them (figure 6).[72] To what extent police headquarters was influenced by its lower ranks' enthusiastic inventiveness is unclear, but it did order some new cuffs and shackles in the homeland and asked the Windhuk police to test them.[73] Thus approved, it ordered more, creating a dynamic exchange between metropole and periphery. Manufacturers in the Kaiserreich offered their products to the colonial government, sending brochures and samples.[74] In this way, policemen contributed to the reciprocal influences and transfers of knowledge that made colonies into a "laboratory of modernity."[75]

As with the sjambok, policemen's experimental approach to restraining implements was framed by racial paradigms on the one hand and economic imperatives on the other. The belief that Africans' bodies were particularly difficult to restrain led policemen to opt for particularly severe binding methods.[76] "Moreover," District Chief Schwerin wrote in closing his request for more shackles, "the native hardly perceives imprisonment as punishment if he is not fettered."[77] Nonetheless, policemen were reminded that prisoners should still be able to work and not be hindered too much by their irons.[78] District Chief Beyer from Warmbad noted that the cuffs that one of his police sergeants had devised had "the advantage of causing . . . no stiffening of the wrist."[79] It is hard to imagine that he had the comfort of his prisoners in mind. Rather, the new cuffs ensured that Africans could promptly return to work after their incarceration.

Regardless of ideological or economic discussions, policemen had to use the restraining technologies available, the poor quality of which required extensive improvisation. And while shackling of itself physically differentiated between groups—free and unfree, innocent and criminal—the specific improvised, situationally adapted practices policemen resorted to when manacling men, women, and children helped refine the economically exploitative racial order even further. Finally, as can be seen in figure 5, the policing technology of shackles, as well as that of the whip, was almost always backed up with another, more lethal one: the gun.

The Policeman and His Gun

By far the most well documented technology of colonial police violence in German Southwest Africa was the firearm. Symbolic of Western technological advantage in general, the use of guns in the colony was subject to extensive and anxiety-ridden policy debate, ideological confusion, sustained regulation, and practical improvisation. In what follows, I analyze the practices of gun use in three parts: equipment and training, the contexts of shooting, and the victims and agents of shooting.

Each German policeman of the Landespolizei was equipped with a military rifle. Most commonly, they received the Gewehr 98, the Mauser system that was the standard service rifle of World War I. Its newer variant, the Karabiner 98, as well as two older models, the M71 and the Gewehr 88, were also in use, but not as often. The rifle was carried in a holster on the saddle. In addition, policemen were armed with revolvers carried on their belt. The equipment and uniform regulations from 1905 stipulated that policemen should also carry a saber. However, after 1907, sabers were handed out only "after review."[80] From 1912 on, the Landespolizei also had one machine gun in its possession, stationed at the remote northernmost outpost Kuring Kuru.[81] According to regulations, African policemen were equipped with a bayonet (*Seitengewehr*) only.[82] The sources show, however, that these men were also quite often supplied with firearms for specific assignments and at the discretion of their superiors. I will come back to the arming of African policemen in the last part of this section.

Despite their prevalence and the assumption that as a technology of rule they automatically empowered whites, colonizers, and the police specifically, firearms were problematic. The revolvers caused concern, for many of them were defective or were not handled properly for lack of instruction.[83] The G98 was known to be a reliable, safe, and easy-to-use rifle. It had a long range and could fire up to five rounds. However, it was quite long and heavy and had a slow rate of fire. Furthermore, police mainly received old rifles discarded by the Schutztruppe and worn out by the war against the Herero and Nama. As a result, they were seldom fully functional, the head of police observed in his yearly report for 1910 "Despite the policemen's good training, interest, and shooting skills, shooting performances were often wanting. This low accuracy is due to absolutely inadequate ammunition and to not fully functional carbines."[84] The eagerness, or "interest"—as the report's author called it—among policemen to shoot their weapons certainly existed. "When it comes to shooting, nobody wants to stay home," Chief of Police Heydebreck remarked with regard to his policemen.[85] Policemen were often members of gun clubs.[86] As chapter 1 showed, both African and German policemen were imbued with martial values. Possession of a rifle and good marksmanship were crucial to every colonizer's self-understanding and functioned as markers of social distinction. But beyond even their military or police use, firearms were omnipresent in the colonial realm. Rarely did a settler festivity pass without some form of shooting competition or demonstration. Shooting was a "leisure activity [*Vergnügen*]," as missionary Brockmann called it. On Sundays, he followed mass in the morning with "proper (military)" shooting practice in the afternoon.[87] Social gatherings of policemen also included gunplay.[88]

Nevertheless, in 1910 Vice Governor Hintrager deplored that policemen were still not practicing enough and still not enthusiastic enough. He demanded that the "African policeman [a German man serving in Africa—M.M.] must be a perfect and passionate marksman, which so far cannot be said to be the case."[89] A look at the weekly schedules in the police depots, where policemen were trained before being deployed to the precincts, demonstrates that (alongside riding) shooting exercises were highly prioritized even before Hintrager's comment.[90] Thereafter, gun training was intensified. All depots had to hold shooting practice once a week for at least two hours.[91] What is more, the decision whether men were sufficiently prepared for police service lay entirely in the hands of military men who were the inspection officers at the depots.[92] After being deployed to their stations, policemen continued to practice shooting three times a month.[93] Only at the police school in Windhuk can one observe a reverse trend. There, military training, particularly shooting, was progressively replaced by classes specializing in bureaucratic skills, notably in surveying and customs regulation.[94]

Shooting practice normally consisted in different aiming exercises during which the distance from the target or the position of the shooter (standing, kneeling, lying, on horseback, and so on) was altered.[95] In this way policemen acquired kinesthetic skills. That is, repetition internalized discrete gestures into automatic muscle memory. The conditions surrounding the exercise always remained the same: the terrain was flat; no distractions or surprises were simulated to prepare the policemen to deal with unexpected attacks; seeking cover was not taught.[96] The self-defense or jujitsu classes, mocked in the newspaper article cited in the chapter's introduction, were in fact the only opportunity for policemen to learn defensive techniques. And these courses were at first only for those few policemen who had been recommended for further training and promotion. Police training, in the end, followed the military logic of forming disciplined soldiers who shot at an enemy almost automatically. Not surprisingly, shooting exercises were modeled on those given to the cavalry.[97] Such training is congruent with the more general observation that the Landespolizei was never really a civilian force but rather highly militarized in its structure, personnel, and organizational culture.[98]

Social scientists who analyze the phenomenon of tacit knowledge—what our bodies "know" how to do without us having to think consciously about it or being able to explain how the body learned it—suggest distinguishing between mimeomorphic and polimorphic skills.[99] Mimeomorphic skills are inscribed into the body through repetition and mimicking. They change only through the decay and renewal of muscle memory. Polimorphic skills are acquired in relation to a social and physical environment. They adapt continuously to changing conditions. William Storey in his article "Guns, Race, and Skill in Nineteenth-Century Southern Africa" notes that "with respect to guns, mimeomorphic skills would include loading and firing a gun repeatedly at a target, day after day, until the shooter achieved proficiency. Polimorphic skills would include hunting animals; every shot fired will be loaded and aimed in different circumstances that must be interpreted by the shooter."[100] The policemen of the Landespolizei did hunt game. Inspection Officer Hildebrandt at police depot Waterberg actively encouraged his men to get a hunting license.[101] Many of them owned private guns for this purpose, notably to supplement their diet with fresh meat.[102] Hence, in addition to the first kind of skill, policemen also gained some proficiency in the second kind: they aimed at moving targets, taking into account the surroundings and the peculiarities of their weapon. In fact, at the turn of the year 1912–1913, Chief of Police Bethe envisioned allowing policemen to use 20 percent of their yearly ammunition supply for hunting.[103] "Hunting," his explanation went, was "the best means to foster shooting proficiency and good eyesight, confidence moving in the terrain and tracking down and following a trail, maintaining a fresh and flexible body, and much more."[104] It was thought to provide a "substitute for combat training in the field."[105] In addition, the measure was aimed at preventing the use of privately bought, inappropriate ammunition with their service weapons. Incorrect ammunition would "ruin the weapon and impair the shooter's proficiency as well as his trust in his rifle."[106] Thus, the line between beneficial and detrimental effects on policemen's polimorphic tacit knowledge was actually quite thin. In the end, Vice Governor Hintrager did not approve of the idea, worrying about "unwelcome over-hunting."[107] And he was concerned not to upset the settler community, for whom the policemen's hunting activity was yet another sign of their privileged position.[108] Consequently, the suggestion was never put into practice.[109] Instead, police headquarters issued a ban on privately owned rifles (not on shotguns), limiting policemen's hunting possibilities even further.[110]

The observations about equipment and training I have made so far can help us draw some conclusions about how policemen might have used their firearms. First, the bad condition of most guns suggests that firing accuracy was seriously limited. Evidence describing bullet wounds supports this assessment.[111] Controlled aiming at one particular body part was for most shooters simply out of the question, and even hitting a victim with a bullet at all seems to have been largely a matter of chance. Second, mimeomorphic military skills were rarely helpful on the beat. To be sure, policemen acquired basic shooting accuracy, but they almost never came into situations in which they had to take on battle formation, firing in a disciplined and concentrated manner at an enemy. Moreover, the specific features of the rifle they were using restricted the speed at which such an automatism could come into effect. Finally, if they had polimorphic shooting skills—having practiced hunting or having had combat training or experience in wartime—policemen still needed to modify that proficiency when implementing it toward human beings in peacetime.

The idea of substituting hunting practice for combat training indicates that these two different kinds of shooting skills were regarded as, first, to a certain extent interchangeable and, second, fully sufficient and appropriate for the work policemen had to do. Indeed, racist ideology often situated the colonized closer to animals than to humans. Some police patrol reports read as if the policemen thought they were on a hunting expedition.[112] Moreover, postwar paranoia and police occupational culture often stigmatized the colonized collectively as criminal enemies rather than colonial subjects in need of protection.[113]

Thus, the ideological, legal, and cultural context is crucial if we want to understand the police's usage of technologies of violence. Understanding embodied tacit competencies as well as the specific physical properties of technologies can get us only so far. We now need to look more closely at the broader contexts in which these were embedded. What were the most common situations in which policemen were required to, wanted to, or did fire their weapon? What was their reasoning before and after the fact, and how did their practice influence policy?

In August 1908, the colonial official responsible for instructing higher-ranking policemen at the police school in Windhuk reported to police headquarters that "policemen were quite surprised when I told them that they were not allowed to shoot at fleeing subjects. After inquiry, I discovered that they were without exception of the opinion that it was their duty to use firearms against escaped prisoners. Some of them had even been so instructed."[114] As a consequence, a month later Chief of Police Heydebreck issued a circular to all administration offices and depots ordering them to "instruct all policemen that they are allowed to use their weapon only in cases of self-defense" and not "against escaped white prisoners" or against any fleeing person. In the case of Africans, the circular specified, one was permitted to shoot at them only "if they appear hostile, that is, if they themselves are shooting or their behavior leads one to believe with certainty that they want to open fire on the patrol."[115] This decree marked the beginning of a discussion among colonial officials regarding the rules of gun usage that lasted until the end of the German colonial era. At that point, the police manual still stipulated that the use of one's firearm was permitted only in defense or if a subject caught in an act of crime resisted arrest "with violence or threats," or escaped after an accomplished arrest.[116] Both the manual and the 1908 circular had as a reference point §53 of the Imperial Penal Code (*Reichsstrafgesetzbuch*), basing colonial police policy on metropolitan norms.[117] Yet, along the way, restrictions were slowly but surely loosened. Police practice, framed by economic and ideological imperatives, drove the change.[118]

In the 1908 decree one can already discern a distinction between the treatment of white and black subjects. Concerning the first group ("whites"), the decree formulated a prohibition. Regarding the second group ("natives"), the decree formulated a permission granted in certain cases. Throughout the colonial period, this differentiation was developed further. The regulations on the use of weapons expressed and enabled the range of distinctions that defined colonial society—prominently, those between policemen and settlers or between whites and nonwhites.

The surprise of policemen when they heard that they were not supposed to shoot at people who fled when the police appeared shows that common practice was contrary to regulation. Likely, this was also the case after police headquarters released its reminder in September 1908. The ruthless seizure of Africans for the colonial economy regularly involved shootings in cases where neither threats nor prior arrests had occurred. Moreover, reports describing settlements that were abandoned in a hurry, leaving valuable belongings behind, indicate that many colonized indeed chose to flee when they had the chance.[119] A number of accounts of shootings fail to mention any form of armed confrontation, suggesting that these were committed against unarmed victims.[120]

How often policemen shot at colonized for reasons other than what one might reasonably construe as self-defense I cannot assess. But by reading the statements carefully, one can detect recurring rationales and behavioral patterns. A 1906 template that served as an illustration of how to fill out the patrol book at the police station at Hohewarte had as one of its entries the following statement: "Camp of the thieves taken by surprise. 1 Herero shot. Rest escaped. 1 ox slaughtered. The second recovered."[121] The district office in Rehoboth telegraphed in 1908: "Patrol [constituted of] two police sergeants, 8 voluntary Basters, in area near [illegible] mountains caught cattle thieves unawares. One Bushman shot dead. Three men and sixteen women a[nd] children apprehended, three old rifles seized."[122] In 1909, a police patrol led by Inspection Officer Trenk captured two San men. Further, "3 Bushmen, among them the murderer of cattle herder Zarus, were shot dead after they attempted escape."[123]

What is noteworthy in these citations is the surmised criminality of the victims, and that this criminality always pertained to the whole collective and not to one individual. The reports needed to imply that the group posed an imminent danger in order to comply with the directive. It is striking that in all cases the police force had overwhelming power and tactical advantage. In the first two cases, the groups were "taken by surprise," and the numerical proportion was always in favor of the assailants. In the first and last examples, no firearms among the police's opponents were even mentioned, indicating that they had none, since the police were instructed to report all apprehended weapons.[124] Only within the framework of an ideology that perceived the colonized as collectively responsible for committed crimes could the police practice of shooting gain the meaning of self-defense.

Furthermore, understanding shooting as a regulated act was crucial, for it established it as bureaucratized and professional. In this manner, the police distinguished their actions from those of other colonizers in the colonial realm. Although settlers using their guns were not necessarily punished, the police had a specific way of doing things, a police procedure.[125] People were shot, in the wording of the police, "according to regulations"—even when the actual rules were ignored or unknown, and even when the actual shooting had been done in an irregular, hasty, or thoughtless way.[126]

Especially the idea that one could shoot if one had called out to an escapee persisted. It was the most common formulation used by police to indicate that they had proceeded in accordance with rules. Sergeant Becker, accompanied by the African policeman Abraham, for instance, pursued two armed African men who were suspected to have stolen a goat.[127] The policemen killed the first man in circumstances not specified. When they approached the second man a day later, Becker observed that, as the man was going to escape again into the hills, "he was hailed. And since he did not stand, he was shot at. While running, he dropped a pot and a blanket, his rifle he kept in his hand until he was lethally hit by the fifth shot and fell to the ground."[128] When the bodies were examined, it turned out that the first victim had had only two bullets, of which one was a misfire, and the second victim had had no ammunition at all.[129]

The bureaucratic practice of inscribing shootings into a specific narrative formula (suspected criminals were hailed, then shot) eventually gave the formula such inertia that it was accepted as regulated practice. In regulations issued in October 1911 and February 1914, the formulation was formally institutionalized by headquarters, retroactively justifying what was common practice.[130] A police practice generated out of misunderstanding the rules had become a new rule. Considerations of state reputation and authority were decisive in this development.

Reacting to the 1908 reminder that weapons were only to be used in self-defense, Magistrate Schmidt had entreated the colonial government that the little authority policemen possessed toward prisoners could only be upheld if they were allowed to shoot, no matter what. "As an official speaking from experience," he argued, policemen would be "degraded to the laughable role of an extra" if they were not allowed to make use of their weapon when a prisoner under their guard tried to flee. Their "official reputation" was at stake.[131] And, in fact, in the summer of 1909, the Landespolizei's reputation suffered a real blow. Four policemen became notorious for having tried to arrest about forty Herero and having utterly failed. The four men had hidden in an empty settlement and, upon the inhabitants' return, had endeavored to apprehend them all. A brawl ensued. One policeman was wrestled to the ground, and the others had to come to his rescue. In the end only one or two Africans had been captured. The *Deutsch-Südwestafrikanische Zeitung* asked why policemen were armed at all if they were not allowed to use their guns.[132] The worst, the article claimed, was the fact that "policemen [were] not even allowed to shoot at wandering, work-shy riff raff."[133]

Chief of Police Heydebreck wrote two texts in response to the newspaper article, giving interesting insights into his understanding of policing and the use of force.[134] In a letter to the newspaper, and thus addressed to the settler community, Heydebreck stressed that "the Landespolizei . . . possesses exactly the same means of protection [*Schutzmittel*] as the police at home," and that the policemen in question would have been legally entitled to use their weapon in self-defense. Several times he reiterated the term "self-defense" and its legal grounding.[135] Moreover, the chief of police made clear that no cultivated state's [*Kulturstaat*] law permitted killing people just because of vagabondage or laziness. He differentiated himself and his men from the settlers by indicating that the police force defined itself through the rule of law and culture; its use of weapons was lawful and cultivated.[136] In his second letter, addressed to all his subordinates, Heydebreck characterized the four men's attempt to arrest forty people as "futile." He noted that such behavior exhibited lack of both experience and knowledge of the pertinent regulations.[137] Above all, he emphasized that policemen really only had two options regarding their firearms: either they should abstain from using them at all, or they should use them decisively. "Only negotiation with the settlement using suitable natives would have led to success," he claimed. But since African resistance had been provoked, "this opposition had to be broken by all means to preserve the policemen's authority." For that, the policemen in question should absolutely have fired their guns, about which they "should have had no doubts" had they known the relevant paragraph in their main regulations book.[138]

The head of police expressed strong discomfort regarding physical contact between colonizers and colonized. Heydebreck commanded that in the unfortunate case that a physical, hands-on fight had been entered, the police's reputation had to be restored immediately through the use of weapons.[139] Magistrate Schmidt echoed this worry in a directive when he explained: "Besides the calamitous collision such a beating of natives by police officials could entail, it is also prone to harm the reputation of the civil servants who have been appointed to uphold peace and order, when they want to chastise natives by themselves; too easily a brawl can ensue if the pummeled native resists;

this must be avoided at all costs."[140] Although these colonial administrators were primarily concerned with bodily integrity and honor, they also sensed the way in which such small physical man-to-man encounters could reveal the brittleness of this very system of belief.

Assimilating the colonial regime's reputation to the bodies of the police-men, Chief of Police Heydebreck formulated the correct response to collec-tive resistance in terms of personal self-defense. In essence, he had found an answer to Magistrate Schmidt's complaint about the embarrassing possibility that policemen would become "extras" in the drama of colonial rule. Rather than waiting for their bodies to be in danger in order to defend the authority of the regime, policemen should consider resistance to the authority of the regime as a threat to their bodies. As already discussed, many policemen had themselves come to this solution insofar as self-defense became the standard-ized post facto justification for having shot a weapon.

An ancillary benefit of explaining events in a formula of self-defense was that it lent an air of standardization to police actions: it reinforced police's pro-fessionalism. Policemen were supposed to use their weapon in a professional way, appropriate for the situation at hand. They were asked to be decisive, but their inadequate training and the bad state of their firearms hindered their per-formance. Hunting game and preparing for war did not prepare the men of the Landespolizei to use their guns when making an arrest. They had not learned how and when to threaten, how and when to shoot, or how to handle their guns in noncombat contact. One of the strategies they acquired to cover their ignorance and to justify their tendency to shoot first and ask questions later was to deploy bureaucratic formulas that gave their actions a professional and honorable quality.

The self-defense argument shored up both police identity and the coloniz-er's authority by defining the regulatory and customary conditions under which a shooting was considered professional and authoritative. But a final question of firearms practice remains: Who was shooting at whom? A more racialized settler colonial ideology guided this aspect of social distinction.[141]

The African group of San (or Bushmen) was a source of special anxiety, even paranoia, among the German colonizers, and consequently they were targets of disproportionate gun violence.[142] Their poisoned arrows, perhaps because they called into question the technological dominance of the colo-nizer, made them seem exceptionally dangerous. And, as will be discussed later in the book, the San were singled out as incapable of being integrated into a modern wage economy. They were believed to be unable to perform disci-plined, regular labor. More than this, they were perceived as an active danger to the economy.

Often, they were the group blamed for cattle thefts or for attacking the economically vital group of Ovambo migrant workers. A farmer's letter published at length in an article entitled "Bushmen Plight" related several cattle thefts from his farm, presumably committed by San. "The Bushmen," the farmer concluded, "are a through and through uncultivable, untamable element, and they can only be kept in check with strict penalties."[143] Magistrate Schultze-Jena alerted police headquarters in May 1911 that "attacks by Bushmen on Ovambo increase alarmingly [*bedenklich*]," and that "this rabble [*Gesindel*]" had no respect for the local police.[144] Then, in October 1911, Sergeant Josef Alefelder was injured by a poisoned arrow during a patrol.[145] He died shortly after.[146] Patrol reports show that, thereafter, when policemen encountered San, or believed that they had, often their immediate response was to shoot at them.[147] In these situations, policemen reverted to the simple logic of warfare: shoot at the enemy.

Hence, agitation by farmers, combined with the above-mentioned racism and a primacy of economic demands, led policemen to shoot specifically at San people—as a measure of preemptive self-defense, so to speak. This practice, and the police sergeant's death, moved the government in October 1911 to make a rule expressly for San.[148] This decree regarding "weapon use against Bushmen" combined many elements I have addressed earlier. It stipulated showing the "greatest attention and caution" and instructed policemen to "always hold their firearm ready for instantaneous use" when approaching San settlements. The decree furthermore elaborated on some "principles" for the "behavior of all administrations against Bushmen." Despite the overall hostile attitude the decree conveyed, it nevertheless reminded local authorities that "it is desirable, as difficult as this may be, that even the Bushmen be brought to work," and that this had to happen "firstly in an amicable [*gütlichem*] way." Nonetheless, if even one member of a San community could be construed in any way as suspected of "cattle theft or other robberies," the whole collective had to be arrested with force. Finally, the decree stipulated that policemen were to use their weapon "upon the least resistance" and "when criminals who have been discovered in the act or tracked down do not stand upon hailing, but instead try to escape arrest through flight."[149] Thus, policemen's use of their rifles was codified according to what was already their customary practice and their ersatz bureaucratic formula: escapees could be shot at if called out to. For Magistrate Schultze-Jena, the decree against San from October 1911 did not go far enough. He wanted to displace them. In January 1913, he wrote that "in order to effectively thwart the Bushmen-threat, all apprehended Bushmen need to be removed from the district and transplanted to an area where they can neither hunt nor rob, but *have to* make a living through work. A good opportunity for this is the diamond fields in Lüderitzbucht."[150]

In the following years, higher colonial officials in Windhuk and Berlin continued to debate the right usage of firearms. In December 1912, Vice Governor Hintrager proposed a new regulation. It stipulated that policemen could shoot at escapees after shouting out a warning "several times." Somewhat vaguely, it added that the rifle should be the last resort if "other weapons" had failed.[151] In January 1913, Senior Executive Officer Hensel in police headquarters suggested to the vice governor to include the terms "criminals, thieves, etc." in the regulation in order to define who the police should be allowed to shoot at. He added: "The Inspection [of the Landespolizei] deems it necessary that pol[ice]men are granted if possible the same rights as the military. . . . The Inspection is very well aware that the expression 'criminal, thieves, etc.' is not altogether clear, but since it figures in all regulations re[garding] the use of weapons by gendarmes [in the Kaiserreich—M.M.], the inspection has no qualms to incorporate it into its own directives."[152] Hintrager's draft and Hensel's proposition did not go into effect immediately. For a year, policemen continued to operate in the field with two distinct regulations, one allowing them to shoot at the San almost with impunity and the other prohibiting them from shooting at other African groups without a clear self-defense argument. However, given that they had never respected the initial limits on their right to fire at Africans, it is all but inconceivable that they noticed the new distinction.[153]

In the beginning of 1914, a new rule was finally established. Paragraph 50.5 of the *Dienstvorschrift* was replaced by a decree that more or less incorporated all the gradually loosened restrictions into one document that finally reflected what had been customary police practice all along. Henceforth, policemen were authorized to shoot at "fleeing, caught in the act murderers, robbers, and cattle thieves, who despite being ordered to, do not stop." They were also permitted to shoot at "natives" in general if they were on a special patrol and the colonized tried to run away, though, again, they had to call out first. And, finally, policemen were invited to resort first to "other means" and "other weapons" with no explanation what these might actually be.[154]

This last clause might have been a concealed or disavowed appeal to use African subalterns to handle arrests and prisoner recoveries in the German policemen's stead. Recall Chief of Police Heydebreck's suggestion that "only negotiation with the settlement using suitable natives would have led to success" in the case of the four embarrassingly incompetent policemen. In his initial draft he had even more specifically suggested that "native police servants" should undertake negotiations.[155] The possibility that Africans were more competent intermediaries, more expert gunman, and more professional police haunted the German policing regime, destabilizing the colony's otherwise monolithic racial hierarchy.

As mentioned at the beginning of this chapter, African police assistants were not supposed to carry firearms, presumably because doing so would have compromised the racist order.[156] However, when it came to the handling of weapons, Africans were sometimes construed as superior to Germans. Vice Governor Hintrager noted in a personal letter to a magistrate that "one cartridge in the hands of a native equals at least ten cartridges in the hands of the white man."[157] In the characteristically confused logic of racial hierarchy, Africans were perceived as "naturally" superior in the use of a complex technology. The police handbook alerted its members that "natives . . . were, due to their natural predispositions, in some proficiencies superior to civilized men."[158]

Notwithstanding anxieties about disrupting racial hierarchy, and perhaps seeking to take advantage of their supposedly superior skills, African policemen were quite often equipped with rifles or revolvers. Both local administrators and rank-and-file policemen endorsed the idea.[159] Chief of Police Bethe begrudgingly acknowledged this reality in 1910 when he noted in a circular that African policemen should be trained so that they would at least use their rifles properly.[160] For this purpose, three hundred M71 rifles were bought in early 1910.[161] Moreover, most regulations on weapons use allowed arming police assistants in exceptional cases if their superiors deemed it necessary.[162] Interestingly, African policemen's training was more adapted to local conditions. They exclusively practiced in the "standing position, freehand," since "in the terrain of the thick bush any other aiming position is hardly in question."[163] It is plausible that more appropriate training really had made them better marksmen than their German colleagues.

Irrespective of whether or not their superior expertise was a reality,[164] the belief in Africans' more accomplished skills had ambivalent implications for the police. On the one hand, it made wary higher colonial officials repeatedly forbid police assistants from having firearms.[165] On the other hand, it disposed other colonial officials, especially those with experience on the ground, to issue rifles to their African police assistants, expecting better results. As in many other cases discussed throughout the book, practice contradicted official policy in such a way that the state was nonetheless strengthened. Unofficially distributing guns to African policemen was yet another form of improvised, informal state activity.

For the formal state and its representatives, such as Vice Governor Hintrager or Senior Executive Officer Hensel, Africans carrying guns remained a point of anxiety. Hintrager noted that for African policemen "the bayonet is perfectly sufficient." "For guarding tasks," he continued, "they can, if necessary, be handed out a sjambok."[166] And Hensel claimed to represent police headquarters' opinion when he stated that "it would certainly be best to take away all firearms from police servants and to hand them a strong sjambok instead."[167] Hence, to return to my opening thoughts, the violent technologies of policing were parceled out according to the system of status hierarchy that defined colonial order. Who carried what weapons and under what circumstances they were used were more important as a matter of social distinction than efficient practice—except that this was more honored in the breach than in the observance. Although Africans should not have had access to weapons, they clearly did.

In point of fact, both German and African policemen of the Landespolizei used technological tools when they exerted their power on the policed. As the case of jujitsu training exemplifies, policemen applying bare hands was viewed with disfavor, both by the settler community and by some parts of the colonial administration. Replying to an invitation from the chief of police to have his policemen participate in the police school's boxing classes, the magistrate of Windhuk noted: "I would like to desist from letting my policemen participate in boxing lessons. . . . The average policeman is easily tempted to apply these arts in wrong places, that is, it might too easily result in cases of assault."[168] Whereas the risk of bare-handed assault was apparently too high, the dangers of flogging, injurious shackling techniques, and sometimes wanton shootings were widely accepted and even codified. Policemen made do with the instruments at hand, despite the fact that they recurrently did not know how to handle them properly or had only dysfunctional ones at their disposal. Their often instrumentally counterproductive uses of technologies of rule become understandable when viewed as complex cultural practices that functioned as markers and rituals of status distinction. Policemen handled whips, shackles, and guns in a differentiating manner. In their improvised manipulation of the tools, showing proper appearance, honor, and, professionalism was crucial. To achieve that goal policemen frequently made reference to their better local knowledge and experience, and deployed bureaucratic techniques to inscribe their technological practices into regularized procedure—oftentimes creating or adjusting official regulation. Distinguishing in different moments between different users, technologies of violence contributed to colonial state power by complicating the new social order.[169] Although European technologies of themselves explain little, the specific improvised practices of the police illuminate how the technologies of violence helped the German regime refine and maintain colonial rule.

CHAPTER 4

Police Work

Daily Routines and the Art of Making Do

Max Weber's famous notion of the state's monopoly of the legitimate use of physical violence has been the starting point for many social scientists to describe what the police are and what they do. Following that dictum, the police are often sociologically defined as a means. Yet, this definition needs qualification. First, the police never fully hold a monopoly, nor do they always have full legitimacy.[1] As social scientists have rightly noted, the police are an expression and a tool of the *claim* to a legitimate monopoly, not its reality.[2] Second, the definition of the police as merely a tool is too limited. The police force is much more complex than a simple instrument. As an organization, it is a collective that does not only follow the rationality of its command (that is, the government). It has its internal logics and bureaucratic mechanisms, an organizational culture, a certain degree of autonomy based on its expertise. The sociologist Dominique Monjardet offers a particularly helpful definition that combines all the considerations mentioned here. According to him, the police force is "inextricably an instrument of state power [*pouvoir*] from which it receives orders; a public service theoretically available to everyone; a profession that develops its proper interests. This triple determination by no means resolves in perfect harmony. On the contrary, these three dimensions can confront each other as distinct and competing."[3] In this chapter I discuss the police force's mandate in German Southwest Africa and the organizational culture it developed from that mission: its tasks, working conditions, routines, and procedures.

Police work in German Southwest Africa comprised virtually everything that pertained to the organization of a productive society—infrastructure, health, agriculture, mining, education, security, welfare, and so on; in essence, police worked with the assumptions of an early modern notion of *Policey* (a concept I will explain below). How the police were supposed to proceed in this seemingly limitless range of tasks was unclear. Decrees were issued at all levels of the colonial administration, but rarely did they include instructions to the lower-ranking men about the means and modes of enforcing them. Regulations aiming at organizing the police themselves mostly referred to appearance and formality. Proper bearing, etiquette, and social convention were the guides that were to assist policemen in the field.

Despite or maybe even because of the impossibility of achieving the official colonial state's goals, the police contributed to forming a colonial state based on improvisation. Because of the specific dynamic that emerged out of permanent uncertainty, inadequate means, and all-encompassing authority, policemen felt constantly compelled and/or enabled to do things. In the policemen's own minds, it did not matter so much what they were doing, but that they were being proactive. Policemen had little professional training. The material conditions and the climate were taxing. The territory they policed was immense, and close supervision by superiors was limited. Because of these circumstances, policemen relied on and came to highly value their own practice and experience. Moreover, the police force was a racially mixed institution. African and German men worked together. The resulting group dynamics and possibilities to act on both the settler and the colonized community prompted practices that were experienced as participative and shared endeavors. Yet, although they were a crucial part of the improvised colonial state in German Southwest Africa, African policemen were also active outside of it—as enterprising subjects seeking a place in the new social and economic order, as independent patriarchs, and as members of the *oturupa*. Or put another way, as African carriers of what was understood on all sides to be "white" power, their very existence hybridized colonial power along its many axes: state/nonstate, colonizer/colonized, official/unofficial.

Police practices were furthermore generated by the effort to distinguish police from other actors in the colonial realm, notably from the military, settlers, and colonized—that is, by the formation of a professional culture. The police force had its distinct way of doing violence and being violent. Policemen prided themselves on doing diligent, professional, and "clean" violent work.

Police Tasks and the Notion of "Policey"

Throughout the existence of the colonial police force in Southwest Africa, colonial leaders struggled over its form of organization, its mission, and its rules. What the police were there for and how they should operate never became entirely clear. This is not particular to the colonial context. Policing in the Kaiserreich at the turn of the twentieth century was still rooted in the diffuse idea that it pertained to the very broad complex of a state invested in the security and welfare of its people and in the maintenance of its power through optimized methods of administration.[4] In a period that was crucial both for the development of police institutions and for European imperialism, earlier, cameralist concepts of police—the notion of *Policey*—prevailed. Eighteenth-century German legal and political thinker Johann Heinrich Gottlob von Justi defined the police in his work *Grundsätze der Policey-Wissenschaft* (1756) as follows:

> Under the name police [*Policey*] we include the laws and regulations that concern the interior of a state, which endeavor to strengthen and increase its power, to make good use of its forces, to produce the happiness [*Glückseligkeit*] of its subjects, in a word, the commerce, finances, agriculture, mining, woods, forests, etcetera, in view of the fact that the welfare [*Wohlfahrt*] of the state depends on the wisdom with which all these things are administered.[5]

The police institutions and agents that grew out of this understanding were responsible for a whole variety of tasks and were directly linked to the authority of the state. They had to ensure welfare and security at the same time. Their main concern was the organization and regulation of the "necessities of life," for example, food supply and health, and of the population's activity and productivity—all with the goal that their activities would "constitute a differential element in the development of the state's force."[6] Historians of late nineteenth-century German policing have recently shown that welfare duties had not yet been entirely detached from the realm of the police, and that their functions were not yet fixed into clearly defined categories despite an ongoing process of bureaucratization and legalization. This is particularly true when observed on the level of daily practices and handbook instructions.[7] In short, at the turn of the century, the police force as we know it today was still in the making. And it was still conceived to be responsible for anything that "strengthen[ed] and increase[d] [the state's] power" and "produce[d] the happiness of its subjects."[8] In addition to the widespread influence of German administration science, Western and Central European police systems had all to a certain degree been under the impact of the Napoleonic model of a militarily organized gendarmerie.[9] In some sense, we can understand the First French Empire's gendarmerie as a "colonial" police. This fact becomes an important backdrop against which colonial police in Africa have to be examined.

If we turn our attention to German Southwest Africa we discover that the Landespolizei was in fact responsible for an overwhelming variety of tasks. In his 1930 history of the force, former policeman Hans Rafalski enumerated some of them: "for instance, the execution of health and veterinarian police measures, the procurement of bacteriological and toxicological samples, of blood tests and such, the monitoring of mining regulations, the management of weapons and ammunition stocks for trade, meteorological observations, route surveying, the supervision of prisons and lost livestock [*Fundkral*], and oftentimes also postal and customs duties as well as juridical duties."[10] The list is far from complete and can be extended with seemingly endless, random activities. Policemen enforced hunting and nature protection laws, oversaw alcohol licensing and distribution, erected road signs, and maintained sewage systems, wells, telegraph lines, fences, soldiers' graves, and other public equipment.[11] They collected dog taxes.[12] They carried out the population census. They registered births, deaths, and marriages. They made lists of European men married to indigenous women.[13] They made sure that settler children went to school, that they were immunized, and so forth.[14] This long enumeration shows that the Landespolizei was charged by the colonial state with organizing more or less all aspects of colonial society, just as Justi's cameralist view of *Policey* had prescribed. Out of this "total responsibility" could arise a certain feeling of all-importance coupled with the feeling of constant frustration because one was of course never able to fulfill all the tasks at hand.[15] Often linked to the challenge of having to deal with potentially everything was the notion that therefore things had to be resolved immediately, especially in a settler society that was rapidly growing and changing.[16] I will come back to the matter of urgency later in this chapter.

Rafalski's list above did not mention the one mission that occupied most of the police's time: namely, finding, capturing, registering, organizing, monitoring, guarding, protecting, and punishing African labor on the one hand, and supervising, inspecting, controlling, supporting, defending, and restoring European property on the other hand. Perhaps more surprisingly, Rafalski did not include fighting crime on his list. I see this as yet another indicator for my claim that policemen saw themselves primarily as the "jill of all trades [*Mädchen für alles*]" of the colonial state for whom preventing crime was just one— certainly not the most important—duty among many.[17] Interestingly, the police's mission statement read much more like a modern police description.

It emphasized security over welfare. Remarkably short, the passage entitled "Preface. Purpose" stated: "The institutions of the police are there to maintain public peace and security [*Ruhe und Sicherheit*]. They have to ensure that the existing laws, ordinances, and rules are followed, they have to protect persons and property against punishable infractions, and to supervise [*überwachen*] the natives."[18] The passage has little informative value on what policemen actually did on an everyday basis, except for perhaps the particular attention given to protecting property and policing the indigenous population.

In order to have an approximate idea of the tasks policemen carried out, especially those that came up repeatedly, it is more helpful to look at examples of the patrol logs that were produced at regular intervals. The following excerpt of one of them gives a fairly representative list of activities in the Windhuk district for the first months of 1908:

> Supervision [*Controlle*] of the paths and water conditions . . . Revision of the horse quarantine outpost [*Sterbeposten*] . . . Supervision of the paths and water conditions, supervision of the natives . . . Supervision of the natives a[nd] legal notices . . . Pursuit of escaped Police Assistant Benjamin and companions—unsuccessful . . . Supervision of natives . . . Legal notices . . . Adjustment of the native registries.[19]

"Supervision of natives," of course, could mean all kinds of things. It could signify that the police had checked passports or labor contracts, that it had searched African dwellings or inspected work sites, that it had shown its face for a brief moment or spent a whole day, or maybe even a night, at a farm, and many other measures. Another log, stretching from mid-1907 to mid-1908, and equally representative of everyday police work, listed the following undertakings of the police depot of Waterberg, situated in the north of the colony:

> For orientation . . . Arranged a grave . . . for legal notice . . . Legal notice a[nd] questioning . . . For orientation . . . In search of farmer Hermann. At the same time farm protection . . . Postal patrol. Searching for escaped natives of a farmer . . . To search the area for nat[ives] . . . For the collection of salaries and copy.[ing] of local police decrees . . . Exploration of water holes . . . Legal notice and questioning . . . Searching for an alleged Herero settlement (unsuccessful) . . . Riding with compass and charting route. . . . Farm protection. Postal patrol . . . Standing patrol, livestock census . . . Reparation of the telephone line . . . Standing patrol (to capture nat.[ives]), quest.[ioning], survey of water conditions, registration of nat.[ives], . . . Farm protection. . . . Closing down of a Kaffir settlement. Search f[or] escaped nat.[ives] o[f] farmers.[20]

Noteworthy is again the vagueness about what actually had been done or achieved by a particular patrol. Most patrol books did not even give the names of all policemen involved.[21]

Nevertheless, the major areas to which most police assignments pertained become fairly evident: first, policemen were striving to get a grasp of the territory, to produce knowledge, and to make it theirs by covering it with infrastructure; second, they provided postal, administrative, and legal services; and last but not least, as I have already pointed out, policemen tried to regulate the indigenous population while supporting European settlement. A fourth, particularly significant field of occupation, which is not explicitly mentioned in the patrol logs but is connected to all of the above tasks, was desk work. Policemen spent large amounts of their time—too large according to some officials—writing reports, compiling lists, issuing papers, copying texts, and so on.

Depending on the area and on the year, priorities could shift. Delivery tasks remained quite stable. Searches for African laborers intensified and abated over the years. It is difficult, however, to make out a pattern. A first wave of tenacious pursuit seems to have occurred immediately in the aftermath of the war when colonizers frantically tried to secure the few African survivors for their farms, mines, and other workplaces.[22] A second wave appears to have occurred about halfway through the existence of the Landespolizei when the institution was relatively well established and thus scarcity of African labor could no longer be ascribed to a malfunctioning administration.[23] Regarding bureaucratic and legal tasks, there was a steady increase of the police's workload as both the court system and the bureaucratic apparatus kept expanding, despite bitter protestations from some colonial officials that these clerical duties did not belong to the "actual purpose" of police.[24] Over the years, exploring and surveying the territory became less and less pressing, although it is important to stress that until the very end of German colonial rule, the police's familiarity with the land and its people remained limited. All in all, variations in what the police concentrated on doing were mostly linked to individual local administrators' preferences, or even to those of individual police station commanders, rather than to earlier or later periods of colonial rule.

That said, some regions had specific policing issues: in the diamond fields south of Lüderitzbucht, for instance, policemen mostly struggled to combat theft and smuggling; in the very north of the colony, they primarily regulated the flow of migrating Ovambo workers who entered the territory from the Angolan border; in and surrounding the town of Rehoboth, policing pertained predominantly to the surveillance of the large Baster population who had settled there in the late nineteenth century and had been given some political autonomy in exchange for allegiance to the German regime; and finally, in urban spaces like Windhuk or Swakopmund or at remote border stations of the colony's outskirts, the police focused on slightly different details than in the rest of the territory.

Police Procedure and Routine: Paperwork and Patrolling

Procedures revolved around either stationary or itinerant forms of police work.[25] The first kind was typical of larger stations that were attached to district offices or police depots. The second kind unfolded in the open territory at and in between remote outposts. Procedures also varied depending on the rank of the policeman. Higher grades, that is, senior staff and staff sergeants, developed daily routines consonant with their command responsibilities, whereas the sergeants, constables, and police assistants fashioned procedures in accordance with obeying orders.

Stationary procedures were created and carried out by larger groups of policemen under relatively close supervision. These groups were usually composed of married men and those considered unfit for horseback duty.[26] Sometimes these men lived with their families in rented apartments among the town population; sometimes they lived together in buildings adjacent to the station.[27] The group dynamics and organizational culture that arose out of stationary police work were marked by sustained contact with the public and the commanding authorities. Collegial relationships could remain fairly professional, since sociability could be found outside of the group. Policemen assumed specific responsibilities and thus did not need to be highly versatile. The southern town Keetmanshoop, for instance, had nine German and nine African policemen. The staff sergeant was in charge of general supervision and inventory; one sergeant led criminal investigations and answered to the court; two men managed weapons sales, customs, and population registries, and acted as clerks for the "native courts"; two men supervised the prisons (one for Africans, one for Europeans); finally, three sergeants undertook "police services proper," that is, patrolling and attending to the public's concerns and requests.[28] The nine African police assistants were also given different functions. As evidenced in another document, these men were assigned to specific tasks as well: to guard prisoners, to provide for livestock, to interpret, or to patrol.[29]

Work at small, remote police stations differed from that in towns. Here, small units of two to five men had to work and live together in a "forced community."[30] They had to somehow get along with each other, and leisure time

FIGURE 7. Police station Büllsport northeast of the Naukluft mountain range. At remote out-posts like these, policemen had to be versatile, and they had to get along with the few other men (and sometimes women) living at the station. Date unknown. Bildarchiv der Deutschen Kolonial-gesellschaft, Universitätsbibliothek Frankfurt am Main. Photo No. 013-2167-11.

was spent with colleagues. Interracial contact was more frequent than at the larger town stations by sheer virtue of the small numbers of men and the isolation (figure 7).[31] Men at outposts had to perform all kinds of tasks and thus, by necessity, had to be resourceful. Daily life revolved around movement. In order to be able to do their job, policemen needed to travel between different posts, farms, and construction and mining sites, and along borders, waterways, and railways.

As a rule, the operation sequence of police work was the following. First, the magistrate or district chief would utter a directive that would be received by the senior commander of any given station. He would then verbally instruct his subordinates and simultaneously enter the assignment in their service book (*Dienstbuch*).[32] After fulfillment of the task, subalterns would report back, either orally or in writing. At that point, they would have their superior sign and stamp their logbook. Depending on the importance of the mission, station commanders would then either write a separate report to the district chief or magistrate, or simply mention it in their next regular report. Thus, directions and accounts would move down and up the echelons by means of bureaucratic procedure.

To the higher officials of the administration, the bureaucratic recording of policemen's work was their most important link to subalterns. It guaranteed accountability and was, in their eyes, the basis for rationalized colonial rule. All district offices were equipped with a calendar that gave them minute instructions about the kind of data they were to collect, the kind of reports and lists they had to hand in to the central administration, and how often.[33] This notwithstanding, officials did not want bureaucratic practice to get out of hand. A note to that effect by Vice Governor Hintrager commenting on a particular case in Outjo was sent to all police depots for instruction: "A favored way of operating there [in Outjo—M.M.] can, for the local circumstances, only be called exceedingly bureaucratic. For the protectorate, police work [*Polizeiwirtschaft*] as done in the homeland will not do. I must therefore expect that the decrees are strictly followed, but not in a way that will devolve into harassment of the population. The colony should not be administered with such a form of police spirit [*Polizeigeist*] which in the eyes of other nations is a German peculiarity."[34] Besides, as I mentioned earlier, paperwork was *not* considered to be the core of police work. But to the lower-rank policemen themselves bureaucratic procedure was the anchor, the practice that distinguished and legitimized them. The way they performed bureaucratic tasks was a *"differentiating* activit[y]," to use Michel de Certeau's conceptualization of everyday practices.[35] Stamps, signatures, reports—paper in general was of the utmost import to them. A staff sergeant at police depot Kub, for example, made it his task to certify signatures for a long time before Chief of Police Heydebreck put an end to this practice, reminding the staff sergeant that the depot was "a police station and not a public office [*Behörde*]."[36] Likewise, Senior Staff Sergeant Boßenberger insisted resolutely on bureaucratic procedure even in the smallest of matters. In one case he prevented an African worker from picking up an ox and bringing it back to his employer. The police had not been informed that the worker was permitted to do so. Without any means to get the ox back to his remote farm, farmer Bergemann had to sell the animal and thus had incurred a great loss, as he wrote in his inarticulate, misspelled complaint to the police.[37] Written expression being manifestly his forte, Senior Staff Sergeant Boßenberger responded: "Since I have merely acted in the farmer's interest, I cannot see that I have caused harm by my correct line of action. Had Mr. Bergemann sent a written communication regarding his designs to the local police, the incident in question would not have occurred."[38] Through bureaucratic practice Boßenberger drew a distinction between himself and the farmer, between the profession of policeman and that of husbandry, between officials and settlers. He lodged his professional identity in eloquent writing and paper, and insisted his civil interlocutor do the same.

Bureaucratic procedure as differentiating practice could also be brought to bear within the police. It shored up social and institutional hierarchies. Status seeker Sergeant Melzer, for example, deployed bureaucratic means in order to assert superiority over his station colleagues. A former farmhand, son of a foreman, he did "not keep company with his peers" when off duty.[39] Unduly often, Melzer made the men under his command collect written statements from settlers in addition to making them regularly confirm his instructions in writing.[40] But first and foremost, bureaucratic procedure separated German policemen from their African subalterns—even if, or maybe especially when, the latter were very well capable of reading and drafting texts. As the historian Gesine Krüger has demonstrated,

> the history of textuality in South Africa is marked by a paradoxical process: the increasing dispersion of script was accompanied by a simultaneous denial of script. . . . While more and more people learned how to read and write the notion of an "oral" African society was solidified. Flanked by laws and decrees, more and more people were factually and potentially excluded from the sphere of colonial dominated textuality— understood as a collectively shared consciousness of universal civilization, not as the necessary knowledge of how to deal with passes and contracts which was by all means desired.[41]

Although the written word was denied to the colonized, they understood how powerful papers were and how necessary it was to know how to navigate the bureaucratic system. The colonized—which in this instance included African policemen—were in a situation where they constantly had to deal with passports, stamps, and official documents while at the same time being excluded from the textual community. Bureaucratic procedure was key to fostering power, even for the lower echelons of the colonial state. As representatives of a rationalistic, modern colonial state, policemen laid exceptional claim to it. It set policemen apart from the rest of the colonizers. And it set the higher-ranking German men apart from the lower-ranking African men. As historian Deborah Durham shows, invoking the power of the state by referring to the office as an impersonal, rationalistic, bureaucratic one was an "everyday tactic" that made "bureaucracy, the system, and the state become . . . both abstract and very real in their effects." And in the process, the officeholders' power was made quite real, too.[42]

However, bureaucratic practice was not purely instrumental. The practice itself could encompass all kinds of styles, some accepted, others not. Sergeant

Henke, for instance, wrote a patrol report that read more like an essay or short story than a matter-of-fact, descriptive text.[43] Chief of Police Bethe was deeply surprised that the report could have slipped through the bureaucratic echelons without causing concern. He ordered the district office to make sure that policemen drafted reports in "short, concise form" and that they refrained from using any "general observations and superfluous colloquialisms."[44] And Sergeant Kobert was ordered by Bethe to do more "written work to improve his orthography and his letter style."[45] Thus, bureaucratic practice was also a form of training policemen, of disciplining them in the art of statecraft.[46] The fact that registers were still not filled out properly in 1914 shows that this was an ongoing process.[47]

Finally, the last stage in an operation sequence might be legal procedure. Both African and German policemen acted as court scribes, witnesses, guards during trials, and—most importantly—executory officers. In these functions they were directly under the command of a judge or court official, and expected to follow the rules of legal procedure. Here again, there was conflict within the administration whether this work was and should be part of police work proper.[48]

Other procedures did not necessitate that higher authorities gave an explicit order every time. These procedures followed the logic of established routines. More mundane kinds of such routines involved cleaning, repairing, and maintaining police equipment and grounds, or reviewing inventory, as well as drill and target and riding practice. But the most prominent routine was the patrol—notably the patrol on horseback (figures 8 and 9). This itinerant procedure was the main scope of small station police, but it was also performed by men from larger stations, particularly from police depots. The police patrol was in German Southwest Africa the archetypical practice of what Michelle Moyd has termed the "fundamentally itinerant style of governance."[49]

Usually, police went on regular patrol at least once a month.[50] The routinized patrol system guaranteed, on the one hand, communication and transportation of goods, payroll money, people, and so on between police and district headquarters, individual stations, and farms. On the other hand, it made individual stations and individual men responsible for a number of farms or work sites in their sector. Magistrate Groeben from district Gibeon issued a detailed decree including schedules, routes, and names of farmers to be visited.[51] District Chief Schneidenberger from Okahandja ordered that patrols should be ridden twice every week to nearby locations, and once or twice a month to remote areas. From his policemen at stations Groß-Barmen und Otjizongati he required that they draw a map of the territory covered by their weekly patrols.[52] Not all district administrators were as systematic as

FIGURE 8. Police patrols on horseback. Two policemen pose in the wide open spaces on the southwestern border of the Namib desert (near Aus). Patrolling meant above all covering long distances and riding for hours. Date unknown. Bildarchiv der Deutschen Kolonialgesellschaft, Universitätsbibliothek Frankfurt am Main. Photo No. 013-2169-02.

FIGURE 9. Four policemen, two African, two German, pose in an unknown place in the typical arid landscape of central Southwest Africa. Patrol units were on average two-to-four-men strong and racially mixed. Policemen spent large portions of their time in these small, homosocial groups. Date unknown. Bildarchiv der Deutschen Kolonialgesellschaft, Universitätsbibliothek Frankfurt am Main. Photo No. 013-2169-02.

Groeben and Schneidenberger, however. District Outjo's patrols were, at least at first, organized on a case by case basis with neither regularized schedules nor territories assigned to specific men.[53]

This notwithstanding, sociological scholarship on present-day police occupational culture has convincingly shown how important an assigned territory is in shaping police attitudes and practices. The allocation of a territory generates a "my beat" or "my turf" mentality and a claim to exclusivity within it. As the sociologist John Crank puts it: "Territory carries a great deal of meaning for the police. Police territories are infused with important values—commitment and responsibility—that surpass simple conceptions of spatial arrangement and population flows. Officers don't simply patrol areas, they control them, and they invest their energies and reputations in them."[54] Patrolling along familiar routes, or exploring new paths within a precinct (*Beritt*), and subsequently solidifying their grasp of that territory through the sketching of maps (figures 10, 11, and 12), attached policemen of the Landespolizei to a specific piece of land. They increasingly identified with it, claimed it as theirs, and distanced themselves from others. Competition and distrust between different precincts was one result of this attachment. Police station Nauchas from district Rehoboth, for instance, refused to cooperate with police station Ururas from district Swakopmund in a capturing mission, noting that the latter had been quite unsuccessful in this kind of enterprise, whereas it was doing well.[55] In 1913, police headquarters fueled competitive attitudes between precincts when it introduced another rationalizing bureaucratic measure that rendered the task of catching Africans a numbers game. Henceforth, each district's monthly report had to list "under the rubric 'patrol work' the number of all collected natives, divided into men, women, children." Recaptured escapees from prisons or farms were to be included in the calculation.[56] In May 1914, Chief of Police Bethe sent out a preprinted form for the monthly reports. Ostensibly, the ones he was receiving were not standardized enough for his taste. In the preprinted form police had to fill in, among other things, the number of captives and had to list the policing activities they had performed on each patrol.[57] Although the 1913 decree was issued to thwart "unjustified attacks" from the public regarding the efficacy of patrols, and thus to polish the police's image, the effects of it were also internal to the police institution.[58]

In the year 1908, the Landespolizei conducted about 675 patrols.[59] With increasing manpower this number grew over the following years.[60] In addition to the monthly patrols, policemen were sent on concrete missions, notably to track down "criminals," "thieves," and "runaways." So-called flying stations were established ad hoc in places of important economic or geopolitical interest.[61] With varying accuracy, all patrols were documented in patrol logs at the

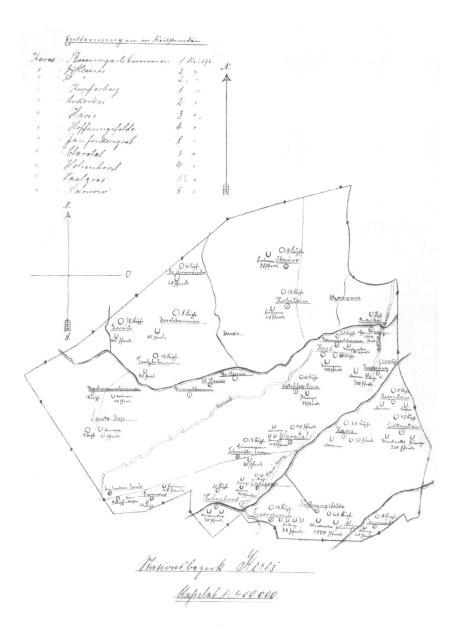

FIGURES 10–12. Maps of police precincts of Keres (1911), Gosorobis (1912), and Nam (1911). Policemen drew maps themselves. They had learned terrain surveying skills during their initial police training or in the military. Over the years, the maps became increasingly detailed and accurate, and thus added to the bureaucratic appropriation of the land. In the maps, distances are documented in terms of riding hours. Most crucial for the purposes of the police, these maps detail the location and amount of water that could be found on patrols. Some maps list the number of "heads" living at a dwelling or a farm (figs. 10, 11). It remains unclear, however, whether the authors had the European, the African, or both populations in mind. The official map of the "police zone" (1907) lists only the number of "whites" and their towns. BArch Berlin Lichterfelde, R 1002/2695, 40; R1002/2694, 81; R 1002/2695, 84.

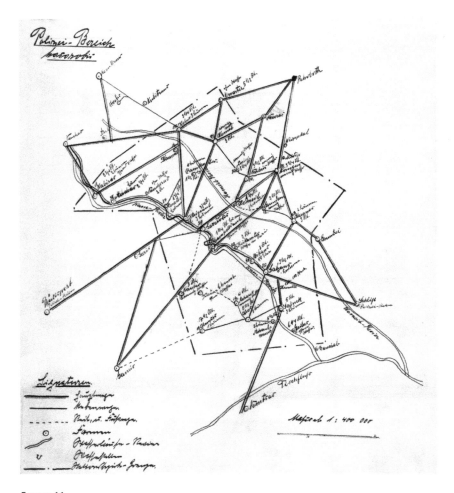

Figure 11.

station. The patrol logs mostly stated the date and length of a given patrol, the name of its commander and sometimes also of its participants, the route and distance covered, and—in very few words—the purpose and/or policing acts performed during the patrol and whether they had been successful.

A careful study of the relationship between distances covered, days spent in the field, and number of accomplished deeds documented in the patrol logs reveals the extent to which the patrol experience was primarily a succession of long, uneventful rides. For example, in the first quarter of 1911, the policemen of depot Spitzkoppe rode forty-eight patrols covering a total of 6,796 kilometers. The number of missions accomplished (both successfully and unsuccessfully) in that time period amounted to about one hundred.

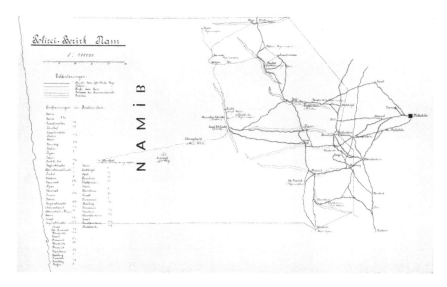

FIGURE 12.

That means only one police act per 67 kilometers.[62] In district Omaruru, in 1908, patrols of one to five men, over distances of 72 to 490 kilometers, lasted between one and eleven days. The record shows not more than one to three tasks per patrol.[63] Moreover, in both of these historical sources most missions pertained to the order of service and supervision rather than to any form of forceful prevention or intervention. Thus, the observation regarding contemporary police that "most police work resembles any other kind of work: it is boring, tiresome, . . . [and] it is rarely dangerous," seems also to apply to the Landespolizei of German Southwest Africa.[64] Given the tediousness of their everyday experience, not achieving the little that was possible on such long rides, often not being able to do any kind of "real" police work, must have been frustrating.[65] This feeling seems to resonate in Sergeant Wenzel's report when he bluntly noted: "success of the patrol = 0."[66]

Patrols were in themselves organized by routinized procedures. Policemen repeatedly had to saddle up and unsaddle, water and feed the horses, pack and manage provisions, secure weapons and prisoners, orient themselves, observe the terrain and the weather conditions, and, of course, ride for long hours. I suggest that not following official procedure punctiliously in some of these instances of unspectacular police work could have had a reanimating, entertaining, or exciting effect and thus might have been a technique to cope with frequent boredom and frustration.[67] To phrase it differently, not following procedure to the letter may also have been a form of minimal dissent, of having a mind of one's own, of temporarily disregarding authority, or being at least careless about it. For example, there are various instances documented in which policemen hunted game during patrol, sought to have some kind of (dangerous) adventure, or simply paused for a moment to look at the scenery.[68] Sometimes, policemen veered off course to investigate something on their own initiative or to look for a diversion. African Police Assistant Bumskopf, for instance, went absent without leave during a patrol, presumably to follow a trail. He returned to his station several days later.[69] For a short period, Bumskopf had taken a break from colonial control. He might have even taken care of his own affairs. And it is likely, though we cannot be certain, that Sergeant Gehrmann did not receive orders to take a guided tour through the mines in Tsumeb, but did so anyway and even included a long description of it in his patrol report.[70]

The historian Alf Lüdtke's notion of *Eigensinn* comes to mind when looking at these police practices.[71] In his studies of industrial labor, he argues that everyday activity in the factory also meant

> illegal break taking, risky "games" and the "carelessness" combatted by superiors, that is, the *Eigensinn* at and with machinery. . . . It was about holding oneself free of exertions, to establish niches for one's own time, for "oneself." What is more: expectations, incentives, impositions that were fixed in commands and liabilities were not just ignored or accepted—in everyday practices they were also always transformed. This form of *appropriation* of industrial work was not predicated on neglect of the work process. To the contrary, intimate familiarity with the modes of operation as well as an exact knowledge of the social power relations in the workshop were the preconditions for being able to fulfill requirements while *at the same time* satisfying one's own needs.[72]

Policemen of the Landespolizei pursued their own interests and desires within, along with, or against the procedural framework of patrol routines. In some cases, this deviating behavior could be fatal. For instance, Sergeant Hergert accidentally killed a soldier of the Schutztruppe when he showed off his gun.[73] And Sergeant Schreiber was shot at by a man who had seized his rifle, which he had carelessly left unattended while taking a break.[74] Needless to say, the risks of *eigensinnig* behavior were much higher for African policemen, and the consequences they faced when caught were much more severe.

The wide expanses that needed to be crossed, the sparseness of the population, the competition between precincts and possessiveness regarding one's own beat, the big and small events experienced side by side on the road, the little "divergences" unknown to police command—all of these features of patrol work made the men of a patrol unit come together. Or rather, formulated in the negative, patrolling isolated the men participating in a patrol from others—the public, the colleagues of another precinct, and their superiors. In his poem "From the Dunes of Southwest," former Staff Sergeant Kleinau bemoaned but also glorified the dire conditions he and his colleagues were working in. On his station, Dawignab, which was situated in the far southeast of the colony, he wrote: "O Dawignab! When your dunes blow, no inspection officer will show, even less the governor, O Dawignab, o Dawignab! They don't want to see you anyway!"[75] Adding to this actual or felt isolation was the fact that suspicion toward the public was in the nature of the job. Every person encountered was, in the mind of the policemen, a potential criminal. Policemen distrusted both settlers and colonized, and not rarely surmised that these were plotting against them. Sergeant Ebermann, for instance, plagued a passing trader whom he suspected of illegal trade and whom he was convinced was lying.[76] Sergeant Melzer was persuaded that the farmers in his precinct were conspiring against him, and so was Sergeant Ptaschek in his.[77] All subjects of the colonial realm were, however, also always potentially in need of help and protection. The sociologist Peter Manning calls this the "impossible" mandate of the police.[78] Scholars of police culture persistently come back to the notion of isolation linked to what they perceive as the uniquely contradictory nature of police work. Some have called its results "siege mentality," others solidarity.[79] In any case, patrol rides were group experiences, across the racial divide, and they generated (a feeling of) isolation.

The patrol logs I have drawn on so far only rarely stated the outcome of a mission. And in no instance did the logs document *how* missions were enforced. For that, we need to look at the longer patrol reports. In these we learn more about police interactions with the public. They tell us about the oscillation between moments of sociability and moments of formality, about how official procedures and personal habits interwove in the everyday, in short, about policemen's concrete ways of getting things done.

Tactics of Interaction: Sociability, Trickery, and Affects

At least during patrols meeting people was an event. As a rule, some kind of verbal exchange occurred, if only the shouting of a command, not seldom unintelligible to its listeners. Oftentimes whole conversations unfolded, notably between speakers of the same language, but also via interpreters. Greetings and other social rituals took place depending on the level of acquaintance between interlocutors. But more important, information was traded, stories were told. On arrival at a farm, for instance, police assistants usually went to talk to the African workers (after having taken care of the horses) while their superiors went to see the employer. Policemen listened to the latest news, concerns, stories, and rumors. Sergeant Geffke, for instance, gossiped with three farmers about one of his colleagues.[80] Sergeant Kuse repeatedly shared gossip with farmer Deckert.[81] Sometimes, although strictly speaking it was not permitted, they stayed overnight, or at least spent some time with the farm inhabitants, maybe ate and drank with them, and listened and talked some more.[82] On one late evening Constable Türk, for instance, sat down with farmer Schmidt in front of his farmhouse. Whether they had a conversation, a drink, a smoke, a break, or were attending to formal business is not clear. But Constable Türk was evidently spending the night at the farm.[83] And Police Assistant Petrus Claasen went to have a chat and drink some water with a number of prisoners.[84] Procedures of formal investigation and interrogation alternated, overlapped, or even merged with informal and convivial forms of intercourse.

What exactly determined how an encounter developed, whether it was mutual understanding and sympathy, or the desire for company (even disliked company), can hardly be assessed. Indeed, in other instances, men avoided contact beyond what was professionally necessary. The farmer couple Glose, for example, was shunned by all members of the nearby police station Nam, because of their "unfriendly behavior."[85] Policemen inserted their personal preferences and habits into the framework of patrol procedure when they encountered others. And hence, information and communication so crucial to police work were as much the product of affections, animosities, and informal conversation as of rationalized procedural templates. Some among the colonized were well aware of the dynamics, noting that "if the boss [*baas*] drinks beer and schnapps with the police, that is not good for us; if the police is at war [*orlog*] with the boss, then we can sheer out [*nücken*] from time to time without being punished."[86]

Knowing the beat and the people was a prerequisite for effective control. However, the racialized idea that there existed a category of "natural" recidivists could block the quest to "know" policed subjects, and reduce knowledge to the stereotypes that "suspects"—or even the entire population—were always the same.[87] Moreover, "suspects" who had already been entered into the bureaucratic system were recurrently arrested. And at least the German policemen were constantly confronted with the contradiction between their belief in the inherent lack of credibility of all colonized and their dependence on these very colonized to provide them with information. In fact, oftentimes it is difficult to discern from the source material how a policeman came by a piece of information and why he chose to believe it. Often the means and the process by which policemen gathered intelligence remain obscure. Take the example of Sergeant Heuer's report of a patrol sent out to apprehend some thieves. First, Heuer writes that he had "provisionally taken in Hottentot Jan" because the latter had no pass. Heuer continues his account, noting that African workers at a farm recognized the arrested man, and that he "thereupon admitted" to having stolen and slaughtered small livestock. "Another questioning," Heuer writes next, revealed that Jan had actually escaped from a prison in Windhuk two years before. The report leaves entirely open who received what information from whom. It is unclear who did the questioning or how it was performed. Heuer never mentions African policemen, and he never alludes to interrogation techniques. The report is also ambiguous on whether the workers who identified Jan were the ones to make him admit his alleged crimes or whether the police, presumably an African police assistant, questioned Jan at that point. In light of these uncertainties it is even unclear how Heuer came by the simple information of the man's name.[88]

Finally, policemen did not merely gather information from the population, but themselves took part in the constant fabrication and circulation of truths, half-truths, rumors, and myths that made up the imaginary of colonial life. Their tales were fixed into reports and thus attained stronger validity. Their bureaucracy could even create new identities. The Nama woman Uibis, for instance, was a prisoner of war who ran away several times. The last time she escaped it took the police six months to find her again. She had married a San man who worked for the land surveying office and had these authorities make her a pass under the name of Katharina.[89] Sociability, emotions, storytelling, and ideology were all elements of police procedures of knowledge production.

When patrols arrived at a farm or approached an African settlement in the hinterlands they could be fairly sure that somebody had already noticed them from afar. Therefore, when policemen were not interested in talking or feared that potential interlocutors or suspects could flee, they inspected dwellings by night, early in the morning, or late in the evening. A German sergeant and his African police assistant, for instance, were sent to a farm "to inspect the natives unexpectedly [*überraschend*] in the early morning hours."[90] Another sergeant and his police assistants raided several settlements in the middle of the night.[91] Deception was a common practice in the Landespolizei repertoire, but it could not be found in the manuals or directives. In fact, clothing disguise was explicitly forbidden, but still occurred.[92] Sergeant Dufring, for instance, dressed up in civilian clothes to uncover what, according to him, was an organized crime ring of "Boers, Cape-Landers [*Kapländer*], Jews, and unfortunately also Germans," whom he suspected of "steal[ing] away" African workers for the mines in South Africa.[93] His undercover operation was not commented on by his superiors, nor did he get disciplined for it. Magistrate Zastrow from district Grootfontein tried repeatedly to institute police patrols in plain clothes. He allowed these to take place even though he never received permission from headquarters. The first time, Zastrow had given permission to his subordinates while at the same time asking authorization from above. A year later, he tried to avoid headquarters and instead to win the nearby inspection officer as an ally in his endeavor. The latter did not like the idea, though, and informed police headquarters.[94]

The rule against disguise did not apply to African police assistants, it seems, who were often poorly uniformed anyway. Police Assistant Westerhuizen, for example, led one such undercover mission. Under the command of Sergeant Ptascheck, who checked in on him only once a week, Westerhuizen and two other African police assistants dressed up as cattle herders and stayed on a farm with the goal of apprehending three men. The architect of the plan, Staff Sergeant Eggersglüß, had "talked the matter through with Sergeant Ptascheck and the [Boer farmers—M.M.], the Boers want to help so that the disguise succeeds."[95] The African policemen's deception scheme did not violate police regulations, but their independent proceeding did. The two examples show how, on the ground, formal and informal working practices went hand in hand. Among these, trickery featured prominently. Or, as the aforementioned Sergeant Dufring somewhat theatrically phrased it, policemen used "guile against guile."[96] In this context German policemen might have been inspired by or relied on what they perceived to be an African tradition of "native trickery."[97] Surprise and guile worked best when performed as a concerted enterprise of African and German policemen, and with the help of the African or the settler population, depending on who was the object of investigation. Sometimes, the "trick" consisted plainly in leaving a farm and letting the farmer or his workers make the arrest for the police, or even kill in their stead. After raiding African settlements twice by night without arresting anyone but having learned more about the suspected thieves, notably that their wives lived and worked on a nearby farm, Sergeant Heuer and his patrol left the area and let the farmer and/or his workers apprehend the men when they came to see their families.[98] And when a Baster farmworker named Trion killed a presumed San thief, the reporting sergeant called it a "stroke of luck," and no legal consequences followed.[99]

Capture patrols were more successful, it seems, when African policemen took the lead or were sent off by their superiors to spearhead an operation. Usually (but not always) they knew the terrain and the population of their precinct better than did their German colleagues. Moreover, they might not have been perceived as policemen right away, or if so, they might not have been expected to be on a capture mission. Their appearance somewhere was sometimes the beginning of a ruse to apprehend colonized people. Seven African policemen, for instance, were the chief protagonists in a series of raids that caught about fifty Africans. The German sergeant in charge of the patrol and who wrote the report made that unusually clear: they were the ones who found the settlements and who spoke to the inhabitants. In one case, which is described in more detail, "African leader [*Führer*] Samuel" went into the village together with a previously apprehended inhabitant of the village to set in motion the upcoming arrests. The formulation leaves open whether Samuel was a simple guide or whether he was the leader of the African police contingent. The German sergeant's rendition of the event also remains silent on what Samuel actually did or said once he had made contact. In any case, his arrival in the village led to the capture of twenty-six men, women, and children.[100]

Placing major responsibility in the hands of African policemen was a regular form of improvised policing with which practical constraints were overcome. Reporting on about five of his best African police assistants, Sergeant Eggersglüss observed that they "showed themselves always willing and did not shy away from danger." He had them accompany search and reconnaissance patrols, and "when it looked like that the patrol was going to be unsuccessful, [I let them] work alone." To motivate their "ambition," Eggersglüss offered rewards, usually tobacco or coffee, but also money.[101] They had received between five and ten marks for "successful Namib-patrols."[102] In the midst of World War I, when there was no one else to do the job, Police Assistant Franz was stationed alone at an outpost near Swakopmund. During his time of duty there he managed to arrest two men by himself.[103]

Another way of proceeding during patrols was to advance in a somewhat unfocused and uncoordinated manner, to deal with facts as they presented themselves, and to creatively build a case. Sergeant Georg Dawedeit's report sheds light on this form of making do. Relying on information given by farmers and their African workers, his patrol went into the veld to find Africans. After several attempts to encircle several of their settlements had failed to capture anyone, the policemen finally came across two children who led them to a small village. The sergeant told a man whom he encountered there "to gather his people, for I wanted to issue each native with a pass."[104] The man obeyed. Thirteen Damara came out of their huts. The huts were searched, and a pelt with bullet holes was discovered. The Damara man was asked where he had hidden the gun but denied owning one. At this point, the whole group of men, women, and children was arrested and brought to a police depot. On their way back to the depot, a farmer identified the man Dawedeit had been supposedly talking to (it is more likely that one of the police assistants had spoken to the man) as a "thief." Thus, only subsequently did Dawedeit learn that he was a presumed thief. That was probably also the moment when he heard the man's name for the first time. In his report, however, the sergeant made it sound as if he had been tracking down Damara "thief" Jakob from the beginning. And in his last sentence—emanating a certain sense of pride—he finally labeled *all* captives as "thieves." The sergeant had made false promises to lure the Africans out of their shelters, had apprehended them based upon a vague suspicion, and had then built a case with information he had come by after the fact. Referring to himself and nobody else in the entire report, he moreover obscured the role African policemen had played in the enterprise.[105]

Finally, a variety of emotions affected daily beat routines. Notably, fear was a constant companion of policing. As might be expected, fear was an "unacceptable" emotion. Within the emotional communities of both German and African men of honor, fright betrayed an unmanly, weak character.[106] This notwithstanding, fear was omnipresent in a colonial regime that was based on coercion and that had just committed a genocide. And although policemen belonged to the coercing party and were thus the agents rather than the victims of threat, intimidation, and terror, they were not spared from feeling the attendant fear. They found themselves in situations in which they were outnumbered or exposed to probable ambushes. Their bodies were vulnerable to the perils of nature. And their psyches and imaginations generated frights and phobias. As much as police headquarters or cultural codes of conduct wanted to "forbid" fear, it affected police behavior. The ways in which policemen overcame, dealt with, or succumbed to their fears were diverse.

Being inexperienced, not having received enough training or none at all, and entrusted with challenging missions to ride into unknown territory, policemen regularly fretted about basic aspects of their work. They were afraid of riding, of using their weapons in a nonstandardized setting, or of navigating uncharted terrain. The sergeant I mention in chapter 2 who reportedly clung to his saddle while crying out in panic was an extreme case. But other men as well, for example, one Sergeant Hammerich, who fell off his horse several times before being "taken by the hand" by another colonial official and escorted to his station, had to deal with their fear of riding and with the humiliating spectacle such fears generated.[107] Such personal phobias may appear to be minor matters, but they gave rise to particular, sometimes even peculiar police behavior. Shame and the fear of humiliation were strong motivators, and one must surmise that many policemen preferred not to be seen when struggling with their mount, their equipment, or their sense of orientation.[108] I have used the example of fear of riding, but the concern for appearances was at the source of a whole variety of solitary or secluded operations. This concern about honor might even have trumped the more existential fear for one's own life. "The fear of death," historian Joanna Bourke notes, is "not universal."[109] In other cases, however, policemen did act upon the worry for their safety. They sought the company of colleagues, often making up an excuse to secure it. Professing that his horse was too young to manage the passing of a mountain range, Sergeant Malsch, for instance, preferred to ride together with Police Assistant Zacharias.[110] Thus, whether they were solitary police initiatives or concerted efforts, police practices can be partly explained as the attempt to deal with fear: either to hide it in the desire to conform to standards of affective control, or to overcome it through denial and disavowal.

As the examples above show, fear was closely related to shame and humiliation, often caused by a perceived slight to one's honor. Shame could prompt or coexist with a sense of helplessness and frustration. In numerous cases, policemen felt frustrated on account of "external" forces (that is, mostly resistance by the population, but also taxing conditions, and so on) and claimed that they had been pushed or compelled to do violence, that violence had been their "last resort." Police Assistant Friedrich Boekis, for instance, defended himself, stating that "in order to fulfill my assignment, . . . I have arguably pushed and beat the woman, but not more than I had to, . . . because I could not help myself otherwise in order to carry out my assignment."[111] Assistant Boekis and a second African policeman had struck a female Herero prisoner repeatedly with the whip until she fell, whereupon they had continued hitting her, including in the face. Their superior merely reprimanded them, and only because a settler had registered a complaint.[112] In a similar fashion Police Sergeant Hermann Wandrei wrote that he "had been forced" to repeatedly beat a Damara man who had refused to come with him.[113]

The presence of an onlooking public was crucial in forming emotions of shame, frustration, and anger. The sense of losing control over one's own body and over a situation, mixed with the realization that some external factors simply could not be brought under one's control, permeated colonial police action. Often, this set of sensations activated and accompanied violent behavior. On August 15, 1910, in the little town of Kuibis, Sergeant Bruno Vogel "let himself get carried away, slapping in agitation [*Erregung*]" a South African woman in the face.[114] In fact, Vogel slapped Anna Hendricks repeatedly and dragged her by the arm. Vogel, known for his paternal character and his role as caretaker, was evidently highly irritated by Hendricks's defiance, by her rejection of his care. In a store where the sergeant had addressed her in front of the European shop owner, some African employees, and possibly a few customers, she had refused to follow his request to come to the police station in order to get registered and to have a passport issued. Without further ado, he hit her. Then Hendricks walked away, perhaps trying to escape Vogel's reach, but not without complaining loudly. Sergeant Vogel followed her, hit her again, and dragged her away. During the entire incident, several onlookers observed the scene as it took its course from the store out onto the street, into a hotel filled with guests, and out onto the street again.[115] Later, Anna Hendricks, a British subject, appealed to the British consul. The British involvement is the only reason there is an archival record of the incident; otherwise it would have hardly raised any interest. Vogel was put in front of a judge and fined the trivial fee of five marks. The judge observed in mitigation that Vogel's behavior was understandable, since he had been "extremely irritated" (*gereizt*) by the South African woman. Moreover, he noted that "the defendant might have had the sensation that, in the interest of the reputation of the white race and of the German state, the insolence of the negro girl [*Negermädchen*] needed to be redressed on the spot with a chastisement commensurate to the mental and moral level of the girl."[116] Vogel's feelings, his inner stirrings, were directly linked to broader political contexts: to colonial state power and racist ideology. The state, through its representatives, like Sergeant Vogel, had "affects" and was called to act upon them.

Anger is an important element in any honor repertoire. Honor is essentially felt, not reasoned.[117] And a notion of "righteous anger" in the face of perceived humiliation and shame was often at the source of violent restitutive measures. In September 1910, Baster Police Assistant Friedrich Boekis and Damara Police Assistant Wilhelm Markus were suspected of having caused the death of an African worker from the Cape Colony. They had beat the man with clubs, and hours later the man had died. Secretary Hilzebecher, who acted as judge, however, acquitted the two policemen. The victim, his explanation stated, had "rightly" incurred the beating. Indeed, it had been his own doing, for he had coveted Boekis's wife and, to boot, had been insolent. From the judge's perspective, Police Assistant Boekis had "acted in protection of his innermost interests." And since the victim had been a "colossal opponent," it was only understandable that the cuckolded policeman had asked for help from his comrade Markus.[118] Boekis himself declared that he had been "angered" (*aufgebracht*) in a twofold way, first by his knowledge of the adultery, and second by the victim's impertinent behavior. He grabbed the man by the chest and struck him several times with a bamboo cane on the back.[119] Sergeant Albert Bruhn,

Boekis's immediate superior, also came to his defense. He vouched for Boekis's good character and expertise, and expressed understanding for his subaltern's behavior: Boekis had "simply made use of his domestic authority
[*Hausrecht*] in defense of legitimate interests" and only after he had been
"gravely irritated" by the other man.[120] Thus, in all these statements, anger
was the result of a combination of broader contextual and immediate situational factors: offense to the "right" of masculine, paternal honor, on the one
hand, and the face-to-face insult, on the other. In such a combination, the con-
sensual tone of all sources implied that "righteous anger" and violent retribu-
tion were appropriate. These ways of reasoning (and feeling) fit well into a
concept of honor that was situated somewhere in between external law and
internal sensibility, between social significance and inner life.

Certainly, it is difficult to evaluate what "anger" meant from a Baster perspective. And the temptation to compare anger from a different time and a
different culture to one's own experience of anger is great. But Catherine Lutz
observes in her anthropological study of emotions that depending on the cultural context there can be either antisocial or "prosocial aspects of anger."[121]
In the case of Police Assistant Boekis, his angry outbursts were amenable to
being framed as "righteous" and thus belonged to the prosocial type, for with
them (moral) redress was considered possible and necessary. As such, "righteous," justified, or justifiable anger organized social life by defining the inclu-
sions and exclusions of specific communities.

Lastly, policemen's violent practices were partly derived from the principle
of sadistic gratification. No individual historical example or singular case study
will do justice to the difficult issue of pleasurable violence. But one has to take
for granted that among the seven hundred policemen, at least some of them
felt bodily and mental elation in inflicting harm on others.[122]

Given the different dynamics of everyday practices I have outlined here, one
can sum up by stating that policemen "muddled through" their everyday duties. They did so by deceiving, bluffing, threatening, hiding from, making
promises to, and surprising the men, women, and children they encountered.
They acted upon instructions, upon individual interests, upon their capacities
and their feelings. And thus, policemen deployed an array of means that can
best be described as tactics. In his theory of everyday practices Michel de
Certeau defines "tactic" as follows:

> [A tactic] operates in isolated actions, blow by blow. It takes advantage
> of "opportunities" and depends on them, being without any base where
> it could stockpile its winnings, build up its own position, and plan raids.
> What it wins it cannot keep. This nowhere gives a tactic mobility, to be

sure, but a mobility that must accept the chance offerings of the moment, and seize on the wing the possibilities that offer themselves at any given moment. It must vigilantly make use of the cracks that particular conjunctions open in the surveillance of the proprietary powers. It poaches in them. It creates surprises in them. It can be where it is least expected. It is guileful ruse.[123]

De Certeau's elucidation of this form of practice, of what tactics can do and how they operate, is in my opinion quite resonant with the kind of police work I have described here. Furthermore, if we think of low-level violent acts as belonging to the realm of tactics, their potential in being effective within an overall unstable, dysfunctional power constellation becomes patent. The frequent grabbing, kicking, and hitting when opportunity presented itself unfolded their greatest power in the moment when they occurred. Policemen had "the power of action" (*Aktionsmacht*) in that moment.[124] They hit and then denied or had to justify the deed after the fact; their power was the greatest in the act; afterwards it decreased again. The logic within which this form of immediate power was inscribed was that of the "men on the spot."[125]

Police Discretion: Common Sense and the Range of Policing Styles

In a letter to police headquarters a district chief in Okahandja explained what kind of patrols he assigned to his policemen. He distinguished between two forms. The first kind of patrol was, "as a rule, made up of one police sergeant and one native police servant. It issues court orders, executes legal enforcement [*Zwangsvollstreckungen*], inspects the native situation [*Eingeborenenverhält-nisse*] and so forth, and, after return, it reports orally on notable [*besondere*] occurrences."[126] The second kind comprised "one police sergeant and 2 native police servants." It was charged with carrying out the same tasks as the first, but in addition it had to survey livestock on visited farms, and then again to "orally report after return about the observations made."[127] Note the minor difference in wording with respect to what needed to be reported back. Whereas the latter patrol was asked to give an account of all that had been observed, the former was supposed to mention only instances that seemed to be out of the ordinary. I suppose that the different formulations were not intentional, but here lay the individual policeman's discretionary power. He had to decide what he considered noteworthy and thus necessary to communicate to his superior. In a situation of constant and utter unpredictability, his evaluation counted.[128] Based on this assessment, actions followed. And often, these actions were his to take, too. In brief, he made a judgment call. Take Sergeant Gehrmann's account of a visit to two remote farms, for instance. He had been informed that "supposedly, the workers had behaved intractably [*renitent*] against their employers. I inquired of the natives about working and boarding conditions. Some of the people spoke actually very well of their employers. The discontented natives were admonished [*ermahnt*]."[129] After a ride of several hours to the location, the sergeant had formed his opinion based on what he heard and what he saw, had acted upon it, and had left again. In this case he decided to wag his finger. But he might well have used more drastic measures or lectured the farmers instead. In the passage quoted above his reasoning is curtailed. We do not learn how he got from learning about discontented farmers and partly contented, partly discontented workers to reprimanding the latter. In situations like these, the policeman's experience and his ability to use common sense became crucial. Gehrmann and his African police assistants relied on their prior experiences and their habits, on "ways of knowing that are available and 'easy to think,'" to favor the course of action they chose.[130]

Common sense, the sociologist Elizabeth McNulty observes, is characterized by "simplicity and contradiction."[131] She suggests that its production is a collective enterprise, that "everyday life routines provide the essential taken-for-granted context in which police together generate common sense knowledge 'on the street.' . . . Common sense . . . is neither univocal nor consistent. Instead, it mirrors the unpredictability and uncertainty on the street."[132] Thus, policemen put practice and experience at the core of what constituted their behavioral guiding principles.[133] They built these principles in concert during formal and informal routines when they shared experiences, narrated them, and collectively tried to make sense of them. Their superiors shared to a certain extent the valorization of experience. Seasoned men like Sergeant Hergert, for instance, who had been in the colony since 1893, were valued, as seen in his evaluation sheet from October 1904:

Hergert is a calm, sober, and dutiful man. For a couple of months now he has been married to a young German woman of immaculate reputation, from all that I have heard, in a very happy marriage. Although his writing skills are a little bit clumsy for lack of practice, as an old African who has been active in a wide variety of positions he possesses a plenitude of practical competences and knows how to gain authority with the whites and the natives. I highly value having in Hergert a practical policeman who is well acquainted with the conditions of the country.[134]

But this assessment could easily turn negative when the policeman, from the perspective of his superiors, "let himself go." This is precisely what happened to Hergert, who, in a crushing evaluation in May 1909, was characterized as "ponderous, dull," and "sluggish."[135] But from the sergeant's perspective, he might have depicted Hergert's policing style entirely differently. Having seen a lot and having been in the country for a long time, he might have decided to turn a blind eye to certain situations.

Police discretion, coupled with the all-encompassing responsibility that I evoke at the very beginning of this chapter, had the consequence that everything could be, but nothing had to be, a policeman's concern. Policemen necessarily made choices. Monjardet notes that "it is thus inevitable, normal that, in this immense and desperate universe, policemen cut out a segment that is well-defined, delimited, clean, visible, easy to measure, and that they make of it the core, heart, and exclusive object of their mission."[136] As a result, police work in Southwest Africa had a wide variety of different styles. Some policemen dragged their feet, avoided tasks, or turned a blind eye to certain transgressions. Others sought every occasion to enforce the law, intervened brutally, or proceeded in an exceedingly formalistic manner. Senior Staff Sergeant Hermann Kratz, for instance, noted in passing that African worker Wilhelm Matrohs had "already asked three times from police patrols" to have a pass issued to him, but that he had still not received one. The staff sergeant himself did not take action either, believing that another office would take care of the issue.[137] Other sergeants came late to their duty or left their post to visit friends.[138] And yet others were much more proactive. They went out of their way to surveil a single person with the single goal of verifying that person's identity.[139] They intruded on domestic lives or pressured workers to press charges against their employers.[140]

Moreover, many policemen combined "a repressive with an 'obliging' or preventive approach."[141] For what mattered was that something was done, whatever it was, and that it happen promptly. As McNulty notes, "Police officers demonstrate that they 'have' common sense by how they act on the street. To be seen as competent, officers must often act quickly and decisively."[142] Or as Sergeant Maletz recalled, sanctions had best "come on the heels" of a misdemeanor.[143] The call for immediacy and pragmatism buttressed the importance of men on the spot and of their experience. Ultimately, it motivated many policemen to make short shrift: "a cheap and quick solution to numerous problems," violence or the threat of violence was never far away.[144]

Violence as Work

Alf Lüdtke has compared the "work" of making war to industrial work. He has shown how certain practices and experiences on a modern battlefield resembled processes and perceptions of work in the factory: "Room for manoeuvre at the respective point of production was crucial to both industrial work and soldiering. Similar if not largely identical in both areas were the demands for skillfully moving and using one's body. Only then would specific varieties of behavior combine efficiency with effectiveness."[145] He has also stressed important differences. Notably, the intense experiences of imminent, life-threatening danger and of killing were a specificity of the battlefield and did not exist in the factory. Police violence in German Southwest Africa was in many ways like waging war. Policemen were former soldiers or warriors. Their leadership trusted most in their military training and bearing to face daily tasks. They were expected to maintain a military set of skills, notably, automatic body movements and the immediate readiness to do violence while remaining calm and in control of a situation. In fact, police raids of African settlements were not seldom organized and executed like military operations, or were even a joint venture of police and Schutztruppe.[146] Occasionally policemen used militarized language and imagery to describe their work. They spoke of the "enemy" that needed to be "defeated," of the "encirclement" of settlements, or of "reconnaissance missions" and of "penetrating into terrain."[147] Killing a large number of Africans, as in the case of Sergeant Hagner, who killed fourteen San on one patrol, was lauded as a "particularly good performance," and he was recommended for a reward.[148]

In her recent historical study of policing in the United States during the 1960s and 1970s, Micol Seigel offers a thorough reconceptualization of what policing is and does. She redefines policing as "violence work": "Police realize—they *make real*—the core of the power of the state. That is what I mean to convey by calling police 'violence workers'. . . . It is simply about what their labor rests upon and therefore conveys into the material world. . . . It takes work to represent and distribute state violence. . . . 'Violence workers' . . . effectively conveys the full panoply of people whose work rests on a promise of violence."[149] What brings me to interpret the police's use of violence as work is the emphasis that policemen laid on the effort that it took and on the dexterity applied when they described violent deeds. They often specified how, and with what tool or part of the body, a blow had been executed. To stress the precise mastery of their body, time and again policemen insisted that they had used their flat hand and not their fist, for instance.[150] Or they indicated that they were able to use their firearm in an efficient, methodical, and nonlethal way, underlining that they had wielded the butt end of their gun. Sergeant Scheiter, for instance, "fended off" an African man by dealing "an acute [*heftig*] blow with the rifle butt."[151]

Moreover, the terms "proficient" or "stalwart" (*tüchtig*) and "assiduous" or "eager" (*eifrig*) were frequently employed to depict violent police types and deeds.[152] According to his superior, Sergeant Lange, who was "feared for his fierceness," who "spared no pains," was simultaneously characterized as "eager to serve [*diensteifrig*], [and] staunch."[153] Being fierce and tough was thus associated with the idea of qualitatively good work, of savoir faire and accomplishment. This is also the case for the description of three policemen who in 1911 in Keetmanshoop severely beat South African prisoners with a sjambok and a belt on repeated occasions, as well as holding these prisoners down on the ground and gagging them. Police headquarters noted in a communication to the colonial government that "the 3 officials are reliable [*bewährt*] men" and that it was "of the opinion that they merely [acted] in exaggerated diligence [*übertriebenem Diensteifer*]."[154]

Policemen considered their work to be valuable not so much because it was heroic, like soldiering, but because it was a modest and honorable service. As Staff Sergeant Rafalski noted, policing in German Southwest Africa was not a "history of war and heroism, but simply of hard, selfless work and the cheerful fulfillment of duty."[155] Part of that work was violence. Violence was an important and necessary part of the profession. Policemen saw the value of their work to lie in a job well done, a kind of violent craftsmanship. With it they claimed to mold and cultivate the land and its people. In the words of Chief of Police Major Bethe: "We are not only qualified, but . . . it is our vocation to supervise and culturally develop dependent peoples."[156]

By and large, policemen had to rely on what they thought or felt was right based on their military socialization, what they happened to have read in the instruction manuals and regulations, or what they had learned on the beat and at the station from their colleagues and in interaction with the public. Policemen were neither all-knowing "killing-machines" nor were they totally ignorant, useless good-for-nothings.[157] They were not idle either. They got the job done, that is, the job that they thought was theirs and that they were able to fulfill. And they did it their way. Policemen followed procedure, but added their own note to it. The everyday conditions of Southwest Africa allowed for some degree of autonomy and imposed improvisation. The result was a mode of operation that could vary between pedantry and laissez-faire, overactivity and idleness, and brutality and kindness.

Although neither author has made the connection, De Certeau's "tactics" and Lüdtke's *Eigensinn* are helpful concepts when analyzing police practices.

Policemen worked for their superiors, followed rules, and executed orders, just like the factory workers who produced goods for their employers in the examples De Certeau and Lüdtke evoke. The manner of operation and the tactics they deployed were their own, however. And policemen added a good portion of "self-will," of appropriating the task at hand, into the mix.

The notion of a failed or limited colonial state suggests inactivity or ineffectiveness. I propose that the policemen's practices did not necessarily have the highest efficiency, but were by all accounts transformative. They did not create a stable colonial state in Trutz von Trotha's sense.[158] But they had effects owing to the fact that they were potently adaptable and performed in concert with other colonial actors, as I elaborate in the following chapter.

CHAPTER 5

Policing Work
Violent Regulation of the Labor Market

Colonial regimes of the nineteenth and twentieth centuries dealt in economic exploitation. Pressured from the metropoles that paid their bills, colonies needed to be productive and thriving. By the end of the nineteenth century, the system of chattel slavery that had so powerfully affected Atlantic societies was on the wane, while a new, global, and more insidiously coercive system of "free labor" under a capitalist framework was under development. Most colonizers by the turn of the twentieth century tried, both in theory and in fact, to produce wage labor systems that encompassed the metropole and the colony.[1] As within Europe itself, one of the most powerful instruments for disciplining colonial populations into a wage labor system was violence—both of a spectacular and an everyday variety. And the typical state instrument for such violence was the police.[2]

Between colonial and settler colonial settings, labor economies differed, however. Whereas in the former setting the primary goal was to extract indigenous labor, like other resources, for the greatest economic gain, in the latter the long-term aim was to expropriate and displace/eliminate the indigenous population to ensconce a settler population instead.[3] Thus, even though indigenous labor "was indispensable to Europeans" and their settlement project, as Wolfe states, "settler-colonization['s] . . . dominant feature is not exploitation but replacement."[4] To what extent this conceptual distinction between colonialism and settler colonialism is an antithetical one or rather one of variation is currently under debate.[5] In German Southwest Africa, the tension between a logic toward elimination of and dependence on African labor was most palpable in the aftermath of the genocidal war against the colonized population. There, the limited supply of labor—caused by the genocide—was the single most important factor limiting economic growth between 1908 and World War I. Hence, securing and regulating African labor was one of the foremost interests that guided state policy in that colony. In the German state's logic, only absolute control of the colonized could ensure a functioning, profitable economy. It fell to the Landespolizei to install that all-encompassing control. Thus, most police work was a matter of policing work. Whereas the last chapter addressed the former, this chapter deals with the latter.

The colonial economy of German Southwest Africa was built on a semi-free labor market—semi-free because even after forced labor, which had been instituted during the war, was officially abolished in 1908, aspects of the system remained quite overtly coercive: men and women who did not wish to enter the colonizers' wage economy and were trying to hide in the outskirts of the colony or outside the Police Zone were forced into it by numerous measures; workers who left their employment before the end of the contracted term were brought back to their employer by force; Africans were restricted in their mobility and could not choose their workplace; and, of course, forced labor continued to exist as a penal practice.[6]

The mode of production settlers put into place—sedentary cattle farming on privately owned, apportioned pieces of land—aggravated economic dysfunction. The fact that African labor was scarce after the war intensified the situation even further and made settlers fight among each other over the labor force. The railroad construction and mining companies vied for the precious resource as well, especially after diamonds were discovered in 1908. In 1911, about fifteen thousand workers were presumably lacking in a country with a colonized population of about seventy thousand and an ever-increasing colonizer (that is, employer) population.[7] To mitigate the labor shortage, employers (notably the copper and diamond mines) recruited migrant workers from the northern parts of the colony (Amboland) lying outside the Police Zone and in the neighboring Portuguese colony, Angola, or from South Africa.[8] These migrant laborers were also subjected to the state monitored semi-free labor regime.

Colonized labor was hard. Working hours were long; often there was no rest even on Sundays. Accommodations and provisions were insufficient.[9] The general framework of semi-free labor, the scarcity of the labor force, the nervousness of employers, and the harsh working conditions—all these were circumstances that facilitated or even generated violence. Regarding this

violence, scholarly readings usually distinguish between two competing un-
derstandings of how to attain economic productivity. These analyses contend
that European farmers and company owners put their individual economic
interests first, and exploited their workers to a maximum using excessive
violence. The colonial government, however, endeavored to check extremely
violent behavior against African workers and to introduce rudimentary protective laws with the objective of establishing a functioning national economy.
One logic stipulated that violence be exercised without restraint, the other
that violence be reduced or limited.[10] Based on this assessment, scholars then
have argued that state regulations aimed at limiting violence could not be
put into practice because the "authorities simply did not possess the resources
to control their 'white' subjects" and because of the resistance of subaltern
functionaries acting mainly on their racist worldview.[11] Zollmann claims that
policemen "almost never were able to have a moderating effect on farmers."[12] This historiography has set up a dichotomy between a stinted but genuine liberalizing effort by the state on the one hand and a reactionary, cruel
conduct, particularly by farmers, but also by overseers and low-level officials,
on the other hand.

Yet, colonial violence was not just excessively applied by some or limited
by some others. Violence is more complicated than that. As I argued in the
preceding chapter, policemen claimed to be competent wielders of violence,
their military training conjoined with their experience in the field making them
experts in dexterous, professional violence. This understanding encompassed
a notion of "constructive" or "educative" violence toward the colonized. It also
made the policemen feel entitled to supervise other colonial actors' use of violence and to correct them if they deemed it necessary.

In an internal note circulated among civil servants of the colonial government in Windhuk, Magistrate Fromm stated in 1911, "He who knows how to
treat people well, will always have workers."[13] This statement captures policemen's general understanding of labor relations, their attitude toward employers
and employees, and their illusions about the workings of the labor market. In
this chapter I expand on the active role policemen assumed within the colonial
economy based on the idea that there was a "right treatment" of colonized
workers. The German colonial police created an economy of violence that
I characterize as an economy of "educative violence." This specific form
of violence was economically viable. In fact, it was integral to the colonial
economy. It refined interaction between employers and employees. It instilled
discipline. Put in crude terms, it assured that workers did not die, but instead
kept on working.

Race, Work, and Discipline

German policemen's writings, notably the certification exams they had to compose on "legal concepts and customs of the natives," betray the policemen's racist worldviews and reflect contemporary ethnographic discourses.[14] Regarding work and ownership, German policemen oftentimes correlated the idea that land was owned by those who cultivated it with the idea that all colonized were lazy, and that they "prefer[red] a life in which they were left to their own devices, even if they had to suffer hunger, rather than regular employment [*geregelte Tätigkeit*]."[15] Police Sergeant Emil Hirschmüller, for instance, observed that "with us, the principle applies: 'where I earn my bread is my home.' This is different with the Herero. He only leaves his home and relatives when forced, and he rather suffers deprivations and dangers here, than to live in abundance in foreign lands."[16] Another sergeant stressed that it would take "still very much patience and effort" before the Herero would work "willingly." For they "only work because they have to, but never of [their] own accord."[17] This idea could go as far as to justify mass murder. In the best-selling adventure novel *Peter Moors Fahrt nach Südwest* (Peter Moor's Voyage to the Southwest), published in the midst of the German war against the Herero and the Nama, and definitely read by quite a few German policemen, the main protagonist declares: "The blacks deserved death before God and humanity, not because they murdered two hundred farmers and rebelled against us, but because they have not built any houses and have not dug any wells. . . . God has let us win here, because we are the nobler and more determined. . . . The world belongs to the industrious, the vigorous."[18]

Considered fundamentally different and inferior, indigenous populations needed to be taught how to work, or else be excluded from colonial society. Racist ideology distinguished between different racial "types" of workers: the colonized were classified along a scale ranging from those who could and those who could not be domesticated to wage labor.[19] In his written exam, one sergeant drew such distinctions. He portrayed the Herero as particularly lazy and dishonest; the Damara as "the most dull-witted [*stumpfsinnigsten*]"; the Basters as the most adaptable, but pretentious; the Nama as malicious and "less suitable for work because of their weak build"; and finally the San (or Bushmen) as "rabble" who were afraid of people and would shun all whites.[20] Sergeant Gentz noted in an annual report: "One can still not accustom the Bushmen to do regular work. They do their work for a couple of months, then they disappear one night, never to return again."[21] And Magistrate Zastrow in Grootfontein branded the San as "a through and through uncultivatable, untamable element."[22] As a consequence, the San were particularly targeted as harmful to the economic system. They were removed from their homes and put to work under high surveillance in other regions.[23] Increasingly, they were seen as a threat—a "plague," as the local newspapers called it in 1911.[24] They were hunted down and murdered.[25] The murder of San is reminiscent of a similar policy in the German homeland toward the so-called gypsy plague, albeit radicalized to settler colonial eliminationism. Both were part of modernity's push to end nomadism and force nomads into labor.[26] To some, like Governor Seitz, for instance, the Nama were similarly unable to fit into a wage economy, for their "love of living in the bush can never be stamped out."[27] Thus, policemen had more or less complex, often motley systems of racial categorization in their heads when they went about disciplining workers.

Responsibility to discipline the colonized into labor, if deemed possible, was believed to lie with all Europeans. In fact, policemen often saw the primary responsibility residing with employers: "There will always be complaints about the laziness and unreliability of the natives from farmers. In part, the farmers are to blame for these circumstances, for where there is not constant control, the best worker will get lazy and remiss."[28] The tool held to be appropriate was violence. In 1900, the Foreign Office in Berlin had asked their colonial governments to assess the general opinion on corporal punishment.[29] The numerous testimonies given by local administrators, military personnel, settlers, and missionaries are proof of an overwhelming consensus on the subject.[30] Corporal punishment was regarded as necessary and particularly suitable for Africans, whose cultures were believed to have accustomed them to this form of correction.[31] Missionary Fenchel from Keetmanshoop noted that his "experience of many years" in Southwest Africa had shown that corporal punishment was "a disciplining tool one cannot do without."[32] Especially the Nama people, he claimed, had "from ancient times" known no other form of penalty than corporal punishment.[33]

That this was a misconception, and that African peoples in Southwestern Africa commonly relied on other forms of conflict resolution and justice, especially material settlement, was actually already established in the scholarship at the time. The historian Martin Schröder discovered that contemporary law experts had come to the conclusion that among the seven African peoples living in the German colonies they had surveyed, penalties usually consisted of capital punishment or property forfeiture, but "seldom in imprisonment or corporal punishment."[34] Precolonial corporal punishment in Africa was usually based on generation or sex: children and women were spanked and beaten.[35] Contemporary ethnographer Carl Meinhof observed that corporal

punishment of adults was "not as common as is mostly assumed."[36] Schröder
concludes therefore that "the penal law of many African ethnicities attributed
great importance to the atonement of wrongdoings through compensation
and additional payment [Bußzahlung]. It was grounded in an African understanding of the purpose of punishment which differed fundamentally from the
European concept. This understanding aimed at the redress of harm inflicted
on the victim. Such a compensation was meant to restore the social order that
had been disrupted by the misdeed."[37] But policemen, like so many others in
the colonial realm, reproduced the prevailing racist narrative of a backward
colonized population who understood only the language of violence, when,
in fact, this fixation on violence as a means of education and communication
was more specific to their own upbringing.[38] Sergeant Emil Hirschmüller
wrote in his exam, for example: "In any case, the best administered remedy is
an immediate, really palpable [wirklich fühlbare] punishment. . . . Besides the
withdrawal of foodstuffs, drinks, and tobacco, the Herero recognizes only a
palpable [fühlbar] beating as real punishment."[39] Thus, added to the idea of
violence as the only appropriate means of correction was the notion that it
could "have the desired effect only if it was executed at once."[40]

How this punishment was supposed to be implemented and by whom was
less obvious. Corporal punishment of the colonized was regulated—like so
many other aspects of colonial rule—by a confusing mixture of executive
orders, internal regulations, and customary law.[41] It could be either a penalty
in a criminal case, a disciplinary measure within a military or state institution,
or a paternal chastisement (väterliches Züchtigungsrecht), that is, a civil, customary right. In this last sense it differed little from the laws regarding domestics,
farm workers, apprentices, students, soldiers, convicts, wives, and children in
the homeland. This common law was buttressed by the ideology that some
members of society needed to be taught to work. "Education to work" was
the widely used expression.[42] It applied to the lower classes in the Kaiserreich,
as well as to Africans in the colonies. Judge Bruhns from the high court in
Windhuk considered the "education" of colonial subjects to be a "cultural mission" of all Europeans and claimed that "if one wants to fulfill honestly and
properly one's educational responsibility [Erziehungspflicht], one is left with no
other choice but to bring to bear the same means of correction that the edu-
cator at home is entitled to."[43] Contrary to its legal and disciplinary counterparts, the paternal right of chastisement was never codified or standardized
(in terms of punishable misdoings, forms and magnitude of punishment, disciplining tools, and so on).[44] Interestingly, nothing in this regard was formulated in the 1907 "native ordinances," where one would have expected at least

a mention of the customary law in the decree regarding employer-employee relationships.[45] This meant that it was left to the chastising person to determine the appropriate form and extent of a beating.

Missionary Fenchel cautioned the colonial government that not all colonizers were competent in the arts of disciplining: "An experienced and sensible [*verständiger*] person would not dare to object to the application [*Anwendung*] of corporal punishment in this country. However, it all depends on the manner of that application in each individual case. In the hands of a pedagogue the whip can do miracles, whereas in the hands of an ignorant [*unverständigen*] person it can lead to abuse."[46] In theory, the different forms of corporal punishment (criminal, disciplinary, paternal) were supposed to be strictly separated. Judge Bruhns stated on that issue: "Those who do not know how far they can go with the usage of educative tools, should keep their hands out of it! Never should the paternal right of chastisement get out of hand so that it replaces the state's penal power!"[47]

Yet, in practice the categories were constantly confused. Farmers punished theft and policemen punished laziness. In fact, Magistrate Heilingbrunner admitted to this very fact in a circular to his subordinates suggesting ways by which one could work around the blurring of penal categories.[48] He advised his policemen "to check whether the native's behavior (disobedience, insubordination, laziness, escape) can simultaneously be construed as a slight [*Mißachtung*] (libel of employer). Routinely, one will be able to assume this."[49] Heilingbrunner's insistence that policemen check up on something that they should regularly assume was perhaps self-contradictory and confusing. To complicate the matter further, settlers could refer to §17 of an 1896 ordinance that allowed them to entrust their paternal right of chastisement to a representative of the state.[50]

As a matter of fact, what mattered to the colonial administration, discernible in both missionary Fenchel's and Judge Bruhns's statements above, was not so much the confusion of legal categories, but rather that violence had to be done in the "proper" way, that the person who disciplined had the ability and knew how to do it "correctly." This is where the role of the police force became crucial. Policemen were in many instances the authority who distinguished "right" from "wrong" violence. They defined what constituted the "correct treatment" of African workers. They specified what was the appropriate behavior toward a colonized population considered in need of care. When a European employer did not know how to deal with his or her employees, that is, how to "educate" them to work, the police intervened. If he or she *did* know how, however, then the police did not interfere and merely assisted him or her. In some sense, they were the teachers of the teachers of work. They were the guardians of "civilizing" violence.[51] And their guiding principles were honor and propriety, as well as their trust in their own practice and experience.[52]

By now, the ideas and ideologies that framed the violent policing of work should be clear, and many of them will be familiar to scholars of colonialism in other contexts. In order to bring greater specificity to my analysis of the German context, and to ground it in material practices, I will now turn to the three main aspects of labor regulation in which the colonial police were involved: recruitment, distribution, and supervision.

Finding and Seizing Labor

First, the police played a major role in recruiting, or better, finding labor. In order to impose their "care" on the colonized, the police had to bring them forcefully under their wing. Many of their patrols were organized with the sole purpose of ruthlessly hunting down Africans who were living in remote areas, far away from the colonizing centers. How brutal these capturing tours often were is barely detectable in the language the policemen used to describe the patrols in their reports. In those reports the policemen talk about having "drawn out" (*ausgehoben*) or "closed down" (*aufgehoben*) some village, about having "cleaned" (*gesäubert*) an area, or about having "collected" (*aufgesammelt*), "picked up" (*aufgegriffen*), and "gotten hold of" (*habhaft geworden*) men, women, and children.[53] Sometimes the reports were not only vague in their choice of verbs but also obscure about the actors involved in the raids. Inspection Officer Hildebrandt, for instance, noted that he himself had "personally brought back people," when it is fairly certain that he must have been accompanied by at least one African police assistant if not a whole group of well-armed German and African policemen—very likely for a higher-ranking man like Hildebrandt.[54]

That police patrols involved a fair amount of everyday violence, in many cases of an intense kind, is indicated in other sources. There, we hear of men and women being subjected to extended interrogations, or deprived of water so that they would give up information about hideouts. Sergeant Link's 1910 patrol report recounts, for instance, a two-hour questioning.[55] And a report from the same year by Senior Staff Sergeant Donicht indicates that he deprived men of water. The report also includes the mysterious death of a man shortly after his interrogation, presumably caused by a kick from a mule.[56] We hear of threats, seizure, and blows to the face.[57] These sources also testify to the repeated instructions to policemen to burn huts and personal belongings once the African settlements had been raided. Sergeant Dufring noted that "what the natives could not carry away, I had brought together on a pile and burnt together with all the huts."[58] And an official in police headquarters commented on Sergeant Wolff's patrol report that it was "very important" that African dwellings would be "burnt down."[59] Whether Africans had never been in the employ of a settler or whether they had escaped it, whether they had stolen something or not, should have made a difference. But often to the patrolling policemen, most, if not all, Africans they encountered were somehow suspect, for they had avoided the state's influence. At this stage, efforts to force colonial subjects into the labor market followed an either/or logic. Compared to subsequent phases, violence in this initial stage was not about education or discipline, not about honing labor relations. What was important then was to bring the colonized under the state's control and protection, with deadly force if necessary. Life outside the state-sanctioned realm of the colonial economy was sought to be made impossible.[60] The logic of violence was different in the hunting stage than once the colonized subject had entered the labor market.

In the extreme, this desire for absolute control could develop into a perverse form of safari, an extreme dehumanization of the colonized, as in this request by Senior Staff Sergeant Eggersglüß at the end of his long patrol report: "I humbly ask the district office for permission to go on a hunt for Bushmen with a larger patrol at the beginning of next month."[61] The commander in chief of the Schutztruppe used hunting vocabulary as well when he complained about the police frightening away his prey: "Otherwise it happens like on a drive hunt whereby somebody had already flushed through [*durchgekäschert*] beforehand." The commander formulated quite frankly the rationale of such indiscriminate measures when he noted that "it is tremendously difficult to distinguish among the prowling rabble [*Gesindel*] between the 'harmless' and the criminals."[62] Particularly regarding the San, the language and the mind-set of the pursuers increasingly included images of disinfestation and pest control, referring to the "extermination" of this group of Africans.[63]

As indicated at other points in the study, the colonial military and the colonial police operated differently, which could sometimes result in setbacks or malfunctions.[64] Holding on to the idea that policing was not the same as soldiering, representatives of the police were convinced that letting the military handle the "collection" of labor was the wrong approach, especially since soldiers had no experience in how to interact with Africans.[65] It did not, however, prevent the two institutions from occasionally joining forces, or at least declaring the intention to do so.[66] Nonetheless, in the first instance, capturing laborers for the colonial economy was a joint effort between African and German policemen, even if the former were rarely acknowledged. An exceptional document from District Office Outjo mentioned all names of patrol riders, Germans and Africans alike. Next to the names, the patrol log listed the number of captured, wounded, or killed "Bushmen" in the period between August 1911 and August 1913. Who exactly did the wounding or killing does not become apparent in this table. All patrols and their results are recorded as joint "successes": altogether twenty-four San were killed and eighty captured.[67] German sergeants often asked specifically for support from their African subordinates.[68] The instances in which police assistants captured more persons than their superiors are numerous.[69] Sometimes, African police assistants even went on patrols on their own. Under the heading "Native Police (Foot Patrol)" one mission read: "Collection of unemployed natives."[70] Police Assistant Fritz, for instance, led several foot patrols with a handful of African men. During those patrols, which lasted between five and thirty days, he apprehended between 18 and 150 people per patrol. Purportedly, Fritz captured 442 Africans altogether in one year.[71]

Furthermore, policemen practiced searches together with settlers and members of the colonized population. On many patrols farmers came along to add the force of their guns or to act as guides. Farmer Grönert accompanied Sergeant Eschen's patrol, for instance, and farmer Glatt accompanied Sergeant Sterzenbach.[72] Local Herero leader Kathena, who accompanied and guided patrols, was promised one mark "for every adult native able to work" whom he helped to capture.[73] Later, Kathena joined the German police force and continued to participate in searches and patrols to arrest "criminals."[74]

Finally, settlers captured people by themselves. Senior Staff Sergeant Schaaps noted casually in a patrol report that farmer Schurz had ventured several times into the Kupferberg massif by himself "in order to recruit prowling natives as workers."[75] Sergeant Wiesemann let several farmers do the same.[76] The necessary violence or threat farmers or their hands used in order to bring in Africans like the ones referred to here, who were hiding in the hills so that they would not be forced into the colonial labor market, was considered acceptable by the policemen. The documents I rely on here do not make entirely clear whether the policemen explicitly gave their permission or whether they simply tolerated the farmers' actions. What does become evident in other sources, however, is that the police were without question annoyed when farmers did not have their tacit or explicit approval, or worse, when farmers hid people in order to keep them for themselves. Farmers Ehorn and Brockerhof in the Karibib area, for example, were suspected of having concealed the whereabouts of unemployed Africans, and of telling others working on their farms to hide when patrols came through.[77] This kind of behavior was not accepted and was severely censured.[78]

Whether searches resulted in seizures or not, the effect was twofold. On the one hand, such searches instigated a capturing practice wherein policemen not only wielded violence, but also delegated and authorized violence, thus including some of the settler and the colonized population in the colonial project. On the other hand, the searches installed a general atmosphere of fear in which hiding from or disregarding the colonial labor system was less and less an option for the indigenous population. Inspection Officer Hildebrandt noted in that regard, "Unfortunately, without it being my intent or the sergeants' fault, the natives are frightened by the constant patrol traffic in such a way that some have declared: '. . . we want peace and move into another area.'"[79]

To sum up, finding and capturing workers for the colonial economy was a concerted effort, even when the actors involved in it pursued different agendas and had different approaches and levels of intensity of violence. These ruthlessly pursued, concerted, yet multifarious enterprises forced the colonized into choosing more often than not to seek wage labor, whether via the police or on their own, rather than resisting or evading the system.

Distributing Labor

Policemen were also at the linchpin of labor distribution. Even though the labor market was supposed to be free, the general scarcity of labor made it necessary to have an intermediary institution between employer and employee. Many settlers made direct requests to the police. "I kindly ask the District Office to reserve for me one or two native families as soon as possible," one woman wrote in July 1907.[80] Her letter is one example of the countless requests for workers stored in the archives.[81] In fact, some settlers believed that they would be automatically supplied by the administration. Governor Seitz observed in 1914 that farmers "repeatedly . . . took the position that the government had the duty to supply them with workers."[82] The historian Zimmerer notes that "the idea that the administration would merely set the framework" within which the distribution of labor was then regulated by the market "was foreign to farmers."[83] He adds that "the colonial administration was not entirely blameless for the farmers' expectations," since the concept of a semi-free labor market "broke with the principle of distribution over the market."[84] Thus, in their day-to-day business at the station or on patrol, police officials listened to the many demands. And they promised, reserved, denied, delivered, reattributed, replaced, and so on, in their dealings with Africans accordingly. As a result, policemen often had the power to decide where and for whom the colonized should work, as well as who would get what kind of workers and for what kind of work. In brief, they were the brokers of the labor market. A circular by the colonial government reminded all local district offices as late as 1914 that "the decision to whom to distribute people" should "on no account" be entrusted to "lower ranking state representatives." That it had recurrently happened "that farmers were promised workers" and "that these were all or partially not available any more when the farmers came to collect them, without the head of administration knowing about their whereabouts," is telling evidence that policemen did indeed oftentimes take up the role of labor supply middlemen.[85]

At any rate, police were officially intended to be involved at some point of the process. Work contracts were supposed to be drawn up and signed at the police station, at least those for a work period lasting longer than a month. However, in 1912, Vice Governor Hintrager observed that, "owing to the employers' carelessness," only few employments were sealed in written form.[86] His reminder to all police organs that contracts absolutely had to be written attests to the fact that on numerous occasions hires were made without paperwork even when the police had served as recruitment agents. Ruth Kühnast, a settlers' daughter, describes, for instance, how in 1906 her mother went to the concentration camp in Swakopmund to "choose from the crowd of prisoners a Herero boy and a Damara" whom she wanted for domestic labor. Whether she entered the camp by herself or with a policeman is unclear. But according to the daughter's narrative, she was in the "company of a native policeman, who was to serve as interpreter," when she took the two African prisoners to her home.[87]

The vice governor also ordered that, if desired, the police had to make copies of the contracts for the hired Africans, "against payment of the usual fee."[88] Having written labor agreements could be advantageous or disadvantageous for employers and employees. There were good reasons either to comply with or to evade the colonial state's imposition of bureaucratic control. But, as the evidence shows, and consistent with my assessment of improvised police procedures in chapter 3, even policemen did not necessarily always follow bureaucratic protocols.

The distribution of captured "vagrant" or recaptured escaped Africans, as well as of imprisoned Africans, was exclusively organized by the police. Several decrees underscored that all African prisoners imperatively had to work.[89] Moreover, prisoners of war who had been massively pressed into forced labor during the war were oftentimes left with no option but to remain in their position long after the official end of war.[90] Acting on behalf of magistrates and district chiefs, German policemen often coordinated the distribution of penal labor chain gangs. And African policemen accompanied and guarded the prisoners.[91] Even European prisoners could ideally be put to some useful occupation, lest their confinement have a "harmful impact on [their] mental state."[92]

Yet the bulk of Africans distributed by the police were captured and recaptured persons. The numerous men, women, and children Police Assistant Fritz and his men had caught "were handed over to the Otavi railway [company], the Tsumeb mines, as well as to farmers and private persons of the district."[93] When a farmer was killed, Sergeant Krey of district Maltahöhe was charged with securing and then redistributing the workers left behind. Interestingly, a former Nama police assistant, owner of about 150 small livestock and several cows, was put in charge to stay on site and to take care of the late farmer Klinge's crops.[94] Local administrations built a vast bureaucracy around the identification and redistribution of escaped workers. They sent descriptions— even photographs—of apprehended presumed escapees across district borders in search of their presumably rightful employers.[95] They transmitted lists of wanted workers, devising profile sheets, including information regarding age, height, or distinct marks.[96] A tremendous effort was put into tracking down runaways and returning them. One of the altogether three files entitled "Control of Native Workers; Investigations into Escapees [*Entlaufenen*] and Strays [*Zugelaufenen*]" of District Office Rehoboth comprises five hundred pages of documentation for the years 1911 to 1914 alone.[97] On the one hand, this effort bolstered the bureaucratization and professionalization of the colonial police in German Southwest Africa. On the other hand, it is proof that the colonial administration's endeavor to master the labor system absolutely was persistently defied by the colonized.[98]

The colonial administration left nothing untried in its endeavor to compel every colonized—that "most important asset" of the colony, as Secretary of State Dernburg called them—to work for the colonial settler economy.[99] Policemen combed through the registries of workers in the employ of public institutions and even personally went through their compounds in search of "appendages" (*Anhang*), that is, mostly family members of employees who were not working for the institution to which the compound belonged. Governor Seitz ordered that these men, women, and children, excluding those relatives who were unfit for work, be "remove[d] immediately from the public compounds [*amtliche Werften*] and delivere[d] to the district offices." The offices were then charged "to see to it that these [Africans] find employment at the soonest."[100] The list of Africans who had to leave their homes at the police headquarters' compound shows that a great majority of them were close relatives (cousins, brothers- and sisters-in-law, and so on) of African police employees. Only about 30 percent of those expelled were actually unemployed.[101] What few kinship relations and precolonial social structures the war had not destroyed, the labor distribution frenzy of the colonial administration finished off.

Although local district administrations sought to restrict the African workforce's mobility, their ambition to distribute labor in a planned and monitored fashion entailed that workers *were* moved from one place to another.[102] The African members of the Landespolizei were crucial in this respect. Police Assistant Jakob, for instance, was entrusted with transporting forty-six workers over a distance of two hundred kilometers from Omaruru to Windhuk by train.[103] Whether and how he advised the workers on how to navigate the colonial economy during the journey must remain speculative.

Likewise, the fact that policemen on their patrol rides were the ones having to judge whether a settler had too many, just sufficient, or not enough workers reveals how much these rank-and-file state representatives were implicated in labor distribution and therefore must have left their mark on distribution practices. Magistrate Vietsch from District Office Rehoboth, for instance, trusted the opinion of his subordinate, Sergeant Ebermann, that a new flying station necessitated the recruitment of two more African policemen. The magistrate ordered his police staff to assess where one could find such men. A Baster widow who, according to this assessment, could forgo two workers, protested and pleaded to be allowed to keep at least one. Vietsch again left it to the policemen to decide whether her concern was grounded and, if so, to go and find someone else elsewhere.[104]

Thus, the archive testifies to the crucial role policemen played in distributing labor. Scrutinizing carefully their everyday distribution practices, I found that negotiations over the "proper" use of violence were key. Police delegated and authorized others in the colonial realm to do violence. But they also revoked such an authorization and took over.

Men the police deemed able to "treat their workers well" could receive permission to supply themselves with labor, that is, to deploy violence on their behalf or in concert with them. This form of violence involved settlers in the colonial project. The act of delegation and authorization on the part of the policemen shored up their own power; the act of violent participation on the part of the settlers legitimized the colonial state. Farmer Grüner, for instance, was told by Sergeant Frahm that he was "allowed to raid an [African] settlement, to keep as reward the people [he] needed, and to deliver the rest to the district office."[105] Both the nearby military post and the nearby police station regularly allocated workers to his farm. He was also permitted to keep Africans who had "strayed" onto his property.[106] It does not necessarily follow that the relationship between farmer Grüner and the colonial administration was always harmonious (sometimes Grüner did not declare the Africans who came to his farm to work, and once he even had to pay a 100 mark fine for defamation of a policeman), but the cooperation worked.[107]

In another case, Inspection Officer Hildebrandt from the police depot in Waterberg urged farmer Speth to accompany the police patrols, for these were his only chance to provide himself with African workers.[108] Farmer Speth benefited from Inspection Officer Hildebrandt's trust. The district chief, however, did not trust him. A year earlier, Speth had tried to procure workers by offering to have a public well built on his property and gambling that he would get to keep the large number of workers needed for such a project. The district chief had refused.[109] The next time farmer Speth had wanted European workers. Upon hearing this, the inspection officer made it clear that, regarding the procurement of workers, farmer Speth was entirely dependent on the care the police would show him, and that he would get such attention if he treated his African workers correctly: "I advise you again to see the native workers as capital which will yield interest . . . through sufficient provisions and good treatment. If you comply with those principles, you will receive the caring support [*sorgliche Unterstützung*] of the police should your employees become neglectful or impertinent. If not, you cannot count on the assistance of the organs of the Imperial Government regarding labor supply."[110] Thus, in an apparent paradox, the police promised to supply or help supply laborers if employers treated them well, something they were capable of proving only once they had gotten workers. Therefore, other factors than the perceived treatment of employees must have been equally decisive in the officials' assessment of whether farmers were trustworthy. Getting along with the local police was a good start. Farmer Nass, for instance, emphasized that he and his farmer friends were "on the best of terms" with the local police. He declared proudly that "the police support me in every possible way," that they protected his farm when he was away, and that they had "assisted me to hire available Kaffirs."[111]

More important, however, were notions of social standing when it came to questions of labor distribution. Both African police assistants and German police sergeants had an impact on the perceived worthiness of farmers and other employers, for, as I noted about patrol procedures in the last chapter, information about conditions on the work sites was primarily gathered by them. In every transaction, both the policeman's and the potential employer's class or social position and reputation were at stake. A staff sergeant in Swakopmund, for instance, had denied additional workers to a farmer who, in the policeman's eyes, had been responsible for an Ovambo worker's death, and, to boot, had not paid the hospital charges. The farmer in question had served as first lieutenant under the now acting chief of police, and was offended that "although now just a simple farmer," he would be treated so poorly by a simple rank-and-file man, a subordinate of his former comrade-in-arms. He wrote that he "could not accept [this] from a policeman." The issue was resolved verbally and personally by the magistrate of Swakopmund, and one must assume that the farmer continued to be allocated workers, since there are no further complaints from him in the archival file.[112] The farmer's negligence (as well as the worker's death) was accepted in the end. His class position and personal relationship to the police leadership allowed him to remain among those settlers whom the police regarded as able to treat their workers well.

Other settlers, on the other hand, were not trusted by the police and lacked the social standing and connections of the farmer in my last example. These were persons the police deemed in need of police attention themselves. The farmer couple Matzkuhn, for instance, were greatly upset when Staff Sergeant Rohde "took away their only boy," the Herero worker Wilhelm.[113] In a letter filled with orthographic mistakes—made even more obvious in comparison to Staff Sergeant Rohde's exceptionally eloquent writing—farmer Matzkuhn lamented how hard it was to get by without workers. Beforehand, his wife had gone to the police station to confront Rohde, in his words, "in a very exasperating manner."[114] As explanation for removing Wilhelm from the farm, the staff sergeant stated that Wilhelm had already been in the employ of another farmer.

Further investigations showed, however, that neither the first farmer, nor the second farmer (Matzkuhn), nor a third employer for whom Wilhelm had worked for a short period in between, had given him a work contract or registered the employment with the police.[115] What seemed ultimately to decide the issue in favor of Staff Sergeant Rohde's interpretation, that is, to restore Wilhelm to his first employer, was a combination of portraying the Matzkuhn couple's low level of education, their irritability (depicted by Rohde in a cool and objective manner), and the general claim that "family Matzkuhn is constantly involved in hassles [*Scherereien*] with the police regarding native matters. Matzkuhn's natives constantly present themselves at the police office to complain about being treated badly, or not getting their due food, or not receiving their wage."[116] In short, who the employers were, their looks, and their way of life as well as how they were represented by the police in their reports mattered, irrespective of actual or perceived conditions on the work site. As a report regarding innkeeper Hülsmann phrased it, his "appearance and moral conduct" were "not suited to instill respect in the natives."[117] Interestingly, policemen also included in the evaluation of an employer's status the overall appearance of his or her farm. Chief of Police Heydebreck had asked his men early on to pay particular attention to the way in which production sites were organized, what they looked like, and what these observations might indicate about the productivity of the site.[118] And, indeed, policemen often backed up their appraisal of an employer's character and status with references to the orderliness and cleanliness, or lack thereof, of a particular place.[119]

One final example illustrates quite strikingly the ways in which different actors pursued their (economic) interests and the ways in which policemen brokered these ambitions. It shows the informal, improvised character those exchanges often had. Little sheets of paper, errands by African policemen and messengers, and encounters in the street or on the station were the means by which many allocations took place. In the course of these exchanges, policemen negotiated questions of reputation, propriety, social standing, and "proper treatment," thus promoting, allowing, reprimanding, prohibiting, tacitly condoning, and so forth, the doings of the colonial population. The way in which Staff Sergeant Kups managed the distribution of labor in Karibib is a good example. In February 1911, he recounted an incident as follows:

> The Hottentott woman Lisbeth Nr. 288 was dismissed by hotelier Rosemann, because she had become increasingly disinclined [*unlustig*] to do work. She intended to go to Usakos where she would have had it easier to dodge work. But since people are absolutely needed here, I gave her a note and told her to go back to Rosemann, making clear that she was not allowed to leave for Usakos and that she was otherwise engaged for [farmer] Polle [in] Claustal. Lisbeth did not come back from Rosemann. But in the afternoon, she brought a note from [manufacturing worker] Keseberg saying that she had been employed by him. Asked to explain herself, she answered that Rosemann had not wanted to take her back and that she had understood that she must find another job in Karibib. Apart from the fact that Lisbeth very well comprehended where she is supposed to work, Keseberg also knew absolutely that this was not proper [*in Ordnung*].[120]

After several to-and-fros between the staff sergeant and the manufacturing worker Keseberg, personally or via the two men's African envoys, the policeman ended up losing his temper and insulting the man. His outburst incurred a formal complaint from Keseberg (with quite a few misspellings) and produced the detailed documentation we can now find in the archive.[121] How Lisbeth's and Keseberg's agreement came about, whether it involved violence or threat, is unknown. One can only speculate about the Nama woman's interest and concerns, about her possible wish to remain in a town and not to be sent to a remote farm, about the relationship between her and Keseberg, and about the amount and nature of everyday violence that would have occurred between the two had the employment taken place. What the short account tells us, however, is the way Staff Sergeant Kups understood his task and the stance he had to take toward Lisbeth and Keseberg. The woman he considered work-shy and sly. The man he considered socially inferior and morally corrupt. Both were in need of his paternal care. Kups was exercising some form of "caring" (fürsorglich) coercion toward Lisbeth when he resolved to "protect" her from Keseberg and forced her to work for a farmer. To what extent his actions toward her involved everyday violence, a threatening gesture, groping, or shoving, performed either by him or his African police assistant, is speculative, but, in my opinion highly probable. Another time, and on the same basis, Staff Sergeant Kups refused to allocate a woman to an engineer named Cliff, whom he had apparently helped out in many other cases.[122]

So far, I have emphasized that police assessments of "proper treatment" as well as their decisions to delegate or authorize the use of violence to other actors in the colonial realm were tightly linked to questions of social standing, appearances, and productivity. This notwithstanding, I wish to go beyond this observation and make a more structural, far-reaching argument about the mechanisms of labor distribution. One should recall the procedures and routines described in my last chapter: policemen watched over acceptable and unacceptable forms of violence in their improvised, commonsensical, pragmatic way of proceeding. In the process, employers' reputations, the police's evaluation of their ability to "treat well," could shift and be readjusted. Policemen did encourage or "admonish" workers to return to employers even when their abusive behavior was well known.[123] However, when an employer kept losing his workers (that is, through escape, but also death) over and over again, policemen grew wary and became reluctant to resupply that person. Farmer Jacobs, for instance, was told that since "in the last nine months, first two and then again three families have run away from you in short succession, it is necessary to investigate whether the natives are treated right and fed on your farm." If his "treatment of natives" had been the cause for them to escape, the letter continued, then they would "under no circumstances be returned to you. Also, the office would not supply you with [other] natives."[124]

When an employer had been able to keep workers over a long period without causing any stir, the police were more often inclined to leave that employer alone, even when there was doubt as to whether the workers in question truly belonged to that employer. District Office Rehoboth, for instance, let a seven-year-old boy who came to a farm to be with his mother even though he was employed somewhere else stay on that farm.[125] When the Herero worker Johannes sought support from the police in his effort to resign from a place, and knew to refer to proper procedure (he insisted that he had properly resigned and not just run away), policemen were willing to help that man out.[126] Moreover, different districts competed between each other to keep labor in their area. The meticulous, maybe even disproportionately time-consuming investigation into whether a worker had had "good" reasons to have left an employer from another district could therefore be motivated not by a humanist commitment to protect the colonized, but rather by the calculating desire to keep that worker in one's own precinct and thus to be able to allocate him or her to one's own colonizer community. In other cases, the rivalry between administrative units led to a redistribution of workers in a rushed manner. Larger groups of unemployed workers were dealt with quickly given the pressure from demanding farmers. An overeager policeman, for instance, distributed a number of captives as soon as they had arrived at his station, even though they were not his to assign.[127] In the light of such police practices one district chief took appropriate measures. In June 1912 he issued a decree stating that "the procedure according to which native workers are assigned to applicants chronologically by date of incoming request, has proven impractical since the natives recurrently run away again. In the future, available natives are therefore assigned such that they are presented with the list of existing labor requests and then asked whose service they wish to enter. This is how requests will be dealt with. Of course, every employer is still free to recruit natives by himself."[128] This district chief made explicit what must have been quite common all over the colony.

Hence, intentionally or unintentionally, the policemen's way of distributing labor was conducive to a market-driven logic. In the dire and utterly constraining economic situation of the post-genocide German colonial era, the colonized regained some degree of agency regarding their choice of a workplace. Since their labor power was so highly in demand, they had some agency in choosing the least bad working conditions—aided by the "caring" and improvised practices of the police. To understand how exactly this dynamic unfolded I need to address what the police did once workers had been assigned to their work site, which is the subject of the last section of this chapter.

Supervising Labor

Third, and finally, the police had the task of supervising labor relations on work sites. As quoted in chapter 3, the general regulations for the police force stipulated that "education of the natives" was not to be understood as "interference in petty quarrels between natives and their white employers."[129] Employers were to deal with their workers by themselves. Their paternal right of chastisement should be guaranteed. Nevertheless, in numerous cases the police did enter the farms or mining sites to take matters into their own hands. Colonial regimes fostered, in Frederick Cooper's words, "episodic exercises of collective punishment or direct coercion against unwilling workers or cultivators on whom the effects of routinized discipline had not been successfully projected."[130] Policemen considered themselves to be responsible for the well-being of workers and hence for their productivity, up to and including "direct coercion." And, at the same time, they considered themselves responsible for the right conduct of employers. The policemen's identification with the state (as developed in chapter 1) and their extremely broadly defined field of responsibilities (as developed in chapter 4) generated the notion that policemen were the personification of the paternal state. They were to be fatherly figures to whom everything was a matter of interest. And as such they strove to give the impression—both to Africans and to European settlers—that they were constantly watching and omnipresent. Magistrate Schenke reported that the African compound in Swakopmund was under steady police surveillance and that "frequent, unexpected controls . . . keep the natives under the impression that they are being observed at all times."[131]

The policeman's paternalistic care was for all colonial subjects, colonizers and colonized alike. For Africans, such police care mostly meant the oppressive feeling of constant surveillance as well as repeated actual violent coercion. But it also meant potential protection against abusive employers. German policemen and, more significantly, African policemen conveyed to African workers the colonial state's concept of "right treatment."[132] Staff Sergeant Ehrlich, for instance, explained to Cape African workers who were protesting against bad working conditions and insufficient pay the difference between penal and disciplinary authority, and that their foreman was not entitled to the former.[133] Thus, workers could (strategically) make reference to the notion of "right" violence to benefit from the police's care. I will come back to the deployment of the "right" violence discourse by the colonized at the end of this section.

To Europeans, police care was either a service or an annoyance. Settlers often took issue with what they perceived as the police's failure to discriminate between the colonizers and the colonized. They often experienced the police as domineering and patronizing. Staff Sergeant Arnold, for instance, went to see the farmer Becker. There he read out loud a paper regarding the proper treatment of workers and then asked the farmer to sign it. Next, the staff sergeant went to interview the workers and refused the farmer's request to be present during those interviews. Afterwards, the staff sergeant demanded to see work contracts and threatened the farmer with removing his workers if he could not produce them. Farmer Becker complained bitterly that he was being treated like a child.[134]

Even though the police were by no means able to ensure effectively that all labor relations were bureaucratically and legally correct, they nevertheless made it their daily concern to check not only on Africans but also on Europeans. Existing scholarship has emphasized too much the impossibility of comprehensive state control over the settler population, and has neglected to inquire into what the recurring, though sporadic, presence of the colonial state and the anticipation or apprehension of that presence did to the colonial social order.[135] The police's concern for settlers framed the range of their possibilities. Whether they liked it or not, European employers had to factor the state's interference into the management of their businesses. They did so in a variety of ways. They forged papers and work contracts.[136] They hid workers on their farm when patrols approached.[137] Or they preemptively reported workers' "misbehavior" when the workers were about to disclose their employer's maltreatment, for example.[138] But they also invited the police onto their farms and mines and actively sought their assistance, especially regarding the disciplining of workers.

Examples of cooperation between policemen and employers are numerous. Some farmers relied from the beginning on the police's violent services to exercise paternal chastisement for them. This form of participative violence fostered the bond between state representatives and settlers. Sergeant Franitzek, for instance, stopped on patrol at a farm where he was asked to mete out corporal punishment to a worker. He, or possibly his assistant, gave the San man fifteen blows with a wooden stick for having been ostensibly negligent and insolent.[139] And farmer Nass lauded the nearby police depot, writing that, "regarding the punishment of the natives, the police have always done their job."[140] Making reference to one case in particular, he noted that "when my . . . workers . . . behaved insolently and let themselves go, I approached the police . . . which then punished the Hottentots thoroughly."[141] Reciprocally, local administrations not only tolerated or acknowledged nonstate violence, but explicitly invited employers to administer violence by themselves. District Office Rehoboth, for instance, advised a sheep farm manager to "observe closely" a Nama worker it was sending to the farm and "in addition, to handle him harshly."[142] Sometimes they condoned violence, even though they described it as somewhat inexpert but justified. Sheep farm director Weber's actions against a Nama worker were thus depicted:

Weber ordered him [the Nama worker—M.M.] to be calm, forbade him to talk, and finally tried to rout him out [of his office—M.M.]. Since the Hottentott behaved ever more insolently, Weber approach him with a stick to hit him. But the Hottentott wrested the stick from him and acted threatening towards Weber. Since the other workers were standing nearby and were watching the incident, Weber had to resort to an energetic means in order to not lose his standing [*Ansehen*] and authority, [so] he drew his Browning pistol and shot the Hottentott in the leg. Then, the latter was brought to Gibeon to be sentenced.[143]

Other farmers, however, needed to be shown how it was properly done. Sergeant Maletz, for instance, recounted that he was asked by an utterly overwhelmed and frightened farmer to help him with his African workers.[144] The sergeant and his police assistant accompanied the farmer immediately back to the farm. At their arrival, Police Assistant Gustav and a Boer employee went to the African compound to assemble all the workers.

> In one procession, with Gustav at the rear, they arrived: men, women, and children. We made the whole flock, about 40 in number, stand at attention in front of the house, the men in the first row. The farmer recounted the events in the presence of everyone. . . . I had the three culprits come six steps forward. They were big, sturdy men. After the farmer had finished his accusation, and after the accused had confessed to their misdoings, I declared to the assembly that they had committed a grave breach against the regulations of the governor which they knew of from their work contracts. I told them that for this kind of proven explicit disobedience and physical [*tätlich*] resistance against their master [*Dienstherrn*] they had to reckon with a high prison sentence in chains, if their master would press charges against them at the district office. But he wanted to desist from doing so this time, because he believed that they had only acted out of foolishness [*Dummheit*] and he took pity on them, for sentences in fetters [*Kettenstrafe*] were hard. They had to vow, though, that they would be obedient from now on. Then, he would leave it at the corporal punishment. According to regulations I pronounced the verdict and had Gustav translate the judgment and statement of grounds. Thereafter, Gustav carried out at once the punishments in the regularized form. Each of the 3 culprits received 10 blows with the sjambok.[145]

This account of police regulating labor was published as a memoir and consequently dramatized to make it more entertaining. But the story conveys clearly the policeman's on-the-spot, paternalistic, and educative interventions with the policed public, both African and German. Sergeant Maletz portrayed himself as the man who saved the day, who taught the farmer how to be firm but not cruel. He also took satisfaction in having resolved the incident simply, without too much legal interference. At the end of the tale, he even prided himself that the punished Africans became fond of him, relating that the three men who had been punished came up to him personally to promise that they would never resist their employer again. The sergeant "sent them on their way with one last strict admonition."[146] From that moment on, he declared, every time he happened to ride by the farm, these three men would wave at him.

The story also illustrates that cooperation between African and German policemen was absolutely necessary in the (violent) supervision of labor. Labor regulation was a shared endeavor across racial boundaries. All policemen assessed situations together, or at least in parallel. Based on these assessments, German policemen decided on the appropriate course of action: to instruct or correct the employer on "proper treatment," and/or to chastise the employee verbally or physically. As a rule, regularized corporal punishments of workers were executed by an African police assistant with the German superior overseeing the operation.[147] But there were cases in which German policemen wielded the whip themselves.[148] What is more, both African and German policemen most likely did not restrict their educative violence to the standardized settings of legal penalty. We must assume that some of the policemen's everyday efforts to press both employees and employers into their concept of economically viable, "right" violence happened outside of the archival record.

The idea of "proper treatment" was tightly linked to the concept of wage labor. "Right" violence had to coincide with sufficient board and lodging, and most importantly with a cash salary. Vice Governor Hintrager reminded all police stations in 1912 that when overseeing labor they had to "at any cost [*tunlichst*] press for payment of the wage in cash."[149] In a comprehensive report, also in 1912, Magistrate Vietsch from District Office Rehoboth claimed explicitly that the "proper treatment" of Africans had nothing to do with uncertainties about farmers' paternal right to chastise or insufficient disciplining authority from law enforcement officers, but was exclusively a matter of foodstuffs and pay.[150] He asserted that there was a direct correlation between escapes from work sites and insufficient food and payment, and that the cases in which workers did complain about chastisement, even a severe one, but had received enough food, especially meat, were extremely rare. African workers, he thus implicitly argued, did not care whether they were beaten as long as they were provided for. Indeed, one could go as far as to suggest that in this colonial official's understanding, chastisement was part and parcel of such care. As a solution, Magistrate Vietsch suggested two measures. First, he urged the government to forbid the so-called truck system by which workers were paid in goods only, or which forced employees to spend their salary at their employer's store. Second, he proposed a rule to standardize food supply on all work sites. Closing his report, the magistrate stressed how important it was to Africans to receive cash and noted that the state would show real proof of its will to take care of them if it introduced the standardized food supply.[151] The report prompted the government to send out a circular to all districts in November 1912 asking for information about average pay and provisions.[152]

It is difficult to assess whether policemen tended to emphasize low or no pay over physical abuse in their reports because of these directives or whether they derived this from their own observation. Cases in which policemen noted that the salary was minimal or nonexistent occurred already before 1912.[153] By and by, they became so numerous that I tend to believe that African workers realized that stressing the lack of pay or board played much more in their favor than evoking physical abuse. In October 1912, two African workers made depositions against a farmer, for instance, in which they first stressed that he did not give them enough to eat, and then, apparently only secondarily, noted that lately he had also beat them a lot.[154] Moreover, policemen probably did not want to hear from Africans themselves that their employers were violent. After all, policemen claimed exclusive authority over the definition of "right" and "wrong" violence. Another interpretation would be that only these reports (that is, the ones registering insufficient wages and provisions) came to the attention of the central government in Windhuk and have thus taken up a more prominent space in the colonial archive. In fact, I discovered entire lists of workers' statements giving the reasons for an escape that were carefully scrutinized by police headquarters and other bureaus in the colonial government, indicating that these were the ones the lower echelons thought would be of interest to the higher echelons. One of those lists was recorded by the police station in Epikuro after its policemen had captured several Herero in the easternmost region of the colony. The following is an excerpt of the list:

> Present: Pol. Sergt. Rudzinski . . . Herero Langmann, about 28 years old, pass tag no. 2316, is summoned . . . and states the following: I had been in the service of farmer Öhl at the black Nossob for about half a year, when I ran away from there at the beginning of April t[his] y[ear]. At farmer Öhl's I had to work hard, but I did not receive any pay; there was enough food. My wife had to herd the cattle. I ran from there into the sand plain, stayed for quite some time in Okonja where I was captured. I have said the truth. Read and approved. X X X [handsign by Langman] [signed by Rudzinski] Translator: Pol. Assistant Moses II . . . Herero Kahomewa Simon without pass tag . . . states . . . the following: About 2 years I was in the service of farmer v. Stetten in Okatjekori, from where I ran away last year. I had to work very hard, even at noon there was no rest, [I] was

always occupied with making bricks and gardening work and I received only 4 Mark wages a month. There was enough food. . . . Herero Kaugruro, Albert about 30 years old, without pass tag . . . makes . . . the following deposition: I have never been employed by a white [this sentence was struck through by Sergeant Rudzinski—M.M.]. I have been 2 years in the service of farmer Einbeck in Otjomango. [I] ran away because I received only 4 Marks wages a month, but had to work hard. I admit . . . that I took 2 iron traps which belonged to farmer Einbeck. . . . Present: Pol. Sgt. Müller I, Epikuro, . . . Herero Langmann [not the same as above—M.M.] is summoned and declares the following: . . . 24 years old, no pass tag . . . I worked for 1 year at farmer Sommer's . . . , received regularly my wages of 6 Marks a month. But since I never received any food from my master and had to provide my own from the land [*Feldkost*], I ran away. . . . I left my pass tag in my hut. Translator: Police Assistant Petrus. . . . Herero August . . . states the following: At farmer Albe's . . . I worked for 1 year, I always received food but never money. Since my master always beat me a lot, and that without reason, I ran away. . . . Zacheirami . . . 42 years old . . . states: 1 year . . . with Boer Kominika . . . received monthly wage of 6 Marks, but never food, since I also received many beatings I ran away. Translator: Police Assistant Petrus.[155]

The collection of minutes was forwarded to Windhuk, where several colonial officials provided commentary and underlined passages, specifically the overwhelmingly frequent reference to little or no pay and food. Senior Executive Officer Kastl declared that "if this is true, [the farmers] cannot complain about the escape of their natives."[156]

I have already quoted Magistrate Fromm's reaction to the list in the beginning of this chapter. After suggesting the redistribution of workers, he remarked that "some will maybe run away again. But this will most likely be the case for a long time still, or always remain that way. He who knows how to treat people well, will always have workers."[157]

In any case, despite my suspicion that the emphasis on wage labor in the definition of "proper treatment" might be skewed by the archival record, there is enough evidence that policemen did pay attention to proper pay in their evaluation of whether an employer was showing the "right treatment" to his workers.[158] Staff Sergeant Kratz, for instance, forwarded charges against employer Levy to the local court in Nama worker Samuel Rooi's name. In his deposition Rooi not only stated that the Levy couple had beaten him because he had not followed an order fast enough (which could have been simply construed as paternal chastisement), but also that they owed him 18 months' worth of pay.[159] To policemen, as to their superiors, the material attention of employers ideally combined salary, means of subsistence, and physical "care," that is, disciplining violence.

The police's definition of "proper treatment" distinguished furthermore between "white" and "not so white" employers, that is, between German (or European) and Boer or Baster employers. Perhaps in order to firm up indistinct racial boundaries, that is, precisely because they were perceived as racially close to the German colonizers, Boers and Basters were constantly suspected of cruelty.[160] In a way, they were qua race considered unable to "treat well." As a consequence, Boer settlers had their workers taken away much more quickly. With them, violence against workers was almost always interpreted as abuse. Reference to insufficient board or pay was not necessary. A patrol passing through farm Aurus in district Rehoboth noted that its workers had complained about physical abuse. The farm was owned by Boer settlers. Two days later, a patrol was sent out "to collect the natives of the Boers in Aurus."[161] And Magistrate Vietsch, who had been so crucial in associating "right treatment" with wage labor, was particularly keen on making a distinction when it pertained to Basters. In a 1913 circular to all his police stations he suggested that policemen work discreetly to remove African workers from Baster farms. He instructed policemen to write the resignation notice themselves and repeated that only the workers of the Basters should be reminded of their right to quit, not those of German employers.[162]

Thus, wage labor and productivity alone did not define "proper treatment." Racist ideology was equally decisive. For instance, Sergeant Nowakowsky reported that a farmer was treating his workers "very well," that they were receiving "enough food," and that they were also "paid fairly well." But "very well" did not mean "right" in this sergeant's statement. To the contrary, he made it immediately clear that the farmer was to blame when his workers ran away, because he had treated them "like equals," had sat with them at the evening fire, and talked or preached to them, which had engendered laziness and willfulness.[163] In the sergeant's opinion, decent pay and board availed nothing if they were not complemented with a hierarchical racial order and the firm, chastising conduct toward Africans that was expected to come with it. Put simply, the absence of violence was as harmful as the wrong kind of violence in the minds of the police.

Finally, "proper treatment" was a pliable concept. It depended on the individual situation in which it was formed. The police's case-by-case approach allowed for a high degree of flexibility and adaptability, and their racially mixed composition widened the field of options for concerted action, helping to fine-tune labor coercion. Local colonial officials encouraged and inculcated this form of productive police violence. They relied on their lower-rank representatives' onsite presence and their ability to assess each individual situation, asking them to combine (violent) action with (written) reasoning. The district chief of Rehoboth, for instance, attached an instruction sheet to the 1907 "native ordinances," circulated to all his police stations, in which he left the appraisal of "proper treatment" in the hands of policemen, but requested that a protocol be drafted that explained how they had come to their evaluation.[164] Thus introducing a bureaucratic means of oversight over his subalterns, he simultaneously impressed on these policemen the notion that their judgment in matters of labor discipline counted. Further, relying again on field experience, superiors circulated precedent cases to instruct their subordinates on the right kind of calibrated police action. A small-business owner who forced his worker's wife to also work for him, but without pay, was, for instance, such a case. The worker complained to the police. The police intervened, coaxing and threatening both worker and employer, insisting on a written contract and a salary for the wife. The correspondence was then sent to all police personnel in the Okahandja area for instruction.[165]

Increasingly, local administrators trusted (though probably reluctantly) in the effectiveness of policemen's accumulated experience and their improvised practices. More and more, the colonial government extended the authorization to pronounce and execute penalties to police ranks. In 1911, disciplinary power over Africans employed in the Landespolizei, which had been reserved to magistrates and district chiefs only, was conferred upon inspection officers.[166] Toward the last years of German rule, policemen deciding on disciplinary *and* criminal penalties in their senior officials' stead became a progressively frequent practice. In 1913, the fact that Senior Staff Sergeant Schlink had repeatedly enforced disciplinary measures in his superior's name at police depot Spitzkoppe caused frowns at police headquarters in Windhuk, but was eventually tolerated.[167] In the same year, the fact that Sergeant Maletz, who was commanding senior at his station, had issued a penalty in a case dating one and a half years earlier, was not even commented on by his higher officials.[168] And again later in 1913, the fact that Sergeant Böttcher executed a penalty on behalf of the magistrate of his district was noticed as an irregularity, but no consequences followed.[169] Senior Executive Officer Kelz, a legal expert in the colonial government, commented on this last occurrence that it had happened "not quite in due form," but that it was "at least practical." Kelz added that, by then, "so and so many" policemen had already been given not only the authority to execute but also to pronounce corporal punishments anyway, implying that it was a well-established practice.[170] And, indeed, Magistrate Heilingbrunner of District Office Keetmanshoop issued a decree in that regard in January 1914, officially transferring to all commanding seniors of police stations "penal authority over natives." The mandate was limited to corporal punishments of up to ten blows with the birch or fifteen with the whip, and "in cases of special exigencies . . . also to pecuniary penalties of up to 20 [marks]."[171] Ultimately, in May 1914, Governor Seitz officially acknowledged the already existing common practice when he observed that the colonial regime could "for now" not forgo transferring penal power to "seasoned, proven, older policemen."[172]

Colonial historians' observation that the colonial government's attempt to "curtail" employer abuses failed due to lack of means and the lower ranks' unwillingness to fulfill their "protective obligation" (*Aufsichtspflicht*) toward workers is not wrong, but beside the point.[173] If we understand their work as defining the "right" kind of violence, not checking or limiting violence, policemen's role in the whole constellation becomes clearer. They defined what "proper treatment" was about—in words and in (violent) deeds. Their control of violence was about degree, scale, attitude, and meaning. They never suggested that violence in and of itself was morally reprehensible. Farmers were censured because they "immoderately [*über Gebühr*]"[174] had made use of their paternal right of chastisement, because they were "partly too severe, partly too mild,"[175] not because they had used violence at all.

Policemen did not resist State Secretary Dernburg's call for "heightened care [*erhöhte Fürsorge*]" toward the colonized.[176] Nor were they entirely unable to enforce it. They adopted the idea of *Fürsorge* and inserted it into their routines of everyday violence. They intervened in order to teach and apply "right treatment," which implied racially motivated and defined effective and disciplining violence in combination with food, shelter, and, most importantly, a cash wage. Racism, capitalist impulses, and humanitarian motivations came together in this notion of everyday educative violence. Policemen's *fürsorglich* violence was a way of refining the colonial economic system. The kind of violence that the policemen applied or instructed others to apply rendered labor relations more fluid. The state's effort to form and educate its subjects—both European and African—so that they would intuitively know their assigned place in society was fostered by policemen's everyday violent practices. The improvised efforts of lower-rank policemen, their "self-will" (Lüdtke), and tactics (de Certeau) both contradicted and complemented official policy. Their ways of "making do" in the service of the "caring" colonial state contributed to a more viable but nonetheless highly exploitative economy.

Conclusion
Histories of Colonial Violence

In June 1908, a manager from a remote stud farm wrote an angry letter to the police in which he waxed nostalgic about the "good old days" when vigilante justice reigned: "In the past, when stock was stolen, a well-armed patrol of two whites and four natives would ride out that same evening to track down the thieves. They were almost always successful. The thieves were usually shot down and the stolen cattle recovered."[1] But now, he complained, "these tasks are solely for the police!" Chief of Police Heydebreck reacted to the letter stating that the police force "by no means follows the principle that every cattle theft is their exclusive concern. Rather, it would be grateful for any support."[2]

Policemen operated within a state aspiring to claim the monopoly of legitimate force. This included that they lay claim to being the sole keepers of the law. However, as the source above strikingly illustrates, policemen also operated within a social system of multiple alliances and dependencies. Moreover, with the main complex of governmental decrees aiming at regulating Africans, the "native ordinances" of 1907, the colonial government had instigated a racially bifurcated legal system with a highly diffuse jurisdictional principle. The "pass ordinance" dictated, for instance, that all colonized had to carry a pass in the form of a tag with a number on it.[3] The police were supposed to register all colonized and hand out these passes.[4] But *all* Europeans were allowed to check the passes, investing them with policing authority.[5] As

Helmut Bley notes, after the war, the "native ordinances" provided the "legal basis" for white dominion: "the rule of 'whites' had thereby become a reality all the way down to the level of individual policing power."[6]

The scholarship on law in colonial Africa has developed recently into a vibrant and independent subfield bringing scholars of law, anthropology, and history together.[7] It shows that colonial law—whether in its European or its ostensibly customary implementations—did not aim at limiting inequalities or eliminating arbitrariness, but was intended to uphold racial inequality. Little has been written, however, on the relationship between law and law enforcement in colonial Africa. Historian David Anderson, whose analyses are the rare exception, writes that basically "all agents of colonialism . . . were, in some senses, involved in policing."[8] He argues that policing needs to be studied as part of one single mechanism that included police, judiciary, and the law.[9] Indeed, judiciary and police work in particular were so tightly linked in everyday colonial rule that it makes little sense to isolate them as two different practices. Although Anderson worked on British colonialism, his interpretation rings true for the Landespolizei in German Southwest Africa as well. There, policemen acted as prosecutors, as executory officers, and as scribes and witnesses in courts. They were often the first to identify a crime and to make the decision whether it should be prosecuted or not. I suggest that we think of colonial policemen also as legislators who made law in the larger sense of the term, even though, or maybe especially because, their knowledge of the written law and of local customs was on the whole quite flawed. As shown in chapter 4, in executing their disciplinary authority, policemen increasingly practiced a form of "summary law" on site—at the farms, mines, and businesses they passed through on their patrols. Their everyday practices of state formation included making law.

Violence, as I argue throughout this study, was the daily business of policemen. Therefore, the relationship between the law and law enforcement as violence needs to be scrutinized more carefully. In his study of colonial law in German Southwest Africa, Harry Schwirck argues convincingly that colonial violence was not the result of nonexistent or incomplete law. To the contrary, he claims, "the brutal exercise of power may prove most effective when attended by law."[10] In their daily practices, policemen made law on the beat. Sometimes that involved following regulations and law by the letter. But often it meant that policemen found abbreviated means of law enforcement. Instead of having courts judge over issues of workers' discipline, for instance, they often passed that judgment themselves at the farm, claiming that it was in the farmers' interest not to lose their labor force to the justice and penitentiary system. Thus, the policemen's personalized legal regime was at times at odds with what policemen perceived as an aloof judiciary in the colonial courts of the district towns. However, both policemen's and the courts' legal practices contributed to a refinement of everyday colonial violence. As Schwirck notes, "Law does not merely respond to violence in an effort to diminish it but also determines and reflects what might be termed an economy of violence. Law plays a central role in defining what a society will recognize as violence and in allocating the ability to legitimately act in a violent manner."[11] Policemen's qualitative delineation of violent behavior, notably defining the "right treatment" of Africans, made them "lawmakers." Their daily practices "legalized" violence, both within and outside of the written law. With their actions oscillating between violence as punishment on the one side and as education on the other, policemen produced a moral economy of violence that can be called improvised, and that might even be seen as the preliminary rudiments of a new customary law.

The lawmaking power of the police was hardly the "rule of law" espoused as one of the grand achievements of modern Western political forms. But, entangled in the processes that restructured life, these state practices produced a viable peacetime social order in German Southwest Africa, one that allowed people to live out their lives, however mutilated by violence. Hence, everyday violence committed or orchestrated by the colonial policemen produced an order. Severely lacking legitimacy and almost entirely bereft of more formal sources of power, the colonial state rested on the improvised, functional violent practices of its ground-level representatives. Those are the major conclusions of my work. They go against the widespread historiographical assumption that colonial violence was an indicator of the weakness of colonial regimes, that colonial states betrayed their lack of strength notably in their inability to control and limit rampant settler brutality. Moreover, the claim that everyday, normalized, and accepted forms of violence are constructive asks that we reconsider our basic ideas about what state violence consists of and about what the foundations of modern state power are.

A Colonial History of Everyday Violence

Coming from multiple cultural groups, the African and German men of the Landespolizei nevertheless shared a host of moral codes that can best be subsumed under the heading of honor. This study reveals significant similarities between policemen from Europe and those from Southern Africa. Out of the Landespolizei's distinctive racial and social composition unfolded a dynamic that made the police decidedly efficacious.

At first glance, the African and German policemen of the Landespolizei occupied an intermediary position between ruler and population. But, partly because of their composition, partly because of their violent improvisation, they became the center of colonial power. Thus, more precise examination reveals that the policemen were *not*, in fact, intermediaries. They *were* the state—at least, the improvised colonial state. This insight might offer a corrective to the thriving research on colonial intermediaries that characterizes colonial soldiers, policemen, scribes, interpreters, and so on, as brokers and negotiators of power rather than as sources of it. Moreover, my study insists on the ways in which colonial power structures often developed within a logic of (contingent) overlap or reciprocity, rather than of translation or mediation. The drawback of my approach lies in the danger of effacing crucial differences, particularly racial ones. But I have tried to account for both similarities and differences, stressing repeatedly the asymmetric power relations that also existed within the group of the colonial police force.

Furthermore, African and German policemen were at one and the same time soldiers and bureaucrats. Thus, besides being an interracial organization, the police force was a semi-civilian, semi-military institution, that is, yet another form of hybrid institution. The policemen's identities and their organizational culture were significantly shaped by martial values and ways of proceeding. Policemen held on tightly to military notions of etiquette, proper appearance, comradeship, and loyalty. Most importantly, they believed that their access to lethal force was a crucial foundation for their authority. Yet, nonmilitary administrational modes of functioning gained importance in the police force's creation of a distinct professional culture. To the policemen, it mattered—both to their identity and to the understanding of their work—that tasks were executed in a bureaucratically correct manner. Thus, added to their self-understanding as wielders of disciplined, martial violence was that of an official administrator. In the process, contrary to the Weberian teleology of rationalizing bureaucratization, policemen did not abandon violence as a means of policing. Rather they redefined what kind of violent acts belonged to their profession and, by extension, defined what modern state violence consisted in.

My analyses of the police force's social and cultural makeup, as well as of its members' core values—regarding especially social status, masculinity, and martial and bureaucratic professionalism—show that the Landespolizei's hallmarks were a congruence of cultural codes, a hybrid composition, and a complex web of mutual obligations and client relationships. It was in part due to these features that the police were so effective despite constraining material conditions and chronic understaffing.

But the main reason the police quite successfully imposed their version of state rule can be found in their practices. My detailed study of the everyday routines and procedures of the Landespolizei shows that police work was make-do (De Certeau) and *eigensinnig* (Lüdtke) in nature. In a period in which a cameralist concept of Policey prevailed, the police's virtually limitless responsibilities opened up room for maneuver, combining security with welfare, reactive responses with proactive ones, and repressive measures with supportive ones. It also made policemen feel the need to act, to do something, in almost every situation. As a rule, policemen acted on the spot, relying on prior experiences, on habit, and on affective states. Out of these practices emerged a notion of common sense and a valorization of pragmatism, combined with idiosyncratic bureaucratic procedure.

The police's daily deeds constituted a form of state action that did not meet the concepts of statehood conceived of by contemporary leaders and state theorists. What is more, this form of improvised statecraft does not tally with present-day theories of the modern state: unable to account for improvised state activity, too many narratives of the (post)colonial state are inevitably those of the "failed state."

Inquiring into the policemen's usage of violent technologies—notably whips, shackles, and firearms—this study draws out the many ways in which everyday violent practices were culturally determined. My discussion of the different manipulations of violent tools reveals that often violent practices were undertaken with the object to establish social distinction, rather than a result of technological possibility or efficient practicality. As such, they culturally produced colonial order and state power.

As I demonstrate by way of the example of labor regulation, the improvised practices of the Landespolizei involved a multitude of violent behaviors. With their violent acts, the police mobilized alliances, included some while excluding others, created dependencies, and generated or reinforced racial and social hierarchies. Moreover, the policemen's violent practices were accepted and normalized as acts of administration, education, communication, or even paternalistic protection. With these everyday practices, the police refined the existing economy of violence.

Examining in detail the everyday workings of violent interactions, this study answers Frederick Cooper's call to reassess the "ways in which power is engaged, contested, deflected, and appropriated."[12] It demonstrates, for instance, that modern bureaucracy, administration, market economy, and knowledge production did not gradually replace direct physical repression, but rather reshaped when, how, and by whom violence was practiced. It also readjusts the Weberian dictum about the state's monopoly on the use of lethal force by showing the manifold and intertwined ways in which lower state actors had recourse to other than lethal violence and invited nonstate actors to participate in the violent enterprises of the project of colonial rule.

Based on my findings, several new lines of inquiry open up. The book sheds light on the police's relationship to other parts of the colonial state, but more can be done. Notably, an analysis of the role of legal staff, civic representatives, schoolteachers, and so on, and of their internal (interracial?) group dynamics could be promising in the goal to historically reassess colonial statehood. Likewise, although to a degree already accounted for in this study, one could focus even more on state actors' interactions with key civilian actors, with African political elites, missionaries, or settler dignitaries, for instance. Lastly, this study offers the possibility to contextualize policing and state power by broadening the scope, both in temporal and in geographical terms. What continuities, legacies, and patterns of violent police practices can be traced in Southwest Africa beyond the German colonial era? How can this specifically Afro-German history of colonial police violence inform our understanding of other European states in the nineteenth and twentieth centuries?

To be sure, Southwest Africa is, perhaps, an unusual example of European colonialism. Extremely sparsely populated, even more so after the genocide, it had an economy that was never profitable to the German motherland or even anybody living there. Moreover, the period of German rule was short in comparison with the more "classical" modern colonial regimes of Britain and France. Despite these limitations as a source of comparisons, the small scale of this colonial regime allowed me to do a microanalysis of everyday violent practices that would simply not have been possible for larger empires such as colonial India, for instance. The German authorities of Southwest Africa were assiduous record keepers, producing a wealth of source documents that nonetheless remain manageable for an individual researcher to process and interpret. Even if my case of settler colonialism is small, my insights about the microlevel mechanisms of colonial rule may be relevant to other colonial regimes or contexts of violent social order that are less easily studied at that level. At best, this book can help reconceptualize state power and state violence in modern history as fundamentally reliant on everyday practices, as reliant on interracial cooperation, and, most importantly, as reliant on common, petty acts of everyday violence. In closing, I would like to share my thoughts on the relationship between my story and the global one.

A History of Violence

"Believe it or not . . . violence has declined over long stretches of time, and today we may be living in the most peaceable era in our species' existence," psychologist Steven Pinker writes in the opening to his best-selling opus *The Better Angels of Our Nature*.[13] In over eight hundred pages densely packed with data and graphs, Pinker builds a case for his provocative thesis of the decline of violence in history. His widely acclaimed book flatly contradicts the historiography that describes the modern world as an exceptionally violent era. "The twentieth century is increasingly characterized . . . in terms of its historically unprecedented levels of bloodshed," observes Mark Mazower in his review of relevant scholarship in "Violence and the State in the Twentieth Century."[14] And Eric Hobsbawm wrote about the twentieth century that "more human beings had been killed or allowed to die by human decision than ever before in human history."[15]

The question whether there is more or less violence over historical time seems to me a moot point. This kind of endeavor assumes that violence can be somehow quantified, as if it happened in discrete units. Body counts can sometimes seem like a plausible starting point, as Hobsbawm's quote suggests, but even they are often impossible to realistically calculate.[16] Moreover, many studies of violence are, in fact, studies of extreme violence, of mass killings during war or under bloody regimes.[17] But it is hard to find macrohistorical accounts of accepted or tolerated violence. Neither Pinker nor the histories of extreme violence pay much attention to official, run-of-the-mill violence. Nor do they spend much time on the individual fates of people who faced the everyday decisions of living in a violent regime.

Instead of a grand narrative of quantified violence, I wanted to draw out the lives of people getting by, living with violence in the everyday. I have tried to uncover how the dynamics of violence were inscribed into a moral economy of the accepted and normal. And my most basic, and unsettling, finding is that violence is not necessarily antithetical to community or social order, that it can be constructive. The daily brutality of modern colonialism was a horrific injustice. But it was also a way of life with its own rules and regularities.

My work on the documentary remnants of German settler colonialism has not produced an appealing story of oppression and resistance, and I have tried to avoid moralizing about the past. But by giving more defined contours to the lives and practices of the people who produced and put up with the regularized violence of colonial life in German Southwest Africa, I hope to have done them justice.

Notes

Abbreviations

BAB	Basler Afrika Bibliographien
BArch-B	Bundesarchiv Berlin
BKE	Bezirksamt Keetmanshoop
BOM	Bezirksamt Omaruru
BRE	Bezirksamt Rehoboth
BSW	Bezirksamt Swakopmund
DAR	Distriktsamt Aroab
DOK	Distriktsamt Okahandja
Gouv. SWA	Kaiserliches Gouvernement Deutsch Südwestafrika
IdL	Inspektion der Landespolizei
NAN	National Archives of Namibia
NCO	Noncommissioned Officer
RKA	Reichskolonialamt
SWA	Southwest Africa
ZBU	Zentralbureau des kaiserlichen Gouvernements

Introduction

1. The colonial state left a sizable amount of documentation regarding Hans's death, yet from these sources we do not learn much about the African man himself or about his life. For instance, we do not know whether "Hans" was his given name or whether he had come up with it for the convenience of his German employers. Statements taken by acting District Chef v. Kageneck (District Office Warmbad), 14.03.1909, Bundesarchiv Berlin-Lichterfelde (hereafter BArch-B), R 1002, 2783, 63–68; Statements taken by acting District Chef v. Kageneck (District Office Warmbad), 17.03.1909, BArch-B, R 1002, 2783, 70–72.

2. Acknowledging that both actors' categories and contemporary identity categories are always problematic, I generally use the terms "African," "German," and "Baster," and avoid "black," "white," and "mixed-race."

3. Magistrate Schmidt (District Office Keetmanshoop) to Police Headquarters (Inspektion der Landespolizei [hereafter IdL]), 26.03.1909, BArch-B, R 1002, 2783, 57–58. All translations from German are mine unless otherwise indicated.

4. Telegram by acting District Chief v. Kageneck (District Office Warmbad) to District Office Keetmanshoop, 15.03.1909, BArch-B, R 1002, 2783, 69; acting District

Chef v. Kageneck (District Office Warmbad) to IdL via District Office Keetmanshoop, 16.03.1909, BArch-B, R 1002, 2783, 57.

5. Internal legal commentary by Senior Executive Officer Kastl (Governorate of German Southwest Africa [hereafter Gouv. SWA]), 07.04.1909, BArch-B, R 1002, 2783, 57–58. Major Heydebreck, the chief of police, reproduced almost verbatim the legal officer's line of reasoning in his reply to the local administrators. Cf. Chief of Police Heydebreck to District Office Warmbad, 11.04.1909, BArch-B, R 1002, 2783, 59–61.

6. Ann Laura Stoler, *Along the Archival Grain* (Princeton 2009).

7. Thus, I go further than Brett Shadle, who notes that "the question was less *if* violence was illegitimate in the colonial project, but rather *how much* violence could or should be used." Brett Shadle, "Settlers, Africans, and Inter-personal Violence in Kenya, ca. 1900–1920s," *International Journal of African Historical Studies* 45, no. 1 (2012): 61. Emphasis in the original.

8. My study is deeply indebted to anthropological scholarship and its theorization of everyday violence, notably by Phillippe Bourgois and Nancy Scheper-Hughes. See, among others, Nancy Scheper-Hughes and Philippe Bourgois, eds., *Violence in War and Peace* (Malden, MA 2004); Arthur Kleinman, "The Violence of Everyday Life," in *Violence and Subjectivity*, ed. Veena Das, Arthur Kleinman, and Mamphela Ramphele (Berkeley 2000), 226–41; Bettina E. Schmidt and Ingo Schröder, eds., *Anthropology of Violence and Conflict* (London 2001).

9. On meanings of violence, cf. Elizabeth Anne Stanko, ed., *The Meanings of Violence* (London 2003). For an interdisciplinary introduction to the study of violence, cf. Christian Gudehus and Michaela Christ, eds., *Gewalt* (Stuttgart 2013).

10. Helmut Bley, *Kolonialherrschaft und Sozialstruktur in Deutsch-Südwestafrika 1894–1914* (Hamburg 1968); Michael Bollig and Jan-Bart Gewald, eds., *People, Cattle and Land* (Cologne 2000); Jan-Bart Gewald, *Herero Heroes* (Oxford 1999).

11. Bley, *Kolonialherrschaft*.15; Horst Gründer, "Deutscher Kolonialismus," *Jahrbuch für europäische Überseegeschichte* 10 (2010): 150.

12. Ulrike Lindner, *Koloniale Begegnungen* (Frankfurt a.M. 2011).

13. Michael Pesek, *Koloniale Herrschaft in Deutsch-Ostafrika* (Frankfurt a.M. 2005).

14. Frederick Cooper, "Conflict and Connection," *American Historical Review* 99, no. 5 (1994): 1533.

15. On the so-called Leutwein system (1894–1904), named after the governor, see Bley, *Kolonialherrschaft*, 18–73.

16. Isabel V. Hull, *Absolute Destruction* (Ithaca, NY 2005), 178.

17. Matthias Häußler, *Der Genozid an den Herero* (Weilerswist 2018); Isabel V. Hull, "The Military Campaign in German Southwest Africa, 1904–1907 and the Genocide of the Herero and Nama," *Journal of Namibian Studies* 4 (2008): 7–24; Susanne Kuß, *Deutsches Militär auf kolonialen Kriegsschauplätzen* (Berlin 2010); Dominik Schaller, "'Ich glaube, dass die Nation als solche vernichtet werden muss,'" *Journal of Genocide Research* 6, no. 3 (2004): 395–430; Jürgen Zimmerer and Joachim Zeller, eds., *Völkermord in Deutsch-Südwestafrika* (Berlin 2003). On concentration camps in German Southwest Africa, see Jonas Kreienbaum, *"Ein trauriges Fiasko"* (Hamburg 2015).

18. There are already three German-language monographs on the Landespolizei: one by a former member of the force written during the Nazi era; one that presents valuable private source material but has a celebratory presentation of the police; and

finally, one recent scholarly study that includes the prewar era starting in 1894 and that is particularly interested in colonial rule of law and its (spatial) limits, but also touches on the social and everyday history of the police. I discuss this latter publication by Jakob Zollmann throughout the book, notably where our interpretations of the source material diverge. Zollmann's book is a shortened version of his exceptionally richly documented dissertation. Hans Joachim Rafalski, *Vom Niemandsland zum Ordnungsstaat* (Berlin 1930); Sven Schepp, *Unter dem Kreuz des Südens* (Frankfurt a.M. 2009); Jakob Zollmann, *Koloniale Herrschaft und ihre Grenzen* (Göttingen 2010); Jakob Zollmann, "Die Kolonialpolizei in Deutsch-Südwestafrika 1894–1919" (PhD diss., Freie Universität Berlin, 2007).

19. Max Weber, *Wissenschaft als Beruf* (Munich 1919), 29.

20. Giorgio Miescher, *Namibia's Red Line* (New York 2012).

21. On intermediaries, see Benjamin N. Lawrance, Emily Lynn Osborn, and Richard L. Roberts, eds., *Intermediaries, Interpreters, and Clerks* (Madison 2006); Albert Wirz, Andreas Eckert, and Katrin Bromber, eds., *Alles unter Kontrolle* (Cologne 2003). Neither of these publications includes policemen or soldiers in their analysis. For that, see Michelle R. Moyd, *Violent Intermediaries* (Athens, OH 2014); Joël Glasman, "Penser les intermédiaires coloniaux," *History in Africa* 37 (2010): 51–81. For an integration of the concept into world history, cf. Jane Burbank and Frederick Cooper, *Empires in World History* (Princeton 2010), 13–14. For an introduction of the concept into the history of African responses to colonialism, cf. Peter Limb, Norman Etherington, and Peter Midgley, eds., *Grappling with the Beast* (Leiden 2010).

22. Among others, Jean-Pierre Bat and Nicolas Courtin, eds., *Maintenir l'ordre colonial* (Rennes 2012); Emmanuel Blanchard, Marieke Bloembergen, and Amandine Lauro, eds., *Policing in Colonial Empires* (Brussels 2017); Marieke Bloembergen, *De geschiedenis van de politie in Nederlands-Indie* (Amsterdam 2009); Marieke Bloembergen, "The Perfect Policeman," *Indonesia*, no. 91 (2011): 165–91; Vincent Denis and Catherine Denys, eds., *Polices d'empires* (Rennes 2012); Joël Glasman, *Les corps habillés au Togo* (Paris 2015); Martin Thomas, *Violence and Colonial Order* (Cambridge 2012); Zollmann, *Koloniale Herrschaft*; Jakob Zollmann, "Communicating Colonial Order," *Crime, Histoire & Sociétés/Crime, History & Societies* 15, no. 1 (2011): 33–57. More references can be found in Blanchard, Bloembergen, and Lauro, *Policing in Colonial Empires*.

For references to the older body of research on British colonial police, see David M. Anderson and David Killingray, eds., *Policing the Empire* (Manchester, UK 1991); David M. Anderson and David Killingray, eds., *Policing and Decolonisation* (Manchester, UK 1992); Anthony Clayton and David Killingray, *Khaki and Blue* (Athens, OH 1989); David Killingray, "The Maintenance of Law and Order in British Colonial Africa," *African Affairs* 85, no. 340 (1986): 411–37.

23. Cf. Clive Emsley, "Policing the Empire/Policing the Metropole," *Crime, Histoire & Sociétés/Crime, History & Societies* 18, no. 2 (2014): 5–25.

24. Daniel Joseph Walther, *Creating Germans Abroad* (Athens, OH 2002), 24–25; Jürgen Zimmerer, *Deutsche Herrschaft über Afrikaner* (Münster 2001), 110.

25. Dörte Lerp, *Imperiale Grenzräume* (Frankfurt a.M 2016); Walther, *Creating Germans Abroad*.

26. On similar policing formations in British settler colonial settings, see, for instance, Jessie Mitchell and Ann Curthoys, "How Different Was Victoria?," in *Settler*

Colonial Governance in Nineteenth-Century Victoria, ed. Leigh Boucher and Lynette Russell (Canberra 2015), 183–202; Amanda Nettelbeck, "'On the Side of Law and Order,," *Journal of Colonialism and Colonial History* 15, no. 2 (2014); Scott C. Spencer, "Polices impériales," in *Policing in Colonial Empires*, ed. Emmanuel Blanchard, Marieke Bloembergen, and Amandine Lauro (Brussels 2017), 157–169.

27. Caroline Elkins and Susan Pedersen, eds., *Settler Colonialism in the Twentieth Century* (New York 2005); Lorenzo Veracini, *Settler Colonialism* (Basingstoke 2010).

28. Bley, *Kolonialherrschaft*; Horst Drechsler, *Südwestafrika unter deutscher Kolonialherrschaft* (Berlin 1966); George Steinmetz, *The Devil's Handwriting* (Chicago 2007), 171–72; Jürgen Zimmerer, "Der koloniale Musterstaat?," in *Völkermord in Deutsch-Südwestafrika*, ed. Jürgen Zimmerer and Joachim Zeller (Berlin: Links, 2003), 26–41; Jürgen Zimmerer, "Deutscher Rassenstaat in Afrika," in *Von Windhuk nach Auschwitz?* (Berlin 2011), 120–38.

29. Zimmerer, *Deutsche Herrschaft*; Zollmann, *Koloniale Herrschaft*.

30. For a detailed analysis of the "native decrees," including their genesis, see Zimmerer, *Deutsche Herrschaft*, 68–84.

31. Zimmerer, "Der Koloniale Musterstaat?," 31.

32. Zollmann, *Koloniale Herrschaft*, 270.

33. To name a few examples, in his social history of the British state, Patrick Joyce has emphasized its material and "mundane" modes of operation. George Steinmetz has shown that the colonial state was above all culturally constituted by competition between different state functionaries and different ethnographic knowledges about the colonized. And Ann Laura Stoler has reminded us of the affective rather than rationalistic character of colonial states, namely, that statecraft was an exercise in "affective mastery." Patrick Joyce, *The State of Freedom* (Cambridge 2013); Steinmetz, *The Devil's Handwriting*; Stoler, *Along the Archival Grain*.

34. Connected history has been dubbed by Sanjay Subrahmanyam, "Connected Histories," in *Beyond Binary Histories*, ed. Victor B. Lieberman (Ann Arbor 1999), 289–316. The term "entangled" was introduced by Sidney Mintz, *Sweetness and Power* (New York 1985), and taken up by Shalini Randeria, "Geteilte Geschichte und verwobene Moderne," in *Zukunftsentwürfe*, ed. Jörn Rüsen, Hanna Leitgeb, and Norbert Jegelka (Frankfurt a.M. 2000), 87–96. See also Sebastian Conrad and Shalini Randeria, "Geteilte Geschichten," in *Jenseits des Eurozentrismus* ed. Sebastian Conrad and Shalini Randeria (Frankfurt a.M. 2002), 9–49; Angelika Epple, Olaf Kaltmeier, and Ulrike Lindner, eds., *Entangled Histories* (Leipzig 2011). On intermediaries, see Lawrance, Osborn, and Roberts, *Intermediaries*.

35. Introductory texts are Ranajit Guha and Gayatri Chakravorty Spivak, eds., *Selected Subaltern Studies* (New York 1988); Gyan Prakash, "Subaltern Studies as Postcolonial Criticism," *American Historical Review* 99, no. 5 (1994): 1475–90.

36. Wolfgang Reinhard, *Geschichte der Staatsgewalt* (Munich 1999). For a thorough critique of Eurocentric models of the colonial state, see the contributions in Søren Rud and Søren Ivarsson, eds., *Rethinking the Colonial State* (Bingley, UK 2017). In this volume, I elaborate further on the nature of the colonial state in relation to police violence: Marie Muschalek, "Violence as Usual," in *Rethinking the Colonial State*, 129–50. On the problem of writing African history "by analogy," see Mahmood Mamdani, *Citizen and Subject* (Princeton 1996), 8–11.

37. Wolfgang Reinhard, "Europäische Staatsmodelle in kolonialen und postkolonialen Machtprozessen," in *Weltgeschichte*, ed. Jürgen Osterhammel (Stuttgart 2008), 239. For this tendency, see the historiography on German colonialism relevant to this study, in Andreas Eckert, "Vom Segen der (Staats)Gewalt?," in *Staats-Gewalt*, ed. Alf Lüdtke and Michael Wildt (Göttingen 2008), 145–65; Andreas Eckert, "Nation, Staat und Ethnizität in Afrika im 20. Jahrhundert," in *Afrika im 20. Jahrhundert*, ed. Arno Sonderegger, Ingeborg Grau, and Birgit Englert (Vienna 2011), 40–59; Peter J. Schröder, *Gesetzgebung und "Arbeiterfrage" in den Kolonien* (Berlin 2006); Zimmerer, *Deutsche Herrschaft*; Zollmann, *Koloniale Herrschaft*. On the theme of "failure" in colonial history, see Maurus Reinkowski and Gregor Thum, eds., *Helpless Imperialists* (Göttingen 2013). Especially in political science, the idea of the postcolonial African state as a "failed state" has been used ad nauseam. Bruce Berman commented already two decades ago on the problematically deterministic narratives one produces when "starting with an account of the current conditions of the post-colonial state in Africa and then searching retrospectively into the past." Bruce J. Berman, "The Perils of Bula Matari," *Canadian Journal of African Studies* 31, no. 3 (1997): 568.

38. For the German historiography, this is most explicitly stated in Sebastian Conrad, *Deutsche Kolonialgeschichte* (Munich 2008), 49; Eckert, "Vom Segen der (Staats) Gewalt?," 153–54; Dierk Walter, "Gewalt, Gewaltentgrenzung und die europäische Expansion," *Mittelweg 36: Zeitschrift des Hamburger Instituts für Sozialforschung* 21, no. 3 (2012): 14–15; Zollmann, *Koloniale Herrschaft*, 346–47.

Alternatively, colonial state violence is framed in terms of successions or stages. The historian Albert Wirz, for instance, states that "in the colonial context, over long years, the men with whips and rifles had more weight than the men with books," but that eventually, "the administration gained . . . in importance as the colonial state began to collect taxes and tolls, to compile statistics, and to administer law." Such narratives omit that violence did not merely come into effect when other forms of governance failed, or gradually disappear with the expansion of the administrational apparatus, but changed in nature. Albert Wirz, "Körper, Raum und Zeit der Herrschaft," in *Alles unter Kontrolle*, ed. Katrin Bromber, Andreas Eckert, and Albert Wirz (Cologne 2003), 12.

39. Matthias Häußler, "'Collaboration' or Sabotage?," in *Cooperation and Empire*, ed. Tanja Bührer et al. (New York 2017), 180. Likewise, Brett Shadle notes with regard to interpersonal violence in colonial Kenya that "settler violence was often exceptionally brutal." Shadle, "Settlers, Africans, and Inter-personal Violence in Kenya, ca. 1900–1920s," 63.

40. There are first signs that this is changing, however. Everyday and interpersonal violence, wielded by private as well as state actors, is coming increasingly under scrutiny. As so often, the British Empire is the first to be investigated. See the special issues on histories of violence in Africa: Florence Bernault and Jan-Georg Deutsch, eds., "Histories of Violence in Africa," *Africa*, Special issue, 85, no. 3 (2015); Matthew Carotenuto and Brett Shadle, eds., "Toward a History of Violence in Colonial Kenya," *International Journal of African Historical Studies*, Special issue, 45, no. 1 (2012). On South Africa, see Keith Breckenridge, "The Allure of Violence," *Journal of Southern African Studies* 24, no. 4 (1998): 669–93; T. Dunbar Moodie, "Maximum Average Violence," *Journal of Southern African Studies* 31, no. 3 (2006): 547–67. On British India, see

Elizabeth Kolsky, *Colonial Justice in British India* (Cambridge 2010); Jonathan Saha, "Histories of Everyday Violence in British India," *History Compass* 9, no. 11 (2011): 844–53; Taylor C. Sherman, *State Violence and Punishment in India* (London 2010).

41. John McCracken, "Coercion and Control in Nyasaland," *Journal of African History* 27, no. 1 (1986): 146.

42. Carotenuto and Shadle, "Toward a History of Violence in Colonial Kenya," 4. In 1994, Frederick Cooper noted that "colonial violence—the most obvious feature of colonial rule—is inadequately studied, largely because anticolonial intellectuals portrayed it as ubiquitous while apologists saw it as incidental." "Conflict and Connection," 1530, fn. 49. In 2015, Florence Bernault and Jan-Georg Deutsch observed that "there are still significant gaps in the existing literature" on violence in Africa. "Control and Excess," *Africa* 85, no. 3 (2015): 391.

43. This form of violence is more often an object of study for anthropologists than for historians. Bernault and Deutsch, "Control and Excess," 386.

44. On the changing perception of violence in twentieth-century Europe and North America, see Richard Bessel, *Violence* (London 2015).

45. Carotenuto and Shadle, "Toward a History of Violence," 5. Emphasis added.

46. Hannah Arendt, *On Violence* (New York 1970), 44.

47. Ibid., 53.

48. On violence as a continuum, see Nancy Scheper-Hughes and Philippe Bourgois, "Making Sense of Violence," in *Violence in War and Peace*, ed. Nancy Scheper-Hughes and Philippe Bourgois (Malden, MA 2004), 1–31. Bernault and Deutsch also stress the "productive and destructive aspects" of violence in Africa. Bernault and Deutsch, "Control and Excess," 387.

49. Although Zollmann has amassed an impressive archival documentation of everyday life in the colony, notably in his dissertation, and claims to do Alltagsgeschichte, his study does not really make this evidence speak analytically. It remains background information. And thus, questions of everyday experiences and of professional police culture play no role in his work. Zollmann, "Die Kolonialpolizei," esp. 156–211.

50. Richard White, *The Middle Ground* (Cambridge 1991), x. On the question of communicating colonial order, see Zollmann, "Communicating Colonial Order."

51. For the metropolitan case, cf. Lindenberger and Lüdtke, who speak of a "coexistence and conflict of different usages of public violence." "Physische Gewalt," in *Physische Gewalt*, ed. Thomas Lindenberger and Alf Lüdtke (Frankfurt a.M. 1995), 34. Cf. also Nirenberg's interesting work on "communities of violence" in the Middle Ages in which he analyzes the "process of barter and negotiation," the (violent) practices of interaction between different religious groups in southern France and Spain. He comes to the conclusion that "violence was a central and systemic aspect of the coexistence of majority and minorities," and he suggests "that coexistence was in part predicated on such violence." David Nirenberg, *Communities of Violence* (Princeton 1996), 6, 9. Recently, Winfried Speitkamp and his research group "Communities of Violence" have offered a variety of empirical studies on the history of "groups and networks for whom physical violence [was] an essential part of their existence." Winfried Speitkamp, "Einführung," in *Gewaltgemeinschaften*, ed. Winfried Speitkamp (Göttingen 2013), 7; Winfried Speitkamp, ed., *Gewaltgemeinschaften in der Geschichte* (Göttingen 2017). For conceptual considerations regarding such communities, cf.

Winfried Speitkamp, "Gewaltgemeinschaften," in *Gewalt*, ed. Christian Gudehus and Michaela Christ (Stuttgart 2013), 184–90.

52. Tanja Bührer et al., eds., *Cooperation and Empire* (New York 2017).

53. Looking at "coercive networks" in colonial and postcolonial India, Taylor Sherman comes to a similar conclusion, showing that the state was an overburdened, often improvising actor and that everyday practices of violence, notably punishing ones, constituted the colonial state. *State Violence and Punishment in India*.

54. My approach has been strongly influenced by the writings of Bernard Cohn and Alf Lüdtke. Bernard S. Cohn, *The Bernard Cohn Omnibus* (New Delhi 2004); Alf Lüdtke, "Was ist und wer treibt Alltagsgeschichte?," in *Alltagsgeschichte*, ed. Alf Lüdtke (Frankfurt a.M. 1989), 9–47.

55. Michel de Certeau, *The Practice of Everyday Life* (Berkeley 1984).

56. I borrow the notion of "common men" and the theoretical approach from the writing of military history "from below." Cf. Bernd Ulrich, "'Militärgeschichte von unten,'" *Geschichte und Gesellschaft* 22, no. 4 (1996): 473–503; Zollmann, *Koloniale Herrschaft*, worked for the most part with sources from the National Archives of Namibia.

57. On reading along and against the archival grain, see Stoler, *Along the Archival Grain*, 1–15; George Steinmetz, "'The Devil's Handwriting,'" *Comparative Studies in Society and History* 45, no. 1 (2003): 46–54. For an introduction into the writing of African history, see Bogumil Jewsiewicki and David Newbury, eds., *African Historiographies* (Beverly Hills 1986); John Parker and Richard Reid, eds., *The Oxford Handbook of Modern African History* (Oxford 2013).

58. Lindenberger and Lüdtke, "Physische Gewalt," 7.

59. With the important exception of the experience of emotions I have tried to account for throughout the book. On violence as a form of experience and being, see Frantz Fanon, *The Wretched of the Earth* (New York 1963), 1–62; Elizabeth Frazer and Kimberly Hutchings, "On Politics and Violence," *Contemporary Political Theory* 7 (2008): 90–108.

1. Honor, Status, Masculinity

1. I use the term "identity formation" rather than "identity" or "identification" in order to indicate on the one hand the processual character of the phenomenon and, on the other hand, the fact that it is not solely a matter of a subject identifying herself with someone or something, but also being identified by others. Cf. my article on policemen's identities, "Honourable Soldier-Bureaucrats," *Journal of Imperial and Commonwealth History* 41, no. 4 (2013): 584–99. For a discussion of the epistemological difficulties surrounding the concept, see Frederick Cooper and Rogers Brubaker, "Identity," in *Colonialism in Question* (Berkeley 2005), 59–90.

2. Pierre Bourdieu, "The Sentiment of Honour in Kabyle Society," in *Honour and Shame*, ed. John G. Peristiany (Chicago 1966), 197.

3. Three recent studies on the history of honor have raised my interest in the concept: for honor in Imperial Germany, although without taking into account the colonial theater, Ann Goldberg, *Honor, Politics, and the Law in Imperial Germany, 1871–1914* (Cambridge 2010); for the British colonial context, Steven Patterson, *The Cult of Imperial Honor in British India* (New York 2009); and for honor in African history, John Iliffe,

Honour in African History (Cambridge 2005). Woodruff D. Smith has suggested paying more attention to the related concept of respectability, also in the context of German colonialism: "Colonialism and the Culture of Respectability," in *Germany's Colonial Pasts*, ed. Eric Ames, Marcia Klotz, and Lora Wildenthal (Lincoln 2005), 3–20. See also the short piece by Heike I. Schmidt, "Who Is Master in the Colony?," in *German Colonialism in a Global Age*, ed. Bradley Naranch and Geoff Eley (Durham, NC 2014), 109–28.

4. Bourdieu, "The Sentiment of Honour in Kabyle Society," 211.

5. "For a challenge to be made, the challenger must consider whoever he challenges to be worthy of it—to be, that is to say, in a position of riposte. . . . Recognition of one's adversary as one's own equal in honour is therefore the basic condition of any challenge." Ibid., 197.

6. Ibid., 228. Cf. Georg Simmel, *Soziologie*, ed. Otthein Rammstedt, orig. publ. 1908, Georg Simmel-Gesamtausgabe, vol. 11 (Frankfurt a.M. 1992), 600.

7. Iliffe defines honor as "a right to respect." He qualifies, however, that this right exists subjectively (self-understanding) and objectively (public opinion). *Honour in African History*, 4.

8. In 1851, Arthur Schopenhauer had articulated that relationship in the short formula that honor was "objectively, the opinion of others regarding our worth, and subjectively, our fear of that opinion." Arthur Schopenhauer, *Aphorismen zur Lebensweisheit*, orig. publ. 1851 (repr., Frankfurt a.M. 1976), 68.

9. Simmel, *Soziologie*, 599–600.

10. Ibid., 602, 601.

11. Iliffe, *Honour in African History*, 6.

12. Bourdieu, "The Sentiment of Honour in Kabyle Society," 231.

13. Ibid., 207.

14. Talal Asad, "Toward a Genealogy of the Concept of Ritual," in *Genealogies of Religion* (Baltimore 1993), 55.

15. Ibid., 58.

16. David M. Anderson and David Killingray, "Consent, Coercion and Control," in *Policing the Empire*, ed. David M. Anderson and David Killingray (Manchester, UK 1991), 7; David Killingray, "The Maintenance of Law and Order in British Colonial Africa," 423; Trutz von Trotha, *Koloniale Herrschaft* (Tübingen 1994), 44. See also Henri Brunschwig, "French Expansion and Local Reactions in Black Africa in the Time of Imperialism (1880–1914)," in *Expansion and Reaction*, ed. H. L. Wesseling (Leiden 1978), 136; Henri Brunschwig, *Noirs et blancs dans l'Afrique noire française* (Paris 1983), 213.

17. For an overview of the newest scholarship, see Emmanuel Blanchard, Marieke Bloembergen, and Amandine Lauro, "Tensions of Policing in Colonial Situations," in *Policing in Colonial Empires*, ed. Emmanuel Blanchard, Marieke Bloembergen, and Amandine Lauro (Brussels 2017), 11–38; Emmanuel Blanchard and Joël Glasman, "Le maintien de l'ordre dans l'empire français," in *Maintenir l'ordre colonial*, ed. Jean-Pierre Bat and Nicolas Courtin (Rennes 2012), 11–41.

18. The Landespolizei was in this way different from the Schutztruppe in German East Africa, for instance, where most of its African members were indeed recruited from outside the colony, or at least from regions within the colony that were far removed from their site of operation. The earliest recruits were not seldom former

slaves or slave-soldiers. Cf. Michelle R. Moyd, *Violent Intermediaries*, 36–60. In German Togo, African policemen were at first recruited from the margins of society, but the process of entry was often progressive and mediated by several steps. Joël Glasman, *Les corps habillés au Togo*, 67–154. For a general assessment of the recruitment of African soldiers in the German colonies, see Thomas Morlang, *Askari und Fitafita* (Berlin 2008).

19. Among Herero, one can make a further distinction: "The otjiHerero-speaking population in Namibia has been commonly divided into Herero (correctly: Ovaherero) and Mbanderu (Ovambanderu), less a cultural or linguistic division than a historical/political one." Misleadingly, the latter, that is, the Mbanderu, were oftentimes called Damara by nineteenth- and early twentieth-century writers. The group that is referred to as Damara today was then called Berg Damas or Berg Damaras. Dag Henrichsen, "Pastoral Modernity, Territoriality and Colonial Transformations in Central Namibia, 1860s–1904," in *Grappling with the Beast*, ed. Peter Limb, Norman Etherington, and Peter Midgley (Leiden 2010), 87; cf. also 95, fn. 27.

20. On the difficulty of which terms to use for the different Khoisan (used by English speakers) or Khoekhoe (used by the Nama) peoples, see Alan Barnard, *Hunters and Herders of Southern Africa* (Cambridge 1992), 7–12. On the difficulty of self-identification and identification by others of the San/Bushmen, see Robert J. Gordon, *The Bushman Myth* (Boulder 1992), 4–8.

21. There is little or no scholarly literature on the history of the Basters, who settled in Southwest Africa. For short overviews, see Peter Carstens, "Basters," in *Standard Encyclopaedia of Southern Africa* (Cape Town 1970); Peter Carstens, Introduction to *The Rehoboth Baster Nation of Namibia*, by Maximilian Bayer (Basel 1984). For an anecdotal and stereotyped account, see Riccardo Orizio, "Namibia," in *Lost White Tribes* (New York 2001), 180–220. For very brief allusions to Baster history, see John D. Omer-Cooper, *History of Southern Africa* (Cape Town 1994), 31, 263; Marion Wallace, *History of Namibia* (London 2010), 50ff., 72.

22. John Kinahan, "From the Beginning," in *History of Namibia* (London 2010), 15–43.

23. Barnard, *Hunters and Herders*; Kinahan, "From the Beginning."

24. I have not come across any Ovambo or San policemen in the archives.

25. The following passage on socioeconomic structures in precolonial and colonial Namibia relies primarily on works by historians Dag Henrichsen and Jan-Bart Gewald for the Herero and Damara; by Brigitte Lau, Tilman Dedering, and Andreas Bühler for the Nama; by Peter Carstens for the Basters; by Marion Wallace for all Namibian groups; as well as on ethnographic studies by Jakob Irle (Herero), Winifred Hoernlé, Alan Barnard, Maximilian Bayer, and Eugen Fischer (Nama, Damara, Basters). Barnard, *Hunters and Herders*; Maximilian Bayer, *The Rehoboth Baster Nation of Namibia* (Basel 1984); Andreas Heinrich Bühler, *Der Namaaufstand gegen die deutsche Kolonialherrschaft in Namibia von 1904–1913* (Frankfurt a.M. 2003); Carstens, "Basters"; Tilman Dedering, *Hate the Old and Follow the New* (Stuttgart 1997); Gewald, *Herero Heroes*; Henrichsen, "Pastoral Modernity"; Dag Henrichsen, *Herrschaft und Alltag im vorkolonialen Zentralnamibia* (Basel 2011); Winifred Hoernlé, *The Social Organization of the Nama and Other Essays*, ed. Peter Carstens, reprint of essays published between 1918 and 1937 (Johannesburg 1985); Jacob Irle, *Die Herero* (Gütersloh 1906); Brigitte Lau, "Conflict and Power in Nineteenth-Century Namibia," *Journal of African History* 27, no. 1 (1986): 29–39; Wallace, *History of Namibia*.

26. Hoernlé, *Social Organization of the Nama*, 21. Cf. Barnard, *Hunters and Herders*, 186–91. For questions of lineage and kinship regarding Herero, see Gewald, *Herero Heroes*, 41–49; more critical of kinship is Henrichsen, *Herrschaft und Alltag*, 223ff.

27. Hoernlé, *Social Organization of the Nama*, 21. See also Iliffe: "Along with kinship and personal achievement, age was especially important to the social organisation and values of stateless peoples." *Honour in African History*, 101.

28. Henrichsen, *Herrschaft und Alltag*, 1–59, 223–25; Barnard, *Hunters and Herders*, 183–84.

29. Dag Henrichsen, "'Ehi rOvaherero,'" *WerkstattGeschichte* 9 (1994): 21.

30. Ibid., 22. On the importance of cattle ownership among Nama and Damara, see Barnard, *Hunters and Herders*, 179; Dedering, *Hate the Old and Follow the New*, 31–36.

31. Edwin Wilmsen, *Land Filled with Flies*, cited in Henrichsen, *Herrschaft und Alltag*, 61.

32. Henrichsen, *Herrschaft und Alltag*, 61–126; Wallace, *History of Namibia*, 47.

33. Henrichsen, *Herrschaft und Alltag*, 65.

34. Michael Garfield Smith, *Government in Zazzau, 1800–1950* (1960), 8, cited in Colin Newbury, "Patrons, Clients, and Empire," *Journal of World History* 11, no. 2 (2000): 229.

35. Eisenstadt and Roniger stress moreover that "the exchange of these resources is usually effected by a 'package-deal,' i.e., neither resource can be exchanged separately but only in a combination that includes both types." And: "As a corollary, there is a strong element of solidarity in these relations, an element often couched in terms of interpersonal loyalty and attachment between patrons and clients—even though these relations may often be ambivalent. . . . Solidarity is often closely related to conceptions of *personal identity*, especially of *personal honor* and obligations, and it is also evident that some, even if ambivalent, personal 'spiritual' attachment may exist between patron and clients." S. N. Eisenstadt and Louis Roniger, "Patron-Client Relations as a Model of Structuring Social Exchange," *Comparative Studies in Society and History* 22, no. 1 (1980): 49–50. Emphasis added.

36. Barnard, *Hunters and Herders*, 195; cf. Bayer, *The Rehoboth Baster*, 26; Henrichsen, *Herrschaft und Alltag*, 65.

37. Dedering, *Hate the Old and Follow the New*, 36.

38. Barnard, *Hunters and Herders*, 195; Bayer, *The Rehoboth Baster*, 6; Wallace, *History of Namibia*, 55ff., 72.

39. On komando culture among Boer, Baster, and Nama societies in general, see Nigel Penn, *The Forgotten Frontier: Colonist and Khoisan on the Cape's Northern Frontier in the 18th Century* (Athens, OH 2005), 108–55; Christiane Hardung and Trutz von Trotha, "*Komando* und 'Bande,'" in *Gewaltgemeinschaften*, ed. Winfried Speitkamp (Göttingen 2013), 275–96; cf. also Bayer, *The Rehoboth Baster*, 29; Lau, "Conflict and Power in Nineteenth-Century Namibia," 29–39.

40. Penn, *The Forgotten Frontier*, 108.

41. Lau, "Conflict and Power in Nineteenth-Century Namibia," 32.

42. Ibid., 33.

43. Ibid. See also Barnard, *Hunters and Herders*, 179; Henrichsen, "Pastoral Modernity," 95–105; Wallace, *History of Namibia*, 51.

44. Dedering, *Hate the Old and Follow the New*, 174.

45. Ibid., 174, 176. Cf. ibid., 19.

46. Thus, Herero adaptation of the komando organization did not have a de-pastoralizing effect, as it had with the Nama. It seems that the Herero had learned their lesson, that is, not to be too dependent on the horse and gun trade. Henrichsen argues that "some, though not all, chiefs engaged in a remarkable reform-driven strategy that reflected not only the chiefs' long experience with Nama-Oorlam polities but also the necessities of life as stipulated by Cape and missionary expansion." "Pastoral Modernity," 99.

47. Ibid., 98.

48. Ibid., and Gewald, *Herero Heroes*, 23–24.

49. Henrichsen, *Herrschaft und Alltag*, 259.

50. On the differences between the various African groups, see ibid., 260, and Penn, *The Forgotten Frontier*, 111.

51. For a while this ideal was even cherished by some German colonial officials. Before the war, in 1903, the German authorities asked Nama *kaptein* Hendrik Witbooi to put together a police komando of twelve Nama men to hunt down a presumed thief. The German colonial administrators particularly admired the independent, guerrilla-like character of this auxiliary police force. Zollmann, *Koloniale Herrschaft*, 64–68.

52. On firearms as important markers of male identity in increasingly militarized African societies, see Iliffe, *Honour in African History*, 147.

53. According to Henrichsen, rifles were also used in other religious rituals, such as cleansing or rain summoning/preventing rituals. *Herrschaft und Alltag*, 258–59.

54. Iliffe, *Honour in African History*, 142–43.

55. Irle, *Die Herero*, 181–182; cf. also Henrichsen, *Herrschaft und Alltag*, 258.

56. Penn, *The Forgotten Frontier*, 110.

57. Henrichsen, *Herrschaft und Alltag*, 228–31.

58. Ibid.

59. Ibid., 40–47.

60. Wallace, *A History of Namibia*, 47.

61. Bayer, *The Rehoboth Baster*, 36–38; cf. Norman Etherington, *The Great Treks* (Harlow, UK 2001).

62. Iliffe, *Honour in African History*, 227.

63. Philipp Prein, "Guns and Top Hats," *Journal of Southern African Studies* 20, no. 1 (1994): 99–121.

64. Ibid., 113.

65. Barnard, *Hunters and Herders*, 183.

66. G. Thomas Burgess and Andrew Burton, introduction to *Generations Past*, ed. Andrew Burton and Hélène Charton-Bigot (Athens, OH 2010), 1.

67. Andreas Kukuri, *Herero-Texte*, trans. and ed. Ernst Dammann (Berlin 1983), 52.

68. Iliffe, *Honour in African History*, 202.

69. Ibid.

70. Ibid.

71. Ibid., 222.

72. Chief of Police Heydebreck to District Office Omaruru, 10.10.1907, BArch-B, R 1002/2508, 23–24. See also Magistrate Vietsch (District Office Rehoboth) to Police

Station Hornkranz, 09.10.1913, National Archives of Namibia (hereafter NAN), Bezirksamt Rehoboth (hereafter BRE), 75 L.2.f, 33 (new series). Zollmann, *Koloniale Herrschaft*, 71.

73. There are no reliable numbers on which institution African policemen were more recruited from. Dag Henrichsen stresses the importance of the colonial military, while Zollmann emphasizes the importance of missionary schools. Dag Henrichsen, "Ozombambuse and Ovasolondate," in *Hues between Black and White*, by Wolfram Hartmann (Windhoek 2004), 168–69; Zollmann, *Koloniale Herrschaft*, 70–71.

74. For better readability, I have translated all relevant titles and ranks into English equivalents: Bezirksamtmann = Magistrate; Distriktschef = District Chief; Regierungsrat = Senior Executive Officer; Inspekteur der Landespolizei = Chief of Police; Inspektionsoffizier = Inspection Officer; Kriminalbeamter = Detective Sergeant; Diensttuender Wachtmeister = Senior Staff Sergeant; Wachtmeister = Staff Sergeant; Sergeant = Sergeant; Polizist = Constable; Polizeidiener = (African) Police Assistant. Interestingly, the rank of Polizeidiener—literally, "police servant"—had also existed in the German states of the early and mid-nineteenth century. Alf Lüdtke, *"Gemeinwohl," Polizei und "Festungspraxis"* (Göttingen 1982), 149.

75. Henrichsen, "Ozombambuse and Ovasolondate," 173–80. On the term "Bambuse," cf. ibid., 163, fnn. 11, 12.

76. Zollmann, *Koloniale Herrschaft*, 78; Rafalski, *Vom Niemandsland*, 105.

77. See, for instance, request regarding Police Assistant Franz Boy by Sgt. Karl Eckel (Police Station Holoog) to District Office Keetmanshoop, 15.06.1910, NAN, Bezirksamt Keetmanshoop (hereafter BKE), 201 B.II.66.c (vol. 1), 16.

78. Michelle Moyd's study of African soldiers in the German colonial service gives a much more sophisticated answer to the question of why military service in a colonial army could have been appealing to African men. Moyd, *Violent Intermediaries*; cf. also Morlang, *Askari und Fitafita*.

79. Report by Sen. Staff Sgt. Max Ehrlich (Police Station Okahandja), 16.12.1901, BArch-B, R 1002/2465, 4.

80. For instance, Sgt. Albert Bruhn (Police Station Keetmanshoop) to Transportation Bureau, Schutztruppe, 28.12.1909, NAN, BKE, 201 B.II.66.c (vol. 1), 7. An interesting discussion of the way in which gift giving shaped relationships between African and German colonial policemen in Togo offers Glasman, *Les corps habillés*, 96–106.

81. Report regarding Police Assistant Seemann by Sgt. Paul Ebermann (Police Station Gosorobis) to District Office Rehoboth, 22.01.1914, NAN, BRE, 75 L.2.f, 48 (new series).

82. See the example of a treasurer at District Office Rehoboth who refused to act as bookkeeper for German policemen who were lending money to their African subordinates. Note by treasurer Widemann (District Office Rehoboth) to policemen Dietrich, Maywald, Hagen, Bülow, Hellwig, 31.03.1914, NAN, BRE, 75 L.2.f, 47 (new series).

83. Moyd, *Violent Intermediaries*, 4.

84. Personal conversation with Dag Henrichsen in Basel, May 14, 2013.

85. This section is based on the results of my quantitative study of the approximately nine hundred existing personnel files of the Landespolizei stored at the German National Archive. I have surveyed all of them. A sample of these I have analyzed in depth. BArch-B, Gouvernement in Windhuk SWA, Personalakten, R 1002/91–1957 and BArch-B, R 1002/2804–3591.

86. Generally, the German policemen were from cohorts 1876 through 1883, that is, they were usually between ages twenty-five and thirty when they entered the police force. The oldest policeman I could find was constable Karl Dietrich, who was born in 1870. The youngest, police sergeant Gustav Manson, was born in 1887. Register of the members of the Landespolizei, no date (ca. 1916), BArch-B, R 1002/2790, no page numbers; personnel file police sergeant Manson, BArch-B, R 1002/3245. For some useful insight into the political mentality of the Gründerzeit generation of German men, see Detlev Peukert, *Die Weimarer Republik* (Frankfurt a.M. 1987), 26–31.

87. There is little or no secondary literature on the social composition of lower-rank soldiers in the German Imperial military. This passage on the social backgrounds of NCOs in the Kaiserreich is based on an analysis I undertook of statistical records from the beginning of the twentieth century. The surveys had been produced in the context of the so-called *Wehrfähigkeitsdebatte*, a dispute among political and military elites regarding the question whether industrialized areas could still produce healthy, "apt" young men to defend the nation. Cf. Detlef Bald, *Vom Kaiserheer zur Bundeswehr* (Frankfurt a.M. 1981); Wilhelm Deist, "Die Armee in Staat und Gesellschaft, 1890–1914," in *Militär, Staat und Gesellschaft* (Munich 1991), 19–41; Wilhelm Deist, "Die Geschichte des preußischen Offizierskorps, 1888–1918," in *Militär, Staat und Gesellschaft* (Munich 1991), 43–56; Werner Lahne, *Unteroffiziere* (Herford; Bonn 1974).

88. My findings are primarily based on Georg Evert, "Die Herkunft der deutschen Unteroffiziere und Soldaten am 1. Dezember 1906," *Zeitschrift des Königlich Preussischen Statistischen Landesamts* 28 (1908).

89. Ibid., 74–133, esp. 132–33. Evert's table shows that the largest proportion of NCOs had fathers occupied in agriculture and "non-classified" occupations (i.e., liberal or service positions). Cf. Bald, *Vom Kaiserheer zur Bundeswehr*, 59; Bald bases his claims on the Evert study, though he cites him incorrectly.

90. On demographic change in Imperial Germany, see David Blackbourn, *The Long Nineteenth Century* (New York 1998), 191–205.

91. Wolfgang J. Mommsen, *Imperial Germany, 1867–1918* (London 1995), 17.

92. See Otto Müller's personnel file, BArch-B, R 1002/3224.

93. In 1910, Chief of Police Bethe asked specifically for blacksmiths, masons, saddlers, and carpenters. Chief of Police Bethe to Gouv. SWA, 24.10.1910, BArch-B, R 1002/2502, 93.

94. Mommsen, *Imperial Germany*, 236.

95. On the transformation of artisanship in the Kaiserreich, see Gerhard Ritter and Klaus Tenfelde, *Arbeiter im Deutschen Kaiserreich 1871 bis 1914* (Bonn 1992), 281–97.

96. BArch-B, R 1002/2804–3591.

97. Ritter and Tenfelde, *Arbeiter im Deutschen Kaiserreich*, 288.

98. Mommsen, *Imperial Germany*. On the role of the military in Imperial German society, see Deist, "Die Armee in Staat und Gesellschaft, 1890–1914."

99. See also Alf Lüdtke's characterization of Prussian policemen in the mid-nineteenth century. *"Gemeinwohl," Polizei und "Festungspraxis,"* 149–59.

100. At least after surveying all the records of the subject folder "Recruitments" in the police archives, in which I have found no evidence of men expressing such feelings in writing. BArch-B, R 1002/2493–2503.

101. The historian Birthe Kundrus comes to a conclusion similar to mine regarding the sources and observes that one cannot empirically substantiate the notion that

people wanted to leave the Kaiserreich out of reactionary nostalgia. Her argument is therefore that the bourgeoisie expressed dreams about a premodern utopian society but mostly remained in the metropole. The working class, she argues, immigrated to the colonies by economic necessity. On imagination in the metropole, see Birthe Kundrus, *Moderne Imperialisten* (Cologne 2003), 43–76, 129–37. For settler aspirations in the colony, see Bley, *Kolonialherrschaft*, 107–23, 220–39. For a combination of both, see Lerp, *Imperiale Grenzräume*; Walther, *Creating Germans Abroad*. For the motivations of Schutztruppe officers and soldiers, see Kuß, *Deutsches Militär*, 127–56. For a critique of a German "Sonderweg" (special path) thesis applied to the colony, see Steinmetz, *The Devil's Handwriting*, 140–44.

102. Otto Olkiewicz to IdL, 12.03.1912, BArch-B, R 1002/2501, 99.

103. Staff Sgt. Max Geyer to Gouv. SWA, 03.04.1908, BArch-B, R 1002/2500, 153. See also application by clerk Otto Bälk from Berlin Spandau, who made 90–100 marks a month and whose wife had already settled in Southwest Africa with the help of the German Colonial Women's Association. Letter by Otto Bälk to Ltn. Winterfeld (Schutztruppe), 08.09.1908, BArch-B, R 1002/2500, 36–39.

104. Kuß, *Deutsches Militär*, 132, 137, 143.

105. Between 1908 and 1909 about two thousand soldiers of the Schutztruppe were demobilized. In the following three years, another five hundred men left the military. Zimmerer, *Deutsche Herrschaft*, 117. For an example of a former NCO who had already been sent home in 1907 and had become a quarryman, see Sgt. Swoboda from Königshütte. "I would like to better my future so that I won't remain a common worker," he wrote in his recruitment request to the Landespolizei. Johann Swoboda to IdL, 18.02.1912, BArch-B, R 1002/2501, 64–65.

106. Gesine Krüger, *Kriegsbewältigung und Geschichtsbewusstsein* (Göttingen 1999), 69.

107. See the instruction from the Colonial Office to avoid "hasty" discharges, for men with experience and knowledge of the colony were deemed better than new recruits from the homeland. Governor Seitz to IdL, 17.11.1913, BArch-B, R 1002/2424, 18–20.

108. See, for instance, Sgt. Paul Altscher's letter to police headquarters in which he explains his and two other men's case regarding uncertainties about general employment conditions. Sgt. Paul Altscher to IdL, 20.12.1907, BArch-B, R 1002/91, 39–41.

109. Internal note by Chief of Police Heydebreck, 29.07.1907, BArch-B, R 1002/2692, no page number. Chief of Police Heydebreck to Colonial Office (Reichskolonialamt [hereafter RKA]), 25.10.1907, BArch-B, R 1002/2417, 1–3.

110. Letters by Hermann Strunck to Johann Strunck, 21.01.1912 and 29.03.1912 (Strunck Family Archive), cited in Kuno Franz Robert Budack, *Raubmord 1912* (Windhoek 1999), 8–9.

111. Chief of Police Bethe to all inspection officers, 07.06.1910, BArch-B, R 1002/2418, 23. For an example, see the case of soldier Hirte, who after his demobilization owned only six hundred to one thousand marks, and was thus denied the right to obtain a farm. Hirte therefore wished to enter the police force. District Chief Kurt Streitwolf (District Office Gobabis) to Gouv. SWA, 06.02.1908, BArch-B, R 1002/2500, 120.

112. Thomas Lindenberger, *Strassenpolitik* (Bonn 1995), 75; Herbert Reinke, "'Armed as If for a War,'" in *Policing Western Europe*, ed. Clive Emsley and Barbara Weinberger (New York 1991), 59; Robert Harnischmacher and Arved Semerak, *Deutsche Polizeige-*

schichte (Stuttgart 1986), 67. However, scholars debate to what extent these standards could be upheld. Cf. Richard J. Evans, "Polizei, Politik und Gesellschaft in Deutschland 1700–1933," *Geschichte und Gesellschaft* 22, no. 4 (1996): 622; Ralph Jessen, "Polizei im Kaiserreich," in *Die Polizei der Gesellschaft*, ed. Hans-Jürgen Lange (Opladen 2003), 21.

113. NCOs were entitled to the so-called *Zivilversorgungsschein* after a twelve-year commitment with good standing. Deist, "Die Armee in Staat und Gesellschaft 1890–1914," 32.

114. *Vorwärts*, July 4, 1892, quoted on the website of the Deutsche Hochschule der Polizei, https://www.dhpol.de/de/hochschule/Ausstellung/Austellungsseiten/index.php.

115. There were two ways to become an NCO: training in specific NCO schools, or the system of *Kapitulation*. The *Kapitulanten* system, which in the early 1900s became the predominant NCO career path, was a procedure by which the aspirant (often a common soldier in good standing) signed up for twelve years of duty. Since 1874, these NCOs were promised a transfer into civil service after the twelve years— the so-called *Zivilversorgung* mentioned above. Deist, "Die Armee in Staat und Gesellschaft 1890–1914," 32.

116. Spohn, *Berufs- und Standespflichten der Unteroffiziere* (Oldenburg 1909), 3.

117. Lahne, *Unteroffiziere*, 318.

118. An NCO's pay around 1900 corresponded more or less with that of a day laborer in the western provinces of Imperial Germany. Manfred Messerschmidt, "Die preußische Armee," in *Handbuch zur deutschen Militärgeschichte, 1648–1939*, ed. Militärgeschichtliches Forschungsamt, vol. 4, part 2 (Frankfurt a.M. 1979), 193.

119. Lahne, *Unteroffiziere*, 281; Bald, *Vom Kaiserheer zur Bundeswehr*, 73.

120. Bald, *Vom Kaiserheer zur Bundeswehr*, 68–69.

121. Deist, "Die Armee in Staat und Gesellschaft 1890–1914," 32.

122. Bald, *Vom Kaiserheer zur Bundeswehr*, 68.

123. On abuse and corporal punishment in the military in Imperial Germany, see Andrew G. Bonnell, "Explaining Suicide in the Imperial German Army," *German Studies Review* 37, no. 2 (2014): 275–95; Hartmut Wiedner, "Soldatenmißhandlungen im Wilhelminischen Kaiserreich (1890–1914)," *Archiv für Sozialgeschichte* 22 (1982): 159–99.

124. Stig Förster, *Der doppelte Militarismus* (Stuttgart 1985); Hull, *Absolute Destruction*, 103–9; Thomas Rohkrämer, *Der Militarismus der "kleinen Leute"* (Munich 1990).

125. Ute Frevert, *A Nation in Barracks* (Oxford 2004), 149.

126. On militarism and "patriarchal-military *habitus*" in the German police, see Lüdtke, *"Gemeinwohl," Polizei und "Festungspraxis,"* 323–25; Lindenberger, *Strassenpolitik*, 68–72.

127. Clive Emsley and Barbara Weinberger, introduction to *Policing Western Europe*, ed. Clive Emsley and Barbara Weinberger (New York 1991), vii–ix; Albrecht Funk, *Polizei und Rechtsstaat* (Frankfurt a.M. 1986), 25–27; Hsi-Huey Liang, *The Rise of Modern Police and the European State System from Metternich to the Second World War* (New York 1992), 4.

128. France did not even have a civil police force until 1907, and then only for limited fields of operation such as political police. Jean-Marc Berlière, "The Professionalisation of the Police under the Third Republic in France, 1875–1914," in *Policing Western Europe*, ed. Clive Emsley and Barbara Weinberger (New York 1991), 36–54;

Jean-Marc Berlière, *Le monde des polices en France* (Paris 1996); Clive Emsley, *Gendarmes and the State in Nineteenth-Century Europe* (Oxford 1999).

129. Internal note by Chief of Police Heydebreck, 29.07.1907, BArch-B, R 1002/2692, no page number. See also the general report about the Landespolizei to the Colonial Office from 1909, in which the desire to have married men is reiterated though qualified. Governor Schuckmann to RKA, Berlin, 04.10.1909, BArch-B, R 1002/2692, 121–27.

130. Chief of Police Heydebreck to all district offices, 22.08.1907, BArch-B, R 1002/2693, 40.

131. Blumhagen (Gouv. SWA) to RKA, 17.08.1910, BArch-B, R 1002/2431, 9.

132. Ibid. See also the concern expressed by the governor a year before; Governor Schuckmann to IdL, 12.06.1909, BArch-B, R 1002/2431, 1.

133. Blumhagen (Gouv. SWA) to RKA, 17.08.1910, BArch-B, R 1002/2431, 9.

134. State Secretary Lindequist to Gouv. SWA, 23.09.1910, BArch-B, R 1002/2431, 11.

135. Ibid., 5–6.

136. Circular by Chief of Police Bethe to all district offices and police depots, 14.09.1911, BArch-B, R 1002/2431, 20.

137. My estimate is based on an evaluation of the database I produced from the personnel files, and of the following sources: register of all staff members of the Landespolizei, 01.04.1911, BArch-B, R 1002/2485, 61–82; register of all staff members of the Landespolizei, 01.04.1913, BArch-B, R 1002/2485, 119–40; Blumhagen (Gouv. SWA) to RKA, 17.08.1910, BArch-B, R 1002/2431, 9. Sven Schepp observes higher marriage rates. For the year 1913 he claims that about 50 percent of the sergeants and about 70 percent of the staff sergeants and senior staff sergeants were married. *Unter dem Kreuz des Südens*, 105.

138. Roebern (IdL) to District Office Swakopmund, 14.02.1910, BArch-B, R 1002/2501, 4; Chief of Police Bethe to Gouv. SWA, 24.10.1910, BArch-B, R 1002/2502, 93.

139. Directive drafted by Chief of Police Bethe, signed by Vice Governor Hintrager, to all district offices and police depots, 21.07.1911, BArch-B, R 1002/2431, 4.

140. Wolfram Hartmann, "Sexual Encounters and Their Implications on an Open and Closing Frontier" (PhD diss., Columbia University, 2002); Wolfram Hartmann, "Urges in the Colony," *Journal of Namibian Studies* 1, (2007): 39–71; Daniel Joseph Walther, *Sex and Control* (New York 2015).

141. Staff evaluations by Magistrate Brill (District Office Windhuk), 05.01.1910, BArch-B, R 1002/2492, 21.

142. Chief of Police Bethe to RKA, Berlin, 21.07.1911, BArch-B, R 1002/2431, 16.

143. Ibid., 16–17.

144. For photos, see Schepp, *Unter dem Kreuz des Südens*, 147; Andreas Selmeci and Dag Henrichsen, *Das Schwarzkommando* (Bielefeld 1995), 134. See also figure 2 in this chapter.

145. See the example of a domestic conflict because the African policeman's wife was supposedly not fulfilling her domestic duties. Report by Inspection Officer Hirschberg (Police Depot Kupferberg) to IdL, 01.09.1909, BArch-B, R 1002/2598, 85. Zollmann, *Koloniale Herrschaft*, 73.

146. Governor Seitz to IdL, 07.06.1912, BArch-B, R 1002/2598, 173.

147. I thank Dag Henrichson for pointing that out to me.

148. As Marion Wallace notes with respect to the Nama-Oorlam komandos, "the term 'Oorlam' essentially indicated an economic and cultural identity, and also a deeply

gendered one"; it referred to "a mounted group of men armed with guns." *History of Namibia*, 51.

149. Kundrus, *Moderne Imperialisten*, 77–96, 283. For a similar distinction between a masculinity of "imperial patriarchy" that saw sex with African women as a white, male privilege, and that of "liberal nationalism," which saw sex not as "a man's private decision, but a social marker of status," in which "race mixing" posed a serious threat to the colonial political order, see Lora Wildenthal, *German Women for Empire, 1884–1945* (Durham, NC 2001), 81–83.

150. Raewyn Connell, *Masculinities* (Berkeley 1995), 72.

151. Iliffe, *Honour in African History*, 100.

152. Magistrate Berengar Zastrow (District Office Grootfontein) to Gouv. SWA, 16.06.1913, cited in Zollmann, *Koloniale Herrschaft*, 76.

153. For the age limit of thirty, see Chief of Police Heydebreck to RKA, Berlin, 25.10.1907, BArch-B, R 1002/2417, 1–3. For the age limit of twenty-seven, see Governor Seitz to IdL, 27.02.1912, BArch-B, R 1002/2417, 30.

154. Hollaender (IdL) to RKA, Berlin, 13.03.1912, BArch-B, R 1002/2417, 29. See also Hollaender (IdL) to Gouv. SWA, 12.07.1912, BArch-B, R 1002/2417, 34.

155. Interestingly, maturity would come through military training. State Secretary Lindequist to Gouv. SWA, 27.08.1910, BArch-B, R 1002/2502, 79–80.

156. Evaluation of Sgt. Boll by Magistrate Todt (District Office Windhuk), 05.01.1914, BArch-B, R 1002/2805, 67.

157. Evaluation of Sgt. Alefelder by Magistrate Blumhagen (District Office Swakopmund), 09.01.1908, BArch-B, R 1002/2793, 25.

158. In the metropole, due to public and political pressure, there was a similar call for more delicate, more composed methods of policing. Reinke, "'Armed as If for a War,'" 68.

159. Marginal note by Chief of Police Bethe on patrol report by Sen. Staff Sgt. Otto Donicht, (District Office Karibib), 19.09.1910, BArch-B, R 1002/2709, 187.

160. Patrol report by Sen. Staff Sgt. Otto Donicht (District Office Karibib), 19.09.1910, BArch-B, R 1002/2709, 187–90.

161. Examples for "prudent": report on Sgt. Link by Inspection Officer Hollaender to District Office Gobabis, 10.02.1910, BArch-B, R 1002/2709, 231; "attentive" and "cautious": patrol report by Sen. Staff Sgt. Eggersglüß (Police Station Nonidass), 21.01.1912, 2710, 204; "conscientious": qualification report for Sgt. Otto Müller by District Office Okahandja, 15.12.1914, BArch-B, R 1002/3224, 70.

162. Complaint against farmer Potthast by Sgt. Bruno Lippke (Police Station Gurumanas), 24.04.1911, BArch-B, R 1002/2466, 42.

163. "Die wehrlose Polizei," *Deutsch-Südwestafrikanische Zeitung*, 25.08.1909; "Polizei und Polizeitruppe in Deutsch-Südwest," *Deutsch-Südwestafrikanische Zeitung*, 19.04.1913.

164. I discuss one particular rape case in Marie Muschalek, "Honneur masculin et violence policière ordinaire," *Revue du Vingtième Siècle* 140, no. 4 (2018): 83–95. More cases are filed in BArch-B, R 1002/2782 and 2783.

165. On sexual violence in the colonies, see, among others, Nancy Rose Hunt, "An Acoustic Register, Tenacious Images, and Congolese Scenes of Rape and Repetition," *Cultural Anthropology* 23, no. 2 (2008): 220–53; Elizabeth Kolsky, "'The Body Evidencing the Crime,'" *Gender and History* 22, no. 1 (2010): 109–30; Charlotte Mertens,

"Sexual Violence in the Congo Free State," *Australasian Review of African Studies* 37, no. 1 (2016): 6–20; Pamela Scully, "Rape, Race, and Colonial Culture," *American Historical Review* 100, no. 2 (1995): 335–59; Brett L. Shadle, "Rape in the Courts of Gusiiland, Kenya, 1940s–1960s," *African Studies Review* 51, no. 2 (2008): 27–50; Elizabeth Thornberry, "Defining Crime through Punishment," *Journal of Southern African Studies* 37 (2011): 415–30.

166. For instance, reprimand of Sgt. Melzer, who had caused a brawl in a bar. Report by District Chief Runck (District Office Warmbad), 28.07.1908, BArch-B, R 1002/1184, 24.

167. When a fight was considered to have harmed the police force's reputation, it could, however, result in dismissal. Cf. Vice Governor Hintrager to Sgt. Johann Sterzenbach (Police Station Choantsas), 18.12.1912, BArch-B, R 1002/3483, 61.

168. Stefanie Michels, *Schwarze deutsche Kolonialsoldaten* (Bielefeld 2009), 229.

169. Ibid.

170. Breckenridge, "The Allure of Violence," 689.

171. See, for instance, decree by Governor Schuckmann, 14.09.1907, BArch-B, R 1002/2605, 1–2; list of salaries for the months of January, February, and March 1908 (IdL), 24.06.1908, BArch-B, R 1002/2598, 25; cash accounting book, District Office Bethanien, August 1909, R 1002/2639, 2; budget 1914 for African workers and police assistants by Hensel (IdL), 19.03.1914, BArch-B, R 1002/2593, 1–4. For the exceptional case in which African policemen received sixty marks, see Chief of Police Heydebreck to District Office Lüderitzbucht, 31.08.1909, BArch-B, R 1002/2598, 80–81.

172. For a list of the remuneration of all German colonial civil servants, see Johannes Tesch, *Die Laufbahn der deutschen Kolonialbeamten, ihre Pflichten und Rechte*, 6th ed. (Berlin 1912), 14–18. For an example of an income sheet, see Sgt. Albrecht's work contract, 06.11.1907, BArch-B, R 1002/2796, 43–44.

173. For an example of the negotiations of a German policeman regarding his income and social benefits, see request by Sgt. Paul Altscher to IdL, 30.11.1907, BArch-B, R 1002/91, 33–34.

174. Zollmann, *Koloniale Herrschaft*, 141–44. See also the case of Police Assistant Fritz, who drowned while on duty, and whose family would have received a one-time payment as compensation if it had asked for it. Report by Staff Sgt. Hans Franken (Police Depot Waterberg), 20.02.1912, BArch-B, R 1002/2600, 25.

175. Decree by Vice Governor Hintrager, 04.03.1910, BArch-B, R 1002/2605, 8.

176. A memorandum regarding colonial civil servants' income from 1910 noted for German Southwest Africa "high prices in many respects," and that "living costs have not become much lower since the end of the uprising." Cited in Tesch, *Die Laufbahn der deutschen Kolonialbeamten*, 457. For an individual case, see the request of a sergeant who could not afford the drinks he had to buy for his informants. Request by Sgt. Paul Altscher to Gouv. SWA, 19.12.1913, BArch-B, R 1002/91, 107–8.

177. Annual report 1909 of the IdL, 25.05.1910, BArch-B, R 1002/2672, 45–47.

178. *Dienstvorschrift für die berittene Landespolizei* (Breslau 1910), 11; Zollmann, *Koloniale Herrschaft*, 73. Baster policemen had a special position, for they had the right to own and even increase livestock without restrictions. Carstens, Introduction to *The Rehoboth Baster Nation*, 2. For African police owning livestock, see patrol report by Sgt. Arthur Wegener (Police Station Altmaltahöhe), 12.10.1911, BArch-B, R 1002/2710, 170; deposition by Police Assistant July (Police Depot Kupferberg), 01.09.1909, BArch-B, R 1002/2598, 84.

179. Iliffe on the African concept of "big men" within a patron-client economy, here of the Beti in Central Africa: "A Big Man's status rested chiefly on wealth in people. . . . The Big Man's household also commonly contained slaves (generally absorbed as poor relations), pawns taken as security for loans, and the clients whom no Big Man could neglect. To acquire and hold dependents, the Big Man had to distribute wealth: 'treasure' or cattle to pay bridewealth, food to support the poor or feast the community, and increasingly the European trade goods that nineteenth-century Beti and their neighbours pursued as avidly as they pursued women." *Honour in African History*, 111. See also Wallace, *History of Namibia*, 48.

180. On colonial photography and visual representations in the German context, see Wolfram Hartmann, Jeremy Silvester, and Patricia Hayes, eds., *The Colonising Camera* (Cape Town 1999); Jens Jäger, "Plätze an der Sonne?," in *Kolonialgeschichten*, ed. Claudia Kraft, Alf Lüdtke, and Jürgen Martschukat (Frankfurt a.M. 2010), 160–82; Wilhelm R. Schmidt and Irmtraud Dietlinde Wolcke-Renk, *Deutsch-Südwest-Afrika* (Erfurt 2001).

181. Magistrate Zastrow (District Office Grootfontein) to IdL, 10.10.1911, BArch-B, R 1002/3483, 47.

182. Magistrate Brill (District Office Windhuk) to IdL, 05.01.1910, BArch-B, R 1002/2492, 21.

183. Request for transfer by Sgt. Wilhelm Czarnetzki (District Court Windhuk) to District Office Windhuk, 15.03.1906, BArch-B, R 1002/325, 1.

184. Memorandum on the Landespolizei in *Stenographische Berichte des Reichtags*, vol. 242 (1907), annex 397, addendum I, 30.

185. See, for instance, a domestic abuse case that was entirely handled by the African police: Report by Sgt. Herold (Police Station Klipdam), 29.09.1913, NAN, Distriktsamt Aroab (hereafter DAR), 4 E.4.d, no page numbers.

186. Roger Chickering, *We Men Who Feel Most German* (Boston 1984), 127–28.

187. Mohamed Adhikari, "Hope, Fear, Shame, Frustration," *Journal of Southern African Studies* 32, no. 3 (2006): 478.

188. The historian Susanne Kuß makes a similar argument with respect to the German colonial military in *Deutsches Militär*, stressing the importance of the conditions on site, in the "theater of war," for the formation of identities and practices.

189. On the military elements in colonial education and discipline, see Timothy Mitchell, *Colonising Egypt* (Berkeley 1988), 63–94, esp. 72–82.

2. Soldier-Bureaucrats

1. Chief of Police Bethe to Magistrate Berengar Zastrow (District Office Grootfontein), 09.06.1910, BArch-B, R 1002/2709, 58.

2. The term "military spirit" figured initially in a draft of the police's main instruction manual, "a term which every soldier is familiar with," the chief of police claimed. Marginal note by Chief of Police Heydebreck on letter by Magistrate Zastrow (District Office Grootfontein) to IdL, 01.10.1907, BArch-B, R 1002/2692, no page number.

3. Jessen, "Polizei im Kaiserreich," 19–36; Reinke, "'Armed as If for a War,'" 55–73.

4. Emsley, *Gendarmes and the State in Nineteenth-Century Europe*; Jean-Marc Berlière and René Levy, *Histoire des polices en France* (Paris 2011); Arnaud-Dominique Houte

and Jean-Noël Luc, eds., *Les gendarmeries dans le monde, de la révolution française à nos jours* (Paris 2016).

5. On the difference between continental and Anglo-American policing, see Emsley and Weinberger, introduction to *Policing Western Europe*, vii–ix; Wolfgang Knöbl, *Polizei und Herrschaft im Modernisierungsprozeß* (Frankfurt a.M. 1998). On the difference between British metropolitan and imperial models of policing, see Emsley, "Policing the Empire/Policing the Metropole"; cf. also Anderson and Killingray, "Consent, Coercion and Control," 3; Richard Hawkins, "The 'Irish Model' and the Empire," in *Policing the Empire*, ed. David M. Anderson and David Killingray (Manchester, UK 1991), 18–32.

6. *Dienstvorschrift*, 16. However, difficulties in finding enough suitable men led the colonial administration to repeatedly reconsider whether it should also accept candidates who had served only five years. Governor Schuckmann to Schutztruppe Command, 21.09.1907, BArch-B, R 1002/2497, 28. Cf. Zollmann, "Die Kolonialpolizei," 116–19. Auxiliary policemen, the so-called Zivilpolizisten or just Polizisten whom I call "constables," were employed with or without contract and paid daily or monthly. They had no civil servant status, and although they did not need to have served six years, they too were often former military men—mostly with the rank of trooper or private. Chief of Police Heydebreck to Schutztruppe Command, 12.09.1908, BArch-B, R 1002/2418, 2; Chief of Police Heydebreck to all police depots, 17.09.1908, BArch-B, R 1002/2418, 4–5.

7. Reinke, "'Armed as If for a War,'" 55; Giorgio Blundo and Joël Glasman, "Introduction: Bureaucrats in Uniform," *Sociologus*, nos. 1–2 (2013): 1–9.

8. Blundo and Glasman, "Introduction: Bureaucrats in Uniform," 3.

9. Krüger, *Kriegsbewältigung und Geschichtsbewusstsein*, 22.

10. Personal e-mail exchange with Memory Biwa (University of Western Cape), January 11, 2012; and with Larissa Förster (University of Cologne), January 19, 2012.

11. This perception was shored up by the fact that there had been no peace negotiation or treaty. Krüger, *Kriegsbewältigung und Geschichtsbewusstsein*, 183.

12. Henrichsen, "Pastoral Modernity," 87–88.

13. Bley, *Kolonialherrschaft*, 313. For an analysis of how German soldiers remembered their experiences of the war, see Krüger, *Kriegsbewältigung und Geschichtsbewusstsein*, 82–103. On the impact of the war on German military culture, see Hull, *Absolute Destruction*, 131–96.

14. For the counterargument in favor of a continuity across the caesura of the war, see Zimmerer, *Deutsche Herrschaft*, 13–14, 282–83.

15. Bley, *Kolonialherrschaft*, 189, 193.

16. Krüger, *Kriegsbewältigung und Geschichtsbewusstsein*, 133.

17. Vice Governor Brückner to Magistrate Frankenberg (District Office Omaruru), 10.11.1910, BArch-B, R 1002/2553, 41.

18. For instance, report by Cpt. Bender (Schutztruppe), 22.09.1907, BArch-B, R 1002/2707, 36–40; farmer Lerm to District Office Keetmanshoop, 20.01.1909, BArch-B, R 1002/2693, 23–25; report by Lt. Petter (Schutztruppe), 23.02.1909, BArch-B, R 1001/1914, 104–5.

19. Report by Magistrate Karl Schmidt (District Office Keetmanshoop) to Gouv. DSWA, 09.02.1909, BArch-B, R 1002/2693, 21.

20. Ibid.; Sergeant Dufring believed in a transnational conspiracy of human trafficking: Sgt. Dufring (Police Station Okahandja) to District Office Okahandja, 16.02.1908, BArch-B, R 1002/2708, 19–37.

21. Luise White, *Speaking with Vampires* (Berkeley 2000), 57.

22. Krüger, *Kriegsbewältigung und Geschichtsbewußtsein*, 162.

23. Gewald, *Herero Heroes*, 229.

24. Larissa Förster, *Postkoloniale Erinnerungslandschaften* (Frankfurt a.M. 2010), 181.

25. Zollmann, *Koloniale Herrschaft*, 14–17. Parliament had the power to review the budget, however. Matthew Fitzpatrick observes that German Southwest Africa was a "kind of 'anomalous legal zone'" that nevertheless "partially shared and was partially excised from the 'legal repertoire' of the metropolitan *Rechtsstaat*," carrying some "German law into an extra-constitutional space." *Purging the Empire* (Oxford 2015), 233.

26. Häußler, "'Collaboration' or Sabotage?," 169. For comparisons between British and other colonial states, see John L. Comaroff, "Reflections on the Colonial State, in South Africa and Elsewhere," *Social Identities: Journal for the Study of Race, Nation and Culture* 4, no. 3 (1998): 321–61; Ulrike Lindner, "Colonialism as a European Project in Africa before 1914?," in *Ordering the Colonial World around the 20th Century*, ed. Sebastian Conrad (Leipzig 2009), 88–106; Crawford Young, *The African Colonial State in Comparative Perspective* (New Haven 1994), 99–105.

27. Albert Frederick Calvert, *South-West Africa during the German Occupation, 1884–1914* (London 1915), 7–8.

28. See particularly Zimmerer, *Deutsche Herrschaft*.

29. Zollmann, *Koloniale Herrschaft*, 14–17.

30. Freytag (IdL) to Blumhagen (District Office Swakopmund), 29.11.1907, BArch-B, R 1002/2553, 12–13; Blumhagen (District Office Swakopmund) to Gouv. DSWA, 21.10.1907, BArch-B, R 1002/2692, no page number; transcript of Berlin police regulation book (1899), NAN, Bezirksamt Swakopmund (hereafter BSW), 125 UA.26/1. For further references to police forces in the German motherland, notably the Prussian and the Württemberg Gendarmerie, cf. Governor Schuckmann to RKA, 04.10.1909, BArch-B, R 1002/2692, 124. Cf. also Zollmann, *Koloniale Herrschaft*, 43.

31. Vice Governor Hintrager to RKA, 02.01.1909, BArch-B, R 1002/2692, 5; Governor Schuckmann to RKA, 04.10.1909, BArch-B, R 1002/2692, 124; Conze (RKA) to Gouv. DSWA, 17.01.1913, BArch-B, R 1002/2429, 2; Chief of Police Heydebreck to Vice Governor Hintrager, 17.03.1909, BArch-B, R 1002, 2703, 7; Chief of Police Heydebreck to General Consul Cape Town, 07.04.1909, BArch-B, R 1002/2703, 22. For knowledge transfer between the British and the German authorities regarding aspects of state rule other than policing, see U. Lindner, *Koloniale Begegnungen*.

32. Policemen also had military superiors, the so-called inspection officers, who were responsible for military discipline, training, and deployment.

33. Vice Governor Hintrager to IdL, 03.01.1910, BArch-B, R 1002/2552, 4. Cf. Jürgen Zimmerer on the unwillingness of local administrators to burden themselves with more work and more decrees. "Der totale Überwachungsstaat?," in *Von Windhuk nach Auschwitz?* (Berlin 2011), 107–17.

34. "Bestimmungen über die Organisation der Landespolizei," 01.03.1905, BArch-B, R 1002/3506, 6–9, published in *Deutsche Kolonialgesetzgebung* 9 (1905): 64–69. For

the history leading up to the official creation of the Landespolizei in 1905, see Zoll-mann, *Koloniale Herrschaft*, 33–41.

35. "Bestimmungen des Reichs-Kolonialamts für die Landesbeamten und sonsti-gen Angestellten in den Schutzgebieten" (1907), in *Deutsche Kolonialgesetzgebung* 11 (1907): 386–92; "Reichsbeamtengesetz" (1907), *Reichsgesetzblatt* 24 (1907): 245–78; "Kolonialbeamtengesetz" (1910), *Reichsgesetzblatt* 37 (1910): 881–96; "Schutztruppen-Ordnung" (1896), *Reichsgesetzblatt* 23 (1896): 653–59; "Mannschaftsverordnungsge-setz" (1906), *Deutsche Kolonialgesetzgebung* 10 (1906): 218–34. Summaries and commentary in Tesch, *Die Laufbahn der deutschen Kolonialbeamten*, 106–15, 414–49.

36. "Verordnung betreffend die Rechtsverhältnisse der Landespolizei in Deutsch-Südwestafrika," 04.10.1907, BArch-B, R 1002/2692, 113–14, published in *Deutsche Ko-lonialgesetzgebung* 11 (1907): 395–96. It went into effect retroactively on April 1, 1907.

37. Internal note, Chief of Police Heydebreck to Gouv. DSWA, 25.09.1907, BArch-B, R 1002/2693, 89; Gouv. DSWA to all district offices, 25.09.1907, BArch-B, R 1002/2693, 89. The initial text was drafted in July: "Entwurf betr. die Organisation der Landespolizei. Im Anschluß an die Denkschrift Beilage I. zur zweiten Ergänzung zum Etat für das Südwestafrikanische Schutzgebiet," 02.07.1907, BArch-B, R 1002/2693, 120–45.

38. Vice Governor Hintrager to RKA, 02.01.1909, BArch-B, R 1002/2692, 3–6.

39. Commander Glasenapp (Schutztruppe) to State Secretary Lindequist, 28.07.1909, BArch-B, R 1002/2692, 116–18; Commander Estorff (Schutztruppe) to IdL, 08.06.1909, BArch-B, R 1002/2692, 68.

40. Meeting notes, Gouv. SWA, 12.08.1908, BArch-B, R 1001/1914, 43–44; Vice Governor Hintrager to IdL, 16.09.1908, BArch-B, R 1002/2693, 3–6.

41. For the main arguments, see State Secretary Dernburg to Gouv. SWA, 05.04.1909, BArch-B, R 1002/2692, 7–11; Commander Estorff (Schutztruppe) to IdL, 08.06.1909, BArch-B, R 1002/2692, 68; Golinelli (RKA) to State Secretary Lindequist, 30.07.1909, BArch-B, R 1002/2692, 119–20; Governor Schuckmann to RKA, 18.06.1909, BArch-B, R 1002/2692, 69–72; Governor Schuckmann to RKA, 04.10.1909, BArch-B, R 1002/2692, 121–27. For more detail on this, see Zollmann, "Die Kolonialpolizei," 94–102.

42. Vice Governor Hintrager to RKA, 02.01.1909, BArch-B, R 1002/2692, 5. Re-garding the three concerns enumerated here, see notes by Chief of Police Heyde-breck, 29.07.1907, BArch-B, R 1002/2692, no page number; Governor Schuckmann to Schutztruppe Command, 21.09.1907, BArch-B, R 1002/2497, 28; Magistrate Blumhagen (District Office Swakopmund) to Gouv. DSWA, 21.10.1907, BArch-B, R 1002/2692, no page number; Governor Schuckmann to RKA, 09.09.1908, BArch-B, R 1002/2467, 9; State Secretary Dernburg to Gouv. SWA, 05.04.1909, BArch-B, R 1002/2692, 7–11; Governor Schuckmann to RKA, 18.06.1909, BArch-B, R 1002/2692, 15–22.

43. Governor Schuckmann to RKA, 04.10.1909, BArch-B, R 1002/2692, 125.

44. Filed in BArch-B, R 1002/2692. Zollmann, "Die Kolonialpolizei," 313–14.

45. Vice Governor Hintrager to RKA, 02.01.1909, BArch-B, R 1002/2692, 5.

46. Gouv. DSWA to RKA, 18.06.1909, BArch-B, R 1002/2692, 20.

47. Circular by Governor Seitz to all district offices and police depots, 04.09.1909, BArch-B, R 1002/2553, 101.

48. §§4–7, *Dienstvorschrift*, 6–8. Metropolitan police stressed appearance and for-mality as well. The entire first part of an instruction manual (1886) for the Prussian police forces focused exclusively on proper saluting, hierarchies, and obedience. Only

one of the thirty-nine articles within this first section gave advice on proper behavior toward the public, simply stating that it was to be "polite and obliging." Otto Held, *Die bestehende Organisation und die erforderliche Reorganisation der preußischen Polizei Verwaltung mit Rücksicht auf die wünschenswerthe Erweiterung derselben zur Deutschen Reichspolizei* (1886), cited in Reinke, "'Armed as If for a War,'" 55.

49. *Dienstvorschrift*, 8.

50. Annex 4, ibid., 51–55.

51. Ibid., 38. This order of priorities is also given to the inspection officers; ibid., 49.

52. Ibid., 38.

53. Ibid., 9.

54. Ibid., 9, 12.

55. Ibid., 9.

56. Ibid., 12.

57. Ibid., 9–12.

58. Ibid., 9–10.

59. "That master noun of modern political discourse, *state*, has at least three etymological themes diversely condensed within it: status, in the sense of station, standing, rank, condition—*estate* . . . ; pomp, in the sense of splendor, display, dignity, presence—*stateliness* . . . ; and governance, in the sense of regnancy, regime, dominion, mastery—*statecraft*. . . . And it is characteristic of that discourse, and of its modernness, that the third of these meanings, the last to arise . . . , should have to come to dominate the term as to obscure our understanding of the multiplex nature of high authority. Impressed with command, we see little else." Clifford Geertz, *Negara* (Princeton 1980), 121.

60. *Dienstvorschrift*, 13–15.

61. Draft by Chief of Police Heydebreck, no date [ca. September 1907], BArch-B, R 1002/2692, 13; and draft by Chief of Police Heydebreck, no date [ca. mid-1908], BArch-B, R 1002/2692, no page number.

62. Notes in the margin might have provided reasons for editing one of the two passages out, but unfortunately they were written with pencil and were later erased.

63. *Dienstvorschrift*, 13–14.

64. Ibid., 14.

65. Ibid., 14–15.

66. Ibid., 15.

67. Ibid., 14.

68. District Office Swakopmund had equipped itself with several police handbooks from the homeland, for instance, from Berlin (1899). NAN, BSW, 125 UA.26/1, 1–30. Police headquarters in Windhuk got interested in these around the time it drafted its own manual. See Freytag (IdL) to Magistrate Blumhagen (District Office Swakopmund), 29.11.1907, BArch-B, R 1002/2553, 12–13. Moreover, I found a copy of another police manual, from Halle (1891), in the files of police headquarters. BArch-B, R 1002/2693, 64.

69. *Dienstvorschrift*, 26–33.

70. The colonized are explicitly mentioned in this last section, but only as an exception to the rule, and only once. When listing the different variables that have to apply before an arrest can take place, Africans are listed as the one category where no prerequisites are necessary. Ibid., 27.

71. They show up only once in the annex, and there only to specify their equipment. Ibid., 39–42.

72. See Zollmann, who elaborates on the discussion among officials regarding African policemen's status as civil servants. *Koloniale Herrschaft*, 64.

73. Notes by Chief of Police Heydebreck, 29.07.1907, BArch-B, R 1002/2692, no page number.

74. See, for instance, Transportation Bureau Schutztruppe to Police Station Keetmanshoop, 28.12.1909, NAN, BKE, 201 B.II.66.c (vol. 1), 7.

75. Decree by Chief of Police Bethe, 18.04.1911, BArch-B, R 1002/2591, 37.

76. Draft of a circular by Chief of Police Bethe to all district offices, 13.07.1914, BArch-B, R 1002/2432, no page number.

77. On German comparisons with the British colonial neighbors of the Cape Colony, see U. Lindner, *Koloniale Begegnungen*.

78. Inspection Officer Medding (Police Depot Spitzkoppe) to IdL, 11.03.1914, BArch-B, R 1002/2594, 14–18.

79. Draft of a circular by Chief of Police Bethe to all district offices, 13.07.1914, BArch-B, R 1002/2432, no page number.

80. Magistrate Zastrow to IdL, 01.10.1907, BArch-B, R 1002/2692, no page number.

81. Magistrate Schulze from Grootfontein suggested that he would write his own regulations. IdL to Magistrate Schulze (District Office Grootfontein), 10.03.1908, BArch-B, R 1002/2553, 95–96; Magistrate Schulze (District Office Grootfontein) to IdL, 20.06.1908, BA-B, R 1002/2692, no page number. Police headquarters had to appease several district offices. See, for example, District Office Maltahöhe to IdL, no date, BArch-B, R 1002/2553, 123; IdL to District Office Omaruru, 29.06.1908, BArch-B, R 1002/2553, 177–78.

82. State Secretary Dernburg to Gouv. SWA, 05.04.1909, BArch-B, R 1002/2692, 7–11.

83. For an early example, see Inspection Officer Müller, who reported that Sergeant Hapke, whom he had deployed to Otjiswa, had repeatedly asked for instructions from the district office but had never received any and thus could not do his job. Inspection Officer Müller to IdL, 12.11.1907, BArch-B, R 1002/2553, 7. By September 1909 some police stations had still not received their manuals. Circular by Governor Seitz to all district offices and police depots, 04.09.1909, BArch-B, R 1002/2553, 101.

84. Vice Governor Hintrager to IdL, 03.01.1910, BArch-B, R 1002/2552, 4.

85. State Secretary Solf to Gouv. SWA, 23.05.1912, BArch-B, R 1002/2417, 32.

86. Governor Schuckmann to RKA, 09.09.1908, BArch-B, R 1002/2467, 9; decree by Governor Seitz, 05.08.1911, BArch-B, R 1002/2596, 5.

87. I do not think that the emphasis on values such as honor or respectability that dictated restraint and moderation was hypocrisy or lip service to appease a liberal public, as Lüdtke has argued regarding a similar discourse in Prussian police handbooks of the mid-nineteenth century. To the contrary, I believe that those were honestly intended counsels understood to be much more helpful than any practical step-by-step guide. Cf. Lüdtke, *"Gemeinwohl," Polizei und "Festungspraxis,"* 318.

88. Magistrate Todt (District Office Windhuk) to IdL, 04.11.1912, NAN, Zentralbureau des kaiserlichen Gouvernements (hereafter ZBU), 108, A.III.e.1, 126, cited in Zollmann, *Koloniale Herrschaft*, 277.

89. State Secretary Lindequist to Gouv. SWA, 27.08.1910, BArch-B, R 1002/2502, 79–80.

90. *Dienstvorschrift*, 23.

91. Ibid., 22.

92. Chief of Police Bethe to all district offices and police depots, 24.02.1911, BArch-B, R 1002/2693, 131–32. On the conflict between inspection officers and magistrates, see also Zollmann, *Koloniale Herrschaft*, 44–48.

93. District Chief Frankenberg (District Office Omaruru) to IdL, 29.10.1907, BArch-B, R 1002/2508, 26–27.

94. Commander Estorff (Schutztruppe) to Gouv. SWA, 30.11.1907, BArch-B, R 1002/2706, 3.

95. Police Depot Bethanien to IdL, 31.10.1911, BArch-B, R 1002/2694, 51.

96. Zimmerer, *Deutsche Herrschaft*; Zollmann, *Koloniale Herrschaft*.

97. Cf. District Chief Frankenberg (District Office Omaruru) to IdL, 09.01.1908, BArch-B, R 1002/2508, 159; District Chief Frankenberg (District Office Omaruru) to Gouv. SWA, 29.10.1907, BArch-B, R 1002/2508, 26–27; Inspection Officer Hildebrandt (Depot Waterberg) to IdL, 28.03.1908, BArch-B, R 1002/2535, 134–36.

98. However, the size of European police forces did expand drastically over the long term. On the deployment of military for police work, see Anja Johansen, *Soldiers as Police* (Aldershot 2005). On discussions regarding the size of police forces within German and French administrations, see Berlière and Levy, *Histoire des polices en France*, 63–66; Ralph Jessen, *Polizei im Industrierevier* (Göttingen 1991), 127–37.

99. See, for instance, Magistrate Schenke (District Office Swakopmund) to Gouv. SWA, 13.07.1908, BArch-B, R 1002/2708, 151–52; Rafalski, *Vom Niemandsland*, 31ff.

100. Magistrate Wasserfall (District Office Bethanien) to Police Depot Spitzkoppe, 29.11.1909, BArch-B, R 1002/2519, 6–7; Magistrate Wasserfall (District Office Bethanien) to IdL, 06.02.1911, BArch-B, R 1002, 2519, 25; Magistrate Roebern (District Office Bethanien) to IdL, 02.07.1912, BArch-B, R 1002/2519, 75–76.

101. Rafalski, *Vom Niemandsland*, 72.

102. Memorandum regarding the size of the military and police forces in German Southwest Africa, in *Stenographische Berichte des Reichstags*, vol. 242 (1907), annex 397, addendum I, 28–30; Chief of Police Heydebreck, "Entwurf betr. die Organisation der Landespolizei. Im Anschluß an die Denkschrift Beilage I. zur zweiten Ergänzung zum Etat für das Südwestafrikanische Schutzgebiet," 02.07.1907, BArch-B, R 1002/2693, 120–45; Chief of Police Heydebreck to Gouv. SWA, 14.05.1909, BArch-B, R 1002/2672, 7. Cf. Rafalski, who erroneously lists an authorized strength of over seven hundred men for 1907 through 1911, of six hundred for 1912, and of five hundred for 1913 and 1914; *Vom Niemandsland*, 72.

103. The 1908 annual report already lists 16 staff sergeants and 278 sergeants. Annual report IdL, 08.05.1908, BArch-B, R 1002/2672, 2. The 1909 annual report claims that the authorized strength of 470 was met in October 1908. Annual report IdL, 14.05.1909, BArch-B, R 1002/2672, 7.

104. For numbers by years, see budget of IdL, no date, BArch-B, R 1002/47, 160; report by RKA, 16.04.[1912], BArch-B, R 1001/1914, 200; register of the members of the Landespolizei, 1909–1913, BArch-B, R 1002/2485, 4–140; statistical survey of the Landepolizei, 1903–1912, 15.09.13, BArch-B, R 1002/2429, 12–15; budget for "native

workers and police" by Hensel (IdL), 19.03.1914, BArch-B, R 1002/2593, 1–4. Cf. Rafalski, *Vom Niemandsland*, 72, 102; Zollmann, *Koloniale Herrschaft*, 46, 69; Zimmerer, *Deutsche Herrschaft*, 297.

105. For population numbers, see Walther, *Creating Germans Abroad*, 24–25; Zimmerer, *Deutsche Herrschaft*, 110. Not the entire colony was policed, however. The Landespolizei limited its activity to the so-called Police Zone, in which settlers could buy property and expect protection. The existence of the Police Zone—and of the "Red Line" that delimited it—remained a little-known fact to the public. It was visible only on colonial authorities' maps. On the history of this internal border in the north of the colony, see Miescher, *Namibia's Red Line*.

106. Anderson and Killingray, "Consent, Coercion and Control," 6; Blanchard, Bloembergen, and Lauro, "Tensions of Policing in Colonial Situations," 20–21; Blanchard and Glasman, "Le maintien de l'ordre dans l'empire français," 27–28.

107. André-Paul Comor, "Implantation et missions de la gendarmerie en Algérie, de la conquête à la colonisation (1830–1914)," in *Gendarmerie, état et société au XIXe siècle*, ed. Jean Noël Luc (Paris 2002), 191.

108. Richard Meinertzhagen, *Kenya Diary*, 1957 (repr., London 1983), 32. However, in the 1950s, Kenya became one of the most heavily policed African colonies. David M. Anderson, "Policing the Settler State," in *Contesting Colonial Hegemony*, ed. Dagmar Engels and Shula Marks (London 1994), 251.

109. For a breakdown of police density in relation to population numbers and size of territory in the Prussian provinces at the turn of the century, see table 5 in Jessen, *Polizei im Industrierevier*, 358; cf. also Jürgen W. Schmidt, *Polizei in Preussen im 19. Jahrhundert* (Ludwigsfelde 2011), 13; Reinke, "'Armed as If for a War,'" 63.

110. Jessen, *Polizei im Industrierevier*, 357; Zollmann, *Koloniale Herrschaft*, 218.

111. Minutes of a meeting with State Secretary Dernburg, Governor Schuckmann, and Head of Police Heydebreck,16.09.1908, BArch-B, R 1002/2693, 4.

112. Magistrate Schulze (District Office Grootfontein) to IdL, 23.12.1908, BArch-B, R 1002/2694, 20–22.

113. List of police stations by IdL, 25.01.1911, BArch-B, R 1002/2670, 59–61. For a similar, slightly reduced list, without personnel numbers, published 1912 in the official journal of German Southwest Africa, see Zollmann, *Koloniale Herrschaft*, 353.

114. List of police stations by IdL, 25.01.1911, BArch-B, R 1002/2670, 59–61; cf. Rafalski, *Vom Niemandsland*, 73–75, 120.

115. See, for instance, patrol book, Police Depot Waterberg, 02.01.1914, BArch-B, R 1002/2711, 54.

116. Memorandum on the Landespolizei, in *Stenographische Berichte des Reichstags*, vol. 242 (1907), annex 397, addendum I, 30.

117. Probably because it revealed too much about the police force's dependency on African policemen, the second part of the sentence was struck out of the final draft. Annual report (1908) by Chief of Police Heydebreck, 14.05.1909, BArch-B, R 1002/2672, 11. See also the 1910 annual report, which stated that African personnel were "utterly inadequate." Annual report, IdL, 14.05.1911, BArch-B, R 1002/2672, 59.

118. Report by Magistrate Vietsch (District Office Rehoboth), 05.02.1912, NAN, BRE, 75 L.2.f, 1–2 (new series); Magistrate Vietsch (District Office Rehoboth) to IdL, 01.02.1913, NAN, BRE, 75 L.2.f, 44. For a detailed account, see Schepp, *Unter dem Kreuz des Südens*, 141–44.

119. Comor, "Implantation et missions"; Peter Gibbs and Hugh Phillips, *The History of the British South Africa Police, 1889–1980* (North Ringwood, AU 2000); Albert Grundlingh, "'Protectors and Friends of the People'?," in *Policing the Empire*, ed. David M. Anderson and David Killingray (Manchester, UK 1991), 168–82; Killingray, "The Maintenance of Law and Order in British Colonial Africa," 415; Damien Lorcy, *Sous le régime du sabre* (Rennes 2011); Spencer, "Polices impériales."

120. Anderson, "Policing the Settler State"; Mathieu Deflem, "Law Enforcement in British Colonial Africa," *Police Studies* 17, no. 1 (1994): 45–68; Lewis H. Gann, *The Birth of a Plural Society* (Manchester, UK 1958), 74–75. Unfortunately, there is no English-language scholarship on policing in the Portuguese settler colonies Angola and Mozambique.

121. Anderson and Killingray, "Consent, Coercion and Control," 7; John D. Brewer, *Black and Blue* (Oxford 1994), 6–10.

122. RKA to the Governor of Cameroon, 24.11.1911, BArch-B, R 1002/2424, 19.

123. Governor Schuckmann to RKA, 18.06.1909, BArch-B, R 1002/2692, 15.

124. Annual report (1909), IdL, 25.05.1910, BArch-B, R 1002/2672, 27–28.

125. Each German policeman had to provide his military roll excerpt on which penalties were registered.

126. State Secretary Lindequist to Gouv. SWA, 09.03.1911, BArch-B, R 1002/2427, 65.

127. Circular by Chief of Police Bethe to all district offices, depots, and officer posts, 29.12.1913, BArch-B, R 1002/2594, 3, and corresponding replies, BArch-B, R 1002/2594, 4–31.

128. BArch-B, R 1002/2594, 4–31.

129. Ibid., and disciplinary records in personnel files, BArch-B, R 1002/91–1957 and BArch-B, R 1002/2804–3591.

130. Chief of Police Bethe to District Office Grootfontein, 02.11.1911, BArch-B, R 1002/3483, 48.

131. Magistrate Böhmer from district Lüderitzbucht, for instance, was quite good at deploying men where their skills were needed. That inspection officers should be aware of this and deploy accordingly was stated in a circular to all police depots. Governor Schuckmann to all inspection officers, 23.06.1909, BArch-B, R 1002/2693, 57. See also the case of Sgt. Wernicke, who was annoyed to be constantly redeployed to places because his skills were needed. Letter by Magistrate Zastrow (District Office Großfontein) to Sgt. Otto Wernicke (Police Station Nurgas), 07.02.1911, BArch-B, R 1002/2465, 28–31.

132. Hermann Strunck to Johann Strunck, 26.09.1910 (private archive of Strunck family), cited in Budack, *Raubmord 1912*, 9.

133. See, for instance, District Chief Frankenberg (District Office Omaruru) to IdL, 18.09.1910, BArch-B, R 1002/3226, 56; report by Roebern (IdL), 18.11.1909, NAN, BRE, 75 L.2.h, 15; and circular by Chief of Police Bethe, 25.03.1911, NAN, BRE, 75 L.2.h, 31. On the bad condition of firearms, see chapter 3.

134. Request for transfer by Sgt. Paul Gentz (Police Station Aninus) to District Chief Struwe (District Office Hasuur), 29.01.1914, BArch-B, R 1002/2992.

135. Annual report 1910, IdL, 14.05.1911, BArch-B, R 1002/2672, 68. Zollmann, *Koloniale Herrschaft*, 299–300.

136. For a variety of photographs illustrating this desire, see Schepp, *Unter dem Kreuz des Südens*.

137. Internal report by Gouv. SWA, 16.04.1912, BArch-B, R 1001/1914, 200; Rafal-ski, *Vom Niemandsland*, 72.

138. District Office Outjo to Depot Waterberg, 10.03.1910, BArch-B, R 1002/2507, 19.

139. Ibid.

140. Patrol report by Sgt. Dufring (Police Station Okahandja) to District Office Okahandja, 16.02.1908, BArch-B, R 1002/2708, 19–37.

141. Annual report 1909/1910 by Inspection Officer Freytag (Police Depot Kub), 01.04.1910, BArch-B, R 1002/2672, 51–52.

142. Medical report on Sgt. Makosch by Dr. Zachlehner, 01.12.1908, BArch-B, R 1002/3219, 30–31.

143. Circular by Vice Governor Brückner to all district offices, 31.07.1910, NAN, BSW, 85 L.2.c, 13.

144. Patrol report by Sgt. Xaver Hagner (Police Station Okaukwejo), 20.10.1913, BArch-B, R 1002/2711, 68–69; cf. patrol report by Sen. Staff Sgt. Wilhelm Schweizer (Police Station Grootfontein), 05.10.1911, BArch-B, R 1002/2793, 59–62.

145. Space is one of Zollmann's main analytical frameworks. *Koloniale Herrschaft*, 213–340. On living and working conditions of policemen, see also chapter 8 of his dissertation, "Die Kolonialpolizei," esp. 156–66, 185–94.

146. Patrol report by Sgt. Albert Link (Police Station Gobabis), 30.09.1910, BArch-B, R 1002/2709, 232–33.

147. Patrol book for January to March 1911 (Police Depot Spitzkoppe), 01.04.1911, BArch-B, R 1002/2710, 32–43. On everyday routines of the police, see also chapter 4.

148. According to regulations, inspection officers had to inspect each station in their assigned area every three months, senior staff sergeants every month. *Dienstan-weisung*, 38, 49.

149. On "going native" and "tropical frenzy," see Felix Axster, "Die Angst vor dem 'Verkaffern,'" *WerkstattGeschichte* 39 (2005): 39–53; Eva Bischoff, *Kannibale-Werden* (Bielefeld 2011).

150. Report by Inspection Officer Freytag (Police Depot Spitzkoppe), 07.05.1909, BArch-B, R 1002/2723, no page number.

151. Annual report 1909/1910 by Inspection Officer Freytag (Police Depot Kub), 01.04.1910, BArch-B, R 1002/2672, 51.

152. On police training, see also Zollmann, "Die Kolonialpolizei," 119–21.

153. Report by Inspection Officer Hollaender (Police Depot Kub), 06.01.1908, BArch-B, R 1002/2535, 30, 64.

154. See annual report 1908 by Inspection Officer Hollaender (Police Depot Kub), 24.04.1909, BArch-B, R 1002/2672, 14–17; Chief of Police Heydebreck to Police De-pots Kupferberg, Kub, and Waterberg, 27.01.1910, BArch-B, R 1002/2534, 12.

155. Written exam by Sgt. Bruno Elsner, 21.12.1909, BArch-B, R 1002/2534, 9–11; Chief of Police Heydebreck to Depot Spitzkoppe, 27.01.1910, BArch-B, R 1002/2534, 12.

156. Acting Magistrate Krafft (District Office Outjo) to IdL, 17.02.1910, BArch-B, R 1002/2535, 16.

157. District Chief Frankenberg (District Office Omaruru) to Vice Governor Brückner, 03.11.1910, BArch-B, R 1002/2553, 39.

158. See the files pertaining to "recommendations and assignment orders to train-ing in Windhuk (1908–1915)," BArch-B, R 1002/2536. For examples of men not being sent to police school for various reasons, see Chief of Police Heydebreck to all district

offices and depots, 10.03.1909, and replies by District Offices Windhuk, Omaruru, and Gobabis, BArch-B, R 1002/2536, 153, 156, 157, 161.

159. Chief of Police Bethe to District Office Bethanien, 02.09.1910, BArch-B, R 1002/2536, 54; Chief of Police Heydebreck to District Chief Wasserfall (District Office Bethanien), 27.01.1909, BArch-B, R 1002/2796, 74.

160. Recommendation by District Chief Beyer (District Office Warmbad), 05.07.1912, BArch-B, R 1002/2536, 203. See also the positive qualification certificate by Inspection Officer Freytag (Police Depot Kub), 08.09.1909, BArch-B, R 1002/1184, 39. For the disciplinary proceedings against Sgt. Melzer, see reprimand by District Chief Runck (District Office Warmbad), 28.07.1908, BArch-B, R 1002/1184, 24; report by Magistrate Schmidt (District Office Keetmanshoop), 23.02.1909, BArch-B, R 1002/2783, 118–19; inquiry by RKA, 30.08.1909, BArch-B, R 1002/2466, 11; report by Inspection Officer Medding (Police Depot Spitzkoppe) to District Chief Beyer (District Office Warmbad), 10.12.1913, BArch-B, R 1002/1184, no page number.

161. Recommendation by District Chief Beyer (District Office Warmbad), 05.07.1912, BArch-B, R 1002/2536, 203.

162. See chapter 3.

163. For instance, letter regarding salute of six policemen by Chief of Police Heinrich Bethe to Cpt. Saurma (Schutztruppe), 07.06.1911, BArch-B, R 1002/2467, 35.

164. Commander Heydebreck (Schutztruppe) to IdL, 06.07.1914, BArch-B, R 1002/2465, 98–101.

165. See, for instance, inspection report by Chief of Police Heydebreck to Gouv. SWA, 01.02.1909, BArch-B, R 1002/2693, 4. The German military paid equal heed to the physical appearance of its soldiers. In 1904, General Headquarters decided that soldiers were not allowed to weigh more than 140 pounds. Kuß, *Deutsches Militär*, 143.

166. See, for instance, application by policeman Otto Olkiewicz, 12.03.1912, BArch-B, R 1002/2501, 99.

167. While Zollmann suggests that missionary schools were the most formative institution for the African police staff, Dag Henrichsen puts forward that the military was the main socializer of African policemen. Henrichsen, "Ozombambuse and Ovasolondate"; Zollmann, *Koloniale Herrschaft*, 70–71.

168. Decree by Chief of Police Bethe, 18.04.1911, NAN, BKE, 201 B.II.66.c (vol. 1), 72; report by Sgt. Johann Slottke (District Office Keetmanshoop), 01.05.1911, NAN, BKE, 201 B.II.66.c (vol. 1), 72v.

169. Circular by Chief of Police Bethe, 08.11.1910, BArch-B, R 1002/2604, 2.

170. Circular by Chief of Police Bethe, 17.03.1914, BArch-B, R 1002/2604, 5. On the use of weapons by African policemen, see also chapter 3.

171. Chief of Police Heydebreck to Magistrate Schulze (District Office Grootfontein), 27.10.1908, BArch-B, R 1002/3219, 34.

172. Inspection Officer Hollaender (Police Depot Kub) to IdL, 23.10.1908, BArch-B, R 1002/2799, 18.

173. Ibid.

174. Circular by Chief of Police Heydebreck to all police depots, 12.11.1908, BArch-B, R 1002/2534, 82.

175. Qualification certificate for Constable Türk by Inspection Officer Hollaender (Police Depot Kupferberg), 01.01.1911, BArch-B, R 1002/3513, 13.

176. Qualification certificates for Sgt. Thelen by Magistrate Brill (District Office Lüderitzbucht), 26.04.1910, BArch-B, R 1002/3503, 31; and 22.08.1908, BArch-B, R 1002/3503, 14.

177. I have come across only one document that shows evidence of the desire to limit military training for the sake of more "theoretical" training, that is, writing exercises. See circular by Chief of Police Heydebreck to all police depots, 08.08.1908, BArch-B, R 1002/2534, 61.

178. Inspection Officer Hollaender (Police Depot Kub) to IdL, 21.03.1908, BArch-B, R 1002/2708, 64.

179. Homi Bhabha, "Of Mimicry and Man," October 28 (1984): 125–33.

180. Selmeci and Henrichsen, Das Schwarzkommando, 97.

181. Commander of transport section of the Schutztruppe to Police Station Keetmanshoop, 28.12.1909, NAN, BKE, 201 B.II.66.c (vol. 1), 7.

182. Sgt. Ehret to District Office Keetmanshoop, 29.09.1910, NAN, BKE, 201 B.II.66.c (vol. 1), 25.

183. Henrichsen, "Ozombambuse and Ovasolondate," 161–84; Krüger, Kriegsbewältigung und Geschichtsbewusstsein, 160–63; Wolfgang Werner, "'Playing Soldiers,'" Journal of Southern African Studies 16, no. 3 (1990): 476–502.

184. Henrichsen, "Ozombambuse and Ovasolondate," 182.

185. Förster, Postkoloniale Erinnerungslandschaften, 250.

186. Paul Stoller, Embodying Colonial Memories (New York 1995), 90.

187. Henrichsen, Herrschaft und Alltag, 294; Michels, Schwarze deutsche Kolonialsoldaten, 115. On its later function of providing unity and mutual support under South African rule, see Werner, "'Playing Soldiers.'"

188. Irle, Die Herero, 299.

189. Henrichsen, "Ozombambuse and Ovasolondate," 168.

190. Inspection Officer Hollaender (Police Depot Kub) to IdL, 02.08.1908, BArch-B, R 1002/2601, 8–9.

191. Inspection Officer Müller (Police Depot Kupferberg) to IdL, 18.06.1908, BArch-B, R 1002/2602, 4.

192. Müller (IdL) to Schutztruppe Command, 28.07.1908, BArch-B, R 1002/2598, 42.

193. Inspection Officer Freytag (IdL) to District Office Windhuk, 10.06.1908, BArch-B, R 1002/2598, 3.

194. Kurt Streitwolf, Der Caprivizipfel (1911), 138, cited in Schepp, Unter dem Kreuz des Südens, 139.

195. For a deconstruction of the loyalty myth regarding Askari in German East Africa, see Moyd, Violent Intermediaries, 207–12.

196. Letter by former Police Assistant Josef Frederik (Bethanien) to former Police Sgt. Bruno Vogel, 31.12.1927, cited in Schepp, Unter dem Kreuz des Südens, 532. See also letter by former Police Assistant Hermann (Windhoek) to former Police Sgt. Walter Kuck, 1928, published in Nachrichtenblatt des Verbandes der Polizeibeamten für die deutschen Kolonien e.V. 9, no. 3 (1928).

197. Confidential report by Hollaender (IdL) and collection of depositions, 12.11.1910, BArch-B, R 1002/2783, 131–60.

198. Reprimand of Sgt. Melzer by Magistrate Runck (District Office Warmbad), 28.07.1908, BArch-B, R 1002/1184, 24.

199. Vice Governor Hintrager to Sgt. Johann Sterzenbach (Police Station Choant-sas), 18.12.1912, BArch-B, R 1002/3483, 61.

200. See, for instance, an incident that occurred between Sgt. Max Kobert and Police Assistant Hendrik Frehse. Deposition by Sgt. Max Kobert and Police Assistant Hendrik Frehse (District Office Hasuur), 16.02.1910, NAN, DAR, 18 E.II.5, 16–18. Or depositions by Sgt. Wilhelm Wilhelmi and Police Assistant Lucas (Police Station Aninus), 19.02.1913, NAN, DAR, 4 E.4.d, no page number.

201. Circular by Chief of Police Bethe to all district offices and police depots, 29.12.1913, BArch-B, R 1002/2594, 3, and replies, BArch-B, R 1002/2594, 4–28.

202. Draft by Chief of Police Bethe to all district offices, 13.07.1914, BArch-B, R 1002/2432, no page number.

203. Inspection Officer Medding (Police Depot Spitzkoppe) to IdL, 11.03.1914, BArch-B, R 1002/2594, 17.

204. Ibid.; decree regarding salute for African policemen by Chief of Police Bethe, 18.04.1911, BArch-B, R 1002/2591, 37.

205. Zollmann, *Koloniale Herrschaft*, 64.

206. Deposition by Police Assistant van Wyk, 04.09.1912, NAN, BKE 292, U.A. 33.8, no page number. Also cited in Zollmann, *Koloniale Herrschaft*, 78.

207. On professionalism and professional honor among colonial soldiers, see Michels, *Schwarze deutsche Kolonialsoldaten*; Michelle Moyd, "'All People Were Barbarians to the Askari . . . ,'" in *Maji Maji*, ed. James Leonard Giblin and Jamie Monson (Leiden 2010), 149–79; Moyd, *Violent Intermediaries*.

208. Max Weber, *Wirtschaft und Gesellschaft* (Tübingen 2005), 183.

209. Ibid., 186–87. But Weber noted that "also the modern, public or private official always seeks and often enjoys toward the ruled a certain higher, 'ständisch' social esteem. His social status is guaranteed by particular criminal regulations." Ibid., 161.

210. Goldberg, *Honor, Politics, and the Law*, 4.

211. Ibid., 13.

212. Internal note (IdL), 16.03.1914, BArch-B, R 1002/2468, no page number; Blumhagen (Gouv. SWA) to District Office Rehoboth, 21.02.1914, BArch-B, R 1002/2468, no page number. On colonial respectability and honor, cf. H. Schmidt, "Who Is Master in the Colony?"; Smith, "Colonialism and the Culture of Respectability."

213. Vice Governor Hintrager to Native Commissioner Ferse (District Office Bethanien), 08.06.1910, BArch-B, R 1002/2466, 16–17.

214. Weber, *Wirtschaft und Gesellschaft*, 161.

215. Fanny Dufétel-Viste, "L'emploi d'indigènes dans une administration publique au sein de l'Empire colonial allemand," in *Empires et colonies*, ed. Christine de Gemeaux (Clermond-Ferrand 2010), 226.

216. Sen. Staff Sgt. Karl Schlink (District Office Warmbad) to Police Depot Spitzkoppe, 11.02.1913, BArch-B, R 1002/2596, 56. Emphasis added.

217. Ibid.

218. Report by Sgt. Julius Streibel (IdL), 30.11.1908, BArch-B, R 1002/2598, 55.

219. Ibid.

220. I elaborate on bureaucratic procedures of the police in chapters 4 and 5.

221. For a discussion of the relationship between regulation and weapons usage, see chapter 3.

222. Letter regarding policeman Kelz's commission to acquire the latest criminal investigation skills in the metropole by Vice Governor Oscar Hintrager (Gouv. SWA) to RKA, 10.05.1910, BArch-B, R 1002/3131, 119–20; District Chief Schneidenberger (District Office Okahandja) to IdL, 01.08.1910, BArch-B, R 1002/2670, 49. See also chapter 3.

223. Dag Henrichsen, "'Iss Worte!,'" in *Afrikanische Beziehungen, Netzwerke und Räume*, ed. Laurence Marfaing and Brigitte Reinwald (Münster 2001), 329–38; Werner Hillebrecht, "'Habe keinerlei Papiere in Deiner Kiste . . . ,'" *WerkstattGeschichte* 1 (1992): 57–58.

224. Gesine Krüger, *Schrift—Macht—Alltag* (Cologne 2009), esp. 174–84.

225. Hillebrecht, "'Habe keinerlei Papiere in Deiner Kiste . . .'"; Margaret J. Daymond, Dorothy Driver, and Sheila Meintjes, eds., *Women Writing Africa* (New York 2003), 157–58.

226. Henrichsen, "'Iss Worte!,'" 330.

227. Zollmann, *Koloniale Herrschaft*, 70–71.

228. Ibid., 71–73; Rafalski, *Vom Niemandsland*, 103–6.

229. Sgt. Karl Eckel (Police Station Holoog) to District Office Keetmanshoop, 15.06.1910, NAN, BKE, 201 B.II.66.c (vol. 1), 16.

230. Bourdieu, "The Sentiment of Honour in Kabyle Society," 207.

231. Jean Comaroff, *Body of Power, Spirit of Resistance* (Chicago 1985), 227.

232. Michels, *Schwarze deutsche Kolonialsoldaten*, 76. Based on this observation she argues that the war between Germans and Herero and Nama was all the more brutal because distinctions between colonial rulers and colonial subjects were not clear at all but rather ambiguous.

233. Stoler, *Along the Archival Grain*, 59.

234. Asking "what emotions do" rather than what they are, feminist political theorist Sara Ahmed suggests using the idea of "impression." The term carries the meaning of leaving a mark and allows her "to avoid making analytical distinctions between bodily sensation, emotion and thought as if they could be 'experienced' as distinct realms of human 'experience.'" *The Cultural Politics of Emotion* (New York 2004), 6.

235. Stoler, *Along the Archival Grain*, 66.

236. On "nervous states," see Nancy Rose Hunt, *A Nervous State* (Durham, NC 2016); Ulrike Lindner et al., eds., *Hybrid Cultures—Nervous States* (Amsterdam 2010).

237. Written exam by Sgt. K[. . .] [name illegible] (Police Depot Waterberg), 16.02.1909, BArch-B, R 1002/2538, 79.

3. Of Whips, Shackles, and Guns

1. On the idea of "civilizing mission," see Boris Barth and Jürgen Osterhammel, eds., *Zivilisierungsmissionen* (Konstanz 2005); Alice L. Conklin, *A Mission to Civilize* (Stanford 1997); Catherine Hall, *Civilising Subjects* (Chicago 2002).

2. On Western philosophy of history and its imperial undercurrents, see Dipesh Chakrabarty, *Provincializing Europe* (Princeton 2000). See also the interesting reinterpretation of Marx's concept of progress and imperialism in Kolja Lindner, "Marx's Eurocentrism," *Radical Philosophy* 161 (2010): 27–41.

3. Daniel R. Headrick, *The Tools of Empire* (New York 1981), 4. In a more recent publication, Headrick has qualified his stand on the role of technology claiming that it was "a necessary, if not sufficient, explanation for the New Imperialism in Africa and Asia." *Power over Peoples* (Princeton 2010), 2. The argument of technological determinism can also be found, to a certain extent, in William Kelleher Storey, *Guns, Race, and Power in Colonial South Africa* (Cambridge 2008).

4. For instance, Michael Adas, *Machines as the Measure of Men* (Ithaca, NY 1989); Michael Adas, *Dominance by Design* (Cambridge, MA 2006); John Ellis, *The Social History of the Machine Gun* (Baltimore 1986); Timothy Mitchell, *Rule of Experts* (Berkeley 2002).

5. For instance, Wiebe E. Bijker, Thomas Parke Hughes, and Trevor Pinch, eds., *The Social Construction of Technological Systems* (Cambridge, MA 1987); David Edgerton, *The Shock of the Old* (London 2006); Ruth Oldenziel, *Making Technology Masculine* (Amsterdam 1999).

6. On improvisation as a regularized police procedure, see chapter 4.

7. Class schedule for first cohort at the police school in Windhuk, 11.02.1908, BArch-B, R 1002/2537, 49; Chief of Police Heydebreck to Brüggemann (Gouv. SWA), 17.03.1909, BArch-B, R 1002/2537, 116–17; Rafalski, *Vom Niemandsland*, 99.

8. "Jiu-Jitsu in den Kolonien," *Deutsch-Südwestafrikanische Zeitung*, January 6, 1909.

9. "Runderlass des Gouverneurs von Deutsch-Südwestafrika betreffend die Vollziehung von Prügelstrafen," 22.12.1905, BArch-B, R 1002/2596, 20. See also the Colonial Office's 1896 general directive "Verfügung wegen Ausübung der Strafgerichtsbarkeit und der Disziplinargewalt gegenüber den Eingeborenen in Deutsch-Südwestafrika," 22.04.1896, BArch-B, R 1002/2596, 15.

The etymology of the term "sjambok" is intriguing. Apparently derived from the Javanese word *cambuk*, meaning any kind of whip made of hide, the term, spelled in Dutch *tjamboek*, was imported to South Africa by Dutch colonizers and colonized. There, the transliteration *sjambok* or *sjamboek* entered the Afrikaans language. Peter Arie Ferdinand van Veen and Nicoline van der Sijs, *Etymologisch Woordenboek* (Utrecht 1989), 686.

10. Decree by the Governor on the execution of corporal punishment, 22.12.1905, BArch-B, R 1002/2596, 20.

11. "Expression of white sovereignty": Stephen Peté and Annie Devenish, "Flogging, Fear and Food," *Journal of Southern African Studies* 31, no. 1 (2005): 12. Corporal punishment itself was the object of periodically recurring debate within the German Empire, notably when colonial administrators of the higher echelons tried to codify its execution. For an overview, see Martin Schröder, *Prügelstrafe und Züchtigungsrecht in den deutschen Schutzgebieten Schwarzafrikas* (Münster 1997). See also Glasman, *Les corps habillés*, 106–14; Rebekka Habermas, "Peitschen im Reichstag oder über den Zusammenhang von materieller und politischer Kultur," *Historische Anthropologie* 23, no. 3 (2015): 391–412; Harry Schwirck, "Law's Violence and the Boundary between Corporal Discipline and Physical Abuse in German South West Africa," *Akron Law Review* 36 (2002): 81–132; Trutz von Trotha, "'One for Kaiser,'" in *Studien zur Geschichte des deutschen Kolonialismus in Afrika*, ed. Peter Heine and Ulrich Van der Heyden (Pfaffenweiler 1995), 521–51; Zollmann, *Koloniale Herrschaft*, 107–26. All authors observe that regulation and practice differed vastly.

12. Model inventory list, IdL, sent to all district offices, 07.03.1912, BArch-B, R 1002/2562, 54–63; model inventory accounting of all police equipment, no date, BArch-B, R 1002/2562, no page number. See also inventories of police station Rehoboth, no date, NAN, BRE, 75 L.2.h.1 and L.2.h.4, no page number; inventories of Police Station Schlip, no date, NAN, BRE 75 L.2.h.2, no page number.

13. Statement by Staff Sgt. Bauer (District Office Warmbad), 17.03.1909, BArch-B, R 1002/2783, 70. Emphasis added.

14. Secret travel report by State Secretary Dernburg, Berlin, November 1907, BArch-B, R 1001/300, 34–53, cited in Fritz Ferdinand Müller, *Kolonien unter der Peitsche* (Berlin 1962), 29; Schröder, *Prügelstrafe*, 90–91. Although Dernburg talked about German East Africa, the situation was most likely similar in German Southwest Africa.

15. On the meanings of the whip and the agency it developed in the capital, notably in Parliament and the press, see Habermas, "Peitschen im Reichstag."

16. Photographs of beatings and the postcard are published in Wolfram Hartmann, *Hues between Black and White* (Windhoek 2004), 67; Gesine Krüger, "Koloniale Gewalt, Alltagserfahrungen und Überlebensstrategien," in *Namibia–Deutschland, eine geteilte Geschichte*, ed. Larissa Förster, Dag Henrichsen, and Michael Bollig (Cologne 2004), 94–95.

17. Habermas argues that the whip's presence in Parliament had the effect of scandalizing excessive corporal punishment, rendering the use of such devices exceptional, and thus effaced the fact that it was a normalized and daily practice. Habermas, "Peitschen im Reichstag," 393.

18. "Verfügung betreffend die Anwendung körperlicher Züchtigung als Strafmittel gegen Eingeborene der afrikanischen Schutzgebiete," 12.07.1907, BArch-B, R 1002/2596, 22.

19. "Verfügung wegen Ausübung der Strafgerichtsbarkeit und der Disziplinargewalt gegenüber den Eingeborenen in Deutsch-Südwestafrika," 22.04.1896, BArch-B, R 1002/2596, 15. Cf. also "Verfügung betreffend die Anwendung körperlicher Züchtigung als Strafmittel gegen Eingeborene der afrikanischen Schutzgebiete," 12.07.1907, BArch-B, R 1002/2596, 22. Cf. Schröder, *Prügelstrafe*, 63ff., 72; Trotha, "'One for Kaiser,'" 527.

20. Fonck, *Deutsch-Ost-Afrika* (1910), 70, cited in Schröder, *Prügelstrafe*, 72.

21. For more on this legal distinction and the penal power of policemen, see chapter 5.

22. Letter to Praeses Olpp, Okombahe, 29.05.1911, cited in Heinrich Brockmann, *Haba du ta gob*, ed. Jürgen Hoffmann, reprint of orig. manuscript [1946] (Berlin 1992), 164.

23. Patrol report by Sgt. Franz Franitzek (Police Depot Waterberg), 10.06.1908, BArch-B, R 1002/2708, 112. There is still the possibility that Franitzek was using the term "executed" in its nominalized form (*Vollstreckung*) to imply that he merely read out the sentence while an African policeman dealt the blows. But policemen, particularly those who served at the outskirts of the colony, were not averse to "getting their hands dirty" by wielding the whip personally. On related contemporaneous forms of masculinity that insisted on hands-on action, see Michael Adas's compelling account of American engineers in *Dominance by Design*, 143–44.

24. Statements by Staff Sgt. Bauer (District Office Warmbad), 17.03.1909, BArch-B, R 1002/2783, 71.

25. Jeremy Silvester and Jan-Bart Gewald, eds., *Words Cannot Be Found* (Leiden 2003), 236.

26. Schröder, *Prügelstrafe*, 64. Glasman observes that only the highest ranks of the police force received the assignment. He also notes that the "room for maneuver which opened up to the policeman was significant, since he could negotiate in advance with the punished about the intensity and the placement of the blows." Glasman, *Les corps habillés*, 111.

27. Drill sergeants regularly meted out beatings to their subordinates. See Bonnell, "Explaining Suicide in the Imperial German Army"; Wiedner, "Soldaten-mißhandlungen."

28. On precolonial interpersonal violence and penal practice in Africa, see Florence Bernault, "The Shadow of Rule," in *Cultures of Confinement*, ed. Frank Dikötter and Ian Brown (London 2007), 55–94; Carotenuto and Shadle, "Toward a History of Violence," 5; Richard Roberts, "Law, Crime and Punishment in Colonial Africa," in *The Oxford Handbook of Modern African History*, ed. John Parker and Richard Reid (Oxford 2013), 182–84.

29. For instance, list of "punished natives" (Police Depot Kupferberg), 02.04.1908, BArch-B, R 1002/2596, 3–4. The largest collection of "Penalty Registers and Beating Protocols" is held in the Namibian Archives, NAN, ZBU 698–712 F.V.k. For numbers drawn from registers like these, see Schröder, *Prügelstrafe*, 94–95; for a critical reassessment of these numbers, see Zollmann, *Koloniale Herrschaft*, 120–21.

30. Chancellor Hohenlohe: "Verfügung wegen Ausübung der Strafgerichtsbarkeit und der Disziplinargewalt gegenüber den Eingeborenen in Deutsch-Südwestafrika," 08.11.1896, BArch-B, R 1002/2596, 15–16. Cf. Schröder, *Prügelstrafe*, 52–53; Zollmann, *Koloniale Herrschaft*, 110.

31. Schröder, *Prügelstrafe*, 67. Cf. the decree pertaining to other African colonies that forbade corporal punishment against Arabs and Indians. Chancellor Hohenlohe: "Verfügung des Reichskanzlers wegen Ausübung der Strafgerichtsbarkeit und der Disziplinargewalt gegenüber den Eingeborenen in den deutschen Schutzgebieten von Ostafrika, Kamerun und Togo," 22.04.1896, BArch-B, R 1001/5498, 6.

32. Governor Lindequist, "Runderlass des Gouverneurs von Deutsch-Südwestafrika betreffend die Vollziehung von Prügelstrafen," 22.12.1905, BArch-B, R 1002/2596, 20.

33. Ibid.

34. As Schröder notes, "The decision . . . for what transgression it could be applied depended entirely on the colonial official in charge." Schröder, *Prügelstrafe*, 57; cf. Zollmann, *Koloniale Herrschaft*, 114.

35. For extensive documentation, see Müller, *Kolonien unter der Peitsche*, 104–10; Schröder, *Prügelstrafe*, 76–78.

36. Internal note RKA, no date, BArch-B, R 1001/5378, 137, cited in Müller, *Kolonien unter der Peitsche*, 110.

37. Schröder, *Prügelstrafe*, 78.

38. Complaint by farmer Engelhard (Georg Ferdinandshöhe), 21.03.1913, BArch-B, R 1002/3226, 78.

39. Statement by Sgt. Ludwig Maletz (Police Station Kalkfeld), 30.04.1913, BArch-B, R 1002/3226, 80–81.

40. Ludwig Maletz, "Aus meinem Dienstbuch. Auf Station Kalkfeld," quoted in Rafalski, *Vom Niemandsland*, 403.

41. Governor v. Schuckmann to RKA, 30.12.1907, R 1001/5379, 161–62, cited in Müller, *Kolonien unter der Peitsche*, 108.

42. Ibid., 107.

43. Statement by Sgt. Ludwig Maletz (Police Station Kalkfeld), 30.04.1913, BArch-B, R 1002/3226, 80–81.

44. Medical report by District Doctor Wohlgemuth, Omaruru, 20.05.1913, BArch-B, R 1002/3226, 79.

45. On critical voices among colonizers regarding corporal punishment, see Zollmann, *Koloniale Herrschaft*, 124–26. Zollmann concludes that corporal punishment was indeed "on no account . . . constitutive of colonial rule" and "counterproductive." Ibid., 125.

46. Michel Foucault, *Discipline and Punish* (New York 1977); see also Richard van Dülmen, *Theatre of Horror* (Cambridge 1990).

47. Habermas, "Peitschen im Reichstag," 408; Pesek, *Koloniale Herrschaft in Deutsch-Ostafrika*, 190–204; Ulrike Schaper, *Koloniale Verhandlungen* (Frankfurt a.M. 2012), 170; Schröder, *Prügelstrafe*, 58. Togo performed its floggings publicly, next to the flagpole of its stations. Trotha, "'One for Kaiser,'" 527.

48. See also the photographs and postcard published in Hartmann, *Hues between Black and White*, 67; Krüger, "Koloniale Gewalt," 94–95. On representations of violence in postcards, see Felix Axster, *Koloniales Spektakel in 9 x 14* (Bielefeld 2014), 108–9, 112–17.

49. Florence Bernault, "The Politics of Enclosure in Colonial and Post-Colonial Africa," in *A History of Prison and Confinement in Africa*, ed. Florence Bernault (Portsmouth, NH 2003), 3.

50. Trotha and the historian of Imperial Russia, Abby Schrader, note a similar disruption of the Foucauldian narrative. Trotha, "'One for Kaiser,'" 523; Abby M. Schrader, *Languages of the Lash* (DeKalb, IL 2002).

51. However, international reputation and even public opinion in the metropole certainly also played a role in the culture of silence surrounding the sjambok. On the parliamentary debates in response to international and national discussion of excessive violence in the German colonies, see Habermas, "Peitschen im Reichstag"; Zollmann, *Koloniale Herrschaft*, 110.

52. The scholarship on corporal punishment and interpersonal violence in the context of African settler colonialism is particularly well developed for colonial Kenya. For instance, David M. Anderson, "Kenya, 1895–1939," in *Masters, Servants, and Magistrates in Britain and the Empire, 1562–1955*, ed. Douglas Hay and Paul Craven (Chapel Hill 2004), 498–528; David M. Anderson, "Punishment, Race and 'the Raw Native,'" *Journal of Southern African Studies* 37 (2011): 479–97; Paul Ocobock, "Spare the Rod, Spoil the Colony," *International Journal of African Historical Studies* 45, no. 1 (2012): 29–56; Shadle, "Settlers, Africans, and Inter-personal Violence in Kenya, ca. 1900–1920s."

53. On corporal punishment in nineteenth-century Germany, see Reinhart Koselleck, *Preussen zwischen Reform und Revolution* (Stuttgart 1967), 641–59; Winfried Speitkamp, *Ohrfeige, Duell und Ehrenmord* (Stuttgart 2010), 25–52.

54. Schröder, *Prügelstrafe*, 2.

55. Habermas, "Peitschen im Reichstag."

56. On the invention of tradition and African customary law, see Kristin Mann and Richard L. Roberts, eds., *Law in Colonial Africa* (Portsmouth, NH 1991); Terence O.

Ranger, "The Invention of Tradition in Colonial Africa," in *The Invention of Tradition*, ed. Eric Hobsbawm and Terence O. Ranger (Cambridge1992), 211–62; Roberts, "Law, Crime and Punishment in Colonial Africa."

57. Zollmann observes that this kind of rationale, i.e., the "obstinate standpoint of 'it is different here,'" also affected the firearms usage debate. *Koloniale Herrschaft*, 173.

58. Circular by Chief of Police Heydebreck to all district offices and police depots, 22.01.1910, BArch-B, R 1002/2670, 5.

59. Ibid.

60. The archival file entitled "Chaining Material" (1907–1912) contains over a hundred pages. BArch-B, R 1002/2670, 3–107.

61. Report by Detective Sgt. Wilhelm Kelz, no date [May 1910], BArch-B, R 1002/2670, 35.

62. Reports by District Chief Weber (District Office Gobabis), 04.04.1910, BArch-B, R 1002/2670, 25–26; by District Office Okahandja, 02.02.1910, BArch-B, R 1002/2670, 9; by Inspection Officer Müller (Police Depot Spitzkoppe), 02.04.1910, BArch-B, R 1002/2670, 27; by Staff Sgt. Schuldt (Police Depot Kupferberg), 04.03.1910, BArch-B, R 1002/2670, 8.

63. Report by acting Magistrate Wellmann (District Office Swakopmund), 15.04.1910, BArch-B, R 1002/2670, 23.

64. Ibid.; Inspection Officer Fuhrmann (Police Depot Waterberg), 23.02.1910, BArch-B, R 1002/2670, 11.

65. Report by Inspection Officer Freytag (Police Depot Kub), 22.02.1910, BArch-B, R 1002/2670, 6; see also reports by District Office Lüderitzbucht, 16.02.1910, BArch-B, R 1002/2670, 17; and by District Office Gibeon, 11.03.1910, BArch-B, R 1002/2670, 20.

66. For instance, reports by Sgt. Paul Melzer (Police Station Kalkfontein), 10.12.1913, BArch-B, R 1002/1184, no page number; by Sgt. Willy Maywald (Police Station Hornkranz), 02.09.1912, NAN, BRE, 77 L.2.i, 5.

67. Report by Sgt. Willy Maywald (Police Station Hornkranz), 02.09.1912, NAN, BRE, 77 L.2.i, 5.

68. Marginal note by Magistrate Vietsch (District Office Rehoboth), ibid.

69. Reports by District Office Gibeon, 11.03.1910, BArch-B, R 1002/2670, 20; by District Office Warmbad, 30.04.1910, BArch-B, R 1002/2670, 30; internal note by Detective Sgt. Wilhelm Kelz (IdL), no date, BArch-B, R 1002/2670, 4.

70. Reports by Magistrate Brill (District Office Windhuk), 09.02.1910, BArch-B, R 1002/2670, 10; by District Chief Fuhrmann (Police Depot Waterberg), 23.02.1910, BArch-B, R 1002/2670, 11; by Sgt. Belz (District Office Warmbad), 30.04.1910, BArch-B, R 1002/2670, 30.

71. Reports by Inspection Officer Freytag (Police Depot Kub), 22.02.1910, BArch-B, R 1002/2670, 6; by District Chief Vietsch (District Office Rehoboth), 20.04.1910, BArch-B, R 1002/2670, 24; by District Chief Fuhrmann (Police Depot Waterberg), 23.02.1910, BArch-B, R 1002/2670, 11.

72. Report by District Chief Fuhrmann (Police Depot Waterberg), 23.02.1910, BArch-B, R 1002/2670, 11–13.

73. Internal note by Detective Sgt. Wilhelm Kelz (IdL), no date [May 1910], BArch-B, R 1002/2670, 35; invoice by Firm Skeyde, Breslau, 01.08.1910, BArch-B, R 1002/2670, 41; Chief of Police Bethe to District Office Windhuk, 21.09.1910, BArch-B, R 1002/2670, 43; report by Magistrate Brill (District Office Windhuk), 18.01.1911, BArch-B,

R 1002/2670, 53–54; order of shackles by police headquarters to Firm W. Wiehle, Ratibor, 31.01.1911, BArch-B, R 1002/2670, 57–58.

74. Firm C. W. Moritz to Gouv. SWA, 07.11.1907, BArch-B, R 1002/2670, 107; Firm Föhse to Gouv. SWA, 27.02. and 20.05.1911, BArch-B, R 1002/2670, 67–68.

75. On colonies as a "laboratory of modernity," see Frederick Cooper and Ann Laura Stoler, "Between Metropole and Colony," in *Tensions of Empire*, ed. Frederick Cooper and Ann Laura Stoler (Berkeley 1997), 5. On an attempt to refine their position, particularly by insisting on "cross-fading and reciprocal influence" between colony and metropole, see Dirk van Laak, "Kolonien als 'Laboratorien der Moderne,'?" in *Das Kaiserreich transnational*, ed. Sebastian Conrad and Jürgen Osterhammel, 2nd ed. (Göttingen 2006), esp. 279.

76. Reports by Magistrate Brill (District Office Windhuk), 09.02.1910, BArch-B, R 1002/2670, 10; by District Chief Fuhrmann (Police Depot Waterberg), 23.02.1910, BArch-B, R 1002/2670, 11–13.

77. District Chief Schwerin (District Office Gobabis) to Police Head Office, 16.02.1912, BArch-B, R 1002/2670, 102.

78. Decree by Vice Governor Hintrager, 29.07.1912, BArch-B, R 1002/2591, 76; reports by Magistrate Schmidt (District Office Keetmanshoop), 21.02.1910, BArch-B, R 1002/2670, 15; by Magistrate Schmidt (District Office Keetmanshoop), 08.10.1908, BArch-B, R 1002/2560, 9–10.

79. District Chief Beyer (District Office Warmbad), 30.04.1910, BArch-B, R 1002/2670, 30.

80. "Bekleidungs-Vorschrift für die berittene Landespolizei in Südwest-Afrika," 01.10.1907, NAN, DAR, 20 P.II.1, 5; *Dienstvorschrift*, 53; Schepp, *Unter dem Kreuz des Südens*, 233; Rolf Selzer, "Der Säbel der Kaiserlichen Landespolizei von Deutsch-Südwest," *Mitteilungsblatt des Traditionsverbandes ehemaliger Schutz- und Überseetruppen* 72 (1993): 105–11.

81. Schepp, *Unter dem Kreuz des Südens*, 227. On the police station Kuring Kuru, see Andreas E. Eckl, "Konfrontation und Kooperation am Kavango (Nord-Namibia) von 1891 bis 1921" (PhD diss., Cologne University, 2004), 96–107; Zollmann, *Koloniale Herrschaft*, 322–40.

82. Circular by Vice Governor Hintrager to all district offices, 03.07.1907, NAN, BKE, 201 B.II.66.c (vol. 1), 172.

83. Roebern (IdL) to District Office Rehoboth, 18.11.1909, NAN, BRE, 75 L.2.h, 15; circular by Chief of Police Bethe, 25.03.1911, NAN, BRE, 75 L.2.h, 31.

84. Annual report (1910) by IdL, 14.05.1911, BArch-B, R 1002/2672, 68.

85. Revision report by Chief of Police Heydebreck, 01.02.1909, BArch-B, R 1002/2693, 11.

86. For instance, Sgt. Bernhard Themm (Police Station Gibeon) to IdL, 23.07.1913, BArch-B, R 1002/2415, no page number. Cf. also file "Participation in Associations and Assemblies" (1906–1914), BArch-B, 1002/2471.

87. Brockmann, *Haba Du Ta Gob*, 136. On club activities in German Southwest Africa, cf. Kundrus, *Moderne Imperialisten*, 176–83; Walther, *Creating Germans Abroad*, 90–91.

88. Schepp, *Unter dem Kreuz des Südens*, 95.

89. Vice Governor Hintrager to IdL, 03.01.1910, BArch-B, R 1002/2552, 4; cf. similar comment by Chief of Police Heydebreck to all district offices, 06.05.1909, BArch-B, R 1002/2540, 125.

90. Chief of Police Heydebreck to all police depots, 12.11.1908, BArch-B, R 1002/2534, 82; class schedules for riding and shooting practice in files BArch-B, R 1002/2539, 2540. The only exception was Chief of Police Heydebreck's instruction to all police depots in August 1908 regarding a group of thirty-one trained policemen who had arrived directly from the metropole. For these, Heydebreck suggested an intensification of instruction, more "theoretical" lessons and less patrolling, riding, and shooting. One can only speculate on the reasons for this. Maybe the head of police wanted to train these men particularly for senior positions in the local district administrations. Maybe he believed that their experience as policemen in the homeland was sufficient to operate in the field, but that they needed an overview over the legal and administrational differences of the colony. Chief of Police Heydebreck to all police depots, 08.08.1908, BArch-B, R 1002/2534, 61.

91. Vice Governor Hintrager to all district offices and police depots, 03.01.1910, BArch-B, R 1002/2489, 11. For an example of the weekly training schedule, see activity report by Sen. Staff Sgt. Hubert Knoche (Police Depot Waterberg), 27.06.1910, BArch-B, R 1002/2535, 40–41.

92. Chief of Police Heydebreck to Police Depot Spitzkoppe, 27.01.1910, BArch-B, R 1002/2534, 12.

93. *Dienstvorschrift*, 43.

94. Class schedules of the police school in Windhuk from 1909 and 1911, BArch-B, R 1002/2537, 195 and 185–86.

95. *Dienstvorschrift*, 44–47.

96. No other exercise beyond shooting was mentioned in the *Dienstvorschrift* or elsewhere.

97. Ibid., 43.

98. Cf. chapter 2.

99. Harry M. Collins and Robert Evans, *Rethinking Expertise* (Chicago 2007), 27.

100. William K. Storey, "Guns, Race, and Skill in Nineteenth-Century Southern Africa," *Technology and Culture* 45, no. 4 (2004): 690.

101. Report on extracurricular activity by Inspection Officer Hildebrandt (Police Depot Waterberg), 28.03.1908, BArch-B, R 1002/2535, 135.

102. Sgt. Friedrich Schmidt (Police Station Rietfontein) to District Office Gobabis, 30.03.1913, BArch-B, R 1002/2415, no page number.

103. IdL to Gouv. SWA, 02.09.1912, BArch-B, R 1002/2415, no page number.

104. Ibid.

105. Marginal note by Chief of Police Bethe in a letter by Vice Governor Hintrager to IdL, 26.03.1913, BArch-B, R 1002/2415, no page number.

106. Ibid.

107. Vice Governor Hintrager to all district offices, 28.12.1912, BArch-B, R 1002/2415, no page number.

108. Ibid.; cf. "Über Polizeibeamten-Gehälter und Anderes," *Deutsch-Südwestafrikanische Zeitung*, February 21, 1911.

109. Vice Governor Hintrager to IdL, 26.03.1913, BArch-B, R 1002/2415, no page number.

110. Decree by Chief of Police Bethe, 09.05.1913, NAN, BRE, 75 L.2.h, 93. The decree was met with many objections and protests. Magistrate Schultze-Jena was particularly disturbed that the policemen's right to own private property was being

curtailed. District Office Omaruru and a great number of rank-and-file policemen were primarily concerned with the restriction the decree put on their food supply. See Magistrate Schultze-Jena (District Office Outjo) to IdL, 27.05.1913, BArch-B, R 1002/2415, no page number; Magistrate Schultze-Jena (District Office Outjo) to IdL, 23.06.1913, BArch-B, R 1002/2415, no page number; District Office Omaruru to IdL, 27.08.1913, BArch-B, R 1002/2415, no page number; Police Station Keetmanshoop to IdL, 03.07.1913, BArch-B, R 1002/2415, no page number; Sen. Staff Sgt. Max Ehrlich (Police Station Okahandja) to IdL, 25.07.1913, BArch-B, R 1002/2415, no page number; Sgt. Bernhard Themm (Police Station Gibeon) to IdL, 23.07.1913, BArch-B, R 1002/2415, no page number.

111. Patrol reports by Sgt. Johannes Becker (Police Station Ramansdrift), 22.11.1908, NAN, ZBU, 479 D.IV.o (vol. 1), 126–28; by Sgt. Xaver Hagner (Police Station Okauk-wejo), 20.10.1913, BArch-B, R 1002/2711, 68–69; by Staff Sgt. Heinrich Eggersglüß (District Office Maltahöhe), 24.03.1913, BArch-B, R 1002/2711, 14–15.

112. Cf. chapter 5.

113. See chapters 2 and 5.

114. Kelz (Police School Windhuk) to IdL, 12.08.1908, BArch-B, R 1002/2560, 1.

115. Circular by Chief of Police Heydebreck, 17.09.1908, BArch-B, R 1002/2560, 4.

116. *Dienstvorschrift*, 31.

117. Zollmann, *Koloniale Herrschaft*, 164.

118. Zollmann comes to a different interpretation regarding the use of weapons. He claims that the discussion was among superiors who then eventually condoned an already practiced procedure of their subordinates, whereas I claim that the rank and file significantly influenced the decision-making process of the superiors. *Koloniale Herrschaft*, 163–79.

119. For instance, patrol report by Sgt. Dufring (Police Station Okahandja), 16.02.1908, BArch-B, R 1002/2708, 19–37.

120. See chapter 5 for a detailed discussion of manhunts.

121. Template of patrol book by Sgt. Kraus (Police Station Hohewarte), 12.03.1906, NAN, DAR, 20 P.II.1, 40.

122. Telegram by Magistrate Hoelscher (District Office Rehoboth) to IdL, 28.09.1908, NAN, ZBU 479 D.V.o, 46.

123. Report by District Chief Seydel (District Office Maltahöhe), 17.03.1909, NAN, ZBU, 479 D.IV.o (vol. 1), 206.

124. Zollmann, *Koloniale Herrschaft*, 68.

125. Cf. chapter 4.

126. Vice Governor Hintrager to RKA, 30.10.1908, BArch-B, R 1001/1914, 53.

127. Patrol report by Sgt. Johannes Becker (Police Station Ramansdrift), 22.11.1908, NAN, ZBU, 479 D.IV.o (vol. 1), 126–28.

128. Ibid., 128.

129. Ibid.

130. Circular by Governor Seitz, 24.10.1911, BArch-B, R 1002/2560, 48–49; circular by Governor Seitz, 04.02.1914, BArch-B, R 1002/2560, no page number. I discuss these two circulars in more detail below.

131. District Chief Karl Schmidt (District Office Keetmanshoop) to Gouv. SWA, 08.10.1908, BArch-B, R 1002/2560, 9–10.

132. "Die wehrlose Polizei," *Deutsch-Südwestafrikanische Zeitung*, August 25, 1909.

133. Ibid.

134. Chief of Police Heydebreck to *Deutsch-Südwestafrikanische Zeitung*, no date [August 1909], BArch-B, R 1002/2560, 25–26; circular by Chief of Police Heydebreck, 14.09.1909, BArch-B, R 1002/2560, 19–29.

135. Chief of Police Heydebreck to *Deutsch-Südwestafrikanische Zeitung*, no date [August 1909], BArch-B, R 1002/2560, 25.

136. Ibid., 26.

137. Circular by Chief of Police Heydebreck, 14.09.1909, BArch-B, R 1002/2560, 19–20.

138. Ibid., 20–21.

139. Ibid., 20.

140. Magistrate Karl Schmidt (District Office Keetmanshoop) to Police Station Hasuur, 16.03.1908, NAN, DAR, 20 P.II.1, 19.

141. On race and how it works in different colonial and settler colonial contexts, cf. Patrick Wolfe, "Race and Racialisation," *Postcolonial Studies* 5, no. 1 (2002): 51–62.

142. On the difficulty of self-identification and identification by others of the San/Bushmen, see Gordon, *The Bushman Myth*, esp. 4–8. In the following, I call this group the San.

143. "Buschmannsnot in Südwestafrika," *Deutsch-Südwestafrikanische Zeitung* (1911), cited in a report by Magistrate Zastrow (District Office Grootfontein), 14.04.1911, BArch-B, R 1002/2710, 91.

144. Telegram by Magistrate Schultze-Jena (District Office Outjo) to IdL, 07.05.1911, and report by Magistrate Schultze-Jena (District Office Outjo), 09.05.1911, BArch-B, R 1002/2507, 39–40.

145. Patrol report by Staff Sgt. Wilhelm Schweizer (Police Station Grootfontein), 05.10.1911, BArch-B, R 1002/2793, 59–62; report by Magistrate Zastrow (District Office Grootfontein), 04.10.1911, BArch-B, R 1002/2793, 53.

146. Medical report by Dr. Zachlehner (Grootfontein), 11.10.1911, BArch-B, R 1002/2793, 57–58; letter of condolence by Chief of Police Bethe to widow Bertha Alefelder, 19.10.1911, BArch-B, R 1002/2793, 49.

147. For instance, patrol reports by Staff Sgt. Heinrich Eggersglüß (District Office Maltahöhe), 24.03.1913, BArch-B, R 1002/2711, 14–15; and by Sgt. Xaver Hagner (Police Station Okaukwejo), 20.10.1913, BArch-B, R 1002/2711, 68–69.

148. Decree by Governor Seitz, 24.10.1911, BArch-B, R 1002/2560, 48–49.

149. Ibid.

150. Magistrate Schultze-Jena (District Office Outjo) to Gouv. SWA, 20.01.1913, BArch-B, R 1002/2560, 59.

151. Draft of decree by Vice Governor Hintrager, 24.12.1912, BArch-B, R 1002/2560, 51–52.

152. Hensel (IdL) to Vice Governor Hintrager, 07.01.1913, BArch-B, R 1002/2560, 53–54.

153. For an interesting discussion of the different legal interpretations regarding the use of firearms in the upper levels of the colonial administration in Windhuk and Berlin, see Zollmann, *Koloniale Herrschaft*, 168–79.

154. Decree by Governor Seitz, 04.12.1914, BArch-B, R 1002/2560, no page number. It replaced the regulations in the *Dienstvorschrift*, 31.

155. Circular by Chief of Police Heydebreck, 14.09.1909, BArch-B, R 1002/2560, 20.

156. Circular by Vice Governor Hintrager to all district offices, 03.07.1907, NAN, BKE, 201 B.II.66.c (vol. 1), 172; circular by Vice Governor Hintrager to all district offices, 10.06.1910, BArch-B, R 1002/2608, 1.

157. Personal letter by Vice Governor Hintrager to Magistrate Zastrow (District Office Grootfontein), 10.06.1910, BArch-B, R 1002/2709, 83.

158. *Dienstvorschrift*, 14.

159. For instance, District Chief Wasserfall (District Office Bethanien) to District Office Keetmanshoop, 21.10.1908, BArch-B, R 1002/2560, 9–10; Magistrate Karl Schmidt (District Office Keetmanshoop) to IdL, 08.10.1908, BArch-B, R 1002/2560, 9–10; Magistrate Karl Schmidt (District Office Keetmanshoop) to IdL, 20.01.1911, NAN, BKE, 201 B.II.66.c (vol. 1), 68; Report by Magistrate Berengar Zastrow (District Office Grootfontein) to Police Depot Waterberg, 08.05.1910, BArch-B, R 1002/2709, 77–79; Magistrate Rudolf Böhmer (District Office Lüderitzbucht) to IdL, 05.07.1910, BArch-B, R 1002/2709, 98. See also Zollmann, *Koloniale Herrschaft*, 69.

160. Circular by Chief of Police Bethe to all district offices and police depots, 08.11.1910, BArch-B, R 1002/2604, 2; amendment to the circular, 17.03.1914, BArch-B, R 1002/2604, 5.

161. Annual report (1911), 25.05.1910, BArch-B, R 1002/2672, 42.

162. Decree by Governor Seitz, 24.10.1911, BArch-B, R 1002/2560, 49; decree by Governor Seitz, 04.02.1914, BArch-B, R 1002/2560, no page number. Even the *Dienstvorschrift* permitted the arming of African policemen, although this was hidden in its section on police equipment. *Dienstvorschrift*, 31.

163. Chief of Police Bethe to Sen. Staff Sgt. Paul Urner (District Office Grootfontein), 24.08.1913, BArch-B, R 1002/2604, 4.

164. For a discussion of weapon expertise and race in another colonial context, see Storey, *Guns, Race, and Power*.

165. Explicit proscriptions: Circular by Vice Governor Hintrager to all district offices, 03.07.1907, NAN, BKE, 201 B.II.66.c (vol. 1), 172; circular by Vice Governor Hintrager to all district offices, 10.06.1910, BArch-B, R 1002/2608, 1. An exception was Vice Governor Brückner, who permitted African policemen to carry a rifle and five bullets in the Outjo district to defend themselves against lions. Vice Governor Brückner to District Office Outjo, 17.08.1910, BArch-B, R 1002/2709, 115.

166. Circular by Vice Governor Hintrager to all district offices, 03.07.1907, NAN, BKE, 201 B.II.66.c (vol. 1), 172.

167. Hensel (IdL) to Vice Governor Hintrager, 07.01.1913, BArch-B, R 1002/2560, 56.

168. Magistrate Brill (District Office Windhuk) to IdL, 07.04.1909, BArch-B, R 1002/2537, 112.

169. Glasman comes to a similar conclusion, calling the whip in German colonial Togo a "tool of distinction." Glasman, *Les corps habillés*, 114.

4. Police Work

1. David H. Bayley, *Patterns of Policing* (New Brunswick, NJ 1985); Jean-Paul Brodeur, "High Policing and Low Policing," *Social Problems* 30, no. 5 (1983): 507–20; Dominique Monjardet, *Ce que fait la police* (Paris 1996).

2. Monjardet, *Ce que fait la police*, 8.

3. Ibid., 9.

4. Liang, *The Rise of Modern Police*, 4.

5. Johann Heinrich Gottlob von Justi, *Grudsätze der Policeywissenschaft*, 3rd ed. (Göttingen 1782), 4, trans. in Michel Foucault, *Security, Territory, Population* (Basingstoke 2007), 330, fn. 8.

6. Foucault, *Security, Territory, Population*, 324, 322. Charles Tilly notes that "before the nineteenth-century proliferation of professional police forces as we know them, the word Police referred to public management, especially at the local level; regulation of the food supply was its single largest component." Charles Tilly, *Coercion, Capital, and European States, AD 990–1992* (Cambridge 2008), 119.

7. Ralph Jessen, "Polizei, Wohlfahrt und die Anfänge des modernen Sozialstaats in Preußen während des Kaiserreichs," *Geschichte und Gesellschaft* 20, no. 2 (1994): 157–80; Alf Lüdtke, introduction to *"Sicherheit" und "Wohlfahrt,"* ed. Alf Lüdtke (Frankfurt a.M. 1992), 13–15; Herbert Reinke, "'. . . hat sich ein politischer und wirtschaftlicher Polizeistaat entwickelt,'" in *"Sicherheit" und "Wohlfahrt,"* ed. Alf Lüdtke (Frankfurt a.M. 1992), 219–43.

8. Justi, *Grundsätze der Policeywissenschaft*, 4.

9. Emsley, *Gendarmes and the State in Nineteenth-Century Europe*, 153–90; Funk, *Polizei und Rechtsstaat*, 25–27.

10. Rafalski, *Vom Niemandsland*, 28.

11. See the list of laws relevant for police work sent to all police depots: Lauterbach (Gouv. SWA) to IdL, 01.02.1908, BArch-B, R 1002/2552, 67–68. Hunting and nature protection: Governor Schuckmann (Gouv. SWA) to RKA, 31.12.1907, BArch-B, R 1001/2183, 31–34. Alcohol: "Gesetz betr. Einfuhr und Vertrieb geistiger Getränke in dem südwestafrikanischen Schutzgebiet," 11.03.1911, cited in Philipp Karl Ludwig Zorn, ed., *Deutsche Kolonialgesetzgebung*, 2nd ed. (Berlin 1913), 591–96. Public equipment: "Wege-Ordnung," 14.06.1912, cited in Zorn, *Deutsche Kolonialgesetzgebung*, 755–62.

12. On the history of the dog tax in Namibia, which originated in 1917, see Bernard Moore, "'Dogs Were Our Defenders!,'" *Perspectives on History AHA*, June 16, 2017.

13. Sgt. Oskar Junge (Police Station Klipdam) to District Office Hasuur, 30.09.1909, NAN, DAR, 20 S.V, 10–11.

14. Census and school attendance: "Gesetz betr. Einführung der Schulpflicht, 20.10.1906," cited in Zorn, *Deutsche Kolonialgesetzgebung*, 558–60; patrol report by Staff Sgt. Karl Schlink (Police Depot Kub), 01.07.1908, BArch-B, R 1002/2708, 147; patrol book, Police Depot Spitzkoppe, January–March 1912, BArch-B, R 1002/2708, 210–17; patrol book, Police Depot Waterberg, 31.03.1912, BArch-B, R 1002/2708, 220–21; patrol book, Police Depot Spitzkoppe, no date, BArch-B, R 1002/2710, 178–85. Immunization: "Impf-Verordnung des Gouverneurs von Deutsch-Südwestafrika," 30.07.1912, cited in Zorn, *Deutsche Kolonialgesetzgebung*, 300–304.

15. Alf Lüdtke and Michael Wildt coined the term *"Allzuständigkeit"* regarding the police in German history. Introduction to *Staats-Gewalt* (Göttingen 2008), 17.

16. For an analogous conception of the importance of immediacy with respect to police work in mid-nineteenth-century Germany, see the politician and state publicist Gustav Zimmermann, *Die deutsche Polizei im neunzehnten Jahrhundert* (1849), cited in Lüdtke, *"Gemeinwohl," Polizei und "Festungspraxis,"* 82.

17. Rafalski himself used the term to characterize policemen in German Southwest Africa. The gendered language appears not to have bothered him. *Vom Niemandsland*, 30.

18. *Dienstvorschrift*, 1. In an earlier draft, the first sentence had referred only to public peace, and not to security. Another draft included the terms "peace," "order," and "security." Drafts by IdL, no dates, BArch-B, R 1002/2692, no page numbers.

19. Patrol log, District Office Windhuk, 06.04.1908, BArch-B, R 1002/2708, 84–89.

20. Inspection Officer Hildebrandt (Police Depot Waterberg) to IdL, 05.04.1908, BArch-B, R 1002/2708, 73–82.

21. For an exception, see patrol book by Staff Sgt. Hermann Raab (Police Depot Spitzkoppe), 03.02.1910, BArch-B, R 1002/2709, 22–23.

22. See, for instance, Aimé Weiss, who in July 1907, like so many others, asked to "have one or two native families reserved" for her. Request by Aimé Weiss, 24.07.1907, NAN, Distriktsamt Okahandja (hereafter DOK), 27 E.2.e, 90. The archive is filled with requests like these from the years 1907–1908.

23. To my knowledge, there was no particular directive issued to that regard. But my survey of the patrol logs and the letters from worried employers shows evidence that more patrols were organized for the sole purpose of capturing Africans in the initial years of police existence and from about mid-1912 onward after a decree regarding "measures against vagrant natives," by Vice Governor Hintrager, 26.06.1912, BArch-B, R 1002/2706, 5–6. See, for instance, the archival files "Searches for Natives," 1911–1914, and "Requests for Workers," 1914–1915, of the Rehoboth District Office, NAN, BRE, 27 E.2.b (vol. 2); 27 E.2.b (vol. 3); 27 E.2.e (vol. 2).

24. Internal note by Chief of Police Heydebreck, 29.07.1907, BArch-B, R 1002/2692, 18.

25. I understand procedures to be structured ways of performing a task according to a prescribed plan of action, or according to one that is perceived as the correct one. That is, procedures pertain to the how, the modality of proceeding. Michel de Certeau defines procedures simply as "schemas of operations and of technical manipulations." *The Practice of Everyday Life*, 43.

26. Circular by Governor Schuckmann to all inspection officers, 23.06.1909, BArch-B, R 1002/2693, 57.

27. Rafalski, *Vom Niemandsland*, 66–70.

28. Ibid., 276.

29. Sen. Staff Sgt. Max Bahn (District Office Keetmanshoop) to IdL, 16.12.1910, NAN, BKE, 201 B.II.66.c (vol. 1), 61–62.

30. On the idea of forced communities, see Alf Lüdtke, "Arbeit, Arbeitserfahrungen und Arbeiterpolitik," in *Eigen-Sinn* (Hamburg 1993), 379.

31. On "the homosocial world of colonialism," cf. Hartmann, *Hues between Black and White*, 69–75.

32. For a template and instructions on how to fill out the service book, see IdL to all offices and depots, 11.08.1908, BArch-B, R 1002/2590, 193–98. Cf. excerpts of Staff Sgt. Urner and Schmidt's service books (District Office Grootfontein), [January 1911], BArch-B, R 1002/2528, 3–6. Since these books were in the possession of the individual policemen, who did not have to return them after they left their service, there are none in the official police archives. A copy of the only logbook I could locate, that of Sgt. Albrecht Arnhold, can be found in the archives of the Baseler Afrika Bibliographien (hereafter BAB), PA50.

33. Vice Governor Hintrager to all district offices, 19.09.1912, R1002/2583, no page numbers.

34. Vice Governor Hintrager to IdL, 30.12.1909, BArch-B, R 1002/2552, 118.

35. De Certeau, *The Practice of Everyday Life*, 59. Emphasis in original.

36. Internal note by Chief of Police Heydebreck, 11.09.1908, BArch-B, R 1002/2725, 5–6.

37. Complaint by farmer Bergemann to IdL, 29.04.1911, BArch-B, R 1002/2465, 61–62.

38. Sen. Staff Sgt. Eduard Boßenbeger (Police Station Maltahöhe) to IdL, 08.06.1911, BArch-B, R 1002/2465, 64.

39. Complaint against Sgt. Melzer by Sgt. Johann Kullick (Police Station Karions), no date [transcript from 05.09.1912], BArch-B, R 1002/1184, no page number.

40. Ibid. Melzer was transferred to another station. See also Sgt. Paul Melzer (Police Station Karions) to District Office Warmbad, 15.10.1912, BArch-B, R 1002/1184, no page number.

41. Krüger, *Schrift—Macht—Alltag*, 325–26.

42. Deborah Durham, "Passports and Persons," in *The Culture of Power in Southern Africa*, ed. Clifton C. Crais (Portsmouth, NH 2003), 155.

43. Patrol report by Sgt. Walter Henke (District Office Grootfontein), 07.03.1911, BArch-B, R 1002/2710, 26–29.

44. Chief of Police Bethe to District Office Grootfontein, 23.03.1911, BArch-B, R 1002/2710, 25.

45. Chief of Police Bethe to District Office Hasuur, 28.12.1910, BArch-B, R 1002/2467, 25.

46. Cf. Stoler, *Along the Archival Grain*, 49–51, 226–34.

47. Governor Seitz to IdL, 03.02.1914, BArch-B, R 1002/2591, 103.

48. Governor Seitz to all district offices and police depots, 15.02.1911, BArch-B, R 1002/2528, no page number. Cf. Rafalski, *Vom Niemandsland*, 81.

49. Moyd, *Violent Intermediaries*, 188.

50. See detailed patrol instructions by District Chief Kurt Streitwolf (District Office Gobabis), 11.03.1908, BArch-B, R 1002/2708, 13–16; Rafalski, *Vom Niemandsland*, 78–80.

51. Magistrate Groeben (District Office Gibeon) to Chief of Police Heydebreck, 12.01.1909, BArch-B, R 1002/2694, 30–33.

52. Report on patrol routines by District Chief Schneidenberger (District Office Okahandja) to IdL, 10.03.1908, BArch-B, R 1002/2708, 12.

53. Magistrate Victor Franke (District Office Outjo) to IdL, 28.11.1908, BArch-B, R 1002/2694, 11.

54. Crank's powerful characterization of policemen's attitudes toward their territory is worth quoting at length: "Bestowed with a specific beat assignment, . . . [cops] act out their subjective, shared sense of morality every time they decide whether, how, and when to intervene in the affairs of the citizenry. They are granted moral dominion over a turf and act, insofar as they are permitted or can get away with, as sovereigns. . . . Details of control that we social scientists carefully ponder—for example, was the intervention for purposes of order maintenance, service, or did somebody actually break the law[—]are simply irrelevant. It is their territory and exists to be controlled. To do less is to fail utterly. Territory is, for cops, more than a geographical assignment. It is their prize for being morally righteous, a divine gift, placed in their care so that they can deal with the assholes and bad guys of the world.

A cop's territory is *theirs*, not management's, not another cop's, certainly not the media's, those sovereigns of a darker order. And cops take it seriously. . . . Territory carries a great deal of meaning for the police. Police territories are infused with important values—commitment and responsibility—that surpass simple conceptions of spacial arrangement and population flows. Officers don't simply patrol areas, they control them, and they invest their energies and reputations in them." *Understanding Police Culture* (Cincinnati 1998), 43–44. Emphasis in the original.

55. Magistrate Vietsch (District Office Rehoboth) to IdL, 06.02.1914, and following correspondence, BArch-B, R 1002/2706, 21–24.

56. Chief of Police Bethe to all districts, depots and officer posts, 06.10.1913, BArch-B, R 1002/2706, 10.

57. Chief of Police Bethe to all offices, depots and officer posts, 25.05.1914, BArch-B, R 1002/2489, 23–25.

58. In fact, as Peter Manning's sociological police study shows, there is a direct relationship between honing the police's image and indexing: "The public's response has been to demand even more dramatic crook-catching and crime prevention, and this demand for arrests has been converted into an index for measuring how well the police accomplish their mandate. . . . The protection of the public welfare, however, including personal and property safety, the prevention of crime, and the preservation of individual civil rights, is hardly achieved by high pinch rate. On the contrary, it might well be argued that protection of public welfare could best be indexed by a low arrest rate. Because their mandate automatically entails mutually contradictory ends—protecting both public order and individual rights—the police resort to managing their public image and the indexes of their accomplishment." "The Police," in *Policing*, ed. Peter K. Manning and John Van Maanen (Santa Monica, CA 1978), 13.

59. Annual report (1908), 14.05.1909, BArch-B, R 1002/2672, 6–12.

60. Annual report (1909), 25.05.1910, BArch-B, R 1002/2672, 31.

61. For instance, Magistrate Beyer (District Office Warmbad) to IdL, 20.03.1912, BArch-B, R 1002/2694, 72–74; Chief of Police Bethe to Gouv. SWA, 10.02.1914, BArch-B, R 1002/2508, no page number.

62. Patrol book January–March 1911, Police Depot Spitzkoppe, 01.04.1911, BArch-B, R 1002/2710, 32–43.

63. Patrol book January–March 1908, District Office Omaruru, BArch-B, R 1002/2708, 93–101.

64. Manning, "The Police," 13.

65. Again pertaining to contemporary police, but possibly pertinent to the colonial case under scrutiny here, sociologist John Van Maanen observes that "the young officer learns that there is a subtle but critical difference between 'real' police work and most of what he does on patrol. 'Real' police work is, in essence[,] his *raison d'être*. It is part of his job that comes closest to the romantic notions of police work . . . [and] calls for a patrolman to exercise his perceived occupational expertise: to make an arrest, save a life, quell a dispute, prevent a robbery, catch a felon, stop a suspicious person, disarm a suspect, and so on. . . . Yet, because of this narrow definition of police work, little of his time on the street provides the opportunity to accomplish much of what he considers to be his primary function. Thus, 'real' police work to the patrolman is paradoxical; a source of satisfaction and frustration." John Van

Maanen, "Kinsmen in Repose," in *Policing*, ed. Peter K Manning and John Van Maanen (Santa Monica, CA 1978), 121–22.

66. Patrol report by Sgt. Julius Wenzel (Police Station Otjimbingwe), 04.06.1910, BArch-B, R 1002/2709, 102.

67. The sociologist Maureen Cain lists three major techniques of coping with boredom and frustration on the beat. The first is "making the work more interesting," that is, trying to get in contact with people, to have friendly encounters with the public. A second means of coping she identifies as "easing behavior," which mainly consists of finding an excuse to take a break (and tea) at the station, in a pub, or elsewhere. "The third means of making a dull and cold eight hours more tolerable was to seek marginally legitimate arrests. This gave excitement, the opportunity to go off duty early or at least to return to the warmth and relative conviviality of the police station, as well as prestige." "On the Beat," in *Images of Deviance*, ed. Stanley Cohen (Harmondsworth 1971), 71–73.

68. Hunting: Circular by Hensel (IdL) to all district offices and police depots, 09.05.1913, NAN, BRE, 75 L.2.h, 93. Observation of nature: Report by Sgt. Walter Henke (District Office Grootfontein), 07.03.1911, BArch-B, R 1002/2710, 26–29.

69. Patrol report by Sen. Staff Sgt. Hermann Eschen (District Office Gobabis), 08.08.1913, BArch-B, R 1002/2711, 30–32.

70. Patrol report by Sgt. Albert Gehrmann (Police Depot Waterberg), 11.06.1908, BArch-B, R 1002/2708, 133–37.

71. The concept is not easily translated into English. It means a combination of obstinacy, stubbornness, self-will, determination, strong-mindedness, and having a mind of one's own. Lüdtke himself uses the English terms "self-will" and "self-reliance." He also gives a useful explanation of the way German authors have employed the term and how he wants it to be understood in his work in "Cash, Coffee-Breaks, Horseplay," in *Confrontation, Class Consciousness, and the Labor Process*, ed. Michael Hanagan and Charles Stephenson (New York 1986), 79, fn. 28.

The term has been regularly misconceived to mean resistant or rebellious behavior. Cf. Thomas Lindenberger, "Eigen-Sinn, Herrschaft und kein Widerstand," *Docupedia-Zeitgeschichte*, February 9, 2014.

72. Lüdtke, "Arbeit, Arbeitserfahrungen und Arbeiterpolitik," 374. Emphasis in the original.

73. Magistrate Karl Schmidt (District Office Keetmanshoop) to Gouv. SWA, 11.12.1907, BArch-B, R 1002/733.

74. The incident prompted Chief of Police Bethe to dispatch a circular regarding "patrol riding according to regulations [*Vorschriftmäßiger Patrouillenritt*]" in which he instructed his staff to address regularly the subject of proper gearing up and weapons handling during patrols. Chief of Police Bethe to all district offices, 05.01.1914, BArch-B, R 1002/2706, 20.

75. Friedrich Kleinau, "Aus den Dünen von Südwest," *Nachrichtenblatt des Verbandes der Polizeibeamten für die deutschen Kolonien e.V.*, April 1925.

76. Sgt. Paul Ebermann (Police Station Gosorobis) to District Office Rehoboth, 16.02.1910, NAN, BRE, 13 B.9.A, 11.

77. Report by Sgt. Paul Melzer (Police Station Karions) to District Office Warmbad, 21.09.1912, BArch-B, R 1002/1184, no page number; report by Sgt. Bruno Ptaschek (Police Station Alt-Maltahöhe), 01.06.1911, BArch-B, R 1002/2466, 47–48.

212 NOTES TO PAGES 115-118

78. Manning, "The Police," 13.

79. Lüdtke calls it siege mentality. Lüdtke, *"Gemeinwohl," Polizei und "Festung-spraxis."* Most sociologies of policing call it solidarity, or comradeship, or esprit de corps. I would be careful with the term "solidarity" since it suggests unity and harmony within the group, which was by no means always the case. For a discussion of the literature, see "Mask of a Thousand Faces," chap. 5 in Crank, *Understanding Police Culture*, 187–203.

80. Confidential communication by District Office Bethanien to IdL, 17.08.1910, BArch-B, R 1002/2976, 42–45.

81. Internal investigation regarding allegations against Sgt. Kuse for, among other things, gossiping, IdL to District Office Großfontein, 23.12.1910–28.02.1911, BArch-B, R 1002/2465, 28–52.

82. Policemen were not allowed to receive free shelter and food from farmers. If they had to spend a night somewhere, they were supposed to camp out and use their own rations. *Dienstvorschrift*, 10.

83. Verdict against Constable Türk by District Judge Dr. Hirschberg (District Court Keetmanshoop), 24.05.1913, BArch-B, R 1002/3513, 37–39.

84. Sgt. Oskar Junge (Police Station Keetmanshoop) to District Office Keetman-shoop, 21.02.1910, NAN, BKE, 201 B.II.66.c (vol. 1), 12–13.

85. District Chief Seydel (District Office Maltahöhe) to IdL, 03.06.1911, BArch-B, R 1002/2466, 48.

86. Farmer Wulff, paraphrasing one of his workers, to Gouv. SWA, 25.12.1912, NAN, ZBU 2045, W.III.b.5 (vol. 1), 184, cited in Zollmann, *Koloniale Herrschaft*, 284.

87. On discourses of criminality qua race, see Bischoff, *Kannibale-Werden*, 165–94.

88. Patrol report by Sgt. Heuer (Police Depot Kupferberg), 15.09.1911, BArch-B, R 1002/2710, 132–33.

89. Hensel (IdL) to District Office Windhuk, 09.05.1912, BArch-B, R 1002/2598, 170.

90. Report by Sen. Staff Sgt. Otto Donicht (District Office Karibib), 09.12.1910, BArch-B, R 1002/2709, 199.

91. Patrol report by Sgt. Richard Malsch (Police Depot Spitzkoppe), no date [May 1910], BArch-B, R 1002/2709, 63–66.

92. Policemen had to wear uniform on and off duty. Only when on leave in the homeland and on foreign ships were they allowed to wear plain clothes. *Dienst-vorschrift*, 54.

93. Patrol report by Sgt. Dufring (Police Station Okahandja), 16.02.1908, BArch-B, R 1002/2708, 19–30.

94. Magistrate Zastrow (District Office Grootfontein) to IdL, 01.06.1910, BArch-B, R 1002/2709, 57; Magistrate Zastrow (District Office Grootfontein) to Police Depot Waterberg, no date, BArch-B, R 1002/2709, 59.

95. Dispatch by Staff Sgt. Heinrich Eggersglüß (Police Depot Maltahöhe), 30.03.1914, BArch-B, R 1002/2706, 25.

96. Patrol report by Sgt. Dufring (Police Station Okahandja), 16.02.1908, BArch-B, R 1002/2708, 30.

97. Referring to African guerrilla tactics and the practice of shouting deceptive or irritating things across the battle lines, Schutztruppe Captain Maximilian Bayer noted,

"There are many examples of annoying native trickery." Bayer, *The Rehoboth Baster Nation*, 33.

98. Patrol report by Sgt. Heuer (Police Depot Kupferberg), 15.09.1911, BArch-B, R 1002/2710, 132–33.

99. Sgt. Albert Siegmann (Police Station Büllsport) to District Office Rehoboth, 11.11.1908, BArch-B, R 1002/2707, 152.

100. Patrol report by Wilhelm Westphal (Police Depot Kupferberg), 07.12.1908, BArch-B, R 1002/2707, 145–50, quote from 146.

101. Report by Staff Sgt. Eggersglüss (District Office Maltahöhe), 16.02.1914, BArch-B, R 1002/2676, no page number.

102. List of bonuses for African police assistants, District Maltahöhe, 16.02.1914, BArch-B, R 1002/2676, no page number.

103. Report on Police Assistant Franz by [Sgt.?] Kühnast (District Office Swakopmund), 27.02.1915, BArch-B, R 1002/2593, 42.

104. Patrol report by Sgt. Georg Dawedeit (Police Depot Waterberg), 06.03.1909, BArch-B, R 1002/2707, 191.

105. Ibid., 190–92.

106. On the concept of "emotional communities," see Barbara H. Rosenwein, "Worrying about Emotions in History," *American Historical Review* 107, no. 3 (2002): 821–45.

107. Inspection Officer Hirschberg (Police Depot Kupferberg) to IdL, 09.01.1909, BArch-B, R 1002/2535, 99–100.

108. George Orwell's short story "Shooting an Elephant" is particularly insightful on the range of emotional experiences among colonial officials caused by the stress of having to perform in front of an audience. *Shooting an Elephant*, 1936 (repr., London 2009), 31–40.

109. Joanna Bourke, *Fear* (Emeryville, CA 2006), 3.

110. Report by Sgt. Richard Malsch (Police Depot Spitzkoppe), no date [May 1910], BArch-B, R 1002/2709, 66.

111. Statement by Police Assistant Friedrich Boekis (Police Station Keetmanshoop), 09.08.1910, NAN, BKE, 201 B.II.66.c (vol. 1), 76–77.

112. Report by Sgt. Otto Hense (Police Station Keetmanshoop), 09.08.1911, NAN, BKE, 201 B.II.66.c (vol. 1), 75–77.

113. Sgt. Hermann Wandrei (Police Station Gochaganas) to District Office Rehoboth, 30.07.1912, NAN, BRE, 34 E.5.e, 6. Emphasis added.

114. District Chief Wasserfall (District Office Bethanien) to IdL, 21.02.1911, BArch-B, R 1002/3520, 53. On Sgt. Vogel, cf. Schepp, *Unter dem Kreuz des Südens*, 119, 359, 532.

115. Verdict against Sgt. Vogel by District Judge Lämmermann (District Court Keetmanshoop), 31.05.1911, BArch-B, R 1002/3520, 60–61.

116. Ibid. Emphasis added.

117. The police force's instruction manual called for a "feeling of honor" [*Ehrgefühl*]. *Dienstvorschrift*, 9.

118. Verdict by Acting Judge Hilzebecher (District Office Keetmanshoop), 08.09.1910, NAN, BKE, 201 B.II.66.c (vol. 1), 24.

119. Statement by Police Assistant Friedrich Boekis (District Office Keetmanshoop), 22.08.1910, NAN, BKE, 201 B.II.66.c (vol. 1), 19.

120. Report by Sgt. Albert Bruhn (Police Station Keetmanshoop), 23.08.1910, 22.08.1910, NAN, BKE, 201 B.II.66.c (vol. 1), 21–22.

121. Catherine Lutz, *Unnatural Emotions* (Chicago 1988), 156–57.

122. Mark Mazower observes that the "state-centered approach has often hidden a reluctance to consider the idea that occasionally ordinary people enjoy or take pride in killing." "Violence and the State in the Twentieth Century," *American Historical Review* 107, no. 4 (2002): 1166.

123. De Certeau, *The Practice of Everyday Life*, 37.

124. Heinrich Popitz, *Phänomene der Macht* (Tübingen 1992), 65.

125. Kirsten Zirkel, "Military Power in German Colonial Policy," in *Guardians of Empire*, ed. David Killingray and David E. Omissi (Manchester, UK 1999), 91–113.

126. Report on patrol routines by District Chief Schneidenberger (District Office Okahandja) to IdL, 10.03.1908, BArch-B, R 1002/2708, 11.

127. Ibid.

128. On "unpredictability and situational uncertainty" in present-day police work, see Crank, *Understanding Police Culture*, 113–21.

129. Patrol report by Sgt. Albert Gehrmann (Police Depot Waterberg), 18.03.1909, BArch-B, R 1002/2707, 182–83.

130. Stoler, *Along the Archival Grain*, 39.

131. Elizabeth McNulty, "Generating Common Sense Knowledge among Police Officers," *Symbolic Interaction* 17, no. 3 (1994): 292.

132. Ibid., 282, 285.

133. Peter Manning notes that one of the main police "postulates or assumptions" is "Experience is better than abstract rules." "The Police," 11.

134. Qualification report for Sgt. Hergert by Magistrate Rudolf Böhmer (District Office Lüderitzbucht), October 1904, BArch-B, R 1002/733.

135. Minutes of interrogation with Sgt. Hergert by Inspection Officer Müller, 09.09.1909, BArch-B, R 1002/733; report by Inspection Officer Freytag (Police Depot Spitzkoppe), 07.05.1909, BArch-B, R 1002/2723.

136. Dominique Monjardet, *Notes inédites sur les choses policières, 1999–2006* (Paris 2008), 29.

137. Report by Sgt. Richard Brunk (Police Station Dawignab), 17.08.1913, NAN, DAR, 3 E.1.d, no page number. See a similar case in which missing papers were not dealt with but simply condoned. Patrol report by Sgt. Wilhelm Westphal (Police Depot Kupferberg), 20.10.1908, BArch-B, R 1002/2707, 89–91.

138. Tardiness: Qualification report, Sgt. La Croix (Police Depot Waterberg), 20.12.1910, BArch-B, R 1002/2492, 47. Absence: Report by Inspection Officer Freytag (Police Depot Spitzkoppe), 07.05.1909, BArch-B, R 1002/2723.

139. Report by Sgt. Johann Kullick (Police Station Karions), no date [transcript from 05.09.1912], BArch-B, R 1002/1184, no page number.

140. For example, report by Magistrate Weber (District Office Swakopmund), 17.10.1912, BArch-B, R 1002/3501, 83–88; excerpt of patrol book (Police Depot Kub), 01.01.1908, BArch-B, R 1002/2707, 26.

141. Lüdtke, *"Gemeinwohl," Polizei und "Festungspraxis,"* 146–47.

142. McNulty, "Generating Common Sense," 285.

143. Ludwig Maletz, "Aus meinem Dienstbuch. Auf Station Kalkfeld," quoted in Rafalski, *Vom Niemandsland*, 403.

144. Shadle, "Settlers, Africans, and Inter-personal Violence," 59.

145. Alf Lüdtke, "War as Work," in *No Man's Land of Violence*, ed. Bernd Weisbrod and Richard Bessel (Göttingen 2006), 134.

146. For instance, report of a series of raids by Inspection Officer Hollaender (Police Depot Kupferberg), 27.06.1911, BArch-B, R 1002/2710, 77–82; and by Sgt. Wilhelm Westphal (Police Depot Kupferberg), 07.12.1908, BArch-B, R 1002/2707, 145–50. For joint operations, see, for instance, Inspection Officer Johannes Medding (Police Depot Waterberg) to IdL, 08.08.1911, BArch-B, R 1002/2710, 131; District Chief Seydel (District Office Maltahöhe) to IdL, 17.03.1909, NAN, ZBU, 479 D.IV.o (vol. 1), 205–6; Chief of Police Bethe to Governor Seitz, 07.11.1913, BArch-B, R 1002/2711, 38, 40–45.

147. Patrol report by Sgt. Dufring (Police Station Okahandja), 16.02.1908, BArch-B, R 1002/2708, 30; patrol report by Sgt. Wilhelm Westphal (Police Depot Kupferberg), 07.12.1908, BArch-B, R 1002/2707, 146; patrol report by Acting District Chief Scheben (District Office Rehoboth), 19.06.1908, BArch-B, R 1002/2708, 117, 120–21.

148. Report by Inspection Officier Hirschberg (Depot Waterberg), 21.12.1913, BArch-B, R 1002/2719, 287; District Office Outjo to IdL, 25.10.1913, BArch-B, R 1002/2711, 69.

149. Micol Seigel, *Violence Work* (Durham, NC 2018), 10–12.

150. Statement by Sgt. Paul Melzer (Police Depot Spitzkoppe), 10.12.1913, BArch-B, R 1002/1184, no page number.

151. Patrol report by Sgt. Arno Scheiter (District Office Okahandja), 14.09.1910, BArch-B, R 1002/2709, 157. On the different uses of violent technologies, see also chapter 3.

152. Interestingly, etymologically, the noun *"Tüchtigkeit"* initially meant "bravery" and "violence" in old medieval German. *Duden-Online*, s.v. "tüchtig," http://www.duden.de/rechtschreibung/tuechtig.

153. Qualification certificate for Sgt. Lange by Magistrate Brill (District Office Windhuk), 05.01.1910, BArch-B, R 1002/2492, 20.

154. IdL to Gouv. Windhuk, 19.03.1912, BArch-B, R 1002/2466, 74.

155. Quoted in Rafalski, *Vom Niemandsland*, 11.

156. Preface by Chief of Police Bethe in Rafalski, *Vom Niemandsland*, 10.

157. "Killing-machines": Brigitte Lau, "Uncertain Certainties," in *History and Historiography* (Windhoek 1995), 39.

158. Trotha describes colonial state-building as a succession of stages of institutionalization and consolidation of state power. Trotha, *Koloniale Herrschaft*.

5. Policing Work

1. On new historical approaches that interpret labor history globally, see Marcel van der Linden, "The Promise and Challenges of Global Labor History," *International Labor and Working-Class History*, no. 82 (2012): 57–76.

2. For a comparative approach to policing labor in late colonialism, see Thomas, *Violence and Colonial Order*.

3. Veracini, *Settler Colonialism*; Patrick Wolfe, *Settler Colonialism and the Transformation of Anthropology* (London 1999).

4. Wolfe, *Settler Colonialism*, 163; see also Veracini, *Settler Colonialism*; Patrick Wolfe, "Settler Colonialism and the Elimination of the Native," *Journal of Genocide Research* 8, no. 4 (2006): 387–409.

5. For a critique of settler colonial theory as it has been established by Wolfe and Veracini, see Lisa Ford, "Locating Indigenous Self-Determination in the Margins of Settler Sovereignty," in *Between Indigenous and Settler Governance*, ed. Lisa Ford and Tim Rowse (Abingdon 2012), 1–11; Manu Vimalassery, Juliana Hu Pegues, and Alyosha Goldstein, "Introduction: On Colonial Unknowing," *Theory and Event* 19, no. 4 (2016): [13].

6. Cf. Zimmerer, *Deutsche Herrschaft*, 182–99.

7. I am not sure how reliable this number, which Zimmerer quotes from a farmer's report, is. But the fact that labor was scarce seems hard to dispute, even if the scarcity was overemphasized by the settler community. Ibid., 177. Cf. Lerp, *Imperiale Grenzräume*, 136–42. For settler population numbers, see Walther, *Creating Germans Abroad*, 24–27.

8. Migrant labor is extensively discussed in Lerp, *Imperiale Grenzräume*, 133–42, and Zimmerer, *Deutsche Herrschaft*, 211–42.

9. On African workers' insufficient sustenance, notably on farms, see Zollmann, *Koloniale Herrschaft*, 289–90.

10. Bley, *Kolonialherrschaft*; Drechsler, *Südwestafrika unter deutscher Kolonialherrschaft*; Zimmerer, *Deutsche Herrschaft*, 199–210; Zollmann, *Koloniale Herrschaft*, 281–306.

11. Häußler, "'Collaboration' or Sabotage?," 180.

12. Zollmann, *Koloniale Herrschaft*, 281. On this point, my work differs fundamentally from Zollmann's study of the Landespolizei. His emphasis on the limits of colonial rule and the state's failure to enforce order is based on an understanding of the workings of law and police practices that is, in my opinion, too schematic. Where policemen were not able to implement state policy to the letter, they failed, according to Zollmann. I argue that they did something else instead—they improvised—which had a crucial impact on the colonial order.

13. Internal note by Fromm (District Office Windhuk) to IdL, 07.08.1911, BArch-B, R 1002/2710, 114.

14. See files entitled "Written Exams and Term Papers, 1908–1914," BArch-B, R 1002/2537, 2538.

15. Annual report by Sgt. Paul Gentz (Police Station Aninus), 22.02.1912, NAN, DAR, 19 J.III, no page number.

16. Written exam by Sgt. Emil Hirschmüller (Police Depot Waterberg), no date, BArch-B, R 1002/2538, 94.

17. Written exam by Sgt. K. [name illegible] (Police Depot Waterberg), 28.09.1908, BArch-B, R 1002/2538, 90.

18. Gustav Frenssen, *Peter Moors Fahrt nach Südwest* (Berlin 1906), 200–201.

19. See George Steinmetz's study on German ethnographic descriptions of Herero, Witbooi, and Baster in *The Devil's Handwriting*, 75–134. On the contradictory nature of the classifications made by local administrators, see also Zimmerer, *Deutsche Herrschaft*, 181–82.

20. Written exam by Sgt. K. [name illegible] (Police Depot Waterberg), 28.09.1908, BArch-B, R 1002/2538, 89–91. Cf. also the French colonial discourse where, for in-

stance, Arabs were construed as "barbarians," equated with wild animals like foxes or wildcats who could thus not be domesticated or disciplined. During the Algerian war of independence, Algerians were called locusts, scorpions, or jackals. Sub-Saharan Africans, on the other hand, were construed as "savages," equated with domestic animals like dogs who were considered to be tamable and a reliable work-force. Olivier Le Cour Grandmaison, *Coloniser, exterminer* (Paris 2005), 58.

21. Annual report by Sgt. Paul Gentz (Police Station Aninus), 22.02.1912, NAN, DAR, 19 J.III, no page number.

22. Magistrate Zastrow (District Office Grootfontein) to IdL, 14.04.1911, BArch-B, R 1002/2710, 91; see also Magistrate Schultze-Jena (District Office Outjo) to Gouv. SWA, 20.01.1913, BArch-B, R 1002/2560, 58–59.

23. Governor Seitz to District Office Warmbad, 23.09.1913, BArch-B, R 1002/2706, 9.

24. For instance, "Buschmannsnot in Südwestafrika," *Deutsch-Südwestafrikanische Zeitung* (1911), cited in a report by Magistrate Zastrow (District Office Grootfontein), 14.04.1911, BArch-B, R 1002/2710, 91.

25. See chapters 6 through 9 in Gordon, *The Bushman Myth*, 49–85. I trace this development through the changing regulatory framework for weapons usage among the police in chapter 3.

26. Fitzpatrick, *Purging the Empire*, 177–204.

27. Governor Seitz to RKA, 12.08.1913, BArch-B, R 1001/2091, 11.

28. Annual report by Sgt. Paul Gentz (Police Station Aninus), 22.02.1912, NAN, DAR, 19 J.III, no page number.

29. Request regarding the "expedience" of corporal punishment by Foreign Office, Berlin, to Government GSWA, Windhuk, 12.01.1900, NAN, ZBU, 694 F.V.f.1, 1.

30. See the numerous responses to the Foreign Office's request, NAN, ZBU, 694 F.V.f.1, 2–84.

31. Schröder, *Prügelstrafe*. On corporal punishment in other German colonies, see Rebekka Habermas, *Skandal in Togo* (Frankfurt a.M. 2016); Trotha, "'One for Kaiser.'" See also chapter 3.

32. Report by missionary Thomas Fenchel, Keetmanshoop, 03.06.1900, NAN, ZBU, 694 F.V.f.1, 76.

33. Ibid.

34. Schreiber, "Rechtsgebräuche der Eingeborenen der deutschen Schutzgebiete in Afrika," (1903), cited in Schröder, *Prügelstrafe*, 15.

35. Whether and to what extent corporal punishment (as well as confinement) existed in precolonial Africa is still insufficiently studied. For more detail and the existing literature, see Ocobock, "Spare the Rod, Spoil the Colony," 30, fn. 9; cf. also Florence Bernault, ed., *A History of Prison and Confinement in Africa* (Portsmouth, NH 2003); Bernault, "The Shadow of Rule"; Bernault and Deutsch, "Control and Excess."

36. Meinhof, *Afrikanische Rechtsgebräuche* (1914), cited in Schröder, *Prügelstrafe*, 16.

37. Schröder, *Prügelstrafe*, 16.

38. On corporal punishment in nineteenth-century Germany, see Kosellek, *Preußen zwischen Reform und Revolution*, 641–59; Speitkamp, *Ohrfeige, Duell und Ehrenmord*, 25–52.

39. Written exam by Sgt. Emil Hirschmüller (Police Depot Waterberg), no date, BArch-B, R 1002/2538, 96–97.

40. Decree by Magistrate Anton Heilingbrunner (District Office Keetmanshoop), 07.01.1914, NAN, BKE, 32 L.2.e, 53.

41. For a comprehensive discussion of the intricacies of legal regulations regarding corporal punishment in the German Empire, see Schröder, *Prügelstrafe*; Zollmann, *Koloniale Herrschaft*, 107–14.

42. On the relationship between "native policy" and labor policy, notably the ideology of labor discipline in both the metropole and the colony, see Sebastian Conrad, "'Eingeborenenpolitik' in Kolonie und Metropole," in *Das Kaiserreich transnational*, ed. Sebastian Conrad and Jürgen Osterhammel (Göttingen 2006), 107–28.

43. Cited in Henning Melber, *Namibia* (Bremen 1981), 42–43.

44. The most important decrees were Governor Lindequist, "Runderlass des Gouverneurs von Deutsch-Südwestafrika betreffend die Vollziehung von Prügelstrafen," 22.12.1905, BArch-B, R 1002/2596, 20; Secretary of State Dernburg, "Erlass zur Handhabung der Prügelstrafe," 12.07.1907, BArch-B, R 1002/2596, 21–22; Vice Governor Hintrager, "Verfügung betr. Vollzug der Prügelstrafe," 30.10.1912, BArch-B, R 1002/2596, 51.

45. "Verordnung des Gouverneurs von Deutsch-Südwestafrika, betr. Dienst- und Arbeitsverträge mit Eingeborenen des südwestafrikanischen Schutzgebiets," 18.08.1907, published in *Deutsches Kolonialblatt* 18, no. 24 (1907): 1179–81.

46. Report by missionary Thomas Fenchel, Keetmanshoop, 03.06.1900, NAN, ZBU, 694 F.V.f.1, 76.

47. Cited in Schröder, *Prügelstrafe*, 103.

48. Decree by Magistrate Anton Heilingbrunner (District Office Keetmanshoop), 07.01.1914, NAN, BKE, 32 L.2.e, 51–55.

49. Ibid., 53.

50. Decree by Chancellor Hohenlohe, "Verfügung wegen Ausübung der Strafgerichtsbarkeit und der Disziplinargewalt gegenüber den Eingeborenen in Deutsch-Südwestafrika," 22.04.1896, BArch-B, R 1002/2596, 16.

51. Here, my reading of the source material differs again from Zollmann's interpretation. His take on corporal disciplining of African labor on farms remains within the archival sources' own logic of a dichotomy between excessive violence (committed by farmers), on the one hand, and a genuine but frustrated effort to rein in said excesses (by the police), on the other hand, which eventually led to the "wide acceptance [*Hinnahme*]" of farmers' behavior by the administration. *Koloniale Herrschaft*, 119–26, 283–92, quote from 292.

52. On honor as a guiding principle for the state administration's relationship to business interests, see Lüdtke, *"Gemeinwohl," Polizei und "Festungspraxis,"* 144.

53. "Drawn out": patrol report by Sgt. Dufring (Police Station Okahandja), 16.02.1908, BArch-B, R 1002/2708, 19–37. "Closed down": patrol report by Sgt. August Goldacker (Police Station Karibib), 04.07.1910, BArch-B, R 1002/2709, 105–9. "Cleaned": report by Sen. Staff Otto Donicht (District Office Karibib) to IdL, 09.12.1910, BArch-B, R 1002/2709, 198–99. "Collected": annual report by IdL, 14.05.1911, BArch-B, R 1002/2672, 68; and patrol book by District Chief Frankenberg (District Office Omaruru), 07.04.1908, BArch-B, R 1002/2708, 93–101. "Picked up" and "gotten hold of": patrol report by Inspection Officer Hildebrandt (Police Depot Waterberg), 27.06.1908, BArch-B, R 1002/2708, 129; patrol report by Sen. Staff Sgt. Otto Donicht (District Office Karibib), 19.09.1910, BArch-B, R 1002/2709, 187–90.

54. Patrol report by Inspection Officer Hildebrandt (Police Depot Waterberg), 27.06.1908, BArch-B, R 1002/2708, 129.

55. Patrol report by Sgt. Albert Link (Police Station Gobabis), 30.09.1910, BArch-B, R 1002/2709, 233.

56. Patrol report by Sen. Staff Sgt. Otto Donicht (District Office Karibib), 19.09.1910, BArch-B, R 1002/2709, 188.

57. See, for instance, patrol report by Sgt. Xaver Hagner (Police Station Okaukwejo), 20.10.1913, BArch-B, R 1002/2711, 68–69; patrol report by Sgt. Johann Sterzenbach (District Office Grootfontein), 03.09.1909, BArch-B, R 1002/3483, 26–27.

58. Patrol report by Sgt. Dufring (Police Station Okahandja), 16.02.1908, BArch-B, R 1002/2708, 20.

59. Marginal notes in patrol report by Sgt. Hermann Wolff (Police Depot Waterberg), 27.03.1911, BArch-B, R 1002/2710, 93–94.

60. On the unpoliced zone in the north of the colony, see Eckl, "Konfrontation und Kooperation am Kavango"; Zollmann, *Koloniale Herrschaft*, 306–40.

61. Patrol report by Sen. Staff Sgt. Heinrich Eggersglüß (District Office Maltahöhe), 17.05.1912, BArch-B, R 1002/2710, 226.

62. Schutztruppe command to Gouv. SWA, 10.10.1913, BArch-B, R 1002/2711, 40.

63. Patrol report by Sen. Staff Sgt. Heinrich Eggersglüß (District Office), 24.03.1913, BArch-B, R 1002/2711, 15.

64. Cf. Zollmann, "Die Kolonialpolizei," 309–16, 319–20.

65. For an early defense of this position, notably regarding the regulation of "Bushmen," see Magistrate Eschstruth (District Office Grootfontein) to Vice Governor Hintrager, 19.05.1907, BArch-B, R 1002/2506, 5–10.

66. Decree that regulated police-military cooperation by Commander in Chief Heydebreck (Schutztruppe), 30.05.1911, BArch-B, R 1002/2560, no page number. For an example of a joint patrol, see report by Inspection Officer Hollaender (Police Depot Kub), 27.09.1908, BArch-B, R 1002/2707, 114. For an example of repeated requests by the police to the military to help out, see telegram from District Office Maltahöhe to IdL, 13.11.1913, BArch-B, R 1002/2711, 46. Cf. Zollmann, "Die Kolonialpolizei," 317–19.

67. Patrol log entry by Sen. Staff Sgt. Oskar Weischer (District Office Outjo), 21.01.1914, BArch-B, R 1002/2711, 71–72.

68. District Chief Lux (District Office Bethanien) to Inspection Officer Pueschel (Officer Post Aus), 01.01.1914, BArch-B, R 1002/2711, 52–53.

69. For instance, the patrol report by Inspection Officer Hildebrandt (Police Depot Waterberg), 16.05.1908, BArch-B, R 1002/2707, 82.

70. Patrol book by District Chief Frankenberg (District Office Omaruru), 07.04.1908, BArch-B, R 1002/2708, 97.

71. Ibid., 97–98.

72. Patrol reports by Sgt. Hermann Eschen (District Office Gobabis), 08.08.1913, BArch-B, R 1002/2711, 30–32, and by Sgt. Johann Sterzenbach (District Office Grootfontein), 03.09.1909, BArch-B, R 1002/3483, 26–27. For more examples, see Zollmann, *Koloniale Herrschaft*, 302.

73. Report by Inspection Officer Hildebrandt (Police Depot Waterberg) to IdL, 28.03.1908, BArch-B, R 1002/2708, 66. Another patrol led by Kathena: report by Inspection Officer Hildebrandt (Police Depot Waterberg) to IdL, 27.02.1908, BArch-B, R 1002/2708, 53–54.

74. Rafalski, *Vom Niemandsland*, 381.

75. Patrol report by Sen. Staff Sgt. Josef Schaaps (Police Depot Kupferberg), 14.06.1913, BArch-B, R 1002/2711, 19.

76. Reports by Sgt. Friedrich Wiesemann (Police Station Rote Berge), 21.01.1913, NAN, BRE, 27 E.2.b (vol. 2), 351, and by Sgt. Wiesemann (Police Station Hornkranz) to District Office Rehoboth, 01.11.1913, NAN, BRE, 77 L.2.i, 39.

77. Report by Sen. Staff Sgt. Otto Donicht (District Office Karibib), 09.12.1910, BArch-B, R 1002/2709, 198–99.

78. Chief of Police Bethe (IdL) to District Office Karibib, 21.12.1910, BArch-B, R 1002/2709, 204.

79. Report by Inspection Officer Hildebrandt (Police Depot Waterberg) to IdL, 06.02.1909, BArch-B, R 1002/2707, 169–70.

80. Request by Aimé Weiss, Otana, 24.07.1907, NAN, DOK, 27 E.2.e, 90.

81. See, for example, the two files entitled "Requests for Allocation" in the papers of the District Office Okahandja, NAN, DOK, 27 E.2.e, vols.1 and 2.

82. Governor Seitz (Gouv. SWA) to IdL, 16.07.1914, BArch-B, R 1002/2610, 53.

83. Zimmerer, *Deutsche Herrschaft*, 190.

84. Ibid., 191.

85. Circular by Governor Seitz (Gouv. SWA) to IdL and all district offices, 16.07.1914, BArch-B, R 1002/2610, 53.

86. Vice Governor Oscar Hintrager (Gouv. SWA) to IdL, 26.06.1912, BArch-B, R 1002/2706, 6.

87. Typed manuscript by Ruth Kühnast, "Die Erziehung der Eingeborenen in Südwest" (1928), BAB, PA.46 III.1.1, 31–32.

88. Vice Governor Hintrager (Gouv. SWA) to IdL, 26.06.1912, BArch-B, R 1002/2706, 6.

89. Decree by Gouv. SWA, 24.11.1909, BArch-B, R 1002/2668, 7; decree by Vice Governor Hintrager, 15.02.1910, BArch-B, R 1002/2668, 9; decree by Governor Seitz, 29.09.1911, BArch-B, R 1002/2668, 11.

90. Zimmerer, *Deutsche Herrschaft*, 183; Krüger, *Kriegsbewältigung und Geschichtsbewusstsein*, 183.

91. Decree by Gouv. SWA, 24.11.1909, BArch-B, R 1002/2668, 7.

92. Decree by Governor Seitz, 20.06.1913, BArch-B, R 1002/2668, 14.

93. Patrol book by District Chief Frankenberg (District Office Omaruru), 07.04.1908, BArch-B, R 1002/2708, 98.

94. Report by Sgt. Arthur Wegener (Police Station Altmaltahöhe), 12.10.1911, BArch-B, R 1002/2710, 169–71.

95. For instance, written profile and two photographs sent by criminal investigator Sgt. Friedrich (Criminal Investigation Dept. Swakopmund) to District Office Rehoboth, 23.01.1913, NAN, BRE, 27 E.2.b (vol. 2), 347.

96. For instance, written profile and identification request by District Office Windhuk to District Office Rehoboth, 19.02.1912, NAN, BRE, 27 E.2.b (vol. 2), 53.

97. NAN, BRE, 27 E.2.b (vol. 2).

98. On police photography as a practice of state formation, and its ambivalent, unstable narratives, see Lorena Rizzo, "Shades of Empire," *Visual Anthropology* 26, no. 4 (2013): 328–54.

99. Bernhard Dernburg, *Zielpunkte des deutschen Kolonialwesens* (Berlin 1907), 6.

100. Governor Seitz to IdL, 07.06.1912, BArch-B, R 1002/2598, 173.

101. Chief of Police Heydebreck to District Office Windhuk, 18.01.1909, BArch-B, R 1002/2598, 72–73.

102. Governor Seitz reminded all district offices in 1911 that they were not authorized to hinder Africans from leaving their precinct. Governor Seitz to IdL, 18.11.1911, BArch-B, R 1002/2597, 61. On the discussions among colonial administrators about confining Africans in order to better control the labor force, see Zimmerer, *Deutsche Herrschaft*, 178–99.

103. Acting District Chief Götte (District Office Omaruru) to District Office Karibib, 05.03.1908, BArch-B, R 1002/2598, 26.

104. Report from Sgt. Ebermann to District Office Rehoboth, NAN, BRE, 75 L.2.f, 21–22; Magistrate Vietsch (Bezamt Rehoboth) to police stations Gosorobis, Hornkranz, and Rote Berge, 03.01.1913, NAN, BRE, 75 L.2.f, 23–24. Cf. also a report on "available" workers on another Baster farm by Sgt. Bruno Lippke (Police Station Gochanas), 05.05.1913, NAN, BRE, 28 E.2.d, 78.

105. Statement by farmer Grüner, Annex to Patrol Report by Sgt. Dufring, 16.02.1908, BArch-B, R 1002/2708, 35.

106. Ibid.

107. Ibid.; verdict by District Judge Dannert (District Court Windhuk), 25.11.1913, BArch-B, R 1002/2468, 14.

108. Inspection Officer Hildebrandt (Police Depot Waterberg) to farmer Freiherr von Speth, 02.12.1908, BArch-B, R 1002/2600, 19.

109. District Chief Frankenberg (District Office Omaruru) to Gouv. SWA, 29.10.1907, BArch-B, R 1002/2508, 26–27.

110. Inspection Officer Hildebrandt (Police Depot Waterberg) to farmer Freiherr von Speth, 02.12.1908, BArch-B, R 1002/2600, 19.

111. Farmer Nass to IdL, 18.03.1908, BArch-B, R 1002/2708, 60–61.

112. Farmer Weitzenberg to Major Heinrich Bethe (IdL), 16.10.1911, BArch-B, R 1002/2465, 68.

113. Farmer Matzkuhn to IdL, 25.11.1910, BArch-B, R 1002/2465, 18–19.

114. Statement by Staff Sgt. Rohde (District Office Omaruru), 09.12.1910, BArch-B, R 1002/2465, 26.

115. Hollaender (IdL) to Magistrate Görgens (District Office Omaruru), 15.02.1911, BArch-B, R 1002/2465, 18–27.

116. Statement by Staff Sgt. Rohde (District Office Omaruru), 09.12.1910, BArch-B, R 1002/2465, 26.

117. Report by District Office Windhuk, 12.07.1907, NAN, ZBU, W.III.B.5, vol.1, 2.

118. Questionnaire by Chief of Police Heydebreck to all district offices, 10.12.1907, BArch-B, R 1002/2610, 3–8.

119. For instance, patrol reports by Inspection Officer Hildebrandt (Police Depot Waterberg), 27.06.1908, BArch-B, R 1002/2708, 130; by Sgt. Franitzek (Police Depot Waterberg), 10.06.1908, BArch-B, R 1002/2708, 109.

120. Report by Staff Sgt. Kups (Police Station Karibib), 28.02.1911, BArch-B, R 1002/2465, 55.

121. Letter from Gustav Keseberg to Gouv., 11.02.1911, and deposition by Keseberg, 09.03.1911, BArch-B, R 1002/2465, 53–54, 57–58.

122. Kups had probably acted as intermediary in Cliff's pelt trade. District Chief Groeben (District Office Karibib) to settler Cliff, 31.03.1914, BArch-B, R 1002/2465, 96–97.

123. IdL to settler Schloifer, 20.10.1908, BArch-B, R 1002/2598, 46.

124. Blumhagen (Gouv. SWA) to farmer Jacobs (Farm Etemba Süd), 03.02.1915, NAN, DOK, 27 E.2.f, no page number.

125. District Office Rehoboth to Deutsch-Südwestafrikanische Wollzüchterei, 12.09.1913, NAN, BRE, 28 E.2.d, 133.

126. Report by Sgt. Karl Hofmann (Police Station Rehoboth), 19.06.1913, NAN, BRE, 28 E.2.d, 118–19.

127. IdL to District Office Windhuk, 24.07.1908, BArch-B, R 1002/2598, 37–38.

128. Magistrate Wasserfall (District Office Omaruru) to all police stations, 28.06.1912, NAN, Bezirksamt Omaruru (hereafter BOM), 53 28 (unregistered police files), no page number.

129. *Dienstvorschrift*, 13–14.

130. Cooper, "Conflict and Connection," 1530.

131. Report by Magistrate Carl Friedrich Schenke (District Office Swakopmund), 24.11.1908, NAN, ZBU, W.III.a.3. vol. 1, 47–51.

132. The district chief of Rehoboth explicitly instructed his men to inform workers about their right to quit a contract. Circular re: "native ordinances," by District Office Rehoboth to all police stations, 15.09.1908, NAN, BRE, 27 E.2.a, 16–17.

133. Patrol report by Staff Sgt. Max Ehrlich (District Office Okahandja), 01.08.1910, BArch-B, R 1002/2709, 128–29. Ehrlich's intervention marked the beginning of a series of events near the town of Wilhelmstal that, in October 1910, spiraled into the bloody suppression of the protest by the German military. On the massacre of Wilhelmstal, see William Beinart, "'Jamani': Cape Workers in German South-West Africa, 1904–1912," in *Hidden Struggles in Rural South Africa*, ed. William Beinart and Colin Bundy (Berkeley 1987), 180–82.

134. Report by Staff Sgt. Albrecht Arnhold (Police Station Namutoni), 06.03.1911, BArch-B, R 1002/2466, 50–51.

135. Notably, studies that stress the importance of space and the idea that colonial rule consisted in "islands of rule" seem to underestimate the effect of the state even if its representatives were not physically present at all times. Cf. Pesek, *Koloniale Herrschaft in Deutsch-Ostafrika*; Zollmann, *Koloniale Herrschaft*, 277–99.

136. Patrol report by Inspection Officer Hildebrandt (Police Depot Waterberg), 27.06.1908, BArch-B, R 1002/2708, 130.

137. Report by Sen. Staff Sgt. Otto Donicht (District Office Karibib), 09.12.1910, BArch-B, R 1002/2709, 198–99.

138. Deposition by farmer Lisse taken by Sgt. Lindinger at farm Choaberib, 18.07.1911, NAN, BRE, 28 E.2.f, 2.

139. Patrol report by Sgt. Franitzek (Police Depot Waterberg), 10.06.1908, BArch-B, R 1002/2708, 112.

140. Letter by farmer Nass (Otjuruntjondjau) to IdL, 18.03.1908, BArch-B, R 1002/2708, 60.

141. Ibid., 60–61.

142. Letter by District Office Rehoboth to Deutsch-Südwestafrikanische Wollzüchterei, 12.09.1913, NAN, BRE, 28 E.2.d, 133.

143. Report by Inspection Officer Hollaender (Depot Kub), 02.04.1908, R 1002/2708, 67–69.

144. Maletz, "Aus meinem Dienstbuch," in Rafalski, *Vom Niemandsland*, 401–5.

145. Ibid., 404.

146. Ibid., 405.

147. Decree by Governor Lindequist, 22.12.1905, BArch-B, R 1002/2596, 20.

148. See, for instance, patrol report by Sgt. Franitzek (Police Depot Waterberg), 10.06.1908, BArch-B, R 1002/2708, 112.

149. Vice Governor Hintrager to IdL and all police depots, 26.06.1912, BArch-B, R 1002/2706, 6. Already in 1907, Undersecretary Lindequist had interpreted §7 of the "native ordinance" regarding labor relations in this direction naming insufficient lodging and boarding, no wages, deficient clothing, and negligence in case of sickness as the main reasons for which workers could leave their employer. Copy of letter by Undersecretary Lindequist to District Office Swakopmund, 18.07.1907, cited in Zollmann, *Koloniale Herrschaft*, 287.

150. Report by Magistrate Vietsch (District Office Rehoboth) to Gouv. SWA, 21.10.1912, NAN, BRE, 27 E.2.a, 43–44.

151. Ibid., 44.

152. Vice Governor Hintrager to all district offices and IdL, 12.11.1912, BArch-B, R 1002/2591, 86.

153. Workers' depositions taken by Sgt. Karl Rudzinski and Sgt. Müller (Police Station Epikuro), 01.06.1911, BArch-B, R 1002/2710, 116–19.

154. Statements taken by Sgt. Bruno Lippke (Police Station Gurumanas), 25.10.1912, NAN, BRE, 28 E.2.f, 69.

155. Workers' depositions taken by Sgt. Karl Rudzinski and Sgt. Müller (Police Station Epikuro), 01.06.1911, BArch-B, R 1002/2710, 116–19.

156. Internal note by Kastl (Gouv. SWA), 03.08.1911, BArch-B, R 1002/2710, 114.

157. Internal note by Magistrate Fromm (District Office Windhuk) to IdL, 07.08.1911, BArch-B, R 1002/2710, 116.

158. Cases recorded in the District Office Rehoboth files under the heading "Native Workers. Complaints" (1911–1914), in NAN, BRE, E.2.f; and those recorded in the District Office Keetmanshoop files under the headings "Native Workers. Complaints" (1912–1914) and "Board and Compensation of Natives (Farm Workers)" (1912–1913), in NAN, BKE, E.2.f (2 vols.) and E.2.m.

159. Statement of Samuel Rooi taken by Staff Sgt. Hermann Kratz (Police Station Hasuur), 18.08.1910, NAN, DAR, 18 G.II.1, 48.

160. Cf. Zimmerer, *Deutsche Herrschaft*, 198.

161. Excerpt from patrol book by Inspection Officer Hollaender (Police Depot Kub), 01.01.1908, BArch-B, R 1002/2707, 26.

162. Circular by Magistrate Vietsch (District Office Rehoboth) to all police stations, 25.07.1913, NAN, BRE, 27 E.2.a, 66.

163. Report by Sgt. Friedrich Nowakowsky (Police Station Ovikokorero) to District Office Okahandja, 19.04.1914, NAN, DOK, 27 E.2.f, 19–20.

164. Circular regarding "native ordinances," by District Office Rehoboth to all police stations, 15.09.1908, NAN, BRE, 27 E.2.a, 16–17.

165. District Chief Fromm (District Office Okahandja) to business owner Weilbächer, 14.05.1908, NAN, DOK, 27 E.2.f, 3–4.

166. Decree by Governor Seitz (Gouv. SWA), 05.08.1911, BArch-B, R 1002/2596, 5.

167. Hensel (IdL) to Police Depot Spitzkoppe, 15.01.1913, BArch-B, R 1002/2596, 56; reply by Sen. Staff Sgt. Schlink (District Office Warmbad), 11.02.1913, BArch-B, R 1002/2596, 56.

168. Report by Sgt. Ludwig Maletz (Police Station Kalkfeld), 30.04.1913, BArch-B, R 1002/3226, 80–81; Chief of Police Heinrich Bethe (IdL) to District Chief Görgens (District Office Omaruru), 24.06.1913, BArch-B, R 1002/3226, 77. See also Maletz's embellished account above in which he very naturally assumed penal power.

169. Blumhagen (IdL) to District Office Grootfontein, 19.10.1913, NAN, ZBU, 692 F.5.d.2, 5.

170. Internal note by Kelz (Gouv. SWA), 10.11.1913, NAN, ZBU, 692 F.5.d.2, 6.

171. Decree by Magistrate Heilingbrunner (District Office Keetmanshoop), 07.01.1914, NAN, BKE, 32 L.2.e, 50.

172. Governor Seitz to all district offices, 01.05.1914, NAN, ZBU, 692 F.5.d.1, 36; also in BArch-B, R 1002/2596, 61.

173. Zimmerer, *Deutsche Herrschaft*, 210.

174. Letter by Magistrate Vietsch to farmer Lisse, Rehoboth, 06.08.1911, NAN, BRE, 28 E.2.f, 1.

175. Report by District Chief Ahlhorn (District Office Okahandja) to IdL, 08.06.1914, NAN, DOK, 27 E.2.f, no page number.

176. Minutes of the meeting between State Secretary Dernburg, Governor Seitz, and high officials in the Windhuk Government, 06.08.1908, BArch-B, R 1002/2693, 191.

Conclusion

1. Letter by stud farm manager Clavé, Nauchas, 11.06.1908, BArch-B, 2708, 127.

2. Marginalia by Heidebreck, ibid.

3. "Verordnung des Gouverneurs von Deutsch-Südwestafrika, betr. die Paßpflicht der Eingeborenen," 18.08.1907, *Deutsches Kolonialblatt* 18, no. 24 (1907): 1183–84.

4. Circular regarding the logistics for implementing the "pass ordinance" by Vice Governor Hintrager to all district offices, 13.05.1907, BArch-B, 2597, 1–2.

5. "Verordnung des Gouverneurs von Deutsch-Südwestafrika, betr. die Paßpflicht der Eingeborenen," 18.08.1907, *Deutsches Kolonialblatt* 18, no. 24 (1907): 1184.

6. Bley, *Kolonialherrschaft*, 213.

7. For an introduction and literature, see Roberts, "Law, Crime and Punishment in Colonial Africa."

8. David M. Anderson, "Policing, Prosecution and the Law in Colonial Kenya, c. 1905–39," in *Policing the Empire*, ed. David M. Anderson and David Killingray (Manchester, UK 1991), 183; see also David M. Anderson, "Stock Theft and Moral Economy in Colonial Kenya," *Africa: Journal of the International African Institute* 56, no. 4 (1986): 399–416; David M. Anderson, "Master and Servant in Colonial Kenya," *Journal of African History* 41, no. 3 (2000): 459–85.

9. Anderson, "Policing, Prosecution and the Law," 198.

10. Harry Schwirck, "Violence, Race, and the Law in German South West Africa, 1884–1914" (PhD diss., Cornell University, 1998), 13.

11. Schwirck, "Law's Violence and the Boundary between Corporal Discipline and Physical Abuse in German South West Africa," 82.

12. Cooper, "Conflict and Connection," 1517.

13. Steven Pinker, *The Better Angels of Our Nature* (London 2011), xxi.

14. Mazower, "Violence and the State in the Twentieth Century," 1158.

15. Eric Hobsbawm, *Age of Extremes* (London 1994), 12.

16. "The statistical problems appear to be overwhelming," Mazower observes for the calculation of deaths caused by political violence alone. "Violence and the State," 1158, fn. 1. Pinker in *The Better Angels* claims to quantitatively document and compare numbers regarding death, assault, torture, abuse, disease, etc., over the span of all of human history.

17. Mazower's review article "Violence and the State" is an example of this. The "violence" in his title refers mostly to scholarship on war and mass murder.

Bibliography

Archival Sources

German Federal Archives, Berlin-Lichterfelde (BArch-B)

R 1001 Imperial Colonial Office (Reichskolonialamt RKA)

Vols. 1227–1233: Arbeiterfragen und Arbeitsverhältnisse in Deutsch-Südwestafrika, 1894–1942
Vol. 1912: Polizeivorschriften in Deutsch-Südwestafrika, 1907–1925
Vol. 1913: Erlaß gesundheitspolizeilicher Vorschriften in Südwestafrika, 1907
Vols. 1914–1916: Polizeitruppe in Deutsch-Südwestafrika, 1894–1939
Vol. 1917: Ausstellung polizeilicher Führungsatteste in Südwestafrika, 1924–1939
Vol. 1920: Ausstellung von Reisepässen—Südwestafrika, 1924–1939
Vols. 2183–2184: Militär- und Polizeistationen in Deutsch-Südwestafrika—Einrichtung und Tätigkeit, 1894–1913
Vol. 2235: Verwaltungsangelegenheiten der Eingeborenen in Deutsch-Südwestafrika, 1906–1913

R 1002 Protectorate German Southwest Africa
Central Government (Gouvernement SWA)

Vols. 91–1184: Personnel files

Landespolizei Headquarters
(Inspektion der Landespolizei IdL)

Vol. 2415: Allgemeine Beamtenangelegenheiten und -Bestimmungen. Gen., 1907–1914
Vol. 2416: Allgemeine Beamtenangelegenheiten und -Bestimmungen. Spec. 1908–1914
Vol. 2417: Bestimmungen für die Annahme von Beamten, 1907–1913
Vol. 2418: Bestimmungen über die Annahme von Angestellten ohne Beamteneigenschaft und Polizisten, 1908–1913
Vol. 2422: Entlassung der zur Probedienstleistung angestellten Schutztruppenangehörigen, 1908–1913
Vol. 2424: Kündigung der Dienstverträge, Entlassungsbestimmungen, Berichterstattung. Gen., 1909–1913

Vol. 2427: Feststellungen über das Vorleben der Beamten usw. Strafregisterauszüge, 1910–1911
Vol. 2429: Statistische Aufstellungen, 1913–1914
Vol. 2431: Verheiratung der Polizeibeamten, 1909–1912
Vol. 2432: Dienstl. Verwendung von Landespolizisten in brit. SWA
Vol. 2465: Beschwerden gegen Beamte, 1909–1914
Vol. 2466: Gerichtliche Strafverfahren, Zwangsvollstreckungen gegen Beamte, 1909–1914
Vol. 2467: Disziplinar-Verfahren und Bestrafungen, 1908–1912
Vol. 2468: Strafanträge wegen Beamtenbeleidigung, 1909–1915
Vol. 2484: Personal-Verzeichnisse, Berichte und Akten, 1911–1914
Vol. 2485: Beamtenverzeichnis, 1909–1913
Vol. 2489: Monatsrapporte. Gen., 1909–1914
Vol. 2492: Qualifikationsberichte, 1909–1915
Vol. 2494: Beschaffung des Beamtenersatzes durch das RKA: Bewerbungsgesuche, Anwärterlisten, 1907–1911
Vol. 2497: Beschaffung von Beamtenersatz im Schutzgebiet. Allg., 1907–1912
Vol. 2502: Einstellung von Polizisten. Gen., 15. Aug. 1907–7. März 1913
Vol. 2503: Einstellung von Polizisten. Spec., 1914
Vol. 2506: Besetzung der Dienststellen mit Polizeibeamten. Beamtenforderungen und Überweisungen. Bericht Grootfontein, 1907–1914
Vol. 2507: Besetzung der Dienststellen mit Polizeibeamten. Beamtenforderungen und -überweisungen. Bericht Outjo, 1906–1914
Vol. 2508: Besetzung der Dienststellen mit Polizeibeamten. Beamtenforderungen und Überweisungen. Bericht Omaruru, 1907–1914
Vol. 2519: Besetzung der Dienststellen mit Polizeibeamten. Beamtenforderungen und Überweisungen. Bericht Bethanien, 1906–1914
Vol. 2528: Verwendung der Polizeibeamten an den Amtssitzen und in anderen Verwaltungszweigen, 1910–1914
Vol. 2534: Ausbildung der Polizeibeamten auf den Depots. Gen., 1908–1910
Vol. 2535: Ausbildung der Polizeibeamten auf den Depots. Spec., 1908–1910
Vol. 2536: Vorschläge und Kommandierungen pp. für den Ausbildungskursus in Windhuk, 1908–1915
Vol. 2537: Lehrgang und Prüfung der zum Kursus nach Windhuk kommandierten Beamten, 1908–1914
Vol. 2538: Prüfungs- und Hausarbeiten ausschließlich der Kursus-Teilnehmer in Windhuk, 1908–1910
Vol. 2539: Reit- und Schießdienst der Polizeibeamten. Gen., 1908–1914
Vol. 2540: Reit- und Schießdienst der Polizeibeamten. Spec., 1909–1914
Vol. 2552: Allgemeine Dienstvorschriften und Anweisungen. Gen., 1907–1914
Vol. 2553: Allgemeine Dienstvorschriften und Anweisungen. Spec., 1907–1914
Vol. 2560: Waffengebrauch, 1908–1914
Vol. 2562: Bekleidung und Ausrüstung. Gen., 1907–1914
Vol. 2583: Terminkalender, 1908–1914
Vol. 2590: Dienstbücher der Polizeibeamten, 1907–1914
Vol. 2591: Eingeborenenangelegenheiten, Allgemeines. Gen., 1907–1914
Vol. 2593: Eingeborenenangelegenheiten, Allgemeines. Spez., Bd. 3, 1914–1915

Vol. 2594: Vorstrafen und Bestrafungen von Polizeidienern, 1913–1914
Vol. 2596: Verfügung von Disziplinarstrafen gegen Eingeborene, 1908–1915
Vol. 2597: Eingeborenen-Verordnungen, 1907–1914
Vol. 2598: Eingeborene der Inspektion, Bd. 1, 1907–1912
Vol. 2600: Eingeborene des Depots Waterberg, 1908–1912
Vol. 2601: Eingeborene des Depots Kub, 1908–1912
Vol. 2602: Eingeborene des Depots Kupferberg, 1908–1913
Vol. 2604: Schiessdienst der Polizeidiener, 1910–1914
Vol. 2605: Eingeborenen-Verpflegung. Gen., 1907–1914
Vol. 2608: Eingeborenen-Bewaffnung. Gen., 10. Juni 1910
Vol. 2610: Farmangelegenheiten, 1907–1914
Vol. 2639: Kassenabrechnungen Distriktsamt Bethanien
Vol. 2668: Gefängniswesen, Gefangenenangelegenheiten, 1907–1914
Vol. 2670: Gefangenen-Schließzeug, 1907–1912
Vol. 2672: Jahresberichte, Bd. 1, 1908–1914
Vol. 2673: Jahresberichte, Bd. 2, 1908–1910
Vol. 2676: Landesrat, 1913–1914
Vol. 2692: Organisation, Ausführungsbestimmungen zur A.V. vom 4. Okt. 1907. Bd. I, 1907–1913
Vol. 2693: Organisation, Gliederung und Verteilung der Landespolizei, Ausführungsbestimmungen zur A.V. vom 4. Okt. 1907. Bd. II, 1907–1911
Vol. 2694: Verzeichnisse der Polizeistationen und deren Patrouillenbezirke. Bd. I, 1908–1914
Vol. 2703: Polizei und Truppe in (Britisch) Südafrika, 1908–1913
Vol. 2706: Patrouillen. Gen., 1907–1914
Vol. 2707: Patrouillen. Bd. I, Spec., 1907–1909
Vol. 2708: Patrouillen. Bd. II, Spec., März–Okt. 1908
Vol. 2709: Patrouillen. Bd. III, Spec., 1910–1911
Vol. 2710: Patrouillen. Bd. IV, Spec., 1910–1912
Vol. 2711: Patrouillen. Bd. V, Spec., 1912–1914
Vol. 2719: Reisen, Revisionsberichte des Inspektionsoffiziers des 1. Polizeibezirks, 1908–1914
Vol. 2723: Reisen, Revisionsberichte des Inspektionsoffiziers des 4. Polizeibezirks, 1909–1914
Vol. 2725: Rechtsangelegenheiten, 1908–1914
Vol. 2782: Geheimakten betr. Beamte pers., 1907–1908
Vol. 2783: Geheimakten betr. Beamte pers., 1907–1911
Vol. 2790: Alphabetisches Verzeichnis der unteren Beamten der Landespolizei
Vols. 2792–3565: Personnel files

Namibia Resource Center, Basel (BAB)

PA.46 III.1.1: Ruth Kühnast: "Die Erziehung der Eingeborenen in Südwest" (1928)
PA.50: Dienstbuch Pol. Sgt. Albrecht Arnhold

National Archives of Namibia, Windhoek (NAN)

FILES OF THE GERMAN COLONIAL GOVERNMENT ZBU
CENTRAL GOVERNMENT

Vol. 479 D.IV.o (vol. 1): Patrouillenritte der Landespolizei und der Truppe
     (1907–1909)
Vol. 479 D.IV.o (vol. 2): Patrouillenritte der Landespolizei und der Truppe
     (1909–1911)
Vol. 692 F.V.d.1: Disziplinarbefugnisse gegenüber Eingeborenen. Generalia
     (1903–1914)
Vol. 692 F.V.d.2: Disziplinarbefugnisse gegenüber Eingeborenen. Specialia
     (1913–1913)
Vol. 694 F.V.f.1: Vollzug der Prügel- und Rutenstrafe. Generalia (1900–1909)
Vols. 698–712 F.V.k: Strafverzeichnisse und Prügelprotokolle (1897–1914)
Vol. 2044 W.III.a.3 (vol. 1): Verordnungen und Vorschriften betr. die Eingeborenen
     (1907–1910)
Vol. 2045 W.III.b.5 (vol. 1): Maßregeln zur Kontrolle der Eingeborenen (1907–1914)

BRE DISTRICT OFFICE REHOBOTH

Vol. 13 B.9.b.a: Beschwerden in Verwaltungsangelegenheiten (1906–1910)
Vol. 27 E.2.b (vol. 2): Kontrolle der eingeborenen Arbeiter, Recherche nach
     Entlaufenen und Zugelaufenen (1911–1914)
Vol. 27 E.2.b (vol. 3): Kontrolle der eingeborenen Arbeiter, Recherche nach
     Entlaufenen und Zugelaufenen (1911–1914)
Vol. 27 E.2.e (vol. 2): Anträge auf Zuweisung von eingeborenen Arbeitern
     (1914–1915)
Vol. 28 E.2.f: Eingeborene Arbeiter. Beschwerden (1911–1914)
Vol. 28 E.2.d: Eingeborene Arbeiter. Dienstverträge, Schriftverkehr (1912–1913)
Vol. 28 E.2.l: Anträge auf Zuweisung von eingeborenen Arbeitern (1914–1915)
Vol. 34 E.5.e: Klagen Eingeborener gegen Weisse (1907–1912)
Vol. 73 L.2.e.1: Dienstt. Wachtmeister Karl Dietrich (1907–1914)
Vol. 73 L.2.e.3: Pol. Sgt. Bülow
Vol. 73 L.2.e.4: Pol. Wachtm. Bilewski (1908–1914); Pol. Sgt. Diener
Vol. 73 L.2.e.5: Pol. Sgt. Ebermann
Vol. 73 L.2.e.7: Pol. Sgt. Karl Hofmann (1907–1914)
Vol. 73 L.2.e.8: Pol. Sgt. Richard Neumann
Vol. 75 L.2.f: Polizeidiener und Feldkornets (1910–1914)
Vol. 75 L.2.h: Bekleidung, Ausrüstung, Bewaffnung allgemein (1909–1915)
Vol. 77 L.2.i: Patrouillendienst und Ritte (1910–1914)

DAR DISTRICT OFFICE AROAB

Vol. 3 E.1.d: Passpflicht der Eingeborenen (1906–1913)
Vol. 4 E.4.d: Eingeborenen Strafakten (1912–1914)
Vol. 18 E.II.5: Eingeborene Strafsachen (1909–1912)

Vol. 18 G.II.1: Gerichtswesen (1907–1912)
Vol. 20 P.II.1: Landespolizei (1907–1911)
Vol. 20 S.V: Standesamt (1906–1914)

BSW District Office Swakopmund

Vol. 85 L.2.c: Landespolizei: Dienstbeschädigungen, Ansprüche, Beihilfen
    (1902–1913)
Vol. 125 UA.26/1: Allgemeines

BOM District Office Omaruru

Vol. 53 28: Polizei. Verschiedenes [unregistered police files]

DOK District Office Okahandja

Vol. 27 E.2.e: Eingeborene Arbeiter. Anträge auf Zuweisung (1904–1914)
Vol. 27 E.2.f: Eingeborene Arbeiter. Beschwerden (1908–1914)

BKE District Office Keetmanshoop

Vol. 32 L.2.e: Polizeibeamte, Dienstinstruktionen, Versetzungen (1912–1915)
Vol. 201 B.II.66.c (vol. 1): Eingeborene Polizisten (1898–1909)

Published Sources

Deutsches Kolonialblatt
Deutsche Kolonialgesetzgebung
Deutsch-Südwestafrikanische Zeitung
Nachrichtenblatt des Verbandes der Polizeibeamten für die deutschen Kolonien e.V.
Reichsgesetzblatt
Stenographische Berichte des Reichstags

Bayer, Maximilian. *The Rehoboth Baster Nation of Namibia.* Translated from the
    German and edited with an introduction by Peter Carstens. [1906]. Basel:
    Basler Afrika Bibliographien, 1984.
Brockmann, Heinrich. *Haba du ta gob: Lebenserinnerungen von Missionar Johann
    Heinrich Brockmann.* Edited by Jürgen Hoffmann. 1946. Reprint, Berlin: Klaus
    Guhl, 1992.
Dernburg, Bernhard. *Zielpunkte des deutschen Kolonialwesens: Zwei Vorträge.* Berlin:
    Mittler, 1907.
Dienstvorschrift für die berittene Landespolizei. Breslau: F. W. Jungfer, 1910.
Evert, Georg. "Die Herkunft der deutschen Unteroffiziere und Soldaten am 1.
    Dezember 1906." *Zeitschrift des Königlich Preussischen Statistischen Landesamts*
    28 (1908).

Frenssen, Gustav. *Peter Moors Fahrt nach Südwest: Ein Feldzugsbericht*. Berlin: Grote'sche Verlagsbuchhandlung, 1906.

Hoernlé, Winifred. *The Social Organization of the Nama and Other Essays*. Edited by Peter Carstens. 1918–1937. Reprint, Johannesburg: Witwatersrand University Press, 1985.

Irle, Jacob. *Die Herero: Ein Beitrag zur Landes-, Volks- & Missionskunde*. Gütersloh: C. Bertelsmann, 1906.

Justi, Johann Heinrich Gottlob von. *Grudsätze der Policeywissenschaft: In einem vernünftigen, auf den Endzweck der Policey gegründeten, Zusammenhange und zum Gebrauch academischer Vorlesungen abgefasset*. 3rd ed. Göttingen: Im Verlag der Witwe Vandenhoek, 1782.

Kleinau, Friedrich. "Aus den Dünen von Südwest." *Nachrichtenblatt des Verbandes der Polizeibeamten für die deutschen Kolonien e.V.*, April 1925.

Meinertzhagen, Richard. *Kenya Diary: 1902–1906*. 1957. Reprint, London: Eland Books, 1983.

Orwell, George. *Shooting an Elephant*. 1936. Reprint, London: Penguin Classics, 2009.

Rafalski, Hans Joachim. *Vom Niemandsland zum Ordnungsstaat: Geschichte der ehemaligen Kaiserlichen Landespolizei für Deutsch-Südwestafrika*. Berlin: Emil Wernitz, 1930.

Schopenhauer, Arthur. *Aphorismen zur Lebensweisheit*. 1851. Reprint, Frankfurt a.M.: Insel-Verlag, 1976.

Silvester, Jeremy, and Jan-Bart Gewald, eds. *Words Cannot Be Found: German Colonial Rule in Namibia: An Annotated Reprint of the 1918 Blue Book*. Leiden: Brill, 2003.

Simmel, Georg. *Soziologie: Untersuchungen über die Formen der Vergesellschaftung*. Edited by Otthein Rammstedt. 1908. Georg Simmel-Gesamtausgabe, vol. 11. Reprint, Frankfurt a.M.: Suhrkamp, 1992.

Spohn. *Berufs- und Standespflichten der Unteroffiziere*. Oldenburg: Gerhard Stalling, 1909.

Tesch, Johannes. *Die Laufbahn der deutschen Kolonialbeamten, ihre Pflichten und Rechte*. 6th ed. Berlin: Otto Salle, 1912.

Weber, Max. *Wissenschaft als Beruf*. Munich; Leipzig: Duncker: Humblot, 1919.

——. *Wirtschaft und Gesellschaft: Die Wirtschaft und die gesellschaftlichen Ordnungen und Mächte. Nachlaß. Teilband 4: Herrschaft*, edited by Edith Hanke. Repr. [1922] Max Weber-Gesamtausgabe. Tübingen: J. C. B. Mohr, 2005.

Zorn, Philipp Karl Ludwig, ed. *Deutsche Kolonialgesetzgebung: Text-Ausg. m. Anm. u. Sachreg*. 2nd ed. Berlin: Guttentag, 1913.

Secondary Literature

Adas, Michael. *Machines as the Measure of Men: Science, Technology, and Ideologies of Western Dominance*. Ithaca, NY: Cornell University Press, 1989.

——. *Dominance by Design: Technological Imperatives and America's Civilizing Mission*. Cambridge, MA: Belknap Press of Harvard University Press, 2006.

Adhikari, Mohamed. "Hope, Fear, Shame, Frustration: Continuity and Change in the Expression of Coloured Identity in White Supremacist South Africa, 1910–1994." *Journal of Southern African Studies* 32, no. 3 (2006): 467–87.

Ahmed, Sara. *The Cultural Politics of Emotion*. New York: Routledge, 2004.

Anderson, David M. "Stock Theft and Moral Economy in Colonial Kenya." *Africa: Journal of the International African Institute* 56, no. 4 (1986): 399–416.

——. "Policing, Prosecution and the Law in Colonial Kenya, c. 1905–39." In *Policing the Empire: Government, Authority, and Control, 1830–1940*, edited by David M. Anderson and David Killingray, 183–200. Manchester, UK: Manchester University Press, 1991.

——. "Policing the Settler State: Colonial Hegemony in Kenya, 1900–1952." In *Contesting Colonial Hegemony: State and Society in Africa and India*, edited by Dagmar Engels and Shula Marks, 248–64. London: British Academic Press, 1994.

——. "Master and Servant in Colonial Kenya." *Journal of African History* 41, no. 3 (2000): 459–85.

——. "Kenya, 1895–1939: Registration and Rough Justice." In *Masters, Servants, and Magistrates in Britain and the Empire, 1562–1955*, edited by Douglas Hay and Paul Craven, 498–528. Chapel Hill: University of North Carolina Press, 2004.

——. "Punishment, Race and 'the Raw Native': Settler Society and Kenya's Flogging Scandals, 1895–1930." *Journal of Southern African Studies* 37 (2011): 479–97. https://doi.org/10.1080/03057070.2011.602887.

Anderson, David M., and David Killingray. "Consent, Coercion and Control: Policing the Empire, 1830–1940." In *Policing the Empire: Government, Authority, and Control, 1830–1940*, edited by David M. Anderson and David Killingray, 1–15. Manchester, UK: Manchester University Press, 1991.

——, eds. *Policing the Empire: Government, Authority, and Control, 1830–1940*. Manchester, UK: Manchester University Press, 1991.

——, eds. *Policing and Decolonisation: Politics, Nationalism, and the Police, 1917–65*. Manchester, UK: Manchester University Press, 1992.

Arendt, Hannah. *On Violence*. New York: Harcourt Brace Jovanovich, 1970.

Asad, Talal. "Toward a Genealogy of the Concept of Ritual." In *Genealogies of Religion: Discipline and Reasons of Power in Christianity and Islam*, 55–80. Baltimore: Johns Hopkins University Press, 1993.

Axster, Felix. "Die Angst vor dem 'Verkaffern': Politiken der Reinigung im deutschen Kolonialismus." *WerkstattGeschichte* 39 (2005): 39–53.

——. *Koloniales Spektakel in 9 x 14: Bildpostkarten im Deutschen Kaiserreich*. Bielefeld: transcript, 2014.

Bald, Detlef. *Vom Kaiserheer zur Bundeswehr: Sozialstruktur des Militärs: Politik der Rekrutierung von Offizieren und Unteroffizieren*. Frankfurt a.M.: Lang, 1981.

Barnard, Alan. *Hunters and Herders of Southern Africa: A Comparative Ethnography of the Khoisan Peoples*. Cambridge: Cambridge University Press, 1992.

Barth, Boris, and Jürgen Osterhammel, eds. *Zivilisierungsmissionen: Imperiale Weltverbesserung seit dem 18. Jahrhundert*. Konstanz: UVK Verlagsgesellschaft, 2005.

Bat, Jean-Pierre, and Nicolas Courtin, eds. *Maintenir l'ordre colonial: Afrique et Madagascar (XIXe—XXe siècles)*. Rennes: Presses Universitaires de Rennes, 2012.

Bayley, David H. *Patterns of Policing: A Comparative International Analysis*. New Brunswick, NJ: Rutgers University Press, 1985.

Beinart, William. "'Jamani': Cape Workers in German South-West Africa, 1904–1912." In *Hidden Struggles in Rural South Africa: Politics and Popular Movements in the Transkei and Eastern Cape, 1890–1930*, edited by William Beinart and Colin Bundy, 166–90. Berkeley: University of California Press, 1987.

Berlière, Jean-Marc. "The Professionalisation of the Police under the Third Republic in France, 1875–1914." In *Policing Western Europe: Politics, Professionalism, and Public Order, 1850–1940*, edited by Clive Emsley and Barbara Weinberger, 36–54. New York: Greenwood Press, 1991.

——. *Le monde des polices en France: XIXe–XXe siècles*. Paris: Editions Complexe, 1996.

Berlière, Jean-Marc, and René Levy. *Histoire des polices en France: De l'ancien régime à nos jours*. Paris: Nouveau Monde Éd, 2011.

Berman, Bruce J. "The Perils of Bula Matari: Constraint and Power in the Colonial State." *Canadian Journal of African Studies* 31, no. 3 (1997): 556–70. https://doi.org/10.2307/486198.

Bernault, Florence, ed. *A History of Prison and Confinement in Africa*. Portsmouth, NH: Heinemann, 2003.

——. "The Politics of Enclosure in Colonial and Post-Colonial Africa." In *A History of Prison and Confinement in Africa*, edited by Florence Bernault, 1–53. Portsmouth, NH: Heinemann, 2003.

——. "The Shadow of Rule: Colonial Power and Modern Punishment in Africa." In *Cultures of Confinement*, edited by Frank Dikötter and Ian Brown, 55–94. London: Hurst, 2007.

Bernault, Florence, and Jan-Georg Deutsch. "Control and Excess: Histories of Violence in Africa." *Africa* 85, no. 3 (2015): 385–94. https://doi.org/10.1017/S0001972015000248.

——, eds. "Histories of Violence in Africa." *Africa*, Special issue, 85, no. 3 (2015). https://doi.org/10.1017/S0001972015000248.

Bessel, Richard. *Violence: A Modern Obsession*. London: Simon and Schuster, 2015.

Bhabha, Homi. "Of Mimicry and Man: The Ambivalence of Colonial Discourse." *October* 28 (1984): 125–33.

Bijker, Wiebe E., Thomas Parke Hughes, and Trevor Pinch, eds. *The Social Construction of Technological Systems: New Directions in the Sociology and History of Technology*. Cambridge, MA: MIT Press, 1987.

Bischoff, Eva. *Kannibale-Werden: Eine postkoloniale Geschichte deutscher Männlichkeit um 1900*. Bielefeld: transcript, 2011.

Blackbourn, David. *The Long Nineteenth Century: A History of Germany, 1780–1918*. New York: Oxford University Press, 1998.

Blanchard, Emmanuel, Marieke Bloembergen, and Amandine Lauro, eds. *Policing in Colonial Empires: Cases, Connections, Boundaries (ca. 1850–1970)*. Brussels: Peter Lang, 2017.

——. "Tensions of Policing in Colonial Situations." In *Policing in Colonial Empires*, edited by Emmanuel Blanchard, Marieke Bloembergen, and Amandine Lauro, 11–38. Brussels: Peter Lang, 2017.

Blanchard, Emmanuel, and Joël Glasman. "Le maintien de l'ordre dans l'empire français: Une historiographie émergente." In *Maintenir l'ordre colonial: Afrique et Madagascar, XIXe–XXe siècles*, edited by Jean-Pierre Bat and Nicolas Courtin, 11–41. Rennes: Presses Universitaires de Rennes, 2012.

Bley, Helmut. *Kolonialherrschaft und Sozialstruktur in Deutsch-Südwestafrika 1894–1914*. Hamburg: Leibniz-Verlag, 1968.

Bloembergen, Marieke. *De geschiedenis van de politie in Nederlands-Indie: Uit zorg en Angst*. Amsterdam: Boom Onderwijs, 2009.

——. "The Perfect Policeman: Colonial Policing, Modernity, and Conscience on Sumatra's West Coast in the Early 1930s." *Indonesia*, no. 91 (2011): 165–91. https://doi.org/10.5728/indonesia.91.0165.

Blundo, Giorgio, and Joël Glasman. "Introduction: Bureaucrats in Uniform." *Sociologus*, nos. 1–2 (2013): 1–9.

Bollig, Michael, and Jan-Bart Gewald, eds. *People, Cattle and Land: Transformations of a Pastoral Society in Southwestern Africa*. Cologne: R. Köppe, 2000.

Bonnell, Andrew G. "Explaining Suicide in the Imperial German Army." *German Studies Review* 37, no. 2 (2014): 275–95. https://doi.org/10.1353/gsr.2014.0055.

Bourdieu, Pierre. "The Sentiment of Honour in Kabyle Society." In *Honour and Shame: The Values of Mediterranean Society*, edited by John G. Peristiany, 193–241. Chicago: University of Chicago Press, 1966.

Bourke, Joanna. *Fear: A Cultural History*. Emeryville, CA: Shoemaker and Hoard, 2006.

Breckenridge, Keith. "The Allure of Violence: Men, Race and Masculinity on the South African Goldmines, 1900–1950." *Journal of Southern African Studies* 24, no. 4 (1998): 669–93.

Brewer, John D. *Black and Blue: Policing in South Africa*. Oxford: Clarendon Press, 1994.

Brodeur, Jean-Paul. "High Policing and Low Policing: Remarks about the Policing of Political Activities." *Social Problems* 30, no. 5 (1983): 507–20. https://doi.org/10.2307/800268.

Brunschwig, Henri. "French Expansion and Local Reactions in Black Africa in the Time of Imperialism (1880–1914)." In *Expansion and Reaction: Essays on European Expansion and Reaction in Asia and Africa*, edited by H. L. Wesseling, 116–40. Leiden: Leiden University Press, 1978.

——. *Noirs et blancs dans l'Afrique noire française, ou, Comment le colonisé devient colonisateur, 1870–1914*. Paris: Flammarion, 1983.

Budack, Kuno Franz Robert. *Raubmord 1912: Die Falk- und Sommer-Morde; Ein Beitrag zur Kriminalgeschichte von Deutsch-Südwestafrika*. Windhoek: Privately published, 1999.

Bühler, Andreas Heinrich. *Der Namaaufstand gegen die deutsche Kolonialherrschaft in Namibia von 1904–1913*. Frankfurt a.M.: IKO-Verlag für Interkulturelle Kommunikation, 2003.

Bührer, Tanja, Flavio Eichmann, Stig Förster, and Benedikt Stuchtey, eds. *Cooperation and Empire: Local Realities of Global Processes*. New York: Berghahn, 2017.

Burbank, Jane, and Frederick Cooper. *Empires in World History: Power and the Politics of Difference*. Princeton, NJ: Princeton University Press, 2010.

Burgess, G. Thomas, and Andrew Burton. Introduction to *Generations Past: Youth in East African History*, edited by Andrew Burton and Hélène Charton-Bigot, 1–24. Athens: Ohio University Press, 2010.

Cain, Maureen. "On the Beat: Interactions and Relations in Rural and Urban Police Forces." In *Images of Deviance*, edited by Stanley Cohen, 62–97. Harmondsworth: Penguin Books, 1971.

Calvert, Albert Frederick. *South-West Africa during the German Occupation, 1884–1914*. London: T. W. Laurie, 1915.

Carotenuto, Matthew, and Brett Shadle. "Introduction: Toward a History of Violence in Colonial Kenya." *International Journal of African Historical Studies* 45, no. 1 (2012): 1–7.

Carotenuto, Matthew, and Brett Shadle, eds. "Toward a History of Violence in Colonial Kenya." *International Journal of African Historical Studies*, Special issue, 45, no. 1 (2012).

Carstens, Peter. "Basters." In *Standard Encyclopaedia of Southern Africa*. Cape Town: NASOU, 1970.

Chakrabarty, Dipesh. *Provincializing Europe: Postcolonial Thought and Historical Difference*. Princeton, NJ: Princeton University Press, 2000.

Chickering, Roger. *We Men Who Feel Most German: A Cultural Study of the Pan-German League, 1886–1914*. Boston: Allen and Unwin, 1984.

Clayton, Anthony, and David Killingray. *Khaki and Blue: Military and Police in British Colonial Africa*. Athens: Ohio University Center for International Studies, 1989.

Cohn, Bernard S. *The Bernard Cohn Omnibus*. New Delhi; New York: Oxford University Press, 2004.

Collins, Harry M., and Robert Evans. *Rethinking Expertise*. Chicago: University of Chicago Press, 2007.

Comaroff, Jean. *Body of Power, Spirit of Resistance: The Culture and History of a South African People*. Chicago: University of Chicago Press, 1985.

Comaroff, John L. "Reflections on the Colonial State, in South Africa and Elsewhere: Factions, Fragments, Facts and Fictions." *Social Identities: Journal for the Study of Race, Nation and Culture* 4, no. 3 (1998): 321–61.

Comor, André-Paul. "Implantation et missions de la gendarmerie en Algérie, de la conquête à la colonisation (1830–1914)." In *Gendarmerie, État et Société au XIXe siècle*, edited by Jean Noël Luc, 510. Paris: Publications de la Sorbonne, 2002.

Conklin, Alice L. *A Mission to Civilize: The Republican Idea of Empire in France and West Africa, 1895–1930*. Stanford: Stanford University Press, 1997.

Connell, Raewyn. *Masculinities*. Berkeley: University of California Press, 1995.

Conrad, Sebastian. "'Eingeborenenpolitik' in Kolonie und Metropole: 'Erziehung zur Arbeit' in Ostafrika und Ostwestfalen." In *Das Kaiserreich transnational: Deutschland in der Welt 1871–1914*, edited by Sebastian Conrad and Jürgen Osterhammel, 107–28. 2nd ed. Göttingen: Vandenhoeck & Ruprecht, 2006.

———. *Deutsche Kolonialgeschichte*. Munich: Beck, 2008.

Conrad, Sebastian, and Shalini Randeria. "Geteilte Geschichten: Europa in einer postkolonialen Welt." In *Jenseits des Eurozentrismus: Postkoloniale Perspektiven in den Geschichts- und Kulturwissenschaften*, edited by Sebastian Conrad and Shalini Randeria, 9–49. Frankfurt a.M.: Campus, 2002.

Cooper, Frederick. "Conflict and Connection: Rethinking Colonial African History." *American Historical Review* 99, no. 5 (1994): 1516–45.

Cooper, Frederick, and Rogers Brubaker. "Identity." In *Colonialism in Question: Theory, Knowledge, History*, 59–90. Berkeley: University of California Press, 2005.

Cooper, Frederick, and Ann Laura Stoler. "Between Metropole and Colony: Rethinking a Research Agenda." In *Tensions of Empire: Colonial Cultures in a Bourgeois World*, edited by Frederick Cooper and Ann Laura Stoler, 1–56. Berkeley: University of California Press, 1997.

Crank, John P. *Understanding Police Culture*. Cincinnati: Anderson Pub., 1998.

Daymond, Margaret J., Dorothy Driver, and Sheila Meintjes, eds. *Women Writing Africa: The Southern Region*. New York: Feminist Press at CUNY, 2003.

De Certeau, Michel. *The Practice of Everyday Life*. Berkeley: University of California Press, 1984.

Dedering, Tilman. *Hate the Old and Follow the New: Khoekhoe and Missionaries in Early Nineteenth-Century Namibia*. Stuttgart: Steiner, 1997.

Deflem, Mathieu. "Law Enforcement in British Colonial Africa: A Comparative Analysis of Imperial Policing in Nyasaland, the Gold Coast, and Kenya." *Police Studies* 17, no. 1 (1994): 45–68.

Deist, Wilhelm. "Die Armee in Staat und Gesellschaft, 1890–1914." In *Militär, Staat und Gesellschaft: Studien zur preussisch-deutschen Militärgeschichte*, 19–41. Munich: R. Oldenbourg, 1991.

——. "Die Geschichte des preußischen Offizierskorps, 1888–1918." In *Militär, Staat und Gesellschaft: Studien zur Preussisch-Deutschen Militärgeschichte*, 43–56. Munich: R. Oldenbourg, 1991.

Denis, Vincent, and Catherine Denys, eds. *Polices d'Empires: XVIIIe–XIXe siècles*. Rennes: Presses Universitaires Rennes, 2012.

Drechsler, Horst. *Südwestafrika unter deutscher Kolonialherrschaft: Der Kampf der Herero und Nama gegen den deutschen Imperialismus (1884–1915)*. Berlin: Akademie-Verlag, 1966.

Dufétel-Viste, Fanny. "L'emploi d'indigènes dans une administration publique au sein de l'Empire colonial allemand: L'exemple de la 'Reichspost.'" In *Empires et colonies: L'Allemagne, du Saint-Empire au deuil postcolonial*, edited by Christine de Gemeaux, 207–37. Clermond-Ferrand: Presses Universitaires Blaise Pascal, 2010.

Dülmen, Richard van. *Theatre of Horror: Crime and Punishment in Early Modern Germany*. Cambridge: Polity Press, 1990.

Durham, Deborah. "Passports and Persons: The Insurrection of Subjugated Knowledges in Southern Africa." In *The Culture of Power in Southern Africa: Essays on State Formation and the Political Imagination*, edited by Clifton C. Crais, 151–81. Portsmouth, NH: Heinemann, 2003.

Eckert, Andreas. "Vom Segen der (Staats)Gewalt? Staat, Verwaltung und koloniale Herrschaftspraxis in Afrika." In *Staats-Gewalt: Ausnahmezustand und Sicherheitsregimes; Historische Perspektiven*, edited by Alf Lüdtke and Michael Wildt, 145–65. Göttingen: Wallstein-Verl., 2008.

——. "Nation, Staat und Ethnizität in Afrika im 20. Jahrhundert." In *Afrika im 20. Jahrhundert: Geschichte und Gesellschaft*, edited by Arno Sonderegger, Ingeborg Grau, and Birgit Englert, 40–59. Vienna: Promedia, 2011.

Eckl, Andreas E. "Konfrontation und Kooperation am Kavango (Nord-Namibia) von 1891 bis 1921." PhD diss., Cologne University, 2004.

Edgerton, David. *The Shock of the Old: Technology and Global History since 1900*. London: Profile Books, 2006.

Eisenstadt, S. N., and Louis Roniger. "Patron-Client Relations as a Model of Structuring Social Exchange." *Comparative Studies in Society and History* 22, no. 1 (1980): 42–77.

Elkins, Caroline, and Susan Pedersen, eds. *Settler Colonialism in the Twentieth Century: Projects, Practices, Legacies*. New York: Routledge, 2005.

Ellis, John. *The Social History of the Machine Gun*. Baltimore: Johns Hopkins University Press, 1986.

Emsley, Clive. *Gendarmes and the State in Nineteenth-Century Europe*. Oxford: Oxford University Press, 1999.

——. "Policing the Empire/Policing the Metropole: Some Thoughts on Models and Types." *Crime, Histoire & Sociétés/Crime, History & Societies* 18, no. 2 (2014): 5–25. https://doi.org/10.4000/chs.1483.

Emsley, Clive, and Barbara Weinberger. Introduction to *Policing Western Europe: Politics, Professionalism, and Public Order, 1850–1940*, edited by Clive Emsley and Barbara Weinberger. New York: Greenwood Press, 1991.

Epple, Angelika, Olaf Kaltmeier, and Ulrike Lindner, eds. "Entangled Histories: Reflecting on Concepts of Coloniality and Postcoloniality." *Comparativ*, 21, no. 1 (2011).

Etherington, Norman. *The Great Treks: The Transformation of Southern Africa, 1815–1854*. Harlow, UK: Longman, 2001.

Evans, Richard J. "Polizei, Politik und Gesellschaft in Deutschland 1700–1933." *Geschichte und Gesellschaft* 22, no. 4 (1996): 609–28. https://doi.org/10.2307/40185919.

Fanon, Frantz. *The Wretched of the Earth*. New York: Grove Press, 1963.

Fitzpatrick, Matthew P. *Purging the Empire: Mass Expulsions in Germany, 1871–1914*. Oxford: Oxford University Press, 2015.

Ford, Lisa. "Locating Indigenous Self-Determination in the Margins of Settler Sovereignty: An Introduction." In *Between Indigenous and Settler Governance*, edited by Lisa Ford and Tim Rowse, 1–11. Abingdon: Routledge, 2012.

Förster, Larissa. *Postkoloniale Erinnerungslandschaften: Wie Deutsche und Herero in Namibia des Kriegs von 1904 gedenken*. Frankfurt a.M.: Campus, 2010.

Förster, Stig. *Der doppelte Militarismus: Die deutsche Heeresrüstungspolitik zwischen Status-quo-Sicherung und Aggression, 1890–1913*. Stuttgart: Steiner, 1985.

Foucault, Michel. *Discipline and Punish: The Birth of the Prison*. New York: Pantheon Books, 1977.

——. *Security, Territory, Population: Lectures at the Collège de France, 1977–78*. Basingstoke: Palgrave Macmillan, 2007.

Frazer, Elizabeth, and Kimberly Hutchings. "On Politics and Violence: Arendt Contra Fanon." *Contemporary Political Theory* 7 (2008): 90–108.

Frevert, Ute. *A Nation in Barracks: Modern Germany, Military Conscription, and Civil Society*. Oxford: Berg, 2004.

Funk, Albrecht. *Polizei und Rechtsstaat: Die Entwicklung des staatlichen Gewaltmonopols in Preussen 1848–1918*. Frankfurt a.M.: Campus, 1986.

Gann, Lewis H. *The Birth of a Plural Society: The Development of Northern Rhodesia under the British South Africa Company, 1894–1914*. Manchester, UK: Manchester University Press, 1958.

Geertz, Clifford. *Negara: The Theatre State in Nineteenth-Century Bali*. Princeton, NJ: Princeton University Press, 1980.

Gewald, Jan-Bart. *Herero Heroes: A Socio-political History of the Herero of Namibia, 1890–1923*. Oxford: James Currey, 1999.

Gibbs, Peter, and Hugh Phillips. *The History of the British South Africa Police, 1889–1980*. North Ringwood, AU: Something of Value, 2000.

Glasman, Joël. "Penser les intermédiaires coloniaux: Note sur les dossiers de carrière de la police du Togo." *History in Africa* 37 (2010): 51–81.

——. *Les corps habillés au Togo: Genèse coloniale des métiers de police.* Paris: Éditions Karthala, 2015.

Goldberg, Ann. *Honor, Politics, and the Law in Imperial Germany, 1871–1914.* Cambridge: Cambridge University Press, 2010.

Gordon, Robert J. *The Bushman Myth: The Making of a Namibian Underclass.* Boulder: Westview Press, 1992.

Gründer, Horst. "Deutscher Kolonialismus: Zwischen deutschem Sonderweg und europäischer Globalisierung." *Jahrbuch für europäische Überseegeschichte* 10 (2010): 147–61.

Grundlingh, Albert. "'Protectors and Friends of the People'? The South African Constabulary in the Transvaal and Orange River Colony, 1900–1908." In *Policing the Empire: Government, Authority, and Control, 1830–1940*, edited by David M. Anderson and David Killingray, 168–82. Manchester, UK: Manchester University Press, 1991.

Gudehus, Christian, and Michaela Christ, eds. *Gewalt: Ein interdisziplinäres Handbuch.* Stuttgart: Metzler, 2013.

Guha, Ranajit, and Gayatri Chakravorty Spivak, eds. *Selected Subaltern Studies.* New York: Oxford University Press, 1988.

Habermas, Rebekka. "Peitschen im Reichstag oder über den Zusammenhang von materieller und politischer Kultur." *Historische Anthropologie* 23, no. 3 (2015): 391–412.

——. *Skandal in Togo: Ein Kapitel deutscher Kolonialherrschaft.* Frankfurt a.M.: Fischer, 2016.

Hall, Catherine. *Civilising Subjects: Colony and Metropole in the English Imagination, 1830–1867.* Chicago: University of Chicago Press, 2002.

Hardung, Christiane, and Trutz von Trotha. "*Komando* und 'Bande': Zwei Formen von Gewaltgemeinschaften im südwestlichen Afrika des ausgehenden 18. und des 19. Jahrhunderts." In *Gewaltgemeinschaften: Von der Spätantike bis ins 20. Jahrhundert*, edited by Winfried Speitkamp, 275–96. Göttingen: V&R unipress, 2013.

Harnischmacher, Robert, and Arved Semerak. *Deutsche Polizeigeschichte: Eine allgemeine Einführung in die Grundlagen.* Stuttgart: Kohlhammer, 1986.

Hartmann, Wolfram. "Sexual Encounters and Their Implications on an Open and Closing Frontier: Central Namibia from the 1840s to 1905." PhD diss., Columbia University, 2002.

——. *Hues between Black and White: Historical Photography from Colonial Namibia, 1860s to 1915.* Windhoek: Out of Africa, 2004.

——. "Urges in the Colony: Men and Women in Colonial Windhoek, 1890–1905." *Journal of Namibian Studies* 1 (2007): 39–71.

Hartmann, Wolfram, Jeremy Silvester, and Patricia Hayes, eds. *The Colonising Camera: Photographs in the Making of Namibian History.* Cape Town: University of Cape Town Press; Athens: Ohio University Press, 1999.

Häußler, Matthias. "'Collaboration' or Sabotage? The Settlers in German Southwest Africa between Colonial State and Indigenous Polities." In *Cooperation and Empire*, edited by Tanja Bührer, Flavio Eichmann, Stig Förster, and Benedikt Stuchtey, 169–93. New York: Berghahn, 2017.

———. *Der Genozid an den Herero: Krieg, Emotion und extreme Gewalt in "Deutsch-Südwestafrika."* Weilerswist: Velbrück Wissenschaft, 2018.

Hawkins, Richard. "The 'Irish Model' and the Empire: A Case for Reassessment." In *Policing the Empire: Government, Authority, and Control, 1830–1940*, edited by David M. Anderson and David Killingray, 18–32. Manchester, UK: Manchester University Press, 1991.

Headrick, Daniel R. *The Tools of Empire: Technology and European Imperialism in the Nineteenth Century*. New York: Oxford University Press, 1981.

———. *Power over Peoples: Technology, Environments, and Western Imperialism, 1400 to the Present*. Princeton: Princeton University Press, 2010.

Henrichsen, Dag. "'Ehi rOvaherero': Mündliche Überlieferungen von Herero zu ihrer Geschichte im vorkolonialen Namibia." *WerkstattGeschichte* 9 (1994): 15–24.

———. "'Iss Worte!' Anmerkungen zur enstehenden afrikanischen Schrifkultur im vorkolonialen Zentralnamibia." In *Afrikanische Beziehungen, Netzwerke und Räume/African Networks, Exchange and Spatial Dynamics/ Dynamiques spatiales, réseaux et échanges africains*, edited by Laurence Marfaing and Brigitte Reinwald, 329–38. Münster: Lit Verlag, 2001.

———. "Ozombambuse and Ovasolondate: Everyday Military Life and African Service Personnel in German South West Africa." In *Hues between Black and White: Historical Photography from Colonial Namibia, 1860s to 1915*, by Wolfram Hartmann, 161–84. Windhoek: Out of Africa, 2004.

———. "Pastoral Modernity, Territoriality and Colonial Transformations in Central Namibia, 1860s–1904." In *Grappling with the Beast: Indigenous Southern African Responses to Colonialism, 1840–1930*, edited by Peter Limb, Norman Etherington, and Peter Midgley, 87–114. Leiden: Brill, 2010.

———. *Herrschaft und Alltag im vorkolonialen Zentralnamibia: Das Herero- und Damaraland im 19. Jahrhundert*. Basel: Basler Afrika Bibliographien, 2011.

Hillebrecht, Werner. "'Habe keinerlei Papiere in Deiner Kiste . . .'" *Werkstatt-Geschichte* 1 (1992): 57–58.

Hobsbawm, Eric. *Age of Extremes: The Short Twentieth Century, 1914–1991*. London: Michael Joseph, 1994.

Houte, Arnaud-Dominique, and Jean-Noël Luc, eds. *Les gendarmeries dans le monde, de la révolution française à nos jours*. Paris: Presses Universitaires de Paris-Sorbonne, 2016.

Hull, Isabel V. *Absolute Destruction: Military Culture and the Practices of War in Imperial Germany*. Ithaca, NY: Cornell University Press, 2005.

———. "The Military Campaign in German Southwest Africa, 1904–1907 and the Genocide of the Herero and Nama." *Journal of Namibian Studies* 4 (2008): 7–24.

Hunt, Nancy Rose. "An Acoustic Register, Tenacious Images, and Congolese Scenes of Rape and Repetition." *Cultural Anthropology* 23, no. 2 (2008): 220–53.

———. *A Nervous State: Violence, Remedies, and Reverie in Colonial Congo*. Durham, NC: Duke University Press, 2016.

Iliffe, John. *Honour in African History*. Cambridge: Cambridge University Press, 2005.

Jäger, Jens. "Plätze an der Sonne? Europäische Visualisierungen kolonialer Realitäten um 1900." In *Kolonialgeschichten: Regionale Perspektiven auf ein globales Phänomen*, edited by Claudia Kraft, Alf Lüdtke, and Jürgen Martschukat, 160–82. Frankfurt a.M.: Campus, 2010.

Jessen, Ralph. *Polizei im Industrierevier: Modernisierung und Herrschaftspraxis im westfälischen Ruhrgebiet 1848–1914.* Göttingen: Vandenhoeck & Ruprecht, 1991.

——. "Polizei, Wohlfahrt und die Anfänge des modernen Sozialstaats in Preußen während des Kaiserreichs." *Geschichte und Gesellschaft* 20, no. 2 (1994): 157–80.

——. "Polizei im Kaiserreich: Tendenzen und Grenzen der Demilitarisierung und 'Professionalisierung.'" In *Die Polizei der Gesellschaft: Zur Soziologie der Inneren Sicherheit,* edited by Hans-Jürgen Lange, 19–36. Opladen: Leske & Budrich, 2003.

Jewsiewicki, Bogumil, and David Newbury, eds. *African Historiographies: What History for Which Africa?* Beverly Hills: Sage Publications, 1986.

Johansen, Anja. *Soldiers as Police: The French and Prussian Armies and the Policing of Popular Protest, 1889–1914.* Aldershot: Ashgate, 2005.

Joyce, Patrick. *The State of Freedom: A Social History of the British State since 1800.* Cambridge: Cambridge University Press, 2013.

Killingray, David. "The Maintenance of Law and Order in British Colonial Africa." *African Affairs* 85, no. 340 (1986): 411–37.

Kinahan, John. "From the Beginning: The Archeological Evidence." In *History of Namibia: From the Earliest Times to 1990,* 15–43. London: Hurst, 2010.

Kleinman, Arthur. "The Violence of Everyday Life: The Multiple Forms and Dynamics of Social Violence." In *Violence and Subjectivity,* edited by Veena Das, Arthur Kleinman, and Mamphela Ramphele, 226–41. Berkeley: University of California Press, 2000.

Knöbl, Wolfgang. *Polizei und Herrschaft im Modernisierungsprozeß: Staatsbildung und innere Sicherheit in Preußen, England und Amerika 1700–1914.* Frankfurt a.M.: Campus, 1998.

Kolsky, Elizabeth. "'The Body Evidencing the Crime': Rape on Trial in Colonial India, 1860–1947." *Gender and History* 22, no. 1 (2010): 109–30. https://doi.org /10.1111/j.1468-0424.2009.01581.x.

——. *Colonial Justice in British India: White Violence and the Rule of Law.* Cambridge: Cambridge University Press, 2010.

Koselleck, Reinhart. *Preussen zwischen Reform und Revolution: Allgemeines Landrecht, Verwaltung u. soziale Bewegung von 1791–1848.* Stuttgart: Klett, 1967.

Kreienbaum, Jonas. *"Ein trauriges Fiasko": Koloniale Konzentrationslager im südlichen Afrika 1900–1908.* Hamburg: Hamburger Edition, 2015.

Krüger, Gesine. *Kriegsbewältigung und Geschichtsbewusstsein: Realität, Deutung und Verarbeitung des deutschen Kolonialkriegs in Namibia 1904 bis 1907.* Göttingen: Vandenhoeck & Ruprecht, 1999.

——. "Koloniale Gewalt, Alltagserfahrungen und Überlebensstrategien." In *Namibia-Deutschland, eine geteilte Geschichte: Widerstand, Gewalt, Erinnerung,* edited by Larissa Förster, Dag Henrichsen, and Michael Bollig, 92–105. Cologne: Minerva, 2004.

——. *Schrift—Macht—Alltag: Lesen und Schreiben im kolonialen Südafrika.* Cologne: Böhlau, 2009.

Kukuri, Andreas. *Herero-Texte.* Translated and edited by Ernst Dammann. Berlin: D. Reimer, 1983.

Kundrus, Birthe. *Moderne Imperialisten: Das Kaiserreich im Spiegel seiner Kolonien.* Cologne: Böhlau, 2003.

Kuß, Susanne. *Deutsches Militär auf kolonialen Kriegsschauplätzen: Eskalation von Gewalt zu Beginn des 20. Jahrhunderts.* Berlin: Links, 2010.

Laak, Dirk van. "Kolonien als 'Laboratorien der Moderne'?" In *Das Kaiserreich transnational: Deutschland in der Welt 1871–1914*, edited by Sebastian Conrad and Jürgen Osterhammel, 257–79. 2nd ed. Göttingen: Vandenhoeck & Ruprecht, 2006.

Lahne, Werner. *Unteroffiziere: Gestern, heute, morgen.* 2nd ed. Herford: Verlag Offene Worte, 1974.

Lau, Brigitte. "Conflict and Power in Nineteenth-Century Namibia." *Journal of African History* 27, no. 1 (1986): 29–39.

———. "Uncertain Certainties: The Herero-German War of 1904." In *History and Historiography: 4 Essays in Reprint*, 39–52. Windhoek: Discourse / MSORP, 1995.

Lawrance, Benjamin N., Emily Lynn Osborn, and Richard L. Roberts, eds. *Intermediaries, Interpreters, and Clerks: African Employees in the Making of Colonial Africa.* Madison: University of Wisconsin Press, 2006.

Le Cour Grandmaison, Olivier. *Coloniser, exterminer: Sur la guerre et l'État colonial.* Paris: Fayard, 2005.

Lerp, Dörte. *Imperiale Grenzräume: Bevölkerungspolitiken in Deutsch-Südwestafrika und den östlichen Provinzen Preußens 1884–1914.* Frankfurt a.M.: Campus, 2016.

Liang, Hsi-Huey. *The Rise of Modern Police and the European State System from Metternich to the Second World War.* New York: Cambridge University Press, 1992.

Limb, Peter, Norman Etherington, and Peter Midgley, eds. *Grappling with the Beast: Indigenous Southern African Responses to Colonialism, 1840–1930.* Leiden: Brill, 2010.

Linden, Marcel van der. "The Promise and Challenges of Global Labor History." *International Labor and Working-Class History*, no. 82 (2012): 57–76.

Lindenberger, Thomas. *Strassenpolitik: Zur Sozialgeschichte der öffentlichen Ordnung in Berlin, 1900–1914.* Bonn: J. H. W. Dietz Nachf., 1995.

———. "Eigen-Sinn, Herrschaft und kein Widerstand, Version: 1.0." *Docupedia-Zeitgeschichte*, February 9, 2014. http://dx.doi.org/10.14765/zzf.dok.2.595.v1.

Lindenberger, Thomas, and Alf Lüdtke. "Physische Gewalt—eine Kontinuität der Moderne." In *Physische Gewalt: Studien zur Geschichte der Neuzeit*, edited by Thomas Lindenberger and Alf Lüdtke, 7–37. Frankfurt a.M.: Suhrkamp, 1995.

Lindner, Kolja. "Marx's Eurocentrism: Postcolonial Studies and Marx Scholarship." *Radical Philosophy* 161 (2010): 27–41.

Lindner, Ulrike. "Colonialism as a European Project in Africa before 1914? British and German Concepts of Colonial Rule in Sub-Saharan Africa." *Comparativ* 19, no. 1 (2009): 88–106.

———. *Koloniale Begegnungen: Deutschland und Grossbritannien als Imperialmächte in Afrika 1880–1914.* Frankfurt a.M.: Campus, 2011.

Lindner, Ulrike, Maren Möhring, Mark Stein, and Silke Stroh, eds. *Hybrid Cultures—Nervous States: Britain and Germany in a (Post)Colonial World.* Amsterdam: Rodopi, 2010.

Lorcy, Damien. *Sous le régime du sabre: La gendarmerie en Algérie, 1830–1870.* Rennes: Presses Universitaires de Rennes, 2011.

Lüdtke, Alf. *"Gemeinwohl," Polizei und "Festungspraxis": Staatliche Gewaltsamkeit und innere Verwaltung in Preußen, 1815–1850*. Göttingen: Vandenhoeck & Ruprecht, 1982.

——. "Cash, Coffee-Breaks, Horseplay: Eigensinn and Politics among Factory Workers in Germany circa 1900." In *Confrontation, Class Consciousness, and the Labor Process: Studies in Proletarian Class Formation*, edited by Michael Hanagan and Charles Stephenson, 65–95. New York: Greenwood Press, 1986.

——. "Was ist und wer treibt Alltagsgeschichte?" In *Alltagsgeschichte: Zur Rekonstruktion historischer Erfahrungen und Lebensweisen*, edited by Alf Lüdtke, 9–47. Frankfurt a.M.: Campus, 1989.

——, ed. *"Sicherheit" und "Wohlfahrt": Polizei, Gesellschaft und Herrschaft im 19. und 20. Jahrhundert*. Frankfurt a.M.: Suhrkamp, 1992.

——. "Arbeit, Arbeitserfahrungen und Arbeiterpolitik: Zum Perspektivenwandel in der historischen Forschung." In *Eigen-Sinn: Fabrikalltag, Arbeitererfahrungen und Politik vom Kaiserreich bis in den Faschismus*, 351–440. Hamburg: Ergebnisse, 1993.

——. "War as Work: Aspects of Soldiering in Twentieth-Century Wars." In *No Man's Land of Violence: Extreme Wars in the 20th Century*, edited by Bernd Weisbrod and Richard Bessel, 127–51. Göttingen: Wallstein, 2006.

Lüdtke, Alf, and Michael Wildt. *Staats-Gewalt: Ausnahmezustand und Sicherheitsregimes. Historische Perspektiven*. Göttingen: Wallstein, 2008.

Lutz, Catherine. *Unnatural Emotions: Everyday Sentiments on a Micronesian Atoll and Their Challenges to Western Theory*. Chicago: University of Chicago Press, 1988.

Mamdani, Mahmood. *Citizen and Subject: Contemporary Africa and the Legacy of Late Colonialism*. Princeton, NJ: Princeton University Press, 1996.

Mann, Kristin, and Richard L. Roberts, eds. *Law in Colonial Africa*. Portsmouth, NH: Heinemann Educational Books, 1991.

Manning, Peter K. "The Police: Mandate, Strategies, and Appearances." In *Policing: A View from the Street*, edited by Peter K. Manning and John Van Maanen, 7–31. Santa Monica, CA: Goodyear Publishing, 1978.

Mazower, Mark. "Violence and the State in the Twentieth Century." *American Historical Review* 107, no. 4 (2002): 1158–78. https://doi.org/10.1086/532667.

McCracken, John. "Coercion and Control in Nyasaland: Aspects of the History of a Colonial Police Force." *Journal of African History* 27, no. 1 (1986): 127–47.

McNulty, Elizabeth. "Generating Common Sense Knowledge among Police Officers." *Symbolic Interaction* 17, no. 3 (1994): 281–94.

Melber, Henning. *Namibia: Kolonialismus u. Widerstand*. Bremen: Informationsstelle Südliches Afrika, 1981.

Mertens, Charlotte. "Sexual Violence in the Congo Free State: Archival Traces and Present Reconfigurations." *Australasian Review of African Studies* 37, no. 1 (2016): 6–20.

Messerschmidt, Manfred. "Die preußische Armee: Strukturen und Organisation." In *Handbuch zur deutschen Militärgeschichte, 1648–1939*, edited by Militärgeschichtliches Forschungsamt, Vol. 4, part 2:3–441. Frankfurt a. M.: Bernard u. Graefe, 1979.

Michels, Stefanie. *Schwarze deutsche Kolonialsoldaten: Mehrdeutige Repräsentationsräume und früher Kosmopolitismus in Afrika*. Bielefeld: transcript, 2009.

Miescher, Giorgio. *Namibia's Red Line: The History of a Veterinary and Settlement Border*. New York: Palgrave Macmillan, 2012.

Mintz, Sidney. *Sweetness and Power: The Place of Sugar in Modern History*. New York: Viking, 1985.

Mitchell, Jessie, and Ann Curthoys. "How Different Was Victoria? Aboriginal "Protection" in a Comparative Context." In *Settler Colonial Governance in Nineteenth-Century Victoria*, edited by Leigh Boucher and Lynette Russell, 183–202. Canberra: ANU Press, 2015.

Mitchell, Timothy. *Colonising Egypt*. Berkeley: University of California Press, 1988.

——. *Rule of Experts: Egypt, Techno-Politics, Modernity*. Berkeley: University of California Press, 2002.

Mommsen, Wolfgang J. *Imperial Germany, 1867–1918: Politics, Culture, and Society in an Authoritarian State*. London: Arnold, 1995.

Monjardet, Dominique. *Ce que fait la police: Sociologie de la force publique*. Paris: La Découverte, 1996.

——. *Notes inédites sur les choses policières, 1999–2006, suivi de le sociologue, la politique et la police*. Paris: La Découverte, 2008.

Moodie, T. Dunbar. "Maximum Average Violence: Underground Assaults on the South African Gold Mines, 1913–1965." *Journal of Southern African Studies* 31, no. 3 (2006): 547–67. https://doi.org/10.1080/0305707052000345090.

Moore, Bernard. "'Dogs Were Our Defenders!' Canines, Carnivores, and Colonialism in Namibia." *Perspectives on History AHA*, June 16, 2017. https://www.historians.org/publications-and-directories/perspectives-on-history/summer-2017/dogs-were-our-defenders-canines-carnivores-and-colonialism-in-namibia.

Morlang, Thomas. *Askari und Fitafita: "Farbige" Söldner in den deutschen Kolonien*. Berlin: Links, 2008.

Moyd, Michelle R. "'All People Were Barbarians to the Askari . . .': Askari Identity and Honor in the Maji Maji War, 1905–1907." In *Maji Maji: Lifting the Fog of War*, edited by James Leonard Giblin and Jamie Monson, 149–79. Leiden: Brill, 2010. http://dx.doi.org/10.1163/ej.9789004183421.i-325.

——. *Violent Intermediaries: African Soldiers, Conquest, and Everyday Colonialism in German East Africa*. Athens: Ohio University Press, 2014.

Müller, Fritz Ferdinand. *Kolonien unter der Peitsche: Eine Dokumentation*. Berlin: Rütten & Loening, 1962.

Muschalek, Marie. "Honourable Soldier-Bureaucrats: Formations of Violent Identities in the Colonial Police Force of German Southwest Africa, 1905–18." *Journal of Imperial & Commonwealth History* 41, no. 4 (2013): 584–99. https://doi.org/10.1080/03086534.2013.836363.

——. "Violence as Usual: Everyday Police Work and the Colonial State in German Southwest Africa." In *Rethinking the Colonial State*, 129–50. Bingley, UK: Emerald Publishing, 2017. https://doi.org/10.1108/S0198-871920170000033007.

——. "Honneur masculin et violence policière ordinaire: Une affaire de viol dans le Sud-Ouest africain allemand (1910)." *Revue du Vingtième Siècle* 140, no. 4 (2018): 83–95.

Nettelbeck, Amanda. "'On the Side of Law and Order': Indigenous Aides to the Mounted Police on the Settler Frontiers of Australia and Canada." *Journal of Colonialism and Colonial History* 15, no. 2 (2014). https://doi.org/10.1353/cch .2014.0031.

Newbury, Colin. "Patrons, Clients, and Empire: The Subordination of Indigenous Hierarchies in Asia and Africa." *Journal of World History* 11, no. 2 (2000): 227–63.

Nirenberg, David. *Communities of Violence: Persecution of Minorities in the Middle Ages.* Princeton, NJ: Princeton University Press, 1996.

Ocobock, Paul. "Spare the Rod, Spoil the Colony: Corporal Punishment, Colonial Violence, and Generational Authority in Kenya, 1897–1952." *International Journal of African Historical Studies* 45, no. 1 (2012): 29–56.

Oldenziel, Ruth. *Making Technology Masculine: Men, Women and Modern Machines in America, 1870–1945.* Amsterdam: Amsterdam University Press, 1999.

Omer-Cooper, John D. *History of Southern Africa.* 2nd ed. Cape Town: David Philip, 1994.

Orizio, Riccardo. "Namibia: How the Basters Lost the Promised Land." In *Lost White Tribes: The End of Privilege and the Last Colonials in Sri Lanka, Jamaica, Brazil, Haiti, Namibia, and Guadeloupe,* 180–220. New York: Free Press, 2001.

Parker, John, and Richard Reid, eds. *The Oxford Handbook of Modern African History.* Oxford: Oxford University Press, 2013.

Patterson, Steven. *The Cult of Imperial Honor in British India.* New York: Palgrave Macmillan, 2009.

Penn, Nigel. *The Forgotten Frontier: Colonist and Khoisan on the Cape's Northern Frontier in the 18th Century.* Athens: Ohio University Press, 2005.

Pesek, Michael. *Koloniale Herrschaft in Deutsch-Ostafrika: Expeditionen, Militär und Verwaltung seit 1880.* Frankfurt a.M.: Campus, 2005.

Peté, Stephen, and Annie Devenish. "Flogging, Fear and Food: Punishment and Race in Colonial Natal." *Journal of Southern African Studies* 31, no. 1 (2005): 3–21. https://doi.org/10.2307/25064970.

Peukert, Detlev. *Die Weimarer Republik: Krisenjahre der Klassischen Moderne.* Frankfurt a.M.: Suhrkamp, 1987.

Pinker, Steven. *The Better Angels of Our Nature: The Decline of Violence in History and Its Causes.* London: Allen Lane, 2011.

Popitz, Heinrich. *Phänomene der Macht: Autorität, Herrschaft, Gewalt, Technik.* 2nd ed. Tübingen: J. C. B. Mohr, 1992.

Prakash, Gyan. "Subaltern Studies as Postcolonial Criticism." *American Historical Review* 99, no. 5 (1994): 1475–90. https://doi.org/10.2307/2168385.

Prein, Philipp. "Guns and Top Hats: African Resistance in German South West Africa, 1907–1915." *Journal of Southern African Studies* 20, no. 1 (1994): 99–121.

Randeria, Shalini. "Geteilte Geschichte und verwobene Moderne." In *Zukunftsent-würfe: Ideen für eine Kultur der Veränderung,* edited by Jörn Rüsen, Hanna Leitgeb, and Norbert Jegelka, 87–96. Frankfurt a.M.: Campus, 2000.

Ranger, Terence O. "The Invention of Tradition in Colonial Africa." In *The Invention of Tradition,* edited by Eric Hobsbawm and Terence O. Ranger, 211–62. Cambridge: Cambridge University Press, 1992.

Reinhard, Wolfgang. "Europäische Staatsmodelle in kolonialen und postkolonialen Machtprozessen." In *Weltgeschichte*, edited by Jürgen Osterhammel. Stuttgart: Steiner, 2008.Reinke, Herbert. "'Armed as If for a War': The State, the Military and the Professionalization of the Prussian Police in Imperial Germany." In *Policing Western Europe: Politics, Professionalism, and Public Order, 1850–1940*, edited by Clive Emsley and Barbara Weinberger, 55–73. New York: Greenwood Press, 1991.

———. *Geschichte der Staatsgewalt: Eine vergleichende Verfassungsgeschichte Europas von den Anfängen bis zur Gegenwart.* Munich: Beck, 1999.

Reinke, Herbert. "'Armed as Iffor a War': The State, the Military and the Professionalization of the Prussian Police in Imperial Germany." In *Policing Western Europe: Politics, Professionalism, and Public Order, 1850–1940*, edited by Clive Emsley and Barbara Weinberger, 55–73. New York: Greenwood Press, 1991.

———. "'. . . hat sich ein politischer und wirtschaftlicher Polizeistaat entwickelt': Polizei und Großstadt im Rheinland vom Vorabend des Ersten Weltkrieges bis zum Beginn der zwanziger Jahre." In *"Sicherheit" und "Wohlfahrt": Polizei, Gesellschaft und Herrschaft im 19. und 20. Jahrhundert*, edited by Alf Lüdtke, 219–43. Frankfurt a.M.: Suhrkamp, 1992.

Reinkowski, Maurus, and Gregor Thum, eds. *Helpless Imperialists: Imperial Failure, Fear and Radicalization.* Göttingen: Vandenhoeck & Ruprecht, 2013.

Ritter, Gerhard, and Klaus Tenfelde. *Arbeiter im Deutschen Kaiserreich 1871 bis 1914.* Bonn: J. H. W. Dietz Nachf., 1992.

Rizzo, Lorena. "Shades of Empire: Police Photography in German South-West Africa." *Visual Anthropology* 26, no. 4 (2013): 328–54. https://doi.org/10.1080/08949468.2013.804701.

Roberts, Richard. "Law, Crime and Punishment in Colonial Africa." In *The Oxford Handbook of Modern African History*, edited by John Parker and Richard Reid, 171–88. Oxford: Oxford University Press, 2013.

Rohkrämer, Thomas. *Der Militarismus der "kleinen Leute": Die Kriegervereine im Deutschen Kaiserreich, 1871–1914.* Munich: R. Oldenbourg, 1990.

Rosenwein, Barbara H. "Worrying about Emotions in History." *American Historical Review* 107, no. 3 (2002): 821–45. https://doi.org/10.1086/532498.

Rud, Søren, and Søren Ivarsson, eds. *Rethinking the Colonial State.* Bingley, UK: Emerald Publishing, 2017. https://doi.org/10.1108/S0198-8719201733.

Saha, Jonathan. "Histories of Everyday Violence in British India." *History Compass* 9, no. 11 (2011): 844–53. https://doi.org/10.1111/j.1478-0542.2011.00806.x.

Schaller, Dominik. "'Ich glaube, dass die Nation als solche vernichtet werden muss': Kolonialkrieg und Völkermord in 'Deutsch-Südwestafrika' 1904–1907." *Journal of Genocide Research* 6, no. 3 (2004): 395–430.

Schaper, Ulrike. *Koloniale Verhandlungen: Gerichtsbarkeit, Verwaltung und Herrschaft in Kamerun 1884–1916.* Frankfurt a.M.: Campus, 2012.

Scheper-Hughes, Nancy, and Philippe Bourgois. "Making Sense of Violence." In *Violence in War and Peace: An Anthology*, edited by Nancy Scheper-Hughes and Philippe Bourgois, 1–31. Malden, MA: Blackwell Publishing, 2004.

———, eds. *Violence in War and Peace: An Anthology.* Malden, MA: Blackwell Publishing, 2004.

Schepp, Sven. *Unter dem Kreuz des Südens: Auf Spuren der Kaiserlichen Landespolizei von Deutsch-Südwestafrika.* Frankfurt a.m.: Verlag für Polizeiwissenschaften, 2009.

Schmidt, Bettina E., and Ingo Schröder, eds. *Anthropology of Violence and Conflict.* London: Routledge, 2001.

Schmidt, Heike I. "Who Is Master in the Colony? Propriety, Honor, and Manliness in German East Africa." In *German Colonialism in a Global Age*, edited by Bradley Naranch and Geoff Eley, 109–28. Durham, NC: Duke University Press, 2014. https://doi.org/10.1215/9780822376392-006.

Schmidt, Jürgen W. *Polizei in Preussen im 19. Jahrhundert.* Ludwigsfelde: Ludwigsfelder Verlagshaus, 2011.

Schmidt, Wilhelm R., and Irmtraud Dietlinde Wolcke-Renk. *Deutsch-Südwest-Afrika: Fotos aus der Kolonialzeit 1884–1918.* Erfurt: Sutton, 2001.

Schrader, Abby M. *Languages of the Lash: Corporal Punishment and Identity in Imperial Russia.* DeKalb: Northern Illinois University Press, 2002.

Schröder, Martin. *Prügelstrafe und Züchtigungsrecht in den deutschen Schutzgebieten Schwarzafrikas.* Münster: Lit Verlag, 1997.

Schröder, Peter J. *Gesetzgebung und "Arbeiterfrage" in den Kolonien: Das Arbeitsrecht in den Schutzgebieten des Deutschen Reiches.* Berlin: Lit Verlag, 2006.

Schwirck, Harry. "Violence, Race, and the Law in German South West Africa, 1884–1914." PhD diss. , Cornell University, 1998.

——. "Law's Violence and the Boundary between Corporal Discipline and Physical Abuse in German South West Africa." *Akron Law Review* 36 (2002): 81–132.

Scully, Pamela. "Rape, Race, and Colonial Culture: The Sexual Politics of Identity in the Nineteenth-Century Cape." *American Historical Review* 100, no. 2 (1995): 335–59.

Seigel, Micol. *Violence Work: State Power and the Limits of Police.* Durham, NC: Duke University Press, 2018.

Selmeci, Andreas, and Dag Henrichsen. *Das Schwarzkommando: Thomas Pynchon und die Geschichte der Herero.* Bielefeld: Aisthesis Verl., 1995.

Selzer, Rolf. "Der Säbel der Kaiserlichen Landespolizei von Deutsch-Südwest." *Mitteilungsblatt des Traditionsverbandes ehemaliger Schutz- und Überseetruppen* 72 (1993): 105–11.

Shadle, Brett. "Rape in the Courts of Gusiiland, Kenya, 1940s–1960s." *African Studies Review* 51, no. 2 (2008): 27–50.

——. "Settlers, Africans, and Inter-personal Violence in Kenya, ca. 1900–1920s." *International Journal of African Historical Studies* 45, no. 1 (2012): 57–80.

Sherman, Taylor C. *State Violence and Punishment in India.* London: Routledge, 2010.

Smith, Woodruff D. "Colonialism and the Culture of Respectability." In *Germany's Colonial Pasts*, edited by Eric Ames, Marcia Klotz, and Lora Wildenthal, 3–20. Lincoln: University of Nebraska Press, 2005.

Speitkamp, Winfried. *Ohrfeige, Duell und Ehrenmord: Eine Geschichte der Ehre.* Stuttgart: Reclam, 2010.

——. "Die Ehre der Krieger: Gewaltgemeinschaften im vorkolonialen Ostafrika." In *Gewaltgemeinschaften: Von der Spätantike bis ins 20. Jahrhundert*, edited by Winfried Speitkamp, 297–315. Göttingen: V&R unipress, 2013.

——. "Gewaltgemeinschaften." In *Gewalt: Ein interdisziplinäres Handbuch*, edited by Christian Gudehus and Michaela Christ, 184–190. Stuttgart: Metzler, 2013.

——, ed. *Gewaltgemeinschaften: Von der Spätantike bis ins 20. Jahrhundert*. Göttingen: V&R unipress, 2013.

——, ed. *Gewaltgemeinschaften in der Geschichte: Entstehung, Kohäsionskraft und Zerfall*. Göttingen: Vandenhoeck & Ruprecht, 2017.

Spencer, Scott C. "Polices impériales: La Southafrican Constabulary, la police montée du Nord-Ouest canadien et le réseau policier impérial britannique, 1895–1914." In *Policing in Colonial Empires*, edited by Emmanuel Blanchard, Marieke Bloembergen, and Amandine Lauro, 157–69. Brussels: Peter Lang, 2017.

Stanko, Elizabeth Anne, ed. *The Meanings of Violence*. London: Routledge, 2003.

Steinmetz, George. "'The Devil's Handwriting': Precolonial Discourse, Ethnographic Acuity, and Cross-Identification in German Colonialism." *Comparative Studies in Society and History* 45, no. 1 (2003): 41–95. https://doi.org/doi:10.1017/S0010417503000045.

——. *The Devil's Handwriting: Precoloniality and the German Colonial State in Qingdao, Samoa, and Southwest Africa*. Chicago: University of Chicago Press, 2007.

Stoler, Ann Laura. *Along the Archival Grain: Epistemic Anxieties and Colonial Common Sense*. Princeton, NJ: Princeton University Press, 2009.

Stoller, Paul. *Embodying Colonial Memories: Spirit Possession, Power, and the Hauka in West Africa*. New York: Routledge, 1995.

Storey, William K. "Guns, Race, and Skill in Nineteenth-Century Southern Africa." *Technology and Culture* 45, no. 4 (2004): 687–711.

——. *Guns, Race, and Power in Colonial South Africa*. Cambridge: Cambridge University Press, 2008.

Subrahmanyam, Sanjay. "Connected Histories: Notes towards a Reconfiguration of Early Modern Eurasia." In *Beyond Binary Histories: Re-imagining Eurasia to c.1830*, edited by Victor B. Lieberman, 289–316. Ann Arbor: University of Michigan Press, 1999.

Thomas, Martin. *Violence and Colonial Order: Police, Workers and Protest in the European Colonial Empires, 1918–1940*. Cambridge: Cambridge University Press, 2012.

Thornberry, Elizabeth. "Defining Crime through Punishment: Sexual Assault in the Eastern Cape, c. 1835–1900." *Journal of Southern African Studies* 37 (2011): 415–30. https://doi.org/10.1080/03057070.2011.602882.

Tilly, Charles. *Coercion, Capital, and European States, AD 990–1992*. Cambridge: Blackwell, 2008.

Trotha, Trutz von. *Koloniale Herrschaft: Zur soziologischen Theorie der Staatsentstehung am Beispiel des "Schutzgebietes Togo."* Tübingen: J. C. B. Mohr, 1994.

——. "'One for Kaiser': Beobachtungen zur politischen Soziologie der Prügelstrafe am Beispiel des 'Schutzgebietes Togo.'" In *Studien zur Geschichte des deutschen Kolonialismus in Afrika: Festschrift zum 60. Geburtstag von Peter Sebald*, edited by Peter Heine and Ulrich Van der Heyden, 521–51. Pfaffenweiler: Centaurus-Verl.-Ges., 1995.

Ulrich, Bernd. "'Militärgeschichte von unten': Anmerkungen zu ihren Ursprüngen, Quellen und Perspektiven im 20. Jahrhundert." *Geschichte und Gesellschaft* 22, no. 4 (1996): 473–503.

Van Maanen, John. "Kinsmen in Repose: Occupational Perspectives of Patrolmen." In *Policing: A View from the Street*, edited by Peter K. Manning and John Van Maanen, 115–28. Santa Monica, CA: Goodyear, 1978.

Veen, Peter Arie Ferdinand van, and Nicoline van der Sijs. *Etymologisch woordenboek: De herkomst von onze woorden*. Utrecht: Van Dale Lexicografie, 1989.

Veracini, Lorenzo. *Settler Colonialism: A Theoretical Overview*. Basingstoke: Palgrave Macmillan, 2010.

Vimalassery, Manu, Juliana Hu Pegues, and Alyosha Goldstein. "Introduction: On Colonial Unknowing." *Theory and Event* 19, no. 4 (2016): [13].

Wallace, Marion. *History of Namibia: From the Earliest Times to 1990*. London: Hurst, 2010.

Walter, Dierk. "Gewalt, Gewaltentgrenzung und die europäische Expansion." *Mittelweg 36: Zeitschrift des Hamburger Instituts für Sozialforschung* 21, no. 3 (2012): 3–18.

Walther, Daniel Joseph. *Creating Germans Abroad: Cultural Policies and National Identity in Namibia*. Athens: Ohio University Press, 2002.

———. *Sex and Control: Venereal Disease, Colonial Physicians, and Indigenous Agency in German Colonialism, 1884–1914*. New York: Berghahn Books, 2015.

Werner, Wolfgang. "'Playing Soldiers': The Truppenspieler Movement among the Herero of Namibia, 1915 to ca. 1945." *Journal of Southern African Studies* 16, no. 3 (1990): 476–502.

White, Luise. *Speaking with Vampires: Rumor and History in Colonial Africa*. Berkeley: University of California Press, 2000.

White, Richard. *The Middle Ground: Indians, Empires, and Republics in the Great Lakes Region, 1650–1815*. Cambridge: Cambridge University Press, 1991.

Wiedner, Hartmut. "Soldatenmißhandlungen im Wilhelminischen Kaiserreich (1890–1914)." *Archiv für Sozialgeschichte* 22 (1982): 159–99.

Wildenthal, Lora. *German Women for Empire, 1884–1945*. Durham, NC: Duke University Press, 2001.

Wirz, Albert. "Körper, Raum und Zeit der Herrschaft." In *Alles unter Kontrolle: Disziplinierungsprozesse im kolonialen Tansania (1850–1960)*, edited by Katrin Bromber, Andreas Eckert, and Albert Wirz, 5–34. Cologne: Rüdiger Köppe, 2003.

Wirz, Albert, Andreas Eckert, and Katrin Bromber, eds. *Alles unter Kontrolle: Disziplinierungsprozesse im kolonialen Tansania (1850–1960)*. Cologne: Rüdiger Köppe, 2003.

Wolfe, Patrick. *Settler Colonialism and the Transformation of Anthropology: The Politics and Poetics of an Ethnographic Event*. London: Cassell, 1999. https://doi.org/10.1080/13688790220126889.

———. "Race and Racialisation: Some Thoughts." *Postcolonial Studies* 5, no. 1 (2002): 51–62.

———. "Settler Colonialism and the Elimination of the Native." *Journal of Genocide Research* 8, no. 4 (2006): 387–409.

Young, Crawford. *The African Colonial State in Comparative Perspective*. New Haven: Yale University Press, 1994.

Zimmerer, Jürgen. *Deutsche Herrschaft über Afrikaner: Staatlicher Machtanspruch und Wirklichkeit im kolonialen Namibia*. Münster: Lit Verlag, 2001.

———. "Der koloniale Musterstaat? Rassentrennung, Arbeitszwang und totale Kontrolle in Deutsch-Südwestafrika." In *Völkermord in Deutsch-Südwestafrika: Der Kolonialkrieg (1904–1908) in Namibia und seine Folgen*, edited by Jürgen Zimmerer and Joachim Zeller, 26–41. Berlin: Links, 2003.

———. "Der totale Überwachungsstaat? Recht und Verwaltung in Deutsch-südwestafrika." In *Von Windhuk nach Auschwitz? Beiträge zum Verhältnis von Kolonialismus und Holocaust*, 92–119. Berlin: Lit Verlag, 2011.

———. "Deutscher Rassenstaat in Afrika: Ordnung, Entwicklung und Segregation in 'Deutsch-Südwest' (1884–1915)." In *Von Windhuk nach Auschwitz? Beiträge zum Verhältnis von Kolonialismus und Holocaust*, 120–38. Berlin: Lit Verlag, 2011.

Zimmerer, Jürgen, and Joachim Zeller, eds. *Völkermord in Deutsch-Südwestafrika: Der Kolonialkrieg (1904–1908) in Namibia und seine Folgen*. Berlin: Links, 2003.

Zirkel, Kirsten. "Military Power in German Colonial Policy: The Schutztruppe and Their Leaders in East and South-West Africa, 1888–1918." In *Guardians of Empire: The Armed Forces of the Colonial Powers c. 1700–1964*, edited by David Killingray and David E. Omissi, 91–113. Manchester, UK: Manchester University Press, 1999.

Zollmann, Jakob. "Die Kolonialpolizei in Deutsch-Südwestafrika 1894–1919. Koloniale Herrschaftsversuche und ihre Grenzen." PhD diss., Freie Universität Berlin, 2007.

———. *Koloniale Herrschaft und ihre Grenzen: Die Kolonialpolizei in Deutsch-Südwestafrika 1894–1915*. Göttingen: Vandenhoeck & Ruprecht, 2010.

———. "Communicating Colonial Order: The Police of German South-West-Africa (c. 1894–1915)." *Crime, Histoire & Sociétés/Crime, History and Societies* 15, no. 1 (2011): 33–57. https://doi.org/10.4000/chs.1240.

INDEX

9 781501 742859